THE PUBLIC BANK SOLUTION

From Austerity to Prosperity

ELLEN HODGSON BROWN, J.D.

Third Millennium Press
Baton Rouge, Louisiana

First edition June 2013

Cover art by David Dees, www.deesillustration.com.

Library of Congress Control Number 2013908909
Includes glossary and index.
Subject headings:
      Banks and banking—history
      Economic history
      Finance, public
      International finance

Published by Third Millennium Press
Baton Rouge, Louisiana
www.webofdebt.com
800-891-0390

Printed in the United States of America

ISBN 978-0-9833308-6-8

TABLE OF CONTENTS

Section I.

BANKING FROM
WALL STREET TO BEIJING:
WHY WE NEED SOMETHING NEW

Section II.

PUBLIC BANKING THROUGH HISTORY:
3,000 B.C. TO 1913 A.D.

Section III.

PUBLIC BANKING MODELS SPAWNED
BY DEPRESSION AND WAR

Section IV.

PUBLIC BANKING MODELS, HYBRIDS AND RIVALS AFTER WORLD WAR II

Section V

SOLUTIONS: BANKING AS A PUBLIC UTILITY

To Toni Decker and Steve Hudson,
two terrific editors;
and to the dedicated public banking team
that drives this work forward

AUTHOR'S PREFACE

This book is a sequel to *Web of Debt: The Shocking Truth About Our Money System and How We Can Break Free*, first published in 2007 and now in its fifth edition. After that, Lehman Brothers collapsed and took much of the global economy with it; debt and unemployment have soared; local and national governments are on the verge of bankruptcy; public services have been slashed and public assets sold off; and the derivatives casino has shot up to the sort of notional values we used to consider imaginary ("quadrillion" was an imaginary number when I was a child). In the latest affront, banks in Cyprus were instructed to confiscate the funds of their depositors, and we've learned that banks globally that are considered "systemically important" and "systemically risky" are being instructed to follow suit if necessary to keep their doors open. All this has brought renewed attention to the banking crisis, and a sense of urgency in finding solutions.

Web of Debt looked at how the power to create money has been usurped by a private banking oligarchy, and how it can be restored to the people at the federal level. This book expands the focus to more local, grassroots alternatives for getting back the money power, by owning some banks ourselves. To that end, it explores the considerable proven successes of the public banking model historically and in the contemporary world.

My focus has been on what is new and interesting—material that helps fill in the gaps, see connections, or appreciate the other side of the stories we heard in school or have gotten filtered through the media. It is hard to know what is really happening on the other side of the world, concealed in economic data in other languages. My approach has been to let the sources speak for themselves, with heavy reliance on quotes and citations, so that readers can form their own opinions and carry on with their own research. There are many stories yet to be told and gaps to be filled.

For ease of reading, each chapter has been summarized in a block at the beginning. The italicized emphases in quotes are mine. Material from *Web of Debt* has been reviewed and expanded on concerning the tally system, the Bank of England, and the early American banking system, both to bring new readers up to speed and to lay the groundwork for the new material that follows. My own thinking has evolved concerning this history, which has taken on new relevance in the public bank context.

I hope you will find this book as engaging to read as I have found it to research and write.

Ellen Brown
Newhall, California
June 2013

FOREWORD BY HAZEL HENDERSON

It is a special privilege to write the Foreword to this important new book. Lawyer Ellen H. Brown has a well-earned reputation for meticulous research and investigative reporting in her many books. In this groundbreaking volume, she emerges as a key public intellectual resource in understanding the politics of money-creation, credit allocation and how democracies can and must regain control over today's global casino. The Public Bank Solution is the most comprehensive overview of how the global financial system has now evolved into a predatory interlocking apparatus which extracts real wealth from productive activities and local economies while exploiting the ecological life-supporting planetary ecosystem on which humanity and all species rely. Ellen is repeatedly called on for her expertise because she offers so many creative proposals for reform along with her in-depth analyses of our current malfunctioning money-creation and credit-allocation policies.

Ellen founded and is president of the Public Banking Institute (PBI), and I am honored to serve on its Advisory Board. PBI champions and fosters the needed return in the USA of public banking. This book focuses our attention on public banking after the Wall Street debacles of 2008 and shows how deeper reforms than Dodd-Frank are needed. Too-big-to-fail banks, now bigger than ever, continue to devastate the lives of millions in our real economy. Ellen led in drawing attention to the over 90 years of success of the publicly owned Bank of North Dakota, focused the wave of media attention on this better model and shows how other public banks around the world lead to better, more equitable forms of economic and social development.

In this book, Ellen gives us a detailed history of the success of public banks in many countries and how they serve the democratic development of robust economies, plowing their revenues back into further community credit needs: for infrastructure, education, health facilities, local enterprises, and providing funds to many other local community banks. The success of these public banks throughout history and today puts them in the crosshairs of the armies of lobbyists for the big for-profit banks. This book documents some of these David and Goliath battles and today's new opportunities to re-launch public banks in the wake of the Wall Street depredations and the scandalous taxpayer funded-bailouts. The bailouts were extorted from meek or terrified politicians, many compromised by Wall Street's campaign "donations," who fell into line and still serve these financial interests today. The appalling 2010 Supreme Court Citizens United decision has turned U.S. elections into a farce in which Congress and the Executive Branch are on the auction block to the highest bidder. There are many efforts to overturn this Supreme Court mistake, such as a Constitutional amendment to clarify that money is not speech and corporations are not persons. Meanwhile, we can act to restore our own communities and keep our money circulating locally and domestically.

This book is a boon to all communities and activists seeking to re-start and support their homegrown economies. While the mystification is purveyed by elites and mass media that the USA is still suffering a "Great Recession," Ellen Brown's research finds root causes and deeper explanations. Ellen explains the working of fractional reserve banking and how the power to create our country's money fell into private hands under the Federal Reserve Act of 1913, allowing the private owners of its 12 Federal Reserve banks and our entire banking system to create our money supply out of thin air, simply as loans which are then credited to the borrower's account. Some 95 percent of our money supply is created through these bank loans and the huge bubble of securitized mortgages, student loans, car loans, etc., which are packaged up as bonds and sold to unsuspecting pension funds. When these bonds turned out to be full of toxic sub-prime loans, credit markets dried up, lending collapsed, and our money supply collapsed with it! This collapse of our domestic money supply still strangles the economies of Main Street, drying up the circulating cash needed for businesses, payrolls, and mortgage payments, causing the tragedies we have witnessed of unemployment, foreclosures and rising U.S. poverty rates.

Fed chairman Ben Bernanke tried his remedy of flooding the economy with newly-created money "thrown out of helicopters, if necessary", as he said in his famous quote of Milton Friedman. Congress and the Treasury hoped it would trickle down to Main Street. Instead, the Fed could have spread funds into local banks and small businesses, and into reducing principals on millions of under-water mortgages. Ellen Brown shows how and why the new money never reached Main Street. It went into Wall Street bailouts and continues to provide big banks with almost interest-free trillions through the Fed's discount window. She also focuses on the ticking time bomb of derivatives and how they could trigger the next global financial meltdown.

Ellen points out that Fed Chairman Bernanke and the Treasury could instead have addressed the almost $1 trillion of un-repayable loans burdening our students, who are suffering unemployment rates of 14 percent. These debts could be packaged up, securitized and bought up by the Fed, in the same way that the Wall Street banks' toxic loans were bought and now sit on the Fed balance sheet. We at Ethical Markets Media agree! We are proud that Ellen Brown is a member of our global Advisory Board and proud to publish her columns regularly. Our mission is to reform markets and metrics while accelerating the global transition underway from the fossil-fueled Industrial Era to the more equitable, decentralized, cleaner, information-richer, green economies endorsed in 2012 by 191 member countries of the United Nations. We track this shift in our Green Transition Scoreboard® and offer our Principles of Ethical Biomimicry Finance™ licensed to asset managers to assist in shifting their assets from unsustainable corporations to thriving younger companies now building more sustainable futures. Our Beyond GDP Surveys with Globescan in eleven countries continue to show that the public is ahead of economists in favoring replacing GDP with broader indicators of quality of life.

This book is a well-researched, disciplined call to all citizens to reclaim our local economies by moving public funds from Wall Street back to where they belong on Main Street, by following the recommendations in this book and of the Public Banking Institute. Here in these pages is our roadmap to a saner, more democratic banking system, one that is actually achievable now that the veils of mystification have been torn away and the new metrics and models of sustainable human development illuminate a brighter future.

Hazel Henderson
President, Ethical Markets Media, LLC
(USA and Brazil)
Saint Augustine, Florida
March 2013

Introduction

FROM AUSTERITY TO PROSPERITY

We are blessed with technology that would be indescribable to our forefathers. We have the wherewithal, the know-it-all to feed everybody, clothe everybody, and give every human on Earth a chance. We know now what we could never have known before – that we now have the option for all humanity to make it successfully on this planet in this lifetime. Whether it is to be Utopia or Oblivion will be a touch-and-go relay race right up to the final moment.

– Buckminster Fuller, 1981

We have entered a millennium that is ripe with possibility. New discoveries in agricultural production, water desalination, energy from non-oil sources, waste conversion, and much more are in the wings just waiting to be developed. We have the manpower, the materials, the science and the intelligence to create prosperity for all. Yet the world in which we find ourselves is one of austerity, mounting unsustainable debt, growing poverty and want. Why?

A major part of the problem is in the system of exchange we call "money," and in the banks that create, store and distribute it. Rather than allowing the free exchange of labor and materials for production, our system of banking and credit has acted as a tourniquet on production and a parasite draining resources away.

President Woodrow Wilson understood the problem a century ago, when he wrote in 1913:

> A great industrial nation is controlled by its system of credit. Our system of credit is privately concentrated. The growth of the nation, therefore, and all our activities are in the hands of a few men who . . . are necessarily concentrated upon the great undertakings in which their own money is involved and who necessarily . . . chill and check and destroy genuine economic freedom.[1]

In the wake of the 2008 financial crisis, much of the global economy has been battling a serious downturn, with rampant unemployment, government funding problems, and harsh austerity measures imposed on the people. Meanwhile, the banks that caused this devastation have been bailed out at government expense and continue to thrive at the public trough. All this has caused irate citizens to rise up against the banks, particularly the large international banks. But for better or worse, we cannot do without the functions they perform; and one of these functions is the creation of "money" in the form of credit when banks make loans.

Money created out of nothing on the books of banks has been heavily criticized, but it is where we get the credit that allows the wheels of industry to turn. Employers need credit at each stage of production before they have finished products that can be sold on the market, and banks need to be able to create that credit in response to demand. Without the advance of credit, there will be no products or services to sell; and without products to sell, workers and suppliers cannot get paid.

A functioning economy needs bank credit to flow freely. What impairs this flow is that the spigots are under private control. Private banks use that control to their own advantage rather than to serve business, industry, and societal needs. They can turn credit on and off at will, direct it to their cronies, or speculate with it; and they collect the interest on loans as middlemen. This is not just a modest service fee. Interest has been calculated to compose a third of everything we buy.[2]

Anyone with money has a right to lend it, of course, and any group with money can pool it and lend it; but the ability to create money-as-credit *ex nihilo* (out of nothing), backed by the "full faith and credit" of the government and the people, is properly a public function, and the proceeds should properly return to the public. The virtues of an expandable credit system can be retained while avoiding the parasitic exploitation to which private banks are prone, by establishing a network of public banks that serve the people because they are owned by the people.

"But that's socialism!" you may say.

Not at all. *Socialism* is government ownership of the means of production—factories, farms, businesses, and land. Public banking is not about government ownership of property but about government oversight of the system of credits and debits that undergirds a functioning economy, ensuring that the system operates efficiently, fairly, securely, and to the benefit of all. Banking, money and credit are not market goods but are economic infrastructure, just as roads and bridges are physical infrastructure. Banking and credit need to be public utilities for a capitalist market economy to run properly. By providing inexpensive, accessible financing to the free enterprise sector of the economy, public banks make commerce more vital and stable.

Banking needs to be a public utility for another reason. Banks form an interlocking network. The collapse of one can take down the rest, and the whole economy with them. That is why, in the banking crisis of 2008-09, Congress put on its "socialist" hat and rushed to bail out the banks at the expense of the taxpayers rather than letting them fail in the capitalist way. Our money is tied into their computers. We do not want to leave the on/off switch to the whims of "the market." Nor should we want to leave it to the machinations of self-seeking private owners.

By making banking a public utility, with expandable credit issued by banks that are owned by the people, the financial system can be made to serve the people rather than people serving the banks. Credit flow can be released so that industry and free enterprise can thrive, and the economy can reach its full potential. That is the subject of this book. The structure is as follows:

- Section I looks at the train wreck looming in our current banking system, and compares that system with the various public banking models of the up-and-coming BRICs (Brazil, Russia, India and China).

- Section II tracks the evolution of public and private banks through history, going back 5,000 years.
- Section III looks at innovative developments in public banking in the early decades of the 20th century through World War II.
- Section IV looks at developments after World War II.
- Section V proposes contemporary public banking solutions— federal, state and local.

To solve our crippling economic problems, we need some new approaches. By studying historical and contemporary models, we can *see what works* and formulate a practical plan for prosperity today.

Section I.

BANKING FROM WALL STREET TO BEIJING: WHY WE NEED SOMETHING NEW

Chapter 1

FROM BAIL-OUTS TO BAIL-INS:
A BANKING DINOSAUR
ON LIFE SUPPORT

"The incentives toward risk-taking remain essentially unchanged from pre-crisis times. . . . Over time I suspect the industry will be treated like and eventually become public utilities."

— FDIC Vice Chairman Thomas Hoenig on the failure of regulation to eliminate the systemic risk in the banking system, April 2013[3]

The Western banking system today has all the earmarks of a giant Ponzi scheme on the verge of collapse: a global credit crisis extorting massive bailouts from the taxpayers; a derivatives casino with a U.S. notional (or nominal) exposure of $300 trillion; governments refusing further bank bailouts; "bail in" policies in which the largest banks are being instructed to confiscate their depositors' funds if necessary, in a last-ditch effort to keep their doors open. "Systemically risky" hardly describes the condition of the giant derivative banks, which are like a house of cards waiting for a strong wind. Fortunately, there is a safer, more sustainable way to design a banking system.

The financial shockwaves first hit in 2008, when we were told that the private global banking edifice was poised to collapse unless the U.S. government came to its rescue with $700 billion in taxpayer funds.

Five years later, governments are finally balking at further bailouts. The global control center of the private international banking system in Switzerland has therefore come up with a new scheme for saving the too-big-to-fail banks. Creditors – including depositors, the largest class of unsecured creditors – are to be "bailed in." In the event of insolvency, the megabanks are being instructed to recapitalize themselves by converting their liabilities (debts) into bank stock, effectively confiscating depositor funds.

Before the 1990s, depository banks were not allowed to have investment arms that gambled in derivatives. But expansion into this new business area was sanctioned in 1999 by Federal Reserve Chairman Alan Greenspan, who argued that the giant U.S. banks had "lost market share." The banks were being beaten out of their profits by large foreign banks and non-bank competitors, including money market funds and the commercial paper market. He said the banks would become "the dinosaurs of financial services" without the repeal of the Depression-era Glass-Steagall Act that forbade these practices.[4] Greenspan assured President Bill Clinton that the derivatives game would be only a small portion of the banks' business, and that they could regulate themselves.[5]

The derivatives industry was then considered immature and in need of nurturing, so additional concessions were made.[6] In 2005, the bankruptcy laws were revised to give derivative claimants "super-priority" in bankruptcy, putting them first in line before all other creditors, public and private.

Today the derivatives casino is the biggest game on Wall Street, posing enormous risks to depositors and the economy. The putative safety net for this high wire act is the FDIC (Federal Deposit Insurance Corporation), which is theoretically backed by the government. But new Dodd-Frank regulations forbid further taxpayer bailouts to save banks from the more speculative types of derivatives losses; and whether the FDIC fund will be adequate to the task without its own taxpayer bailout is questioned by the agency itself. (See Figure 1.)

This will all be explored later. The point here is that we are living in a tinderbox that could catch fire at any time, and our fire insurance may not cover the damage. The next time the house of cards goes down, the government may not be willing or able to prop it back up.

FDIC Deposit Insurance Fund	Deposits At US Commercial Banks	Total US Financial Derivative Exposure

$297,514 BN

$25 BN

$9,283 BN

Source: OCC.gov; H.8 Statement; Zero Hedge

Figure 1. **FDIC fund vs. total U.S. deposits
vs. total U.S. notional derivatives.**
Source: Occ.gov; H.8 Statement; ZeroHedge.[7]

Why the Private Global Banking Edifice Is Not Sustainable

Derivatives, the rocket science of finance, are so complex that few people understand them. But the fundamental flaw in the banking scheme is something much simpler and more comprehensible: the unsustainable nature of a monetary system in which most money is created as a debt to private banks. Paying a perpetually compounding rent to the banking sector may work mathematically, but it is not sustainable in the real world. Workers, resources and customers all reach their natural limits; but interest continues to grow, in an imaginary world of numbers divorced from the realities of the producing economy.

Consider these arresting facts:

- Roughly one-third of everything we buy goes to interest.[8]
- The interest goes to private banks which create money as a debt—a debt for which more is always owed back than was advanced in the original loan.
- At the height of the financial bubble, over 40 percent of U.S. corporate profits went to the financial industry—up from 7 percent in 1980.[9]
- Between $21 trillion and $32 trillion are now hidden in offshore tax havens – between one-third and one-half of the global GDP – and a majority of these dollars emanate from Wall Street.[10]

The finding that a third or more of everything we buy goes to interest comes from Professor Margrit Kennedy in her book *Occupy Money* (2012), drawing from the research of German economist Helmut Creutz, interpreting Bundesbank publications.[11] The data involve the expenditures of German households for everyday goods and services in 2006, but similar figures can be assumed for the United States, where the financial sector claims a comparable portion of the Gross Domestic Product (GDP).

Economist Michael Hudson derives the U.S. figures using data from the National Income and Product Accounts (NIPA). It shows that $2.6 trillion were paid in interest by the private sector in 2011.[12] The U.S. GDP was nearly $15 trillion that year, of which 60 percent or $9 trillion was from the private sector. Interest was therefore $2.6 trillion of $9 trillion, or 29 percent, of private sector GDP.

Comparable results can be assumed for other countries. Figure 2 shows financial sector profits from 1985 to 2008 in five major Western economies, rising at similar rates as a percent of GDP.[13]

Share of the financial sector in GDP (in per cent)

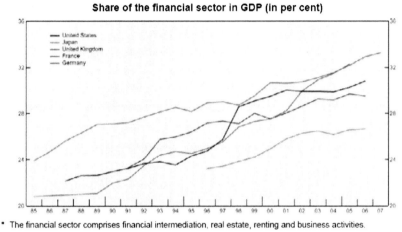

* The financial sector comprises financial intermediation, real estate, renting and business activities.

Source: OECD.

Figure 2. **Share of GDP going to the financial industry**

How can interest represent a third or more of everything we buy? Most people think that if they pay their credit card bills on time and don't take out loans, they aren't paying interest; but Dr. Kennedy says this is not true. Tradesmen, suppliers, wholesalers and retailers all along the chain of production rely on credit to pay their bills. They must pay for labor and materials before they have a product to sell, and before the end buyer pays for the product 90 days later. Each supplier in the chain adds interest to its production costs, which are passed on to the ultimate consumer.

Consumers also collectively bear the interest charges for financing public projects. Dr. Kennedy cites figures ranging from 12 percent interest for garbage collection, to 38 percent for drinking water, to 77 percent for rent in public housing in her native Germany; or an average of 35-40 percent for publicly-financed projects.

But aren't we just "paying interest to ourselves," benefiting from the "miracle of compound interest" when we buy and hold bonds, while paying interest on our mortgages?

No. Dr. Kennedy's figures show that eighty percent of the population are net borrowers, and ten percent break even. Only ten percent are net lenders. That makes interest a highly regressive tax that the poor and middle class pay to the rich.

Bank assets, interest, and debt have all been growing exponentially, along with the incomes of the 1 percent; and this income growth has been gained at the expense of the 99 percent, where incomes have at best grown linearly and in real terms may have declined. (See Figure 3.)

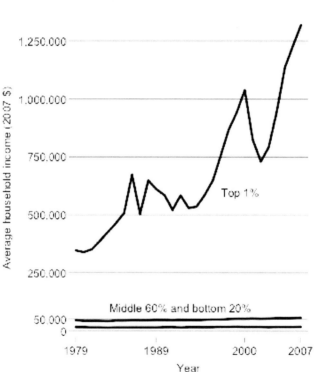

Figure 3. **Inflation-adjusted household incomes, 1979-2007**
Adapted from: "The Best Inequality Graph," lanekenworthy.net[14]

In nature, sustainable growth progresses in a curve that rises quickly at first, then increases more slowly until it levels off (called a "logistic" curve). Exponential growth does the reverse: it begins slowly and increases over time, until the curve shoots up vertically, as in Figure 4. Exponential growth is seen in parasites, cancers – and compound interest. When the parasite runs out of its food source, the growth curve suddenly collapses. And that is the tipping point threatening the economy today.

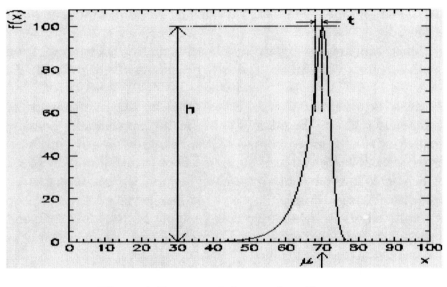

Figure 4. **Exponential growth collapses when the food source runs out**

"Compound interest" is interest charged on interest, a charge that is added progressively to principal. People generally assume that if they pay their bills on time, they are not paying compound interest; but this, too, is not necessarily true. Compound interest is baked into the formula for most mortgages, which compose 80 percent of U.S. loans.[15] On credit cards, if not paid within the one-month grace period, interest charges are compounded daily. Even if you pay within the grace period, you are paying 2 percent to 3 percent for the use of the card, since merchants pass their fees on to the consumer.[16] This is also true for debit cards, although they are the equivalent of paying cash.

Visa, MasterCard and the banks at both ends of these interchanges charge an average fee of 44 cents per transaction, although the cost to them is about four cents.[17]

These exponentially growing charges must come out of consumer incomes that are not growing and in many cases have shrunk. When the exponential function overtakes the linear function, the debt can no longer be paid, and the lender declares "Default!" The borrower has breached his contract and must relinquish his collateral to foreclosure. His house, his business, his equipment and his vehicles are claimed as payment for the use of money created by the banker on a computer screen.

That explains how wealth is systematically transferred from Main Street to Wall Street. The rich get progressively richer at the expense of the poor, not just because of "Wall Street greed" but because exponential growth is inherent in the mathematics of compound interest. The attempt to extract an exponentially growing interest burden from economies that at best grow linearly has been responsible for repeated banking crises. Booms are followed by busts, which are followed by austerity, belt-tightening, job loss, foreclosures, and homelessness. Busts follow as a mathematical certainty, because virtually all of our circulating money supply is created as debt; and collectively, more money is always owed back on that debt than was created in the original loans.

Banks Create Most of the Money Supply

How banks acquired a monopoly over the creation of money (or "credit") will be explored later; but to convince yourself that it is true, you can examine Figure 5, a chart put out by the St. Louis Federal Reserve. Arguably, the Federal Reserve (or "Fed") is itself a private institution, since its twelve branches are 100 percent owned by private banks. But whatever category it falls under, it issues only the money represented by the lowest line on the graph (MB, the monetary base); and most of that money does not circulate beyond the reserve accounts of banks. Where, then, does the rest come from? It is advanced on the books of financial institutions when they make loans.

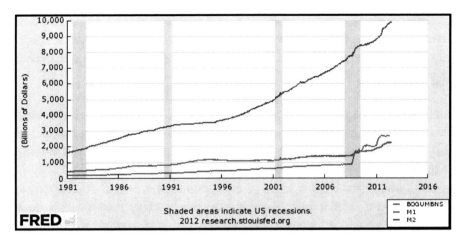

Figure 5. U.S. money supply—MB, M1, M2.

By 2012, M2 had shot up to $10 trillion—nearly four times MB, even after copious injections of "quantitative easing." And that number does not reflect the entire money supply. M3, the largest measure of the money supply, includes additional "near-monies" that are also created privately. (More on all this later.)

The problem with money created as private bank credit is that more is always owed back than was created, and this excess winds up in private coffers rather than being recycled back into the economy. Debunkers of this "debt virus" theory say that bankers spend their profits into the economy like everyone else, making it available to pay the interest on loans; but this is another economic model that does not seem to be grounded in fact. The lion's share of bank profits go to wealthy CEOs, management, and shareholders. Little of this money is spent on goods and services, adding to the consumer demand needed to stimulate production and create jobs. Most of it goes into speculative "money making money" schemes that draw resources out of the economy without feeding them back in.

Confirming that observation is a July 2012 report by the Tax Justice Network, finding that between 21 trillion and 32 trillion dollars are sequestered in offshore havens.[18] In *Treasure Islands: Uncovering the Damage of Offshore Banking and Tax Havens* (Palgrave Macmillan 2012), Nicholas Shaxson states that the primary architect and primary beneficiary of this offshore system is the financial services industry.

He maintains that financiers on Wall Street and in the City of London have constructed a system to help them undermine democracy, drastically boost profits, destabilize global markets, shape international regulation, and evade taxes.

In the 1980s, "supply side" economists argued that if taxes were cut for the rich, the benefits would flow down to the masses. Jobs would be created and prosperity would be maximized, as a rising tide lifted all boats. This was called the "trickle down" theory, after a line from humorist Will Rogers, who said during the Great Depression, "Money was all appropriated for the top in hopes that it would trickle down to the needy." But it has become eminently clear that wealth does not trickle down. It accumulates at the top and seeps into offshore tax havens, which continue to grow like tumors on the side of the economy, sucking resources out.

The Other Banking Model

That is the extractive model of banking prevalent today in Western countries, but it is not the only way to design a banking system. Interest *could* be returned to the economy and the people, feeding and sustaining the economy rather than feeding off it; and in some systems historically, it has been.

Two banking models have competed for dominance for thousands of years – *public* and *private*. In the public model, interest and profits belong to the community, and they are returned to the community. Credit is delivered to the economy in an organic way that sustains it and is sustainable.

Publicly-owned banks operate in the public interest by law. That means they must support the real, wealth-producing economy. Bank profits generated from the credit of the public are returned to the public.

The model was proven in the first half of the eighteenth century, in Benjamin Franklin's colony of Pennsylvania. The provincial government printed its own money and operated a "land bank," which issued low-interest loans to farmers. The interest returned to the government, funding the provincial budget. Except for import duties on liquor, the government collected no taxes at all. It also had no debt and paid no interest. There was abundant money for trade and the economy thrived.[19]

In the competitor model prevailing today, privately-owned banks (sometimes called "usury" banks) operate for private gain. They are extractive rather than cooperative and supportive, focused on maximizing profits for their owners and executives. Classical economists called these financial profits unearned and said they should be heavily taxed; but today, with lawmakers captured by the profiteers, they are taxed only lightly if at all.

Neoliberal economic theory assures us that what is good for the big privately-owned banks is good for society – that private ownership produces better results in that sector as in all others; but the data tell a different story. Usury banking dominates in Western countries today, but 40 percent of banks globally are publicly owned. These are largely in the BRIC countries – Brazil, Russia, India and China – which also house 40 percent of the global population. In the first decade of the 21st century, the BRICs boasted growth in GDP of 92.7 percent, while Western economies limped along at a very modest 15.5 percent.[20]

The BRICs moved into public, cooperative banking out of necessity. With massive populations that needed to be fed and housed, they could not afford to support a parasitic financial elite. The BRICs have problems, but they don't have our problems. Unburdened by counterproductive financial sectors, they have strongly upward economic trajectories, while the West's are stagnating.

The advantages of public over private banking are not rocket science. A government that owns its own bank can keep the interest and reinvest it locally, resulting in potential public savings of 35 percent to 40 percent. Costs can be reduced across the board; taxes can be cut or services increased; and market stability can be created for governments, borrowers and consumers. Banking and credit become public utilities, sustaining the economy rather than mining it for private gain. And banks again become safe places to store our monies, both our public revenues and our private savings.

The following chapters will explore a variety of successful public banking models. But first, a closer look at the fragile underpinnings of the current system, and why it needs to be overhauled.

Chapter 2

EXPOSED: A CORRUPT AND DYSFUNCTIONAL BANKING SYSTEM

"I suddenly realized I had joined the wrong mob."

-- Notorious gangster Lucky Luciano,
after spending a day on Wall Street

> The Wall Street model of banking has made the economy serve the needs of high finance rather than the reverse, with taxpayers propping up the banks rather than the banks supporting the economy. Regulation won't fix this systemic dysfunction. Megabanks considered too big to fail are proving to be too big to regulate; and in any case, the regulations now being pursued aim at the wrong problem.

The banking crisis of 2008 was a rude awakening for people putting their faith in the soundness of the banking edifice. The banks had fostered a real estate boom based on a faulty securitization model backed by derivatives, which were supposed to decrease risk by spreading it out. Instead, they increased risk.[21] For funding and to multiply profits, the banks relied on a "shadow banking system" which was intrinsically unsafe and inherently flawed. The securitization scheme turned out to be no more sound than the "liar's loan" subprime mortgages of which it was comprised. Bankers hid these facts, however, behind a façade of high-tech expertise. Banking acquired the mystique of a religion, with the chairman of the Federal Reserve serving as high priest. Fed actions were protected like military secrets. The people simply had to have faith in the economic leaders who had the nation's finances in their hands.

The deceptive façade was blown away on September 11, 2008, when Lehman Brothers, a major investment bank, was the target of a massive bear raid. Its stock dropped by 30 percent.[22] Bankruptcy followed, triggering a run on the money market. Large institutional investors pulled their money out en masse.

U.S. Treasury Secretary Henry Paulson, former CEO of investment bank Goldman Sachs, told Congress that if the government did not bail out the banks, the entire global monetary system could collapse, and that martial law might have to be imposed.[23] He dropped on one knee before House Speaker Nancy Pelosi and begged her not to blow up his proposed bailout package.[24]

How close the economy actually came to complete collapse was revealed by Democratic Representative Paul Kanjorski, speaking on *C-Span* in February 2009. Repeating what Congress had been told by Paulson and Fed Chairman Ben Bernanke, he said:

> On Thursday (Sept 18), at 11 am, the Federal Reserve noticed a tremendous draw-down of money market accounts in the United States, to the tune of $550 billion . . . being drawn out in the matter of an hour or two. The Treasury opened up its window to help and pumped $105 billion in the system and quickly realized that they could not stem the tide. We were having an electronic run on the banks. They decided to close the operation, close down the money accounts and announce a guarantee of $250,000 per account so there wouldn't be further panic out there.
>
> If they had not done that, their estimation is that by 2 pm that afternoon, $5.5 trillion would have been drawn out of the money market system of the U.S., would have collapsed the entire economy of the U.S., and within 24 hours the world economy would have collapsed. It would have been the end of our economic system and our political system as we know it.[25]

The end of our economic and political systems as we know them! It sounded perilous indeed. But why would a run on the money markets jeopardize the banking system?

We learned that banks don't just lend the money they have on deposit, matching "savers" with "borrowers" as we had been taught. Banks simply advance "bank credit" to any creditworthy borrower who walks in the door, creating the money in the form of a deposit on the bank's books. Depositors then write checks on their deposit accounts, and checks fly back and forth between banks all day. Most withdrawals net out against incoming deposits; but if the bank comes up short at the end of the day, the Fed treats the deficiency as an overdraft in the bank's reserve account, in effect lending the bank the money. This overdraft then has to be cleared by borrowing the money from somewhere else – typically the "excess" reserves of another bank or the money market.[26]

According to a banking textbook called *Bank Management & Financial Services* by Rose and Hudgens, the largest banks often borrow close to 100 percent of their "liquidity needs."[27] That means they are not lending their own money *or* their depositors' money. They are just advancing credit, then covering the loan by taking advantage of the bankers' exclusive right to borrow very cheaply at bankers' rates and pass this money on at much higher rates to their customers.

In short, banks rely on the money market to get quick cash to back loans they have already made; and without that pool of cheap money, credit can freeze. That is what happened in 2008. The run on the money markets caused interbank lending rates to soar. LIBOR—the London interbank lending rate for short-term loans—shot up to around 5 percent.[28] When the cost of borrowing the money to cover loans became too high for banks to turn a profit, lending came to an abrupt halt. Businesses were unable to get the credit they needed to pay for workers and materials. They started laying people off or closing their doors. Over the next six months, the stock market dropped by nearly 50 percent.[29]

The Federal Reserve and the United States government then whipped into action. The Fed bought "toxic" assets off the books of the banks and made credit available to them nearly interest-free. The Fed's target for the Fed funds rate (the overnight interest rate that banks in the Federal Reserve system charge each other) was dropped to a rock-bottom 0 percent to 0.25 percent, and it has been there ever since.

These extremely low rates were supposed to ease the credit crisis and get banks to lend again, but the banks passed little of this windfall on to borrowers. Lending to consumers and to all but the largest businesses was slow to revive. Turning the virtually-free credit spigots on full bore simply made cheap credit available for bankers and their cronies to engage in speculation and corporate raids.[30]

Paulson's appeal worked and the banks were bailed out, restoring their profits with taxpayer money. But consumers, businesses, and state and local governments struggled to remain solvent. Local governments were maintaining large and wasteful "rainy day" funds even as they slashed services to balance their budgets. They had to do this because they did *not* have the secure, nearly-interest-free credit lines that private banks have with each other.

In the United States between 2008 and 2012, over 6 million workers lost their jobs, over 8 million pieces of real estate went into foreclosure, and student debt topped $1 trillion.[31] Students who had been seduced by the belief that a good education was an investment in their futures wound up with five- or six-figure debts, and no jobs to pay them off; and the debts were not dischargeable in bankruptcy. Many of these young people could be facing debt peonage for the rest of their lives.

Politicians, backed by bank lobbyists, blamed the victims for buying houses they could not afford, running up debts, and receiving too many employee benefits. The victims were made to bear the losses, while the largest banks and their employees were reaping record profits. Public outrage prompted such movements as Occupy Wall Street and Move Your Money, triggering a quick mass education in the issues and focusing attention on the culprits—the Wall Street banks themselves.

Too Big to Regulate

The solution pursued by a deadlocked Congress has been to maintain the existing system and simply tighten regulatory controls. But by the summer of 2012, two years after the Dodd-Frank legislation that was supposed to fix the system with tougher regulations, it was clear that this solution wasn't working. The giant Wall Street banks had only grown larger, more ungovernable, and more corrupt. Major lawsuits charged them with racketeering (organized crime under the U.S. Racketeer Influenced and Corrupt Organizations Act or RICO), antitrust violations, wire fraud, bid-rigging, and price-fixing.[32] Many of these charges were already proven, and hefty damages and penalties had been assessed; but the international megabanks were able to absorb these fines and penalties simply as a cost of doing business. Only a few bit players had gone to jail.

Bid-rigging was the subject of *U.S. v Carollo, Goldberg and Grimm*, a ten-year lawsuit in which the U.S. Department of Justice obtained a judgment in May 2012 against three GE Capital employees. The court confirmed that billions of dollars had been skimmed from cities all across America by bank collusion to rig the public bids on municipal bonds, a business worth $3.7 trillion. Bid-rigging, noted Matt Taibbi in *Rolling Stone*, was the sort of crime for which the Mafia was notorious.[33] Besides GE Capital, banks involved in the bidding scheme included Bank of America, JPMorgan Chase, Wells Fargo and UBS. These banks paid a total of $673 million in restitution after agreeing to cooperate in the government's case.

The bid-rigging scandal was quickly followed by the LIBOR scandal, involving collusion to rig the inter-bank interest rate. LIBOR affects $500 trillion worth of contracts, financial instruments, mortgages and loans. In June 2012, Barclays Bank admitted to regulators that it had tried to manipulate LIBOR before and during the 2008 financial crisis and said that other banks were doing the same. Barclays paid $450 million to settle the charges. After resigning, top executives at Barclays promptly implicated both the Bank of England and the Federal Reserve.[34]

In short, the biggest banks and the central banks that oversaw them were being charged with conspiring to manipulate the most important market interest rates globally, along with the exchange rates propping up the U.S. dollar.

The losers – local governments, hospitals, universities and other nonprofits that had wound up on the short end of interest rate swaps – were busily counting up their damages and assessing their legal remedies.[35] Local banks were also seeking to recover damages for the LIBOR scam. The low interest rates that allowed the big derivatives banks to make a killing on interest rate swaps were also killing the profits from local bank lending.[36]

Then there were the lawsuits against the Mortgage Electronic Registration Systems or MERS, an electronic registry designed to track servicing rights and ownership of mortgage loans in the United States. Among other cases, one in Louisiana involved thirty judges representing thirty parishes suing MERS and seventeen colluding banks under RICO. The pleadings said that MERS was a scheme set up to defraud the government of real estate transfer fees, and that mortgages transferred through MERS were illegal.[37] The RICO statute provides for treble damages, so the bite from these suits could be substantial.

The Shadow Banking System:
The Weak Link the Regulators Missed

The Dodd-Frank legislation has not succeeded in reining in the megabanks, but critics say that even if it had, it would not have insured against another Lehman-style collapse, because it was shooting at the wrong target. As noted by Representative Kanjorski, the bank run that triggered the global credit freeze was not in the conventional system. It was in the not-so-familiar shadow banking system, which remains perilously unregulated.[38]

Yale economist Gary Gorton explains that bank runs don't generally occur in the traditional banking system today because depositors are protected through the Federal Deposit Insurance Corporation (FDIC). But FDIC insurance covers only $250,000 in deposits. There is a massive and growing demand for banking by large institutional investors—pension funds, mutual funds, hedge funds, sovereign wealth funds—which have millions of dollars to park somewhere between investments. They want an investment that is secure, that provides them with a little interest, and that is liquid like a traditional deposit account, allowing quick withdrawal.[39]

The shadow banking system evolved in response to this need, operating largely through the "repo" market. The repo system is a complicated subject, but basically it operates like a pawn shop. Instead of FDIC insurance, investors are protected with repos—sales and repurchases of highly liquid collateral, typically Treasury debt or mortgage-backed securities. If the investors don't get their money back from the pawn shop (in this case a "special purpose vehicle" or SPV), they can recover by foreclosing on the securities.

To satisfy the demand for liquidity (funds available for ready withdrawal), the repos are one-day or short-term deals, continually rolled over until the money is withdrawn. This money is used by banks for other lending, investing, or speculating. But that puts the banks in a quite risky position. Like Jimmy Stewart in the classic 1930s film *It's a Wonderful Life*, they are funding long-term loans with short-term borrowings. When money market investors get spooked and pull their money out all at once, as happened in 2008, the banks can no longer make commercial loans, and credit freezes.

The shadow banking system has allowed the private expansion of credit by piling debt upon debt in a fragile house of cards that is mathematically unsustainable. Operating outside the prying eyes of bank regulators, the shadow system allows credit to be generated without regard to capital requirements, reserve requirements, or the need to balance loans (assets) against liabilities (deposits), as conventional banks must do.

Although it is a risky and inherently fraudulent undertaking, this fragile, domino-like credit structure fills a market need. Credit is the lifeblood of the economy; and conventional banks have increasingly been hamstrung by regulations that limit lending, requiring some alternative source of free-flowing credit to keep the wheels of production turning. By definition, a shadow banking system is one that evades regulation. History shows that loopholes will be found as fast as they can be filled. Yet it is this sort of system that will have to be dealt with as long as the conventional banking system remains limited and unresponsive to the needs of the modern market.

Derivatives: The Wall Street Casino

Derivatives are another part of the shadow banking system that is obscure and complicated, and that most people had never heard of before the 2008 banking crisis; but in terms of money traded, these investments represent the biggest financial market in the world.

Derivatives are financial instruments that have no intrinsic value but derive their value from something else. Basically, they are just bets. You can "hedge your bet" that something you own will go up by placing a side bet that it will go down. "Hedge funds" hedge bets in the derivatives market. Bets can be placed on anything, from the price of tea in China to the movements of specific markets.

"The point everyone misses," wrote the late Robert Chapman many years ago, "is that buying derivatives is not investing. It is gambling, insurance and high stakes bookmaking. Derivatives create nothing."[40] They not only create nothing, but they serve to enrich non-producers at the expense of the people who *do* create real goods and services. In congressional hearings in the early 1990s, derivatives trading was challenged as being an illegal form of gambling. But the practice was legitimized by Fed Chairman Alan Greenspan, who not only lent legal and regulatory support to the trade but actively promoted derivatives as a way to improve "risk management." Partly, this was to boost the flagging profits of the banks; and at the larger banks and dealers, it worked. But the cost was an increase in risk to the financial system as a whole.[2]

Derivative trades have grown since then to be many times larger than the entire global economy. By 2008, the over-the-counter derivatives market had exceeded $650 trillion in "notional" contract trades (the face amount of the trades)—over 10 times the GDP of all the countries in the world combined.[41] How is that figure even possible? The gross domestic product of all the countries in the world is only about 60 trillion dollars. The answer is that gamblers can bet as much as they want. They can bet money they don't have, and that is where the huge increase in risk comes in.

Credit derivatives are sold as insurance against default. Credit default swaps (CDS) are bets between two parties on whether or not a company will default on its bonds. In a typical default swap, the "protection buyer" gets a large payoff from the "protection seller" if the company defaults within a certain period of time, while the "protection seller" collects periodic payments from the "protection buyer" for assuming the risk of default. CDS thus resemble insurance policies, but there is no requirement to actually hold any asset or suffer any loss, so CDS are widely used just to increase profits by gambling on market changes. In one blogger's example, a hedge fund could sit back and collect $320,000 a year in premiums just for selling "protection" on a risky BBB junk bond. The premiums are "free" money – free until the bond actually goes into default, when the hedge fund could be on the hook for $100 million in claims.

And there's the catch: what if the hedge fund doesn't have the $100 million? The fund's corporate shell or limited partnership is put into bankruptcy; but both parties are claiming the derivative as an *asset* on their books, which they now have to write down. Players who have hedged their bets by betting both ways cannot collect on their winning bets; and that means they cannot afford to pay their losing bets, causing other players to also default on their bets. The dominos could go down in a cascade of cross-defaults that infects the whole banking industry and jeopardizes the global pyramid scheme. The potential for this sort of nuclear reaction was what prompted billionaire investor Warren Buffett to call derivatives "weapons of financial mass destruction." It is also why the banking lobby insists that a major derivatives player must not be allowed to go down, and why derivatives claims are allowed to go first in bankruptcy before all others, including those of depositors—even secured depositors such as state and local governments.

Wall Street has the biggest lobby and the loudest voice in Congress, but other experts dispute that netting out the derivatives could not be done without disastrous results. More on this in Chapter 29.

Turning Mortgages into Pawns for the Repo Market

"Securitization" of mortgages is another part of the shadow banking system that is an offshoot of the pawn-shop model of banking. Massive pools of home mortgages have been turned into "securities"-- tradable documents evidencing an ownership interest in a portion of a debt, which can be sliced and packaged like sausages and sold off to investors. The system has allowed the banks to originate more loans, but it has had a devastating effect on both the U.S. real estate market and county land title records.

The system arose in response to the capital requirements imposed from abroad by the Bank for International Settlements beginning in the 1980s. (More on this later.) Under the "Basel Accords," to back $100 in loans, banks are required to have about $10 in capital (meaning their own rather than their depositors' money). Once the bank has reached this lending limit, it must wait for 20 or 30 years until the loans are repaid before making new ones. That puts a damper on credit creation, something banks have gotten around by securitization. Selling the loans to investors allows the banks to move them off their books so that new ones can be made.

Securitization was another type of "shadow" system, in this case one that evaded capital requirements. But it has had the negative effect of divorcing the original lender from any responsibility for the loans, or from any penalty for churning out great volumes of loans to non-creditworthy borrowers. The result was a massive housing bubble, which was followed by a housing bust when investors realized they had been sold loans backed by "toxic" collateral—mortgages that were not "triple A" as represented. All this happened behind the electronic curtain called MERS, which allowed houses to be shuffled among multiple, rapidly-changing owners while circumventing local recording laws. Among other frauds it concealed was the pledging of the same home as "security" for several different investor groups at the same time.[42] As Michael Rivero put it on his blog *What Really Happened*:

> [The banks] realized that while you can only sell a house to one owner at a time, you can in theory sell the mortgage over and over, since it is a piece of easily copied paper or more likely a computer record in MERS, . . . a computer system created to evade transfer fees[43] and to speed up the churning of the mortgages as they shuffled from one investment company to another. MERS initially helped conceal the over-selling of mortgages, but eventually the scam became known, and numerous major banks have been exposed for selling the same mortgage into multiple mortgage-backed securities,[44] generating vast profits for the bundlers. . . . In February 2009 CNBC broke the story that many of the mortgage bundlers had pledged individual mortgages as collateral over and over into different CDOs, when legally, they can be pledged as collateral only once.[45]

Fraud as a Business Model

Rivero noted that the mortgage bundlers might not have seen this as a fraud. They were simply following the system of "fractional reserve" lending used by banks for hundreds of years. Businesses need ready access to a fluid credit mechanism, and that is what banks do: they provide credit. But to pull this off, they have had to engage in sleight of hand. This is because money has been perceived to be a "thing"— gold or another commodity that is valuable in itself and is in limited supply. A limited money supply can expand to meet the demands of an expanding economy only through a massive shell game, in which bankers purport to be lending something they do not really have.

When the official medium of exchange was gold, the shell game was susceptible to periodic collapse when the banks' customers discovered there were insufficient peas under the shells to cover all their claims. Complex regulations would then be imposed to keep the bankers in line, but these often served only to impede the issuance of credit. Various ruses would be devised to get around the rules, but it was a constant scramble to balance the books and avoid insolvency.

In the same way, the modern securitization shell game has run into trouble when more than one investor group has tried to foreclose on the same property at the same time. The securitization model has also crashed against the hard rock of hundreds of years of state real estate law, which has certain requirements that the banks have not met. It seems that the banks not only have not but cannot meet these requirements, if they are to comply with the tax laws for REMICs, the Real Estate Mortgage Investment Conduits through which mortgage-backed securities are typically funneled.[46]

The bankers have engaged in what amounts to a massive fraud, not necessarily through criminal intent, but in order to come up with the collateral (in this case real estate) necessary to back the extension of credit in a pawnshop model of banking. In the system we have today, banks are not free simply to create credit and advance it to us, counting on our future productivity to pay it off. (This can be and has been done in systems in which the bank is an institution of a sovereign government, authorized to advance the credit of the nation; but more on that later.) In today's private banking structure, banks must meet capital requirements, reserve requirements, and check clearing requirements. They must balance their books, and to do that they must borrow—from their depositors, other banks, or the money market. The net effect is that they are vacuuming up our money and lending it back to us at higher rates. In the shadow banking system, they are chopping up our real estate to serve as collateral for large institutional investors, including our pension funds and mutual funds. As British money reformer Ann Pettifor puts it:

> [B]ankers now borrow from their customers and from taxpayers. They are effectively draining funds from household bank accounts, small businesses, corporations, government Treasuries and from e.g. the Federal Reserve. They do so by charging high rates of interest and fees; by demanding early repayment of loans; by illegally foreclosing on homeowners, and by appropriating, and then speculating with trillions of dollars of taxpayer-backed resources. . . .
>
> By borrowing from the real economy, and then refusing to lend except at high rates of interest, bankers are effectively performing a lobotomy on the real economy. They are cutting critical credit connections to and from the vital "cortex"—the region of the economy responsible for investment and the creation of jobs.[47]

The situation was summed up by economist Michael Hudson in a January 2012 article titled "Banks Weren't Meant to Be Like This":

> Banking has moved so far away from funding industrial growth and economic development that it now benefits primarily at the economy's expense in a predatory and extractive way, not by making productive loans. This is now the great problem confronting our time. Banks now lend mainly to other financial institutions, hedge funds, corporate raiders, insurance companies and real estate, and engage in their own speculation in foreign currency, interest-rate arbitrage, and computer-driven trading programs. Industrial firms bypass the banking system by financing new capital investment out of their own retained earnings, and meet their liquidity needs by issuing their own commercial paper directly. Yet to keep the bank casino winning, global bankers now want governments not only to bail them out but to enable them to renew their

failed business plan—and to keep the present debts in place so that creditors will not have to take a loss.[48]

Yves Smith, author of the popular blog *Naked Capitalism,* takes a similarly dark view of the current scheme. In a September 2010 post titled "Why Do We Keep Indulging the Fiction that Banks Are Private Enterprises?", she wrote:

> Big finance has an unlimited credit line with governments around the globe. "Most subsidized industry in the world" is inadequate to describe this relationship. Banks are now in the permanent role of looters. They run highly leveraged operations, extract compensation based on questionable accounting and officially-subsidized risk-taking, and dump their losses on the public at large.
>
> But the subsidies go beyond that. To list only a few examples: we have near zero interest rates, which allow banks to earn risk free profits simply by borrowing short and buying longer-dated Treasuries. We have the IRS refusing to look into violations of REMIC rules, which govern mortgage securitizations. We have massive intervention to prop up real estate prices, with the main objective to shore up banks; any impact on consumers is an afterthought.
>
> The usual narrative, "privatized gains and socialized losses" is insufficient to describe the dynamic at work. The banking industry falsely depicts markets, and by extension, its incumbents as a bastion of capitalism. The blatant manipulation of the equity markets shows that financial activity, which used to be recognized as valuable because it supported commercial activity, is whenever possible being subverted to industry rent-seeking. And worse, *these activities are state supported.*[49]

Banks can be circumscribed by rules imposed by the government; but rules can be dodged, regulators can be captured, and misguided regulations can impair the flow of credit. Yet banking and credit are vital to the economy, and government backing is necessary to keep the banking system afloat. A better solution than regulation would be to also socialize the gains, something that could be done by making banking a public utility. There are many examples historically and globally demonstrating that this solution will work. While Western economies have been languishing, countries with strong public banking sectors have not only managed to avoid the recent banking crisis but have shown remarkable growth.

Chapter 3

PUBLIC SECTOR BANKS: FROM BLACK SHEEP TO GLOBAL LEADERS

"Once the black sheep of high finance, government owned banks can reassure depositors about the safety of their savings and can help maintain a focus on productive investment in a world in which effective financial regulation remains more of an aspiration than a reality."

— *Centre for Economic Policy Research, VoxEU.org (January 2010)*[50]

> The common perception of government-owned banks is that they are less efficient, less profitable and more susceptible to political corruption than banks operated for private profit. Recent studies, however, have found the reverse. Strong public banking sectors are linked to strong, productive economies.

Public sector banking is a concept that is relatively unknown in the United States. Only one state—North Dakota—actually owns its own bank. North Dakota is also the only state to escape the recent credit crisis, sporting a budget surplus every year since 2008. It has the lowest unemployment rate in the country, the lowest credit card default rate, and no state government debt at all. But skeptics write these achievements off to other factors, including an oil boom in the state. The common perception is that government bureaucrats are bad businessmen. To determine whether government-owned banks are assets or liabilities for economies, then, we need to look farther than our own backyard.

Removing our myopic U.S. blinders, we find that internationally, not only are publicly-owned banks quite common, but that countries with strong public banking sectors generally have strong, stable economies. According to an Inter-American Development Bank paper presented in 2005, the percentage of state ownership globally in the banking industry by the mid-1990s was over 40 percent.[51]

These public banks are largely in the BRIC countries—Brazil, Russia, India, and China—which contain nearly three billion of the world's seven billion people, or 40 percent of the global population. The BRICs have been the main locus of world economic growth in the last decade. Publicly-owned banks compose about 60 percent of the banks in Russia, 75 percent in India, 69 percent or more in China, and 45 percent in Brazil.[52]

According to *China Daily*, "Between 2000 and 2010, BRIC's GDP grew by an incredible 92.7 percent, compared to a global GDP growth of just 32 percent, with industrialized economies having a very modest 15.5 percent."[53] In 2009, when GDP dropped by 2 percent worldwide due to the banking crisis, the BRICs expanded by 4.3 percent. In 2010, BRIC GDP surged by 8.8 percent.[54] The International Monetary Fund predicts that by 2016, the GDP of the BRIC countries will total $21 trillion, out-stripping the United States. On a currency-adjusted basis, the BRICs are already larger than the U.S. and U.K. combined.[55]

All the leading banks in the BRIC half of the globe are state-owned.[56] The largest banks globally are also state-owned, including:

- The two largest banks by market capitalization (ICBC and China Construction Bank)
- The largest bank by deposits (Japan Post Bank)
- The largest bank by number of branches (State Bank of India)
- The largest bank by assets (Royal Bank of Scotland, nationalized in 2008)
- The largest development bank (China Development Bank).[57]

The world's seven *safest* banks are also publicly-owned, leading with KfW, Germany's public development bank.[58]

The term "BRIC" was introduced in 2001 by Goldman Sachs economist Jim O'Neill, in an article titled "Building Better Global Economic BRICs." He predicted that these four countries would dominate the world's economy in the future, shifting global economic power away from the developed economies toward the developing world.[59] Events since then have confirmed this prediction.

The BRIC countries have abundant labor and resources, but O'Neill notes that their growth has far outstripped predictions based on these factors alone.[60] Something else has been responsible for their "economic miracles." According to a May 2010 article in *The Economist*, the BRICs sailed through the banking crisis largely because of their strong and stable publicly-owned banks.[61] Professor Kurt von Mettenheim of the Sao Paulo Business School of Brazil observes:

> Government banks provided counter cyclical credit and policy options to counter the effects of the recent financial crisis, while realizing competitive advantage over private and foreign banks. Greater client confidence and official deposits reinforced liability base and lending capacity. The credit policies of BRIC government banks help explain why these countries experienced shorter and milder economic downturns during 2007-2008.[62]

Not-for-profits Outperform For-Profits

In a June 2011 paper titled "Alternative Banking: Competitive Advantage and Social Inclusion," Professor von Mettenheim and Olivier Butzbach show that "alternative banks"—public savings banks, cooperative banks, and public development banks—have done more than just match their private counterparts. In recent years, they have actually outperformed their for-profit rivals:

> These "alternative banks" (or ABs) . . . not only fared better than their joint-stock counterparts during the crisis and its aftermath; they have been constantly over-performing them for some time—whether we compare cost efficiency, riskiness

or even, in some respect, profitability—a paradox as ABs are in principle not profit-maximizing entities.[63]

These results differ from those of earlier studies. An often-cited 2004 World Bank study concluded:

> Unfortunately, the performance of most public sector banks has been weak, particularly in terms of large non-performing loans (NPLs). For example, in China, recent official estimates suggest NPLs of around 24 percent in the four public sector commercial banks, equivalent to over 30 percent of GDP; estimates of private analysts are much higher.[64]

The explanation for this discrepancy could turn on the word "performance." Although the Chinese state-owned banks may have more non-performing loans than private Western banks, the Chinese economy itself is performing better than Western economies dominated by private sector banks; and this superior performance is supported by a public sector banking system that functions very well for its intended purposes. Before 1981, the Chinese government issued its own sovereign currency, paid its bills in that currency, and did not incur national debt. When it opened to Western trade, it had to make a show of conforming to Western practices. Advances of credit intended for national development were therefore re-characterized as "non-performing loans." But the Chinese government did not actually expect repayment of these funds. They were simply credits created on the banks' books for the purpose of paying for infrastructure and services. They were in the nature of "contingent grants." If they generated income, great. If not, they were written off as a cost of running an economy. They were government-issued money stimulating economic development. [65]

Western politicians call these unpaid loans "deficits," debts" and "fiscal cliffs," and they engage in endless debates over how to get rid of them. Meanwhile, China and its neighbors carry on building, growing and producing. They recognize that the government's debt is the people's credit, and that a freely-flowing national credit is the key to a flourishing national economy. How well this has worked for the Chinese is explored further in Chapter 6.

Other Surprising Findings

Neo-classical economic theory predicted that when banking was opened to competition and liberalization (the relaxing of banking rules), "alternative" banks would disappear, either through privatization or through competitive pressures. But that is not what happened. According to von Mettenheim and Butzbach:

> Savings banks and cooperative banks have . . . retained or increased their significant market shares since liberalization of the industry. Instead of convergence toward private banking, joint-stock ownership, shareholder governance and market-centered finance, public savings banks, cooperative banks and special purpose (development) banks have modernized through a rich variety of strategies to retain or expand market shares while seeking to recast their social policies and missions.

The alternative banks have merged and integrated with each other:

> Far from being condemned by more liquid financial markets or risk seeking private banks, the integration of regional and local savings banks and cooperative banks have produced competitive advantage, better performance, increased market shares and renovated institutions for social and economic policy coordination.[66]

A major competitive advantage of public, not-for-profit banks is that their costs are less:

> Government banks . . . produce more public policy for less cash. The slim central offices, low cost/income ratios and principles of profit sustainability at special purpose banks and development banks provide powerful competitive advantages over private banks and help lower the costs of public policy.

Another competitive advantage is in the governance structure of alternative banks. Decisions are made by "stakeholders"—community members, employees and creditors who have a stake in preserving the business as a viable concern—rather than by shareholders whose chief interest is in maximizing their own short-term profits.

Publicly-owned banks can do more with the government's money than the government can by spending it outright. Banks can leverage the funds, multiplying them many times over in the form of bank credit. Von Mettenheim, et al., use the example of Brazil's government banks, particularly the Caixa Economica Federal, its government savings bank:

> Analysts often compare government bank performance unfavorably with private commercial banks. However, in terms of public policy, government banks can do more for less: Almost ten times more if one compares cash used as capital reserves by banks to other policies that require budgetary outflows. Central Bank of Brazil regulations require eleven percent (weighted) capital reserves against credit risk. *This implies that the Caixa (and other government banks) can loan almost ten times whatever profits are retained or funds may be allocated by congress.* From this perspective, . . . the Caixa appears uniquely positioned to provide social services and extend credit to those left behind during Brazilian development. *Tapping the popular credit channel may accelerate social inclusion and economic development, deepen the Brazilian financial system, and provide substance to citizenship and democracy.*[67]

A government bank can take one million dollars of its own capital and turn them into ten million in loans. Again, "capital" means the bank's own money (shareholder equity plus profits), not the money of its depositors. Deposits will be needed to back the loans; but a government savings bank will have plenty of deposits, and if the bank does not have them, it can borrow them. This sort of system has worked particularly well in Japan, which has tapped into the copious deposits in the government-owned Japan Post Bank, now the largest depository bank in the world. (See Chapter 21.)

Public Banks Spur Growth Better and Are Less Corrupt

Another study comparing public and private banks was reported in 2010 by a team of economists at the Centre for Economic Development and Institutions (CEDI) at Brunel University in the U.K.[68] They noted that the post-2008 nationalization of a number of very large banks, including the Royal Bank of Scotland, was an excellent opportunity to reduce the political power of bankers and to carry out much needed financial reforms. The concern was whether governments could run nationalized banks efficiently. The authors observed:

> While many countries in continental Europe, including Germany and France, have had a fair amount of experience with government-owned banks, the UK and the USA have found themselves in unfamiliar territory. It is therefore perhaps not surprising that there is deeply ingrained hostility in these countries towards the notion that governments can run banks effectively. . . . Hostility towards government-owned banks reflects the hypothesis . . . that these banks are established by politicians who use them to shore up their power by instructing them to lend to political supporters and government-owned enterprises. In return, politicians receive votes and other favors. This hypothesis also postulates that politically motivated banks make bad lending decisions, resulting in non-performing loans, financial fragility and slower growth.

But that is not what the data of these researchers showed. To the contrary:

> [W]e have found that . . . countries with government-owned banks have, on average, grown faster than countries with no or little government ownership of banks. . . . This is, of course, a surprising result, especially in light of the widespread belief—typically supported by anecdotal evidence—that "bureaucrats are generally bad bankers" . . . .

The authors suggested that, contrary to popular belief, politicians may prefer that banks *not* be in the public sector:

> Conditions of weak corporate governance in banks provide fertile ground for quick enrichment for both bankers and politicians—at the expense ultimately of the taxpayer. In such circumstances politicians can offer bankers a system of weak regulation in exchange for party political contributions, positions on the boards of banks or lucrative consultancies. Activities that are more likely to provide both sides with

quick returns are the more speculative ones, especially if they are sufficiently opaque as not to be well understood by the shareholders such as complex derivatives trading.

Government owned banks, on the other hand, have less freedom to engage in speculative strategies that result in quick enrichment for bank insiders and politicians. Moreover, politicians tend to be held accountable for wrongdoings or bad management in the public sector but are typically only indirectly blamed, if at all, for the misdemeanours of private banks. It is the shareholders who are expected to prevent these but lack of transparency and weak governance stops them from doing so in practice. On the other hand, when it comes to banks that are in the public sector, democratic accountability of politicians is more likely to discourage them from engaging in speculation. In such banks, top managers are more likely to be compelled to focus on the more mundane job of financing real businesses and economic growth.

Public banks are run by civil servants on government salaries who do not get commissions based on loan volume and have no opportunity to engage in speculation for their own account. They get paid for serving the public interest, and they get promoted for succeeding at that pursuit. That helps explain the findings of the Brunel research team, which were summarized on *VOX* as follows:

Using data from a large number of countries for 1995-2007, we find that, other things equal, countries with high degrees of government ownership of banking have grown faster than countries with little government ownership of banks. We show that this finding is robust to a battery of econometric tests.[69]

Public Banks Foster Growth While Expanding Social Services

This fast growth is particularly evident in the BRIC countries. Looking at them individually, China's GDP has grown by nearly 10 percent almost every year since the early 1980s.[70] India has also achieved impressive uninterrupted growth, averaging 7.8 percent for the period 2000-2010.[71]

In Russia, GDP growth averaged 6.5 percent from 2000 to 2008. It fell back in 2009 in response to the Western financial crisis and a drop in the price of oil, but it moved back up to about 4 percent of GDP in 2010 and 2011, with low inflation and low unemployment—very good by world standards. Jim O'Neill predicts that by 2030, Russia could surpass Germany to become the richest European nation.[72]

Brazil is also experiencing the greatest economic growth in its history, averaging 4.5 percent per year since 2002. In 2010, the country's GDP expanded by an estimated 7.5 percent, bringing its total GDP to almost $2.2 trillion (the highest in Latin America) and its GDP per capita to over $11,000 (the sixth-highest in Latin America). Joblessness was at an all-time low, and foreign exchange reserves had soared to the sixth-highest globally.[73]

The popular perception is that this unusual growth has been achieved through the exploitation of the poor and working classes. But the data show that, to the contrary, millions of people in these countries have been raised from poverty into the middle class. According to a September 2012 article in *The Economist* called "New Cradles to Graves," Asian countries are providing social benefits to their citizens far beyond those available in the United States.

In 2008, India expanded its job-guarantee program to every rural district, promising 100 days of minimum-wage work a year to every household that asked for it. It has also extended health insurance to about 110 million people, more than twice the number of uninsured Americans.

China's rural health-insurance scheme covered only 3 percent of the eligible population in 2003, but it now covers 97.5 percent according to official statistics. China's National Audit Office declared in August 2012 that the country's social security system was also basically in place. Statutory retirement ages in developing Asia average 59 for men and 58 for women.

Other Asian countries with strong public banking sectors are also strong on social benefits. South Korea (discussed in Chapter 22) has legislation guaranteeing a minimum income to the poor. The government subsidizes the employment of the elderly and is beginning to socialize the burden of caring for them. In 2008, South Korea introduced insurance for long-term geriatric care. And in Indonesia, a law was passed in October 2011 pledging to provide health insurance to all of the country's 240 million citizens, making it the largest single-payer system in the world.[74.]

Indonesia is not one of the BRICs, but it too has a strong public banking sector. Publicly-owned banks control over 40% of Indonesian bank assets, and all public sector entities (including about 150 state-owned enterprises) are required by law to deposit their financial assets in state-owned banks.[75] The result is a massive, captive deposit base that can be turned into credit available for public purposes.

Unfair Competition or a Better Mousetrap?

Western competitors complain that the advantages of government ownership allow publicly-owned banks to compete unfairly, and they attempt to handicap those banks with regulations. But the fact that public banks can offer more in the way of security for customers, lowered costs, and larger capital and deposit bases is not really "unfair" competition. It is simply a more competitive banking model.

Hamstringing the BRICs and other Asian competitors with international banking regulations is ultimately doomed to failure, because those countries are powerful enough to step outside our system and set up their own rules, as they are doing today in the BRIC economic bloc and the ASEAN Economic Community to be established in 2015. It might be more productive to simply incorporate some portion of their safe and efficient banking models into our own. That doesn't mean adopting their political agendas; but by rigidly insisting even on the outmoded aspects of our system just because of ideology, we may find that our entire ideology—democracy and all— has been relegated to the dustbin of history.

The next three chapters will take a closer look at the BRICs, since they are the most powerful contemporary examples of efficient public banking systems. But there are other public models that are also quite instructive, going back thousands of years. That history will be the subject of Section 2, laying the groundwork for the interesting 20th century developments in Section 3.

Chapter 4

THE BRICS AS A GLOBAL POWER: BRAZIL AND RUSSIA

"Don't you find it very chic that Brazil is lending to the IMF? I spent part of my youth carrying banners against the IMF in downtown Sao Paulo."

-- Brazilian President Lula da Silva after the 2009 G20 Summit[76]

Today, the BRIC bloc is evolving into not just an economic but a political force, and undergirding it all is a strong public banking sector. Brazil and Russia, the first two countries in the BRIC acronym, are both forging bright futures with public banks as key features of their economies. Brazil is considered the most successful model among the BRICs, while Russia is expected to be the richest country in Europe by 2030.

The BRIC group has evolved into more than just a growth trend identified by an economist. It has become an international organization, an alliance of countries representing the common interests and goals of its members. Russia has been the main driving force behind this alliance. In a famous speech in Munich in February 2007, Russian President Vladimir Putin predicted the emergence of the new alliance on the ruins of the unipolar world being pursued by the United States. The first BRIC meeting, held in 2008, was called a triumph for Putin's policy of promoting multilateral arrangements that would challenge this unipolar concept.[77]

The BRIC countries had their first official summit and became a formal organization in Yekaterinburg, Russia, in 2009. They met in Brazil in 2010, in China in 2011, in India in 2012, and in South Africa in 2013. In 2010, South Africa joined the group at China's invitation, making it "BRICS" and adding a strategic presence on the African continent.

The BRICS seek more voice in the United Nations and want an alternative to Western-centric international financial institutions with their neoliberal policies. At their March 2013 meeting in Durban, South Africa, they formally declared their intention to create a BRICS Development Bank to underwrite infrastructure projects within their own nations, in direct competition with the International Monetary Fund (IMF) and the World Bank.

The BRICS also seek to create an alternative to the dollar as the world reserve currency. After the Yekaterinburg summit, they called for a new reserve currency that is "diversified, stable and predictable."[78] And they appear to have the clout to get it. The BRICS account for around three-quarters of total currency reserves, have few serious fiscal issues, and are net government creditors.[79]

Thus the BRICS are coming on like gangbusters; and their strong public banking sectors are major engines of that drive. This chapter will look at the first two countries in the BRIC acronym, Brazil and Russia. The following two chapters will look at India and China, which have over one billion people each and have evolved their own unique ways of funding the needs of their massive populations.

Public Banking in Russia: On the Rise

Contrary to the predictions of neoliberal economists, public banks in Russia are enjoying a popular resurgence. Rather than proceeding from public to private, as predicted by neoliberal economists, change in Russian bank ownership is going the other way. That is the conclusion of a paper posted in 2009 by the Federal Reserve Bank of St. Louis titled "Russian Banking: The State Makes a Comeback?" It states:

Concentration is increasing within the public sector of the industry, with the top five state-controlled banking groups in possession of over 49 percent of assets. We observe a crowding out and erosion of domestic private capital, whose market share is shrinking from year to year. Several of the largest state-owned banks now constitute a de facto intermediate tier at the core of the banking system.[80]

According to a March 2010 *Forbes* article titled "Financial Crisis Alters Russian Banks":

The ownership structure of the Russian banking system differs from those in other emerging eastern European markets. It more closely resembles China's: Both markets are characterized by the dominance of state institutions and the relatively small role of foreign banks. . . .

As in other countries, the [2008] crisis prompted the state to take on a greater role in the banking system. State-owned systemic banks . . . have been used to carry out anticrisis measures, such as driving growth in lending (however limited) and supporting private institutions.[81]

Large foreign banks that once saw Russia as a huge undeveloped market are now fleeing the country, because they cannot compete with the state-owned banks. In a February 2011 report, Moody's Investors Service said that state-owned banks control about half the banking system's total assets and enjoy unparalleled access to low-cost funding and high-quality borrowers.[82]

At the end of 2010, Russia's top 20 banks had a total of $737 billion in assets among them. Of these, state-owned banks held a 75 percent share, up from 73 percent a year earlier. The top five state-owned banks account for 48 percent of all assets, with Sberbank, the largest, holding 58 percent of all retail deposits.[83] The government owns 58 percent of Sberbank and has 60 percent of the voting rights. With assets of $283 billion, Sberbank is nearly ten times the size of the largest privately owned Russian bank, Alfa Bank.[84]

Russia's top two banks by assets, Sberbank and Vneshtorgbank (VTB), are both state-run, and they are expanding into new markets. Sberbank has almost 20,000 retail branches and is moving into investment banking. VTB, once the Soviet foreign trade bank, has diversified into retail and small business lending, the industry's fastest-growing segments. In the Soviet era, VTB financed trade and heavy industry. Today it has more than 530 branches nationwide, and its investment banking unit is the largest underwriter of bond and equity sales. In 2011, in the largest acquisition by a lender to date, the Moscow government sold its shares in Bank of Moscow for $3.5 billion—not to a foreign bank, but to the state-run VTB.[85]

Like China and Japan, Russia has made a show of privatizing portions of its state-owned banks while retaining government control. VTB sold $3.3 billion worth of shares in February 2011, but the sum represented a mere 10 percent of its equity, leaving a solid 75.5 percent still owned by the state.[86] VTB was supposed to be the test case of the financial authorities' willingness to open up the banking sector to privatization, but according to a 2005 article in *Business Week*:

> So far there are few signs of progress toward that goal. . . . Some doubt the powers that be will ever let VTB out of government hands.
>
> . . . [S]trong state backing has kept VTB well capitalized and helps the bank to borrow cheaply on international financial markets. State ownership also reassures mom-and-pop depositors. Last summer a banking panic led to the collapse of some private banks and shook others, leading deposits to flow into state-owned banks.[87]

State-owned banks are expected to dominate the Russian banking industry for the foreseeable future.[88] In the 1998 Asian crisis, many Russians who had put all their savings in private banks lost everything, and the credit crisis of 2008 has reinforced their distrust of private banks. They want a bank in which they can feel their money is safe. As problems linger in global financial markets, local Russian companies are also switching to state-owned banks for funding.[89]

Brazil, Lula and the BNDES

Brazil is the fifth largest country in the world, with a population of over 190 million. Considered the most successful model among the BRICs, it is growing faster than Russia, does not have the ethnic and border troubles of India, and is less dependent on exports than China is. Exports make up only 13 percent of Brazil's GDP. The country ranks highest among all South American nations economically and has acquired a strong position in the global economy.

But while it shines today, Brazil wasn't always doing so well. During the 1980s and 1990s, it had the dubious distinction of being the most indebted country in the world. It was unable to generate enough revenue even to pay the interest on its debt, and it was borrowing heavily just to stay afloat.

Then in 2003, Luiz Inacio Lula da Silva ("Lula"), a former auto worker and founding member of the Workers' Party, became Brazil's president. His achievements during his eight years in office have been called nothing short of miraculous. By 2006, Brazil had paid off its debts. In the space of a few years, the Brazilian government managed to accumulate more than 200 billion dollars in reserves and to transform the Real (Brazil's currency) into one of the world's strongest currencies. In October 2009, Brazil announced that it was actually becoming an IMF creditor, purchasing 10 billion dollars worth of IMF bonds.[90]

According to a March 2013 article in *Der Spiegel*, Lula's supporters "liken him to U.S. President Franklin D. Roosevelt, who dammed the Tennessee River in the 1930s to provide electricity to the region and who launched the New Deal, a massive investment program to overcome the Great Depression."[91] Like Roosevelt, Lula funded his ambitious programs with "self-liquidating loans"—advances of government credits that were repaid with the proceeds of the project.

The loans in both cases were generated by a financial institution owned by the government and having free access to the Treasury. For Roosevelt, it was the Reconstruction Finance Corporation (RFC). (More on this in Chapter 14.) For Lula, it was the the Banco Nacional de Desenvolvimento Econômico e Social—the National Economic and Social Development Bank, or BNDES. Lula rescued his insolvent country by enlisting its giant national development bank to aim the fire hose of national credit at a whole host of creditworthy projects, including road construction, dam building, bridge building, museum refurbishing, public transport projects, mining companies, and slaughterhouses.

Featured in *Time* as one of "The 100 Most Influential People in the World for 2010," Lula has been called "the most successful politician of his time."[92] He is generally regarded as the most popular politician in the history of Brazil, and at the time of his mandate he was one of the most popular in the world.

National Development Using National Credit

Today, approximately 40 percent of domestic lending and finance is conducted in Brazil through three big federal government banks. Besides the BNDES, they include the Banco do Brasil, the largest bank in Brazil by all measures; and the Caixa Econômica Federal, or federal government savings bank, which retains a dominant market share in housing, savings, and urban development. Brazil also has flourishing local public and cooperative banks. But the innovative use of the BNDES to turn the economy around is of particular interest here and will be the focus of this chapter. The BNDES has been indispensable to the creation of domestic capital markets in Brazil, and it is the main source of long-term loans in the economy. Its focus is on infrastructure and long-term lending to strategic sectors. It is not just a passive lender but holds an ownership interest in many Brazilian enterprises.[93]

A December 2009 article in *Al Jazeera* maintained:

> Without question, the BNDES is the most powerful public bank in all of Latin America, and quite possibly one of the most influential—yet little known—public lending institutions in the entire world.
>
> . . . So far this year alone the BNDES has handed out loans and lines of credit totalling more than $57bn (100bn reals).
>
> At the World Bank, by contrast, loans have totalled just under $47bn a year . . . .
>
> As Brazil's economy has surged in recent years . . . so too has the amount of money the BNDES has loaned, more than doubling from $22bn in 2004 (based on today's currency conversion) to more than $57bn today.
>
> [BNDES president] Coutinho has said that the BNDES loans, coupled with credit supply, have spurred Brazil's impressive and well-publicised growth in the past few years. And bank officials have said its lending is a big reason why Brazil was one of the last countries to feel the effects of the

global economic downturn, and one of the first countries to exit it. . . .

The BNDES, which falls under the auspices of the Ministry of Development, Industry and Foreign Trade, keeps a low public profile even within Brazil, and does not go out of the way to publicise its work. But it has wide leeway to chart its own course with almost semi-autonomy from the federal government bureaucracy.[94]

Reviving the Tradition of the Public Development Bank

The BNDES has its critics, who say that it may be *too* autonomous. Its power and influence have increased exponentially, while its transparency and its regard for the social and environmental impacts of its loans have not. Its "cozy" relationship with big business has also been criticized. If the model is to be followed, it will need to be with a stricter mandate concerning the environment and the public interest. But what is of interest here is what this government-owned bank has been able to achieve for an economy that not long ago was not able to pay even the interest on its debts.

The BNDES was featured in a March 2011 article in *The Guardian* by economist Jayati Ghosh, titled "Development Banks Still Have a Role to Play, as Brazil's Success Shows." Ghosh observes that while state-controlled banks have gotten some bad press, the success of the BNDES shows they can play a major role in long-term investment. He notes that development banks were used extensively in the developing world in the second half of the 20th century, to provide credit on terms that would make long-term and risky but socially necessary investment financially sustainable. They were both lenders and investors, using lending to influence investment decisions, monitor the performance of borrowers, and direct long-term investment. As developing economies were directed to rely on stock and bond markets and other forms of long-term investment financing, the development banks were largely wound down or marginalized. That was true in most countries but not in Brazil, where the BNDES was instead powered up. And it has served the country well:

It had a significant positive effect in helping Brazil deal with the effects of the 2008-09 financial crisis, and was responsible in no small measure for the quick turnaround in GDP growth. [95]

When the global financial crisis broke, the response in many countries was to lower interest rates and ease reserve requirements for commercial banks. But the banks did not pass those benefits on to the productive sector, and the credit crunch wound up hitting output and employment hard. That was not true, however, in Brazil:

> [T]he existence and spread of the BNDES allowed for a different kind of solution: to create a penultimate lender of last resort through government loans to the bank, which in its turn lent the resources to firms. This credit facility reached 3.3 percent of GDP during the crisis and helped many firms to meet their needs of circulating capital in 2008-09. So the drying up of private sector loans did not affect Brazilian producers as much as it did in most other developing countries.
>
> After the worst impact of the crisis receded, this special credit facility was gradually redirected to finance investment, which accelerated from the second half of 2009. In the past two years its lending has gone up by more than 70 percent.

To the argument of critics that the BNDES is hampering the development of the Brazilian financial sector, Ghosh counters, "[T]he world should be much more cynical now about the benefits ostensibly delivered by an unregulated financial sector bent on extracting private profits, even when at the cost of development and social conditions." While the central banks of the world are focused on backstopping the private banks they serve, development banks such as the BNDES direct credit to the real, producing economy.

According to Christian Poirier, program director for Brazil's "Amazon Watch":

> Without BNDES financing, many projects . . . would exist only on paper. Given the risks and impacts of mega-projects in the Amazon, as well as their enormous cost, it's very unlikely that other development banks or private banks could front sufficient funding for these projects.[96]

Funding the Bank that Funds the Economy

To assure an adequate and stable source of funding for the bank, Brazil's 1988 federal constitution required a portion of the Workers' Assistance Fund (FAT) to be invested in the BNDES for use in economic development programs. Rather than being invested in derivatives and other speculative ventures, public pension fund money was thus invested in the infrastructure needed to rebuild Brazil.

According to the BNDES website, FAT represented the main source of BNDES funding until 2008. In 2009, however, the bank raised R$ 100 billion from the National Treasury, and this credit limit was raised thereafter. In addition, the BNDES has resources from "return on its operations, monetization of its portfolio assets, equity, funds raised in the international market, either through multilateral organizations . . . or by issuing bonds," and other sources.[97]

The BNDES can fund infrastructure loans when private banks either cannot or will not, because the bank is underwritten and guaranteed by the government. The loans are at modest interest, helping to ensure they get repaid. The money can then be lent again. The bank can afford to charge less than market rates of interest because it is subsidized by the government and has lower costs—low overhead, no competitive advertising costs, no exorbitant bonuses, fees, commissions, or shareholder dividends. The loans zero out, but the net result for the economy is that it has roads, bridges, dams and social services that it did not have before.

Chapter 5

INDIA: BANKING FOR THE "AAM ADMI" (COMMON MAN)

"In the world's leading countries, the finance sectors have crashed but we are still surviving because we nationalised our banking sector."

-- Indian Finance Minister Pranab Mukherjee, July 2009

India emerged from five centuries of colonial rule with a massive, desperately poor population that could not afford to indulge a parasitic financial elite. Mother India needed to use her national credit to support her own industries and her own people. Nationalizing the country's major banks allowed resources to be directed to areas most in need, putting millions to work and spurring economic growth.

India is home to over 1.2 billion people, including an estimated one-third of the world's poor, who subsist on less than $1.25 a day.[98] In its last major famine in 1943, between seven and ten million people died.[99] When the country gained its independence from British rule in 1947, the government could not afford the luxury of a banking system that put priority on inflated returns for a non-producing investor class. Its priorities had to be on feeding and housing its burgeoning masses. The trend after independence was therefore to move banking into the public sector.

In 1955, the government nationalized the Imperial Bank of India, renaming it the State Bank of India (SBI); and in 1960, SBI's seven subsidiaries were also nationalized. But the banking sector was still largely private, and it was not meeting the country's development needs.

In 1969, Prime Minister Indira Gandhi therefore took the bold step of announcing on national radio that the country's major banks should be not just socially controlled but publicly owned. Fourteen major banks were nationalized, not because they were bankrupt (the usual justification today) but to ensure that credit would be allocated according to planned priorities, including getting banks into rural areas and making cheap financing available to Indian farmers.[100]

It was a game-changing move that drew enthusiastic support from the people. Crowds danced in the streets. At last something was being done for the poor, and the rich were being put in their place.[101]

According to a 2004 MIT research paper, the economic impact was dramatic:

> After nationalization, the breadth and scope of the Indian banking sector expanded at a rate perhaps unmatched by any other country. Indian banking has been remarkably successful at achieving mass participation. Between the time of the 1969 nationalizations and the present, over 58,000 bank branches were opened in India; these new branches, as of March 2003, had mobilized over 9 trillion Rupees in deposits, which represent the overwhelming majority of deposits in Indian banks. This rapid expansion is attributable to a policy which required banks to open four branches in unbanked locations for every branch opened in banked locations.[102]

A major shift also occurred in the types of lending pursued:

> At the time of nationalisation the priority sector concept was introduced by bringing agriculture, small-scale industry, retail trade, small business and small transport operators under its fold. The list widened with the passage of time. It was made mandatory for banks to provide 40 per cent of their net credit to these "priority" sectors.
>
> Within this, banks had to provide 18 per cent of their net credit to the agricultural sectors, so as to reduce the hold of

moneylenders and make more funds available for agricultural development. From the early 1970s, banks were also actively involved in poverty alleviation and employment generation programmes.[103]

Jobs were created in the process, putting millions to work:

Employment generation in Public Sector Banks (PSBs) also recorded an enormous increase during this period . . . . It is largely because of the role of Nationalised Banks, during this period, in rural India, that a Green Revolution could be brought about and [India became] self-sufficient in food production.[104]

Bank deposits also increased, increasing investment in the economy:

By sweeping money from individuals into the financial system, bank branch expansion caused an increase in the savings rate from 12 percent in 1969 to 20 percent in 1980. The steep rise in the savings rate, in turn, set the stage for the growth of 5.5-6 percent that [India] saw in the eighties. There is thus a clear link between bank nationalisation and the acceleration in India's economic growth.[105]

As the nationalized bank branches proliferated, people who had never before had a bank account started putting their money in banks, giving the banks the liquidity to extend credit far and wide. Money once hidden at home was being recycled, increasing the money available for industry, trade, agriculture and infrastructure.

After a new round of bank nationalizations in 1980, the Government of India controlled over 91 percent of the country's banking industry.[106] The 1980s were also when India's economic growth took off. Today, government ownership is somewhat less; but it still accounts for about 75 percent of all banking assets in India.[107] Measured by share of deposits, *83 percent of the banking business is in the hands of state or nationalized banks.*[108]

The 1990s: The Swing Toward Privatization

The gains were impressive, but nationalization had its critics. Massive lending to farmers and small businesses meant that bank profitability had taken a beating.

Defenders of the public sector banks said they had done what they were supposed to do. They were told to grow their balance sheets, extending loans wherever needed; and for two decades, they did that. With banking deregulation in the 1990s, the banks were told to focus on profits; and they dutifully did that. A January 2010 editorial in the *Economic Times* (India) maintained, "As a result, we have today a banking system that is among the most profitable in the world."[109]

Deregulation and privatization in the 1990s increased bank profits, but they were very hard on the small farmers who composed the mass of the population. The push for privatization was ideologically driven from abroad, led by the International Monetary Fund and the World Bank. Banks were downsized, merged or closed; government ownership was diluted; priority-sector lending was cut.[110]

Particularly hard hit by these measures were agriculture, small-scale industry and the "informal" sector (labor relations not based on written contract). The minimum allocation for agriculture was removed. Private banks already had few rural branches, and foreign banks had none; but from the early 1990s, even the public sector banks effectively stopped any rural expansion and concentrated on urban and metropolitan banking.[111]

The result was to dry up credit, particularly for owners of small farms and businesses. By 2007, 90 percent of farmers still remained outside the bank network, and for those farmers and small businessmen who could get credit, interest rates were about double those for large-scale industries.[112]

Contributing to the decline in bank credit was the "Basel norm," a banking stricture that like the push for privatization was imposed from abroad. In the 1980s, the Bank for International Settlements in Switzerland set "capital adequacy" standards requiring loans to private borrowers to be "risk-weighted." The degree of risk was determined by private rating agencies. Since small business owners could not afford the agencies' fees, 100 percent risk was assigned to their loans. Banks then resisted extending credit to these "high-risk" borrowers, since more capital was required to cover the loans.

When a spate of suicides among Indian farmers aroused the conscience of the nation, the government established a policy of ending the "financial exclusion" of the weak. But its lament of the neglect of farmers had little real effect on the lending practices of commercial banks, due largely to the chokehold of the Basel rules.[113]

The Pendulum Swings Back

Attitudes toward the public banking sector changed again with the global credit crisis of 2008. As private, profit-constrained banks cut down on loans, the public banks ramped lending up, acting counter-cyclically. The public banks also avoided the toxic mortgage-backed securities and credit default swaps that were felling Western financial institutions. This public banking sector prudence and pro-action were credited with helping India escape the global downturn.[114]

Public banks were transformed from the black sheep of the Indian banking world into shepherds protecting the herd. In a 2008 article titled "The Importance of Public Banking," CP. Chandrasekhar wrote:

> In a reversal of its recently held position, the Congress party has declared that publicly owned banks are one of India's strengths and that the nationalisation of banks was one of the party's important achievements.
>
> [Congress Party president] Sonia Gandhi . . . argued that while the ongoing "economic upheaval" could "grievously affect the most vulnerable sections of our society," her party had partially insulated India's poor from becoming "victims of the unchecked greed of bankers and businessmen." Elaborating, she said: "Let me take you back to Indira Gandhi's bank nationalisation of 40 years ago. Every passing day bears out the wisdom of that decision. Public sector financial institutions have given our economy the stability and resilience we are now witnessing in the face of the economic slowdown.[115]

At first, the statements of Sonia Gandhi were regarded skeptically, as intended to glorify Indira Gandhi. But they took on weight when her lead was followed by the Finance Minister, who had formerly been pushing bank privatization:

> Finance Minister P. Chidambaram. . . emphasized that India's public sector banks were strong pillars in the world's banking industry. This was because, unlike the chief executives of private banks in the United States, public sector bank managers did not violate regulations in search of profits.[116]

In 2009, another finance minister, Pranab Mukherjee, confirmed this assessment. He ruled out privatization of the state-run banks, saying that a market economy was not the solution to the nation's economic problems:

> Recalling that the late prime minister Indira Gandhi had nationalised banks 40 years ago in 1969, Mukherjee said, "We survived the economic meltdown because of this step. In the world's leading countries, the finance sectors have crashed but we are still surviving because we nationalised our banking sector." Rather than privatising banks, he said, the government policy was to strengthen the state-run banks. "The government will always have at least 51 percent stake in them" . . . . He said economic reforms were needed, but the stress would be on fulfilling the needs of the "aam admi" (common man).

Instead of the trickle-down approach of the supply-siders, Mukherjee took the demand-side approach. Rather than imposing austerity on the people, the government would raise the purchasing power of the poor to increase demand, which would then increase production:

> Unless the purchasing power of the working class is raised, the country cannot prosper, Mukherjee said. "So our main aim is to eradicate poverty. We have the National Rural employment Guarantee Act (NREGA). We will introduce similar schemes to raise the purchasing power of the poor people so that companies' productions are unaffected by lack of demand."[117]

Mukherjee's lead in promoting bank nationalization was followed in 2010 by chief economic adviser Kaushik Basu, who said nationalization had resulted in a rise in savings and investment and had helped push up India's growth rate.[118]

In "The Importance of Public Banking," C.P. Chandrasekhar attributed this change in attitude to three factors:

(1) The Indian public banks had weathered the financial storm considerably better than the Indian private banks.

(2) The managers of leading private Western banks, including those held up as "models of modern banking," had lost credibility. In the pursuit of private profit, they were playing fast and loose with the people's money, dropping all due diligence and making decisions that actually threatened the viability of the banking system.

(3) It had become clear, said Chandrasekhar that "the only way in which the losses made by these [leading private western] banks could be socialized and their viability ensured was for the government to invest in their shares so as to recapitalize them. Across the world, the response to the financial crisis has shifted out of mere measures to inject liquidity into the system to backdoor nationalization of these banks so as to save them from bankruptcy and to ensure that they keep lending."

The banks were supposed to be making the people's money safe. Instead, the people were making the banks' money safe. If the people had to bear the losses by "backdoor nationalization," they should be getting the profits and have a say in the banks' management.

Chandrasekhar blamed the crisis in the western private banking sector on the profit motive. Shareholders were demanding higher returns, turning banks into "factories that produced financial assets for investors." It was this, he said, that had led to "financial liberalization," which meant simply that regulations had been lifted to increase bank profitability:

> [P]rocesses euphemistically referred to as financial innovation were adopted to boost the profits of the banks. As a part of that, banks shifted to the "originate and distribute" model in which they created credit assets not to hold them but to pool them, securitize them and sell them to other investors, transferring risk in the process. The banks' own incomes now depended not on net interest margins . . . but on the fees and commissions

they were paid to serve as factories that produced financial assets for investors with varying tastes for risk.

Higher returns came at the cost of ever-increasing bank failures. Chandrasekhar concluded:

> [T]here is a fundamental contradiction in private enterprise capitalism. If the banking sector is regulated, it cannot deliver the profits that are considered adequate by private investors . . . . On the other hand, if regulations are relaxed to facilitate the pursuit of profits, it will result in bank fragility and "the poor become the victims of the unchecked greed of bankers and businessmen", as Sonia Gandhi noted. The only solution, therefore, is the nationalization of banking.

Private investors demand the highest possible private profit, which is not consistent with providing financial security, equitable service, and ready credit to the population. If the banks are to serve the people, they need to be publicly-owned.

A Work in Progress

State-owned banks are back in favor in India, but the pendulum continues to swing. The World Trade Organization agreement on financial services has paved the way for foreign firms to increase control of the Indian financial market, and foreign banks have made inroads.[119] Under the post-2008 banking directive called Basel III, Indian banks are supposed to increase their capital base and trim risky loans, which means cutting lending to small businesses and the poor. But the public service banking model carries quietly on. According to a February 2012 *Frontline* article, "the banks have been directed by the authorities to go for financial inclusion for lending to many welfare programmes."[120]

Some Indian banks have been downgraded by the American rating agency Moody's. The agency points to inflation, monetary tightening, and rising interest rates.[121] But local commentators are more skeptical of Moody's than of the Indian banks. They note that the rating agency was complicit in giving AAA ratings to collateralized debt obligations that proved to be fraudulent, allowing them to be peddled worldwide by Wall Street banks.

India suffers from price inflation, but the cause is not clear, and the conventional medicine has not been working. As a financial commentator wrote in India's *Business Standard*:

> The puzzle is simply this: why is inflation in India so stubbornly high and so much higher than other emerging markets, even those that are supposedly overheating, such as China, Korea and Indonesia, where inflation is closer to 3 per cent?[122]

The conventional medicine – raising interest rates to reduce the money supply – may actually be at the root of the problem. In 2010 and 2011, the Reserve Bank of India aggressively raised interest rates on the theory that this would make credit harder to get, shrinking the money supply and reducing prices. Yet after 11 raises in 18 months, the effect was merely to slow the economy.[123]

Why? As James Cumes points out in *Demon Money* (2013), raising interest rates can cause prices to rise rather than fall. Businesses must recoup the higher interest charges by raising their prices; and businesses that cannot afford to borrow at the higher rates decrease production, reducing supply relative to demand, driving prices up.

Other commentators question whether inflation in a rapidly growing economy is necessarily a bad thing. One of the guiding principles of the IMF and the World Bank in their management of developing countries has been to keep the inflation rate very low. But while this policy benefits investors, it may not work to the benefit of the national economy. In a 2007 book called *Bad Samaritans*, economist Ha-Joon Chang points out that in some countries, including Korea and Brazil, "miracle growth" has been accompanied by quite high price inflation. Chang maintains that inflation is a double-edged sword, with higher inflation rates actually having a favorable effect on growth and jobs. (More on Korea in Chapter 22.)

Banking in India continues to be a work in progress. But banking for the "aam admi"—the common man—has clearly made great strides, an achievement that is a credit to Mother India's compassion and high level of civilization.

Chapter 6

THE SECRET OF CHINA'S ROBUST ECONOMY: THE GOVERNMENT OWNS THE BANKS RATHER THAN THE REVERSE

"Poverty is not socialism. To be rich is glorious."

-- Deng Xiaopeng

China is a massive country with correspondingly massive problems, including pollution, overbuilding, and overcrowding; but the focus here is not on what is wrong with the country but on what is right. China has made phenomenal progress economically in the last few decades, and government control of the banking system is a key factor in that progress. Its recent debt problems stem from the inroads made by neoliberal economics and a Chinese "shadow" banking system beyond government control.

China is the most populous country in the world, with 1.3 billion people. It has also displayed the most remarkable economic growth in history. By 2010, it had maintained a growth rate of around 10 percent for a full 30 years. It is now the largest center of manufacturing globally, and it maintains the largest foreign reserves of any country. Of the 700 million people expected to join the world's middle class by 2030, half are expected to be Chinese.[124]

While local American businesses were being devoured by giant corporations in leveraged buyouts, creating what economist James Galbraith calls the corporate "predator state," China was evolving local cooperative structures that were main drivers in the country's economic development. These structures are "planned," but they are planned at the local level.

According to economist Michael Hudson, all economies are planned. The problem in the U.S. is that planning has been largely forfeited to the private financial sector, and the plan of that sector is to take care of itself rather than the country as a whole. What is good for Wall Street is not necessarily good for the people or the economy.

Funding Industry with National Credit

Like India, China has used its national credit card to support its own people and its own industries rather than indulging a parasitic financial elite. It has not stood on ideology but has adopted new ideas wherever they seemed to work. The Chinese government owns the banks and can subsidize its industries simply by advancing credit to them. This easy credit has helped China's exports out-compete those of virtually every other country in the world.

Western competitors cry, "Not fair!" But the government owns the nation's banks and many of its enterprises, and it is simply making efficient use of its own credit. While Western banks extract all the profits they can get from Western industry, China's banks are working with its industries to make them more productive.

How well the model works was underscored by Ron Unz in an April 2012 article in *The American Conservative* titled "China's Rise, America's Fall." He wrote:

> China's economic progress is especially impressive when matched against historical parallels. Between 1870 and 1900, America enjoyed unprecedented industrial expansion, such that even Karl Marx and his followers began to doubt that a Communist revolution would be necessary or even possible in a country whose people were achieving such widely shared prosperity through capitalistic expansion. During those 30 years America's real per capita income grew by 100 percent.

But over the last 30 years, *real per capita income in China has grown by more than 1,300 percent.*

In achieving all this, China followed a Japanese model called "state-guided capitalism." After Mao's death in 1976, the group of reformers who inherited power in China saw that their neighbors in Japan, Korea, and Taiwan were either on the road to riches or had already arrived there. By the late 1970s, Taiwan's per capita income was seven times that of mainland China.[125] China's new leaders, led by Deng Xiaopeng, decided to abandon Maoist economics and try to duplicate the results of the Japanese model, using a Chinese version that maintained their own socialist values. Deng famously said, "It doesn't matter if a cat is black or white, so long as it catches mice." China intended to be practical rather than ideological, and it intended to join the ranks of the wealthy.

Riches were good, but according to Eamonn Fingleton in *In The Jaws of the Dragon* (2009):

> For idealistic Communists charting a course for the nation in the immediate aftermath of Mao's death, perhaps the ultimate attraction of the Japanese system was its income distribution, which has long been one of the world's most egalitarian.[126]

The results of this new model were dramatic. Unz wrote:

> By 1985, *The Economist* ran a cover story praising China's 700,000,000 peasants for having doubled their agricultural production in just seven years, an achievement almost unprecedented in world history.
> . . . During the three decades to 2010, China achieved perhaps the most rapid sustained rate of economic development in the history of the human species, with its real economy growing almost 40-fold between 1978 and 2010. In 1978, America's economy was 15 times larger, but according to most international estimates, China is now set to surpass America's total economic output within just another few years.

In *Why Nations Fail* (2012), economists Daron Acemoglu and James Robinson characterize China's ruling elites as "extractive"—parasitic and corrupt, building an empire on the backs of the workers. The authors contrast this model to the United States, which they contend is built on "inclusive" democratic institutions, allowing it to continue from success to success while the Chinese economy is moving toward its inevitable failure. Unz agrees that "extractive" economic models fail in the end, while "inclusive" models survive; but he thinks Acemoglu and Robinson have put China and the United States into the wrong categories:

> [T]he vast majority of China's newly created economic wealth has flowed to ordinary Chinese workers, who have moved from oxen and bicycles to the verge of automobiles in just a single generation. While median American incomes have been stagnant for almost forty years, those in China have nearly doubled every decade, with the real wages of workers outside the farm-sector rising about 150 percent over the last ten years alone. The Chinese of 1980 were desperately poor compared to Pakistanis, Nigerians, or Kenyans; but today, they are several times wealthier, representing more than a tenfold shift in relative income.

Unz notes that when wealthy elites govern a society along extractive lines, there is a massive upward flow of extracted wealth. That trait, he says, characterizes the American economy more than the Chinese:

> [T]he rapid concentration of American wealth continues apace: the richest 1 percent of America's population now holds as much net wealth as the bottom 90–95 percent, and these trends may even be accelerating. A recent study revealed that during our supposed recovery of the last couple of years, 93 percent of the total increase in national income went to the top 1 percent, with an astonishing 37 percent being captured by just the wealthiest 0.01 percent of the population, 15,000 households in a nation of well over 300 million people.

In China, on the other hand, wealth is fed back into the productive economy and the general population, so that a rising tide has actually lifted all boats. The tide has risen because profits have been returned to the economy rather than siphoned out of it.

According to Fingleton, the fountain that feeds this tide is a strong public banking sector. He states:

Capitalism's triumph in China has been proclaimed in countless books in recent years. . . . But . . . the higher reaches of its economy remain comprehensively controlled in a way that is the antithesis of everything we associate with Western capitalism. *The key to this control is the Chinese banking system* . . . [which is] not only state-owned but, as in other East Asian miracle economies, functions overtly as a major tool of the central government's industrial policy.[127]

Although China's banking system has been partially privatized, the country still has the highest percentage of government bank ownership of any major economy in the world. It is the controlling shareholder of the Big Four commercial banks, which were split off from the central bank, the People's Bank of China, in the 1980s; and the People's Bank of China itself remains state-owned. [128] Fingleton notes:

In 2006 of nearly 70,000 bank branches in China all but 214 were Chinese-owned. . . . Thus, China's vast savings flows will remain indefinitely under the control of a handful of state-controlled Chinese banking institutions.

As of 2008-09, the Big Four were among the world's largest banks in terms of assets, and they represented approximately 50 percent of the Chinese banking sector's assets and deposits. The Big Four carried out the majority of Chinese financial transactions, allowing the government to play a critical role in the allocation of resources.

Today, however, another publicly-owned Chinese bank has pulled ahead. In *China's Superbank: Debt, Oil and Influence – How China Development Bank is Rewriting the Rules of Finance* (2013), Henry Sanderson and Michael Forsythe assert that the China Development Bank may now be the most powerful financial institution in the world. Besides enabling the government's policies at home, including inventing the system of local finance that helped China weather the global financial crisis, it has financed the China-Africa Development Fund, bankrolled the global expansion of Chinese companies, and extended tens of billions of dollars in energy-backed loans to borrowers around the globe, including Brazil, Russia and Venezuela.[129]

Most corporate funding in China comes from bank loans rather than from stock and bond markets, which remain underdeveloped. That gives corporations more autonomy than in the United States, where shareholder-owned corporations are required to focus on short-term profits to please their absentee owners. Chinese companies can take the long view and do what is best for their overall health and productivity.[130]

China had to agree to largely privatize its four big state-owned banks as a condition for joining the World Trade Organization; but while the government has made a show of conforming its banking system to Western standards, it continues to dominate the banking sector, using its banks in a way that serves the Chinese economy and industries. In 2006, China opened its banking sector to foreign banks, but Beijing has been adept at slowing their progress. Fingleton states that only about two percent of total assets are in foreign banks, which remain "ghettoized in narrow niche activities such as foreign-currency loans and deposits." Much about the Chinese economy is kept secret, with the government maintaining control over many enterprises that are nominally private.[131]

China's "Post-Capitalist" Economic Model

China today is neither communist nor capitalist but is what Fingleton calls a *post*-capitalist society, drawing on an economic model originated by the Japanese, which in turn copied elements of the Soviet and German economies of the 1930s. According to economist James Galbraith, both China and the United States have "mixed" economies. The government sector is actually responsible for well over half of economic activity in the United States. Even our ostensibly private banks are heavily dependent on government, as the recent banking crisis made clear.[132] The Chinese government has taken the next logical step and formalized this arrangement with its banks. Taking control of industry and banking has allowed China to triple the growth achieved by Western capitalism.

Japan's state-guided capitalism is discussed in Chapter 22. The Chinese call their variation on this theme a "socialist market economic system." About 50 percent of production is still accomplished by state-owned enterprises (SOEs). Foreign money is welcomed but within strict limits. Foreign ownership is limited to 25 percent of the shares of China's state-owned banks.[133] By 2009, nearly three-quarters of

Chinese bank assets were controlled by banks in which the state was the largest or only shareholder.[134]

China's SOEs benefit from preferential treatment by the government, making them formidable competitors of Western industries. State-owned banks continue to favor SOEs and to give short shrift to the private sector. According to recent U.S. regulatory filings, SOEs and their subsidiaries get preferred access to bank capital, below-market interest rates on loans from state-owned banks, favorable tax treatment, policies that create a favorable competitive environment for SOEs relative to other firms, and large capital injections when needed.[135]

State control has been maintained through a system of "vertically integrated groups," involving large state-owned and related companies. Each group has a "central holding company," the State-Owned Assets Supervision and Administration Commission (SASAC), which is the majority shareholder in a "core company." That company owns a majority of shares in the state-owned companies comprising the group, including a finance company that finances members. In 2010, total SOE assets equaled 62 percent of China's GDP. There are intra-group linkages via joint ventures, alliances, and shareholding. These hierarchical structures are embedded in dense networks that exchange and collaborate on matters of production and policy.[136] Most SOEs are also obligated to provide cradle-to-grave social services to workers and their families.[137] SOEs are exempt from anti-trust enforcement; and according to a 2011 overview in *The Economist*, the government "enforces rules selectively, to keep private-sector rivals in their place."[138] Foreign firms can be blocked from acquiring local firms.

The government uses its SOEs and state-owned banks to facilitate economic change. In 2009, it used them to provide stimulus to the domestic economy. Its banks remain public utilities, providing unlimited capital to the cherished SOEs.[139] China also has a powerful Postal Savings Bank, which was formed only in 2007 but has already become a major tool for getting income into rural areas.[140]

China Goes Local: Shifting Power to Township and Village Enterprises

Government control remains pervasive in China, with the central government owning virtually the entire financial system, much of the economy's productive assets, and almost all of the land.[141] Yet China is not the wholly-centrally-planned economy of half a century ago. A great deal of power and control is wielded today at the local level, making the model an interesting one for those local cooperative movements now forming in the United States. According to economist Adam Hersh in testimony before the U.S.-China Economic and Security Review Commission in February 2012:

> More than 30 years since beginning economic reform, China's fundamental economic institutions today are dramatically different than the system of central planning operating during the Mao era. . . . Beijing neither controls nor coordinates everything in the Chinese economy. . . . Local officials make their own decisions in their own interests, often without the knowledge or support of Beijing. Local officials are integral to many of the entrepreneurial decisions that have led to China's remarkable economic success. The investment resources under local government control vastly exceed those used by the central government to support its own state-owned enterprises as well as private sources of financing.

While U.S. cities and states struggle with shrinking budgets and obstructionist politics, local government officials in China have a degree of authority unknown in the West. They have authority over economic affairs, finance, and productive industry. Local governments also own significant portions of China's economy, and they command huge financial resources that can be used for economic development.

These changes came with political and economic reforms that steered China away from the inefficient over-centralization of the Mao era. What emerged in post-Mao China was a system of industrial policy in which local government was the main driver. Key to this system are the TVEs—the publicly-owned township and village enterprises. According to Hersh:

TVEs as an enterprise form evolved from pre-reform era rural-agricultural collectives and were organized under the authority of local government officials . . . In a relatively short time period, these companies developed tremendous economic importance. In the 1980s TVEs accounted for 30 percent of China's growth in manufacturing and service sectors. By the mid-1990s literally millions of TVEs accounted for a combined 40 percent of China's total exports. Economic analyses find that these TVEs achieved levels of efficiency that rivaled or surpassed privately owned and even foreign-invested companies.[142]

What enabled the TVEs to blossom were reforms in the structure of tax collection that gave incentives to local government to be entrepreneurial and efficient. Before reform, local officials would remit the taxes they collected to higher levels of government and get some revenue-sharing allotments back. With fiscal reform, this structure was reversed, so that local officials in effect had a "property right" to the taxes they collected. Taxes on industrial and commercial activities, along with miscellaneous fines and fees, could be retained at the local level as "extrabudgetary" revenues available to local officials at their discretion. As much as two-thirds of off-budget local government revenues come directly from the business activities of TVEs.

Other Chinese development strategies discussed by Hersh include regulation of the financial sector so that it supplies capital for productive investments in the manufacturing sector, and *a commitment to employment-targeted policies that promote the development of a middle class, which in turn enlarges markets for business.* Today, says Hersh:

> Foreign investment, to which many observers and analysts ascribe China's economic success, accounts for a relatively minor and diminishing portion of overall investment in China. In the time since China's WTO accession in December 2001, foreign investment averaged only 3.7 percent of national investment, and less than 2 percent in 2009. Similarly, China's capital markets supply only a marginal share of total investment, on average less than 3 percent annually since WTO accession.

That could explain why the "collapse" in the Chinese stock market in March 2013 did not prove to be a major event portending the collapse of the economy, as Western analysts were predicting.[143] China's stock market appears to be more a mere plaything of investors than a major source of capital for the Chinese economy. Most investment funds come neither from the stock market nor from the central government. According to Hersh:

> [T]he overwhelming majority of funds for fixed-asset investment in China are under the control of local government. More recently, under China's 2009 and 2010 fiscal and monetary stimulus plan, local governments also borrowed substantial sums for investment from [publicly-owned] banks through what are called local government-financing platforms.

Hersh notes that "truly private entrepreneurship is a poor man's affair in China." The Chinese have gone beyond capitalism to a productive structure largely led by local government. But there is still plenty of room for competition. Local government enterprises compete with each other:

> Competition in markets helped drive local government enterprises to efficiency, but so did competition for political advancement, premised in large part on achieving economic and export growth targets set from above in the political hierarchy. In essence the political advancement of local officials was linked to their entrepreneurial skills.

In China, it seems, the single-party system allows individuals to excel based on their personal competence for the job. Compare that to the U.S. two-party political system, in which two massive, corporate-funded political machines are continually at loggerheads, often blocking effective action.

Hersh acknowledges that the Chinese system of funneling large sums of money to local government businesses offers opportunities for corruption and waste, but this problem is also prevalent in the West. Local Chinese officials must be doing something right, says Hersh, or the system would not have yielded the rapid, sustained development seen in China over the past three decades:

> The local government-led industrial strategy system . . . has been remarkably successful and effective at delivering strong economic growth and steadily rising standards of living for Chinese citizens. While local government officials oversaw

much successful microeconomic development, they did not do so on their own – they operated within a supportive macroeconomic environment that allowed the seeds of local government investment to flourish.

How China Beat the "Global" Banking Crisis

All of this helps explain how China managed to maintain its phenomenal growth rate, even as the rest of the world was in a massive tailspin. While the U.S. government and the Fed were bailing out U.S. banks, China's state-owned banks were bailing out its industries by underwriting them and forgiving their debts. Having no private financial free-riders to cater to, the government could keep its real economy moving forward and its billion-plus people employed. Fingleton writes:

> [T]he banks are important tools for a vast program for subsidizing the expansion of Chinese industry. The effect is particularly significant among promising but undercapitalized export companies whose growth is funded with easy bank credit for years or even decades on end. Many such companies will eventually become fully viable, but for the most part only after their debts are forgiven and converted into equity [giving the government a share in the company]. By forgiving debts, Chinese banks therefore provide hidden subsidies to China's targeted industries.

Chinese industries enjoy a quiet "debt jubilee" when they get into financial trouble. Their debts are forgiven, allowing them to pick up and go on. Fingleton observes that this is a clear breach of WTO rules. China gives lip service to the foreign requirement that it account for its "non-performing loans" (advances of credit that never get paid back), while proceeding with its own methods of keeping businesses open, people employed, and prices unbeatably low. As noted earlier, however, China did not consider grants to its state-owned enterprises to be "non-performing loans" before it joined the WTO in 2001. They were just advances of the credit needed to get the job done. There were no creditors demanding payment from the state-owned banks. The creditor *was* the state; and the state, at least in theory, was the people. The state was lending to itself, and it could write off its loans if it wished.

Because the Chinese government has control of its banks, it was able to open the credit spigots in response to the 2008 banking crisis while the United States and other countries were caught in a bank-created credit crunch. State-owned banks massively increased lending, with local governments and state enterprises borrowing on a huge scale. The People's Bank of China estimated that total loans for the first half of 2009 were $1.08 trillion, 50 percent more than the loans issued by Chinese banks in 2008. The U.S. Federal Reserve was also engaging in record levels of lending, but its loans went chiefly to bail out the financial sector itself. According to Dr. Samah El-Shahat, writing in *Al Jazeera* in August 2009:

> China is the one leading economy where the divide—the disconnect between its financial sector and the world normal Chinese people and their businesses inhabit—doesn't exist. Both worlds are booming again and this is due to the way the government handled its banks. *China hasn't allowed its banking sector to become so powerful, so influential, and so big that it can call the shots or highjack the bailout.* In simple terms, the government preferred to answer to its people and put their interests first before that of any vested interest or group. And that is why Chinese banks are lending to the people and their businesses in record numbers.
>
> . . . In the UK and US, the financial sector is booming, while the world of normal people seems to be going from bad to worse, unemployment is high, businesses are folding and house foreclosures are still taking place. Wall Street and Main Street might as well be existing on different planets. And this is in large part because banks are still not lending money to the people. In the UK and US, banks have captured all the money from the taxpayers and the cheap money from quantitative easing from central banks. They are using it to shore up, and clean up their balance sheets rather than lend it to the people. The money has been hijacked by the banks, and our governments are doing absolutely nothing about that. In fact, they have been complicit in allowing this to happen.[144]

China's Shadow Banking System

That is how it looked in 2009, but in the spring of 2013, concerns surfaced about a massive debt overhang in the Chinese economy. This debt has sprung up suddenly, along with the rise of a "shadow" banking system outside government control, similar to the shadow banking system in the United States.

According to an April 2013 interview of Vincent Kolo, senior editor of Chinaworker.info, the trend today is for more and more banking business to go "off balance sheet" into a multitude of shadow finance entities, trust companies, and so on. Loans within the traditional banking sector fell to just 58 percent of all financing in 2012, down from 95 percent in 2002. More than 40 percent of all credit is now non-bank lending from a complex and unregulated shadow financial system, including the growth of so-called wealth management products (WMPs), which have gone viral in the last 3 or 4 years. The value of outstanding WMPs rose to 16 percent of total bank deposits in 2012. Kolo explained:

> The growth of WMPs is a way to get around government lending limits and to extend fresh credit to shaky local government entities that otherwise wouldn't be able to meet their debt repayments.
>
> . . . [When] the central government launched its huge stimulus package and gave banks the green light to increase loans, local governments, which are banned by law from taking loans, were allowed to get around this by setting up their own finance vehicles (LGFVs)—thousands of them—to tap into this credit boom and build infrastructure. . . . [A] lot of this investment was wasted, stolen, or went into property speculation, "ghost cities", "ghost malls", and so on.
>
> . . . The stimulus 2009-10 loans began to fall due last year, but a lot of the infrastructure projects are either unfinished or have not recouped enough income to pay back the loans. . . . Old loans are being serviced by issuing fresh loans, but not from the banks' own balance sheets.
>
> . . . The central government has issued warnings and is struggling to get control over this process, because some local government financial platforms are throwing hospitals, schools

and other public assets into these financial "products" to make them more attractive to investors. Investors ask, "what am I actually buying into here?"—they want to see some physical assets. So, it's a form of backdoor privatisation.[145]

All this has caught the central government in the same sort of squeeze in which the U.S. Congress found itself in 2008. In December 2012, Huaxia Bank in Shanghai, a middle-sized bank with Deutsche Bank as part-owner, faced protests in the streets after a WMP it had sold defaulted, losing the depositors around US$22 million. Some influential voices said the government should do nothing, to show it won't step in to rescue the WMPs, which are largely a private business not guaranteed by banks. But the government did step in behind the scenes, to prevent the Huaxia affair triggering a run on the WMP sector as a whole, which now accounts for around 16 percent of total bank deposits. If sales of new WMPs were to dry up, it could cause a "liquidity crunch" for local governments and property companies which need to roll over old debts. As in the U.S., the shadow banks and regular banks are no longer isolated from each other, something the government cannot control.[146]

Meanwhile, a new team of leaders is in charge in China. Kolo observes:

> The new leaders, Xi Jinping and Li Keqiang especially, stand for the type of measures outlined in the World Bank's dossier launched last year . . . which was co-authored by Li's ministry and calls for sweeping privatisations and marketisation. We should remember that the World Bank and its sister organisation the IMF bear as much guilt as anyone for the global financial crisis.
>
> . . . They plan to "liberalise" the financial sector, interest rates and so on, ostensibly to make the allocation of capital more "efficient", to cut back on wasteful investment. This means formalising the shadow banking sector—"freeing" the mainstream banks to engage in this sort of thing legally.
>
> The regime wants to internationalise the yuan (or renminbi) and has made significant moves to increase the offshore trade in the Chinese currency, through "swap lines" with foreign banks – most recently the Bank of England. . . .

But to turn the yuan into a major international currency means removing exchange controls, which, as things stand today, would very likely trigger a financial collapse. So, in addition to splits within the regime, there are major risks in implementing the leadership's liberal—actually neo-liberal —agenda.[147]

It seems that China is heading down the slippery slope of privatization, liberalization, and an ever-expanding shadow banking system. But it still has a solid base in manufacturing, a healthy public banking system, and the momentum of the most phenomenal miracle economy ever. It is still on a path to becoming the world's biggest and strongest economy.

The Wall Street Journal reported in March 2013 that Beijing was aggressively striking at surging housing prices, pitting itself against real estate developers, local governments and speculators, all of whom have an interest in continued rapid increases in prices.[148]

Meanwhile, the government continues to boost its funding of social services. Early in China's move toward capitalism, workers complained that they were being made to pay for housing, health care and higher education formerly picked up by the state. But the government has taken major steps to fix these gaps and flaws. As Ron Unz observed in April 2012:

> For many years Western journalists regularly reported that the dismantling of China's old Maoist system of government-guaranteed healthcare had led to serious social stresses, forcing ordinary workers to save an unreasonable fraction of their salaries to pay for medical treatment if they or their families became ill. But over the last couple of years, the government has taken major steps to reduce this problem by establishing a national healthcare insurance system whose coverage now extends to 95 percent or so of the total population, a far better ratio than is found in wealthy America and at a tiny fraction of the cost.

In March 2013, Bloomberg reported that while the United States and Europe were struggling to cut deficits, China was raising its deficit by 50 percent to boost demand:

Higher spending this year may help the government meet a challenge set by then-party chief Hu in November to double per-capita income by 2020 from 2010 levels . . . .

Chinese people want "more income, greater social security, better medical and health care," Xi Jinping said in November after taking over as head of the Communist Party.

Boosting outlays on social security and public housing and changing the tax system to help lower-income families also dovetail with policy makers' long-standing pledge to shift the economy to consumption-led growth and away from a dependence on investment and exports. . .

Central government funding for social security and employment will rise 13.9 percent this year . . . [and] the amount of central government money earmarked for affordable housing will rise 5.3 percent . . . , according to the report.[149]

Flaws aside, there is something to be said for a political system in which leaders can commit to doubling per-capita income, raising social security, providing affordable housing, and increasing public health care—and who propose to do it all by deficit spending—without raising howls of protest from their political opponents. That sort of thing may actually be possible in a system in which the members of a single political party move together as a block rather than in two giant opposed parties continually locking horns, and in which the government owns the banks that are funding it all on the national credit card.

* * *

The BRICs have been highlighted in this section, but their experience is relatively short in the timeframe of history. The next section takes the long view, tracing the development, vicissitudes, and rivalry of public and private banking from the dawn of civilization to the 20th century.

Section II.

PUBLIC BANKING THROUGH HISTORY: 3,000 B.C. TO 1913 A.D.

Chapter 7

PUBLIC BANKING IN ANTIQUITY: THE FORGOTTEN HISTORY

"[P]ublic rather than private enterprise was the early crucible of commercial innovation and capital accumulation. It took a major social catalyst to legitimize the sustained investment of surpluses."

-- Prof. Michael Hudson, "Debts and Indebtedness in the Neo-Babylonian Period" (1998)[150]

Contrary to popular belief, the first monetary systems in recorded history were not private but public systems. Tallies of sums paid and owed predated metal coins used in trade by at least two millennia. These bank-like payment systems allowed civilization to flourish in ancient Sumeria, Egypt and China. They did not spring spontaneously from the bottom up. They were imposed from the top and were operated by public institutions.

In considering possible models for a sustainable banking alternative, it is instructive to look not just abroad but back in history. It has been argued that banking is not a proper function of government, and that gold and silver coins are the oldest and most stable forms of money; but history disputes both of these contentions. Before people used coins or paper currency for trade, public institutions kept records of debts paid and owed, set prices and fixed interest rates. The stability of the trading system was maintained in this way for thousands of years.

Another popular belief that is contested by anthropological evidence is that "money" originated from primitive barter. In *Debt: The First 5,000 Years* (2011), David Graeber reports that no primitive society has been found that engages in barter within its own community. Primitive societies are organized as extended families or villages, which operate on the basis of communal sharing or "gifting."

According to Professor Michael Hudson, an expert in ancient Near Eastern economies, prices and interest rates did not get set in ancient times by private barter in the "free market." Rather:

> [F]or thousands of years before price-adjusting markets emerged, it was the temples that paved the way by developing and overseeing weights and measures. What was sought was regularity and standardization, not fluctuating prices responding to shifts in supply and demand. It has taken over five thousand years for public control of resources—the means of production, land and subsoil rights—to be stripped away to the degree seen today.[151]

The Mystery of Sumer

"History begins at Sumer," wrote Professor Samuel Kramer in his classic treatise of the same name. If writing is taken as a prerequisite for civilization, Sumer was its earliest cradle, followed by Early Dynastic Egypt.[152] The Sumerians not only had the first recorded writing system but had the first wheel, the first roads, the first irrigation, the first animal domestication, the first institutionalized religion, and the first laws. They also had the first banking system.

Located where Iraq is today, Sumer was one of the longest-lasting civilizations in recorded history, spanning from about 5,200 B.C. to its conquest by the Semitic-speaking kings of the Akkadian Empire in about 2,270 B.C.[153] Sumer re-emerged briefly before being absorbed into Mesopotamia, which was united under Babylonian rule about 1,700 B.C.

The Sumerians invented the writing of numbers about 3,500 B.C., and ideographic writing (pictures representing concepts) about 3,000

B.C., evolving into logographic writing (pictures representing words) by about 2,600 B.C.[154]

How they came by their remarkable achievements remains a mystery. By their own account, preserved in cuneiform writing in clay tablets, their civilization was brought to earth fully formed by the god Enki and his consort Inanna, along with Enki's advisor Adapa U-an (Oannes).[155]

The Sumerian story of Gilgamesh parallels the Judeo-Christian story of the flood, although predating it by more than a thousand years.[156] One notable difference is that in the Sumerian tale there are two rival gods, the benevolent Enki and his jealous brother Enlil. Enlil was bent on exploiting rather than nurturing humanity. He sent the flood, and Enki sent the ark.

In *The Mystery of Money* (2003), Bernard Lietaer sees this sort of dualism reflected in the evolution of money and banking. Two rival monetary systems have competed for thousands of years, one based on shared abundance, the other on scarcity, debt and private self-interest. The former characterized the "matrifocal" societies of antiquity-- societies in which "the focus of both the methodology and of the system of rewards and appreciation . . . is honoring the feminine." The latter tended to characterize the warlike patriarchal societies that forcibly displaced them.[157]

Sumer evolved from matrifocal to patriarchal over its long history. The feminine deity was Inanna, the goddess of fertility, life and death. She first appeared in the late fourth millennium B.C. as the patron deity of the central storehouse of the ancient Sumerian city of Uruk--a literal connection to wealth in an agricultural society, says Lietaer, since stores of grain served as money. She wore the horns of a cow, the "cornucopia" from which poured the earth's plenty. The cow was the sacred animal that personified the Great Mother everywhere in ancient myth. Hathor, the Egyptian equivalent, had cow ears and a human face and was the goddess of love, fertility and abundance. Isis, an even more powerful Egyptian mother figure, was portrayed wearing the horns of a cow with the sun disc between them. In India, the cow goddess was Kali, and cows are sacred there to this day.

After the Indo-European invasions of the second millennium B.C., the male god Enlil of Nippur superseded Inanna as the source of supreme kingship. The cornucopia of the Horned Goddess became the bull horns of the Thunder God, representing masculine power, virility and force.[158]

In the domain of money and banking, the public, community-oriented system was gradually displaced by the private system of the moneylenders and their gold. Money became a "thing" separate from the goods and services it represented, a commodity in itself that had to be borrowed from middlemen moneylenders and could be withheld, manipulated, and devalued. Rather than simply a yardstick or measure of value, it thus became a tool for exploitation and domination by the "haves" over the "have-nots."

The Sumerian Temple System

Early Sumerian society was communal and cooperative, focused on providing for all. It was organized around the temple, a public institution that also served welfare functions, including the support of widows, orphans, the elderly and infirm. The temple operated autonomously, supporting itself by renting lands and workshops, and by charging interest on loans. Temples were endowed with land to provide food for their dependent labor, and with resources such as herds of sheep to provide wool for their workshops. Goods were advanced to traders, who returned the value of the goods plus interest. When interest was paid on the loans, it went back to the temple to fund the community's economic and social programs.[159] Professor Hudson writes:

> The Sumerians mediated early gain-seeking trade through the temples and palaces. The term "public institutions" may be preferable to "the state" in describing their role, for they existed autonomously alongside the community at large as a parallel sector with specific designated functions.[160]

The temples thus served some of the same functions as public banks. Modern public banks such as the Bank of North Dakota and the German Sparkassen, discussed later in this book, also operate autonomously alongside the community at large.

Along with their many other firsts, the Sumerians developed the concepts of interest-bearing loans and debt. The Sumerian word for interest was the same as the word for "calf," the fruit of the abundance of the cow. But Dr. Hudson contends that interest was not actually paid in calves, and that the sum owed was not arrived at by bartering. The development of interest-bearing loans required the standardization of weights and measures, which only public institutions could bring about and enforce. Money, prices, and interest rates were set as a matter of public agreement through law. He writes:

> The earliest interest rates in Mesopotamia, Greece and Rome were set not economically to reflect profit or productivity rates, but by the dictates of mathematical simplicity of calculation. The interest . . . did not take the form of young animals, but rather of the unit fraction, the smallest unit fraction in each of the above fractional systems: 1/60th in Mesopotamia, 1/10th in Greece, and 1/12th in Rome. The birth or calf/kid metaphor for interest thus referred to "baby fractions," not literally baby animals.[161]

Before interest and tithes were paid in fractions, it seems plausible that tribute was paid to the temple in the form of calves or grain, in gratitude for the earth's abundance. But in any case, when interest rates were devised, they were set by the temple; and the interest went back to the temple, not as a form of usurious exploitation but to fund the community's economic and social programs. Hudson writes:

> From Babylonian times through classical antiquity, usury was denounced as an exploitation of needy borrowers by the well-to-do, a violation of the traditional ethic of mutual aid.
>
> As in Egypt, the role of credit evidently was to be part of the social self-support system, not to undermine it.
>
> *A widely permitted exception to traditionalist sanctions against gain-seeking occurs when the gains are sought on someone else's behalf, above all for institutions sanctified by the community to perform functions deemed socially necessary and cohesive.* Sumer's temples played this role, and in time the palaces. The charging of interest thus seems to have been endorsed when temple or palace administrators advanced assets to merchants, related entrepreneurs or sharecroppers for a stipulated return.[162]

The Evolution of Coinage

In the early Sumerian system, the economy functioned without the use of "money" in the form of coins or paper notes as we know them today. Trade was conducted by recording transactions with symbols impressed in clay. In fact, writing evolved as an accounting tool.

The earliest examples of cuneiform script date from approximately the end of the 4th millennium B.C. and evolved from an earlier system that used clay tokens for accounting and record keeping. Eventually, just the impression of the tokens was used. For complex tokens, the ancient Sumerian scribes used a stylus to make wedge-like shapes in the clay. A wedge shape came to represent "one" and a circle to represent "ten." To write five sheep, for example, the scribe would impress a wedge five times and then make the sign for sheep.[163]

These accountings had no value independent of the data they recorded. They could not "grow" independently of the things they represented. Abstract numbers did not yet exist. There was a symbol for one-sheep and another for one-day, but no symbol for "one."[164]

Prof. Lietaer states that coin-like tokens have been found dating back as far as 3,200 B.C., but they were used for religious purposes rather than for trade.[165] He describes a bronze token of that date bearing the likeness of the Goddess Inanna-Ishtar inscribed "debt to the Gods." He writes:

> Its original purpose was as a token proving that the bearer had paid the wheat taxes to the Goddess's temple, and it was returned to the temple during the fertility rituals in exchange for sexual intercourse with a representative of the Goddess herself.

Two thousand years later, the Bible would call this priestess "the temple prostitute," but Lietaer maintains that "sexual intercourse with a priestess was not what we would understand today as prostitution, even from a woman's viewpoint."[166]

Prof. Hudson questions the validity of this bit of history, but in any case the tokens were not used in commerce. According to the British Museum's website, coins used for trade date only to the seventh century B.C. They were invented in the area that is now Turkey by early Anatolian traders, who stamped marks on metals to avoid having to weigh them each time they were used.[167] These coins became the official currency when the coin-stamping function was later taken over by national rulers. Herodotus says the first national coinage was issued by Croesus, King of Lydia, in the 6th century B.C.

The "shekel" dates to around 3,000 B.C., but the word referred to a unit of weight rather than a coin. The shekel was just a measure, like inches and ounces. Initially, it may have referred to a weight of barley ("she" was Akkadian for barley).[168]

Hammurabi's Code

When the Babylonians superseded the Sumerians, they adopted the Sumerian monetary system. Records of loans from Babylonian temple priests to merchants date to the 18th century B.C. Hammurabi's Code, dated about 1,790 B.C., includes laws governing banking.[169]

Weights and measures were itemized in meticulous detail, and prices were extensively fixed. Charges were established not just for goods but for services, including the wages of tavern-keepers, physicians, veterinarians, builders, boatmen and artisans.[170] There was no price inflation, since prices were literally set in stone and were intended to last indefinitely. Payment could be in a variety of commodities, including precious metals; but these metals were not in the form of coins. Prices were designated in grains, weights, or container sizes.[171] The Code specified, for example:

> If an ale-wife has given 60 *sila* of coarse liquor on credit, at the harvest she shall take 50 *sila* of corn.

Interestingly, the ale-wife could not demand a weight of silver instead of corn:

> If an ale-wife does not accept grain for the price of liquor [but] accepts silver by the heavy weight or [if] she reduces the value of beer [given] against the value of corn [received], they shall convict that ale-wife and cast her into the water.

A surgeon, however, could take payment in silver:

> If a surgeon has made a deep incision in [the body of] a [free] man with a lancet [?] of bronze and saves the man's life or has

opened the carbuncle [?] in [the eye of] a man with a lancet [?] of bronze and saves his eye, he shall take 10 shekels of silver.[172]

Prof. Hudson writes of these fixed prices:

Contrary to the modern disparagement of planned economies, Mesopotamia's experience shows that administered pricing can indeed promote stable development. Corporate enterprise and uniform pricing originated in the temples and palaces because these large institutions were able to provide what individuals could not: economic standardization.[173]

Not only prices but interest was fixed by the government. Rates did not fluctuate as they do today but were maintained at the same stable percentage for centuries. Hudson writes, "These rates were set by public custom, not by cultivators, pastoral herders or merchants acting autonomously and independently in response to productivity, profit rates or marginal shifts in monetary supply and demand."[174] This government-regulated system was stable and sustainable:

[I]nterest rates have been administered by law throughout most of history. The rate of 1/60th per month — one shekel per mina — seems to have remained stable within Mesopotamia for over a thousand years, starting with the laws of the Third Dynasty of Ur, shortly before 2000 BC, and extending through the laws of Eshnunna and Hammurapi to Neo-Babylonian times.[175]

Babylonian rates of interest would today seem quite high: 20 percent for an advance of silver; a third of the crop for an advance of fees for land, cattle or water that were not repaid at harvest time. But the interest paid in crops was only for advances that were not repaid on time, and it was a third of the crop that the borrower actually had. A small crop meant small interest, so there would still be enough to cover the obligations.

Long-distance trade, however, was generally conducted not in crops but in silver. Precious metals eventually came to dominate as a unit of exchange, because they were not subject to rot and decay and were easily transported and stored. Their disadvantage was that, unlike crops, they did not grow. That meant there were never enough coins in the community collectively to cover the additional interest charges added to loans. According to Richard Hoskins in *War Cycles, Peace Cycles*, it was this inelasticity in the face of an increasing demand for coins that led to debt peonage and servitude. Farmers often had to borrow until harvest time; and if there were insufficient coins in circulation, extra coins would not be available to pay the interest. The odd man out in the musical chairs of finding eleven coins to repay ten wound up in debtor's prison.[176]

When the creditor was the king or the temple, this problem could be relieved by periodic "jubilees." Debts were forgiven, the board was reset, and the game could begin again. Debt jubilees were an institution that allowed economies to renew themselves and function long-term in ancient cultures. The jubilee system was adopted by the Jews as religious law; but religious law does not have the force of government behind it, and in modern times the system has been abandoned even among the religious, as being impracticably "utopian."[177]

Money in Ancient Egypt

The Egyptian Empire began about 3,500 B.C. and lasted until 20 B.C., when it was invaded by the Roman Empire. Like the Sumerians, the ancient Egyptians used a publicly-organized system of exchange based on very carefully regulated weights and measures. Wages for Egyptian laborers were paid in bread and beer—literally. Loaves of bread were standardized according to size and nutritional value and actually served as money.[178]

The process of record-keeping in Egypt was facilitated by the invention of papyrus paper, which replaced the cumbersome clay tablets of the Sumerians. But while papyrus records were more practical than clay, they were still simply accounting tools tracking the exchange of goods and services. They were not something that could be over-printed, hyperinflated, or hoarded and lent only at usurious interest rates. The Egyptians paid taxes, but these took the form of goods or labor rather than coins.[179] As in Sumeria, grain was a medium of exchange, and government-owned granaries functioned as banks.

In an article titled "Community Currencies: A New Tool for the 21st Century," Bernard Lietaer writes that the basis of the Egyptian money system consisted of stockpiles of food:

> Each farmer who contributed to the stockpile would receive a piece of pottery having an inscription of the quantity and date of delivery of his contribution, which he could then use to purchase something else. These receipts, or *ostraca*, have been found by the thousands and were in fact used as currency. . . .
>
> This currency was used in Egypt for more than a thousand years, until the Romans forcibly replaced it with their own banking and currency system . . . .[180]

The *ostraca* were simply receipts from the treasury (the government grain bank) for goods delivered to it. The receipts were not borrowed into existence, as most national currencies are today, but were issued debt-free. They circulated as money and held their value because they could be redeemed for an equivalent value in goods at the grain bank, less a "demurrage" charge for storage and decay. This government-monitored currency was sound and stable enough to last for a thousand years.

The same pattern will be seen repeatedly with government-issued money, from the paper money of the Chinese emperor Kublai Khan to the medieval English tally to the paper scrip of the American colonists. These currencies were not "money created out of thin air" but consisted of receipts backed by real goods and services, which circulated as money and held their value because they were redeemable by the government in the payment of taxes.

When Egypt fell to Greek rule under the Ptolemies (332-30 B.C.), the government granaries were transformed into a network of public grain banks. The "central bank" was located in Alexandria, where centralized accounts were kept. This public banking network served as a trade credit system, in which payments could be transferred from one account to another without physical grain or coins having to change hands.

This sort of credit-based trade was also widespread in Greece in the 4th century B.C. Financial transactions including loans, deposits, currency exchange, and the extension of credit were conducted both by private moneylenders and by governmental and religious entities.[181]

The World's First Paper Money

Paper money was invented in China, where it was first issued in the 10th century A.D. by the Sung Dynasty. It was a pure "fiat" currency, having value not because it was made of something valuable but by "fiat" ("so be it" in Latin), because the emperor said so. But this currency was still not unbacked. Like the Egyptian ostraca and the Sumerian tokens, it represented a receipt for value. The emperor issued it in return for goods and services, and it circulated in the community for an equivalent value in goods and services.

How well it worked was reported by Marco Polo, who visited China under the rule of Kublai Khan. In *Princes of the Yen: Japan's Central Bankers and the Transformation of the Economy* (2003), Richard Werner quotes Marco Polo as saying:

> It is in the city of Khan-balik that the Great Khan has his mint; and it is so organized that you might well say that he has mastered the art of alchemy.
>
> . . . With this currency he orders all payments to be made throughout every province and kingdom and region of his empire. . . . And I assure you that all the peoples and population who are subject to his rule are perfectly willing to accept these papers in payment, since wherever they go they pay in the same currency, whether for goods or for pearls or precious stones or gold or silver. With these pieces of paper they can buy anything and pay for anything.

Werner comments:

> In this advanced monetary system, there was no doubt about what money was: the paper money issued by the emperor and stamped by his seal. He was the central bank. No other institution was allowed to create money, on penalty of death. The emperor was directly in control of the money supply. This meant that he could stimulate demand by creating more paper money, or cool the economy by taking paper out of circulation.

Werner contrasts the economic sovereignty of the Chinese emperor with the debt-strapped European kings and princes, who thought money must be gold or other precious metals that they could not control:

Gold cannot be created at will. Rulers tried, though in vain. Thanks to their efforts, chemistry got an early start in the form of the doomed attempts at creating gold through alchemy.

. . . The great Kublai Khan, Emperor of China and the Mongolian Empire, would probably have shaken his head in disbelief if he had known that European rulers could not issue money to implement public-sector projects. Instead, European governments had to rely on taxes. Often tax levels were already close to the pain threshold, and money was still needed for government investments or expenditures.[182]

When paper money was later introduced into medieval Europe, it would be in a quite different form, issued not by the king but by private moneylenders.

Chapter 8

MEDIEVAL ITALIAN BANKERS DISCOVER THE ALCHEMY OF DOUBLE-ENTRY BOOKKEEPING

"I have never seen the Philosopher's Stone that turns lead into Gold, but I have known the pursuit of it turn a Man's Gold into Lead."

--Benjamin Franklin, Poor Richard's Almanac

Creating money out of nothing in the form of bank credit, later called "fractional reserve" banking, was an innovation of the medieval Italian bankers. It was an essential catalyst to the burgeoning Italian merchant trade, but it was also subject to abuse. When the Venetian senators attempted to forbid private banking and to impose "full reserve" banking through a single publicly-owned bank, however, the bank was unable to service the needs of trade, and private banking, with its fractional reserve credit creation, had to be restored.

Medieval alchemists sought to turn base metal into gold. Medieval Italian bankers went one better: they turned accounting entries into gold. They discovered that money could be made to magically appear on their books if they simply created an "overdraft" (a negative balance) in the account of the borrower. It was what the Chinese

---

might have called the *yin* and *yang* of credit and debt. Zero (nothing) could produce plus one (something), if balanced on the books against a minus one (negative something). The bankers had created money from nothing.

This artful practice was officially called "double-entry book-keeping." It was a set of accounting rules in which every transaction changed at least two different accounts, using debits and credits. A debit in one account created a credit in another. Developed in the 13th century and codified in the 15th century, the system allowed the extension of credit without the exchange of physical coins. The "credit" was just an overdraft, a "debit" in the borrower's account. According to Cambridge Professor Peter Spufford in *Power and Profit: The Merchant in Medieval Europe* (2003):

> By allowing overdrafts and thus letting their cash reserves fall below, and often well below, the total of their deposits . . . local deposit bankers were not only facilitating payments, but also effectively increasing the money supply.[183]

The medieval Italian bankers derived a system of credit that allowed merchants to pay in the future for products and services acquired today. Promises to pay were turned into money—negotiable instruments that could be traded in the marketplace.

The extension of credit was a brilliant innovation, and there was a huge demand for it, since credit was the lifeblood of the burgeoning Italian mercantile trade. Businessmen could pay for labor, raw materials, or finished goods on credit, then sell their wares and pay off the advance with the proceeds, while pocketing some profit for themselves.

For the bankers, however, it was risky business. The loans did not always get repaid, and failure to balance the banks' books was often severely punished. Spufford writes that in Barcelona in 1300, bankers who could not pay their obligations were "forbidden ever to keep a bank again, and were to be detained on bread and water until all their account holders were satisfied in full."[184] Worse:

> In 1321 the legislation there was greatly increased in severity. Bankers who failed and did not settle up in full within a year were to be beheaded and their property sold for the satisfaction

of the account holders. This was actually enforced. Frances Castello was beheaded in front of his bank in 1360.

Beheaded in front of his bank! Some victims of today's banking scandals might like to see this standard reinstated. But over the centuries, the bankers' power of "issue"—the power to create money on their books—gave them so much leverage that the laws were changed to protect rather than punish the greatest offenders.

Expanding the Money Supply with Bills of Exchange

The medieval Italian bankers had their failures and limitations, but they also made important contributions to commerce and trade. An expanding economy demanded an expanding money supply, and they provided that.

Among other game-changing medieval innovations was the *bill of exchange*, the forerunner of the modern check. It did not necessarily involve a bank. It was essentially an order made by one person to another to pay money to a third person. The modern check is a bill of exchange drawn on a bank and payable by the bank to a third person on demand.

Spufford writes that in the 13th century, the bill of exchange sparked a commercial revolution among merchants. With the development of mutual confidence, merchants from the great trading cities of northern and central Italy found that credit sales could take place, enabling a greater volume of business to be transacted. No longer did purchasers and sellers need to be burdened with large and stealable quantities of precious metals. They could simply send and receive an IOU ("I owe you") or promise to pay.[185] Since only the named payee could cash the bills, they were of no use to robbers. Bills of exchange could be carried between cities by a single courier on a horse. Gold, by contrast, had to be transported by armed guards. In one instance, a large shipment of gold sent by convoy to pay for a war in 1328 was ambushed and stolen although accompanied by 150 cavalry guards.

Paper transfers were also a major improvement over storing and counting great stacks of coins. As one 16th century contemporary put it:

Buyer and seller are satisfied in a moment, while the pen moves over the page: whereas a day would not be enough to complete the contract for a great mass of merchandise by counting a great number of coins.[186]

By the first half of the 14th century, it was normal to pay between cities in Europe by bills of exchange, with only the final imbalances settled in gold and silver. Spufford cites an account book recording receipts from abroad by bills of exchange between 1456 and 1459 in which only 7.5 percent were paid in physical cash. All of the rest—92.5 percent—were met simply by transfers on the banks' books.

Although there was an explosion in the use of bills of exchange, the volume of trade in gold and silver did not diminish. That meant the bills of exchange themselves were serving as money, expanding the money supply. The bankers were "creating money out of thin air." Bills of exchange backed by goods and services not only substituted for gold but acted as money in their own right. How the system worked is illustrated in the following example from Spufford:

A shipping merchant might write a bill of exchange for the 100 ducats he expected to receive at the end of his voyage for selling his wares abroad. The banker would "discount" the bill of exchange by a percentage—say, 20 percent—paying the merchant only 80 ducats. The bill of exchange could then be traded among merchants just as if it were money. The percentage the bill was discounted would be reduced proportionately, as the delivery date approached and collection became more certain. When the ship returned with the gold the merchant got for his wares, payment would be made and the bill would be canceled.

"Discounting" bills in this way also allowed the parties to avoid the charge of usury—lending money at interest—which was both morally and legally forbidden. In that sense, the bill of exchange might be called the first "shadow" banking system—a system designed to get around the rules.

Transfers "in Bank":
Sidestepping the Need for Physical Gold

Another payment system that avoided the usury laws was similar to modern government bonds. Italian city-states sometimes needed large sums of money quickly for local wars, which they got through forced loans from their richer citizens, called *prestanze*. The government paid interest on these loans until they could be repaid. Because it was the government that needed money, usury laws were not usually enforced on these loans to cities and city-states. Loans for commercial and industrial purposes also largely escaped the usury laws.[187]

The rights to repayment and to the interest on the government's *prestanze* could be transferred and sold. The result was to transform debt owed by the government into a form of money, just as government bonds are a form of "near-money" today.

Transfers of *prestanze* could be done *in bank*—by accounting entries on the bank's books, without transferring physical gold. Other payments could be transferred in this way as well. The result was another form of the modern check. Written instructions, or checks, eventually supplanted oral instructions for these transfers. By the 15th century, checks were common even for modest purposes. Florence had as many as eighty banks by the early 14th century, and the bankers had accounts in each other's banks, allowing payments to be made by transfers between them. Transfers *in bank* became such a popular method of payment that in 1321, the Great Council of Venice had to pass a law compelling bankers to pay cash in gold within three days of being asked, rather than just shifting numbers between accounts. The development of checks in 19th century America served as another form of shadow banking system, discussed in Chapter 12.

This form of accounting-entry exchange was so popular in medieval Italy that the *ducat banco* of the Bank of Venice—the "money of account" transferred *in bank*—is said to have traded at a 20 percent premium *over* gold for the better part of two centuries.[188] Gold was discounted by 20 percent as soon as the depositor put it in the bank. Gold coins were subject to being devalued by clipping, so it was hard to tell their actual worth; and the bank would have had to insure them and count them by hand. A ducat that was just a number in an account was more convenient and its value was more stable.

The Emergence of Public Banking in Europe: The Mons Pietatis

In the thriving Italian economy, there were not enough gold coins to go around; and for the poor, it was particularly difficult to obtain money, since lending money at interest was forbidden to Christians. The Catholic Dominicans and Augustinians condemned it as a breach of the prohibition on usury proclaimed by Jesus in Luke 6:33.[189] An exception was made for the Jews, whose Scriptures forbade usury only to "brothers" (meaning other Jews).[190] But this gave them a virtual monopoly on lending, allowing them to charge excessively high rates because there were no competitors. Interest sometimes went as high as 60 percent.

These rates were particularly devastating to the poor. To remedy the situation, Franciscan monks defied the prohibitions of the Dominicans and Augustinians and formed charitable pawnshops called *montes pietatus*, which lent at low or no interest on the security of valuables left with the institution. *Mons* in Latin (*monti* in Italian) means a stash of collected funds.

The first true *mons pietatis* made loans that were interest-free. Unfortunately, it went broke in the process. It was founded in London in 1361, when Bishop Michael Nothburg left 1000 marks of silver for the establishment of a bank that would lend money interest-free on pawned objects. Expenses were to come out of the original capital investment; but that left no money to run the bank, and it eventually had to close.

Franciscan monks then established *montes pietatis* in Italy that lent at 4 to 12 percent interest, which at that time was considered quite low. These were either autonomous establishments or municipal corporations, which paid employees with a fixed salary or a percentage of the profits. If the net profits were large, the rate of interest was lowered. In some cities, collections were regularly taken on appointed days to increase the stash of funds.

The Franciscan monks were not out to make a profit on their loans. If the object pawned was not redeemed within the stipulated time, it was sold at public auction; and if the price obtained for it was greater than the loan plus the interest, the surplus was turned over to the owner. The sums lent were at first very small, in the hope that speculation and extravagance would be avoided.

Despite these conservative practices, the *montes* faced bitter opposition, not only from their banking competitors but from other theologians. It was not until 1515 that the *montes* were officially declared to be meritorious. The Bull of Pope Leo X said that anyone who preached or wrote against them in the future incurred excommunication.

Once the question of moral right had been determined in their favor, the *montes pietatis* spread rapidly in Italy and other European countries. They were introduced at the end of the 15th century in Germany and Austria, where they are still in operation today as municipal establishments, some belonging to the government. By the 16th and 17th centuries, the *montes* had capital reserves large enough to be drawn on by the government, especially for war. They soon evolved into banks, which were public in nature and served public and charitable purposes. This public bank tradition became the modern European tradition of public, cooperative and savings banks.

The Catholic Encyclopedia concludes that despite the long history of notoriety of the *montes pietatis*:

> [T]hey are a necessity; for without them the needy would be exposed either to the extortions of private lenders or to ruin, into which they might be plunged by some misfortune from which a momentary loan might save them. . . [T]he montes pietatis, besides the relief that they brought to the poor, exerted great influence upon the ideas concerning interest on loans; for the rigid views of the theologians of the Middle Ages in that connection underwent a first modification, which prepared the way for a generalization of the principle that moderate interest might justly be charged, and also the mere existence of the montes pietatis compelled private speculators to reduce their rates of interest from the usurious rates that had hitherto prevailed.[191]

City-state Public Banks:
The Model of the Bank of Venice

While the *mons pietatis* were evolving locally to serve the poor, public banks were being explored at the city-state level by local governments. Spufford writes that when private bankers fell on hard times in the crisis years of the late 14th and 15th centuries, instead of tightening regulations or demanding heavier guarantees, some cities and states provided banking services themselves.

The first of these publicly-owned banks was in Barcelona in 1401. The city's public bank survived for more than four centuries, when it became part of the Bank of Spain in 1853. Genoa also had a public bank in the 15th century.[192] But the most well known of the public banks was in Venice, the most commercially sophisticated city in Europe by the time of the Renaissance.

The Bank of Venice grew out of hearings in the Venetian Senate in 1585, which were detailed by Charles Dunbar in *The Harvard University Quarterly Journal of Economics* in 1892. They tell much about the development of the private banking system and the abuses and failings that made a public bank necessary.

Dunbar said the history of private banking in Venice "was a tale of repeated disaster." The Act establishing the bank began by "reciting the mischiefs resulting from the ruin of the private banks, the great need of a bank of some kind, and the conclusion that private banks could not supply the want." A large proportion of the Venetian banks had ended in failure, producing bank runs and bank panics. "In 1584 came the failure of the house of Pisani and Tiepolo for 500,000 ducats, and this event apparently brought private banking in Venice to its end."[193]

One complaint that strikes a familiar chord today was that the bankers were creating money simply as credit on their books, unbacked by any physical deposit in the bank. A speaker named Tommaso Contarini testified at the hearings:

> The banker can accommodate his friends without the payment of money, merely by writing a brief entry of credit. The banker can satisfy his own desires for fine furniture and jewels by

merely writing two lines in his books, and can buy estates or endow a child without any actual disbursement.

"In short," wrote Dunbar, "the Venetian private banks had become banks of issue, and the bankers found many temptations in the way of a prudent use of this power." Beyond just holding people's money for safekeeping, banks had actually "issued" money, creating it on their books.

The "modern system of issue" began when the Venetian bankers learned that "besides the money actually received from depositors, they could also make use of credits opened on their books, but not representing any deposit." In other words, they could advance credit as "overdrafts" without having the gold to cover it. Dunbar wrote:

> The immediate effect of over-issue, to which the bankers were thus tempted, would of course be a difficulty in meeting the demands of depositors and the resort to expedients for avoiding payment. Embarrassment of this sort, as well as actual fraud, is probably the explanation of a long series of practices legislated against by the Venetian Senate.

For example:

> The law of 1526 declares that bankers shall not, upon a demand for cash, send the creditor to another bank with an order upon it, and so wear him out by sending him from one to another, nor say that there is an error and that accounts must be compared, nor delay or refuse to transfer to a person likely to demand actual payment.

Dunbar commented dryly, "We are instantly reminded of the shifts of insolvency."

Another abuse that has a familiar ring today was the use of depositors' money to speculate for the bankers' own profit. Tomasso Contarini testified at the 16th century hearings:

> Those who open banks do not undertake this labor, and subject themselves to the burden of being cashiers for all the money in the market merely for the sake of holding it, but in order to trade with it, and by trading to make gains.

Early Experiments in "Full Reserve" Banking

In an attempt to correct these abuses, in 1587 a new Venetian public bank called the Banco di Rialto was instituted "to secure the advantage of payment in this convenient form, without risks of private mismanagement," by "taking under the guarantee of public authority" some of the functions performed by private bankers. In 1619, the Senate also established a second public bank to be a companion to the Banco di Rialto, called the Banco del Giro. It was this bank that later absorbed the Banco di Rialto and became famous throughout Europe as the Bank of Venice. It remained in business for nearly two centuries, until Napoleon's conquest in 1797.

The Bank of Venice operated very conservatively, on what today would be called the "100 percent reserve" system. (See Chapter 30.) It could lend only what it had in its vaults. Dunbar wrote:

> The bank was required to receive all cash deposits offered in good and current money; the money was to remain always subject to call . . . ; transfer in bank could be made, but only in the presence of the depositor or by his written consent . . . . The republic wisely declined to undertake the investment of the funds entrusted to it, sought no profit from the use of its credit, and, in short, merely undertook to keep the money of depositors in safety, and to pay it out or transfer it to others at the will of the owner. At a given moment the depositors might even draw out their whole of the cash, in full satisfaction of their claims, if they chose, and nobody would be any the worse. Certain of the functions of the private banks were thus selected and made the work of the new establishment, and the rest were disregarded.

It was a tightly regulated system of "sound" money—so tightly regulated that it eliminated the critical banking function of generating credit as needed for trade. The Venetian senators were so strict in their rules that they cut off the flow of credit that was vital to the flourishing Italian economy. In the end, the senators wound up restoring the private banks and allowing them to operate alongside the Bank of Venice. Dunbar wrote:

> The question whether the public bank with its restricted functions should have the sole occupation of the field of banking was finally decided by convenience rather than by deep policy. The act of 1584 had forbidden the establishment of private banks . . . But in February, 1596-97, the Senate, after reciting the impossibility of meeting all the needs of commerce by means of a single bank, gave . . . leave to establish a private bank . . . .

The Bank of Venice kept afloat, but Dunbar reports that it was a troubled venture. The bank was founded to pay off a government debt, but the Senate insisted on limiting its resources to its deposits, and the burdened bank could not pull itself out of debt. Alexander Hamilton would face this problem again when he set up the First Bank of the United States to pay the debts of the new United States government; but he arrived at a quite different solution, explored in Chapter 11.

Dunbar concluded of the whole Italian experiment:

> The private bankers [were] more ready [than the Venetian senators] to adapt themselves to the needs of the community . . . but had paid the penalty of inexperience in dealing with credit. The public bank had replaced [the private banks], had discarded a part of their functions, and had reduced the remainder for safety to an inflexible routine. In this form, however, the public bank had no longer the power to adapt itself to the needs of commerce in a rapidly changing world.[194]

A bank that operated on a 100 percent reserve system, lending only the gold that it had, could not provide the expanding money supply necessary to support an expanding economy. Some way was needed of extending credit without risking the periodic bank runs that were triggered when depositors all demanded their gold at the same time.

This problem would be solved in medieval England using a system that mirrored the ancient Sumerian and Egyptian systems of credits and debits.But in England the accounts would be kept, not on paper or clay or papyrus, but on pieces of wood.

Chapter 9

CREDIT INNOVATIONS IN ENGLAND: FROM GOVERNMENT TALLIES TO FRACTIONAL RESERVE LENDING

"[O]ur forefathers had no other books but the score and the tally . . . ."

-- Shakespeare, 2 Henry VI (4.7.36)

For more than five centuries, English kings funded their governments with wooden tallies, which were simply receipts for goods and services delivered to the government as an advance against taxes owed. They retained their value because they were accepted in the payment of taxes. Like the Egyptian *ostraca*, the tallies circulated as money, until they were supplanted in the late seventeenth century by the banknotes of the privately-owned Bank of England, which became the template for the central banking system we have today.

The early Italian bankers solved the problem of a limited supply of gold with a clever innovation involving credit issued for more gold than they actually had. But the scheme was based on sleight of hand, and it periodically got both the bankers and their local economies into trouble. In medieval England, a more honest, transparent and stable solution was devised. As in imperial China, the king rather than the banks became the issuer of the currency. But rather than coins or paper notes, he simply issued receipts. They were neither more nor less than what they purported to be: tallies of sums owed and paid. The number of tallies expanded naturally as trade expanded, and it shrank as the tallies returned to the government in the payment of taxes.

The English tally system originated with King Henry I, son of William the Conqueror, who took the throne in 1,100 A.D. The Gutenberg printing press had not yet been invented, and taxes were paid directly with goods produced by the land. Payment was recorded on a piece of wood that was notched and split in half. One half was kept by the government and the other by the recipient. To confirm payment, the two halves were matched to make sure they tallied. Since no stick splits evenly, and since the notches tallying the sums were cut right through both pieces of wood, the method was virtually foolproof against forgery.

The tallies provided a convenient form of bookkeeping. They were used by the government not only as receipts for the payment of taxes but to pay soldiers for their service, farmers for their wheat, and laborers for their labor. They have been called "the English equivalent of today's credit card."[195]

Sovereign Money Is "Equity," Not Debt

According to Chris Cook, a senior research fellow at University College London writing in the March 2013 *Herald Scotland*, the medieval English tallies represented a pre-payment of future taxes. They were not a debt owed by the king. They were the prepayment of a debt owed to the king. Money, goods and services were advanced by citizens to the king so that the government could meet its expenses and obligations or wage war. The tallies were "discounted" by being issued in excess of the current value of goods and services delivered. Cook writes:

> Naturally these medieval taxpayers did not give the sovereign £10 worth of value in exchange for a £10 prepayment but received a discount for their trouble. The phrase "rate of return" literally means the rate over time at which the stock

could be returned to the issuer, enabling the initial discount to be realized.[196]

Cook says this process has been obscured today by the intervention of banks as middlemen. The bank now creates money as a loan by writing it into an account as a deposit, which the government borrows, spends, and owes back with interest. But historically, before the banker interceded as middleman, the sovereign simply collected what he needed from his constituents and paid with receipts consisting of credits against future taxes. The taxpayer already owed the taxes; he was just paying them early and being rewarded with a discount on his tax bill.

When the banks got into the money-creating business, these advances became "loans." The discount became interest, and the "sovereign" became a debtor. But Cook maintains that "sovereign debt" is a mischaracterization. Government bonds, or debt, should properly be thought of as equity in U.K., Inc., or U.S.A., Inc. The government pays with equity, or shares, in the Common Wealth.

Interestingly, the word "stock," meaning a financial certificate, actually comes from the Middle English word for the tally stick. As explained in a 2008 journal article on the tally sticks, "A refinement of the split tally was to make one-half of the marked stick shorter. The longer half was called the stock and was given to the party advancing the money to the receiver. The shorter part, the foil, went to the debtor, who got 'the short end of the stick.'"[197]

Much of the stock in the Bank of England was originally purchased with tally sticks. The holder of the stock was said to be the "stockholder," who owned "bank stock." One of the original stockholders purchased his shares with a stick representing £25,000, an enormous sum at the time. A substantial share of what would become the world's richest and most powerful corporation was thus bought with a stick of wood. According to legend, the location of Wall Street, the New York financial district, was chosen because of the presence of a chestnut tree enormous enough to supply tally sticks for the emerging American stock market.

Stock issuance was developed during the Middle Ages as a way of financing businesses when usury and interest-bearing loans were forbidden. In medieval Europe, publicly-owned banks run by municipal or local governments helped finance ventures by issuing shares of stock in the ventures. These public banks were large, powerful, efficient operations that fought the moneylenders' private "usury banks" tooth and nail. The usury banks prevailed in Europe only after revolutionaries in France were forced to borrow from the international bankers to finance the French Revolution (1789-1799), putting the revolutionary government heavily in their debt.

The Tallies Fund a Long Period
of English Prosperity

The tally system was in use in England for more than five centuries before the gold-based paper banknotes of the usury bankers took root, helping to fund a long era of leisure and abundance that flowered into the Renaissance. Tallies were used not only by the king but by individuals and institutions, to register debts, record fines, collect rents, and enter payments for services rendered. By the thirteenth century, the financial market for tallies was sufficiently sophisticated that they could be bought, sold, and discounted. According to historian M. T. Clanchy in *From Memory to Written Record, England 1066-1307*:

> Tallies were . . . a sophisticated and practical record of numbers. They were more "convenient" to keep and store than parchments, less complex to make, and no easier to forge.[198]

Clanchy wrote that only a few hundred tallies survive, but millions were made.

In the 1500s, King Henry VIII gave the tallies the force of a national currency, when he ordered that they *must* be used to evidence the payment of taxes.[199] That meant everyone had to have them.

In *War Cycles, Peace Cycles* (1985), Richard Hoskins wrote that by the end of the seventeenth century, about 14 million pounds' worth of tally-money was in circulation.[200] Spufford states that English coinage had never exceeded half a million pounds up to that time.[201] Thus the tally system was not a minor monetary experiment, as some commentators have suggested, but made up the bulk of the English money supply during most of the Middle Ages.

Modern schoolbooks generally portray the Middle Ages as a time of poverty, backwardness, and economic slavery, from which the people were freed only by the Industrial Revolution. But reliable early historians painted a quite different picture. The Black Death and other scourges had to be contended with, but the economy itself seems to have provided quite easy living conditions.

Thorold Rogers, a nineteenth century Oxford historian, wrote that in the Middle Ages, *"a labourer could provide all the necessities for his family for a year by working 14 weeks."* Fourteen weeks is only a quarter of a year.

The rest of the time, some men worked for themselves; some studied; some fished. Some helped to build the cathedrals that appeared all over Germany, France and England during the period—massive works of art that were built mainly with volunteer labor. Some used their leisure to visit these shrines. One hundred thousand pilgrims had the wealth and leisure to visit Canterbury and other shrines yearly.

William Cobbett, author of the definitive *History of the Reformation*, wrote that Winchester Cathedral "was made when there were no poor rates; when every labouring man in England was clothed in good woollen cloth; and when all had plenty of meat and bread . . . ." Money was available for inventions and art, supporting the Michelangelos, Rembrandts, Shakespeares, and Newtons of the period.[202]

The Renaissance is usually thought of as the flowering of the age; but the university system, parliamentary government, the English common law system, and the foundations of a great literary and spiritual movement were all in place by the thirteenth century, and education was advanced and widespread. As one scholar of the era observes:

> We are very prone to consider that it is only in our time that anything like popular education has come into existence. As a matter of fact, however, the education afforded to the people in the little towns of the Middle Ages, represents an ideal of educational uplift for the masses such as has never been even distantly approached in succeeding centuries. The Thirteenth Century developed the greatest set of technical schools that the world has ever known. . . . These medieval towns, . . . during the course of the building of their cathedrals, of their public

buildings and various magnificent edifices of royalty and for the nobility, succeeded in accomplishing such artistic results that the world has ever since held them in admiration.[203]

The common people had leisure, education, art, and economic security. According to *The Catholic Encyclopedia*:

> Economic historians like Rogers and Gibbins declare that during the best period of the Middle Ages—say, from the thirteenth to the fifteenth century, inclusive—there was no such grinding and hopeless poverty, no such chronic semi-starvation in any class, as exists to-day among large classes in the great cities . . . . In the Middle Ages there was no class resembling our proletariat, which has no security, no definite place, no certain claim upon any organization or institution in the socio-economic organism.[204]

Richard Hoskins attributes this long period of prosperity to the absence of usurious lending practices.[205] Rather than having to borrow the moneylenders' gold, the people relied largely on the interest-free tallies. Unlike gold, wooden tallies could not become scarce; and unlike paper money, they could not be counterfeited or multiplied by sleight of hand. As in the Sumerian and Egyptian accounting systems, they were simply a receipt or invoice for goods and services exchanged.

The tally system avoided both the depressions resulting from a scarcity of gold and the inflations resulting from printing paper money out of all proportion to the goods and services available for sale. Since the tallies came into existence *along with* goods and services, supply and demand increased together, and prices remained stable.

The tally system provided an organic form of money that expanded naturally as trade expanded, and contracted naturally as taxes were paid. Bankers did not have to meet behind closed doors to set interest rates or manipulate markets to keep the money supply in balance. It balanced the way a checkbook balances, as a matter of simple arithmetic.

Private Banknotes Replace the Government's Tallies

Britain thrived with government-issued currency (tallies and coins) until the king's sovereign authority was eroded by Cromwell's revolt in the mid-seventeenth century. Before that, the king had not needed to borrow money for domestic use, since he had the sovereign right to issue it himself; but gold was sometimes needed for international purposes. In 1087, King William (Rufus) admitted Jewish moneylenders into the country when he needed gold to do business with the French. They were allowed to practice their trade on condition that the interest be demanded in gold and that half be paid to the king. But the moneylenders eventually became so wealthy at the expense of the people that the Church, with urgings from the Pope, prohibited them from taking interest; and in 1290, when they had lost their usefulness to the king, the Jews were again expelled from the country.

For a brief period in the 1500s, King Henry VIII relaxed the laws concerning usury when he broke away from the Catholic Church. But when Queen Mary took the throne, she tightened the laws again. The result was a radical contraction of the money supply, but Queen Elizabeth I (Mary's half-sister) was determined to avoid the usury trap. She solved the problem by supplementing the money supply with metal coins issued by the public treasury.[206]

The coins were made of metal, but their value came from the stamp of the sovereign on them. This was established as a matter of law in 1600, when Queen Elizabeth issued relatively worthless base metal coins as legal tender in Ireland. All other coins were annulled and had to be returned to the mints. When the action was challenged in the highest court of the land, the court ruled that it was the sovereign's sole prerogative to create the money of the realm. What the sovereign declared to be money was money, and *it was treason for anyone else to create it*. According to 19th century historian Alexander Del Mar, quoted by Stephen Zarlenga in *The Lost Science of Money*, this decision was so detested by the merchant classes, the goldsmiths, and later the British East India Company, that they worked incessantly to destroy it. Del Mar wrote in 1895:

This was done by undermining the Crown and then passing the free coinage act of 1666, opening the way for the foreign element to establish a new Monarch, and to reconstitute the money prerogative in the hands of a specific group of financiers—not elected, not representing society, and in large part not even English.[207]

In the mid-seventeenth century, Oliver Cromwell led a revolt against the Tudor monarchy. The middle classes sided with Parliament under Cromwell, who was a Puritan Protestant. The Protestants were more lenient than the Catholics toward usury and toward the Dutch moneylenders who practiced it. The nobles and gentry sided with the King—Charles I, son of James I—who followed the Church of England, the English Catholic Church.

The moneylenders agreed to provide the funds to back Parliament, on condition that they be allowed back into England and that the loans be guaranteed. That meant the permanent removal of King Charles, who would have repudiated the loans had he gotten back into power. Charles' recapture, trial, and execution were duly arranged and carried out to secure the loans.[208]

After Cromwell's death, Charles' son Charles II was invited to return; but Parliament had no intention of granting him the sovereign power over the money supply enjoyed by his predecessors. When the king needed a standing army, Parliament refused to vote the funds, forcing him to borrow instead from the English goldsmiths at usurious interest rates. The final blow to the royal prerogative was the Free Coinage Act of 1666, which allowed anyone to bring gold or silver to the mint to have it stamped into coins. The power to issue money had for centuries been the sole right of the king. It was now transferred into private hands, giving bankers the power to cause inflations and depressions at will by issuing or withholding their gold coins and the paper banknotes ostensibly backed by them.[209]

"The Mother of Central Banks"

The earlier English kings and queens, having the power to issue money themselves, would not have agreed to charter a private central bank that had the power to create money and lend it to the government. But

King William III, who succeeded to the throne after Charles II, was a Dutchman and a tool of the powerful Wisselbank of Amsterdam.

William began his career as a Dutch aristocrat. He was elevated to Captain General of the Dutch Forces and then to Prince William of Orange with the backing of Dutch moneylenders. His marriage was arranged to Princess Mary of York, eldest daughter of the English Duke of York, who reigned as James II of England from 1685 to 1688. When James was deposed in 1689, William and Mary became joint rulers.

William was soon at war with Louis XIV of France. To finance his war, he borrowed 1.2 million pounds in gold from a group of moneylenders who would form the Bank of England. The money was raised by a novel device that is still used by governments today: the lenders would issue a permanent loan on which regular interest would be paid, but the principal portion of the loan did not need to be repaid but could be rolled over and expanded indefinitely.[210] It was the beginning of the tradition of deficit spending and of carrying a national debt to private creditors.

The Bank of England was chartered in 1694 to William Paterson, a Scotsman who had lived in Amsterdam.[211] It was called "the Mother of Central Banks," but it was not actually the first national central bank. Sveriges Riksbank, also called the Bank of Sweden, began operations in 1668 and is not only the world's oldest central bank but the fourth oldest bank still in operation. Sveriges Riksbank was founded under private ownership but remained under the control of Parliament, and it was not allowed to issue money in the form of bank-notes.[212]

The Bank of England did not suffer from that limitation. Its banknotes circulated as the national paper currency, and the government agreed to use the Bank for all its transactions. The Bank's charter not only gave control of the country's money to a privately owned company but gave the force of law to the "fractional reserve" banking scheme that allowed the Bank to issue many times more banknotes than it had gold to back them.

The Bank of England Develops Credit as an "Instrument of World Supremacy"

In *Tragedy and Hope* (1966), Georgetown University Professor Carroll Quigley called fractional reserve lending "one of the instruments of English world supremacy." The English had discovered the power of credit. Quigley wrote:

> It early became clear that . . . a volume of [paper gold] certificates could be issued greater than the volume of gold reserved for payment of demands against them. Such an excess volume of paper claims against reserves we now call bank notes. . . .
>
> In effect, this creation of paper claims greater than the reserves available means that bankers were creating money out of nothing. The same thing could be done in another way, not by note-issuing banks but by deposit banks. Deposit bankers discovered that orders and checks drawn against deposits by depositors and given to third persons were often not cashed by the latter but were deposited to their own accounts. Thus there were no actual movements of funds, and payments were made simply by bookkeeping transactions on the accounts.
>
> Accordingly, it was necessary for the banker to keep on hand in actual money (gold, certificates, and notes) no more than the fraction of deposits likely to be drawn upon and cashed; the rest could be used for loans, and if these loans were made by creating a deposit for the borrower, who in turn would draw checks upon it rather than withdraw it in money, such "created deposits" or loans could also be covered adequately by retaining reserves to only a fraction of their value.
>
> Such created deposits also were a creation of money out of nothing, although bankers usually refused to express their actions, either note issuing or deposit lending, in these terms. William Paterson, however, on obtaining the charter of the Bank of England in 1694, to use the moneys he had won in privateering, said, "The Bank hath benefit of interest on all moneys which it creates out of nothing." This was repeated by Sir Edward Holden, founder of the Midland Bank, on December 18, 1907, and is, of course, generally admitted today.

By engaging in what the stricter Bank of Venice had forbidden – the extension of credit unbacked by an equal sum in gold – the Bank of England was able to fund industry, trade, and wars. Quigley wrote:

> This organizational structure for creating means of payment out of nothing, which we call credit, was not invented by England but was developed by her to become one of her chief weapons in the victory over Napoleon in 1815. The emperor, as the last great mercantilist, could not see money in any but concrete terms, and was convinced that his efforts to fight wars on the basis of "sound money," by avoiding the creation of credit, would ultimately win him a victory by bankrupting England. He was wrong, although the lesson has had to be relearned by modern financiers in the twentieth century.[213]

The creation of money out of nothing, or credit, allowed England to prevail over the "sound money" French. But because the Bank of England was privately owned, the profits from its extension of credit went into private coffers, leaving the government heavily in debt. The Bank lent to the government by trading its own paper banknotes for paper bonds representing the government's promise to pay principal and interest back to the Bank. According to Eustace Mullins in *The Secrets of the Federal Reserve* (1952), the negotiation of additional loans caused England's national debt to go from 1.2 million pounds in 1694 to 16 million pounds in 1698. By 1815, the debt was up to 885 million pounds, largely due to the compounding of interest. The lenders reaped huge profits and gained substantial political leverage from the debt.

Since only a fraction of its notes were actually backed by gold, the Bank of England was vulnerable to runs when suspicious customers demanded their gold, something that happened only two years after the Bank was founded. But the government wanted the scheme to work, and it agreed to back the notes. Thus the government wound up underwriting the Bank rather than the Bank underwriting the government.

In 1697, the government prohibited any new corporate bank from being established in England that would compete with the Bank of England, granting a monopoly privilege to the Bank. In 1708, the government made it unlawful for any corporation besides the Bank of

England to issue bank notes. In 1742, private counterfeiting of Bank of England Notes was made a crime punishable by death.[214]

The "Financial Revolution" Transfers the Right to Issue Money From the Government to the Banks

After the Bank of England began issuing paper banknotes in the 1690s, the government followed suit by issuing paper tallies against future tax revenues. Paper was easily negotiable, making the paper tallies competitive with private banknote money.

The paper tally lost out to the paper banknote not for functional but for political reasons. King William's right to the throne was disputed, and the Dutch moneylenders who backed him could be evicted if the English Catholic leaders got back in power and forbade moneylending again. To make sure that did not happen, the moneylenders used their new influence to discount the tallies as money and get their own banknotes legalized as the currency of the realm.

The tallies were called "unfunded" debt, while the Bank of England's paper notes were euphemistically labeled "funded" debt. According to a scholarly article published at Harvard University in 2002, "Tallies and departmental bills were issued to creditors in anticipation of annual tax revenues but were not tied to any specific revenue streams; hence they were 'unfunded.'" When debt was "funded," on the other hand, *Parliament set aside specific revenues to meet interest payments*, a feature that further enhanced confidence in lending to the government." Note that it set aside money *just for the interest*, not the principal, which was rolled over from year to year. The interest constituted "rent" for the use of the bankers' paper banknotes.

The article contains a chart showing that in 1693, 100 percent of the government's debt was "unfunded" (paid in government tallies or bills of credit). "By the 1720s," they write, "over 90 percent of all government borrowing was long term and funded. This, in a nutshell, was the Financial Revolution."[215]

That is one way of looking at the "Financial Revolution." But until the mid-seventeenth century, the tallies did not *need* to be "funded" through taxes, since *they were not government debts*. As Chris Cook explains, the debt was owed by the taxpayers to the King; the King had just collected it early by paying for the things he needed with discounted receipts. The things he paid for with tallies *were* the taxes; the tax bill was paid when the tallies were exchanged for the goods. Before Cromwell's Revolution, the king did not need to borrow, because he could issue wooden tallies or metal coins at will to pay his bills. What the Financial Revolution actually did was to transfer the right to issue money from the government to private banks.

The tallies were an interest-free accounting system that competed with the interest-bearing money of the private bankers. After the passage of certain monetary reform acts, the tally sticks went up in flames in a huge bonfire started in a stove in the House of Lords in 1834. In an ironic twist, the fire quickly got out of control and wound up burning down both the Palace of Westminster and the Houses of Parliament. It was symbolic of the end of an equitable era of trade. "Money" was transformed from an accounting tool into a weapon for economic control.[216]

As the era of the wooden tally was fading in England, however, its paper equivalent was emerging in colonial America. The thirteen colonies were thirteen experiments in government-issued money, and some were more stable than others. The most sustainable systems incorporated a government-owned bank, which recycled the colonial scrip back to the government and the economy. The best of these was devised by the Quakers in colonial Pennsylvania.

Chapter 10

HOW THE QUAKERS' MODEL PUBLIC BANK BROUGHT PROSPERITY TO PENNSYLVANIA

There are three faithful friends – an old wife, an old dog, and ready money.

– Benjamin Franklin

The first and arguably the best of the modern public banking models was established by the Quakers in the American colony of Pennsylvania. Issuing money as credit that returned to the government and was recycled back into the economy created a sustainable feedback loop, avoiding a pyramiding, compounding debt. The Pennsylvania experiment was terminated not because it was unsuccessful but because of the opposition of British banking interests.

The Quakers, like the Jews, were a minority religious sect that took up banking in England when they were excluded from other forms of commerce. The sect was founded by George Fox in 1650, following a revelation that the divine presence was within him and in every man. It was a revolutionary way of preaching, which did away with hierarchies and did not recognize worldly claims of office. The doctrine was so revolutionary that the established order felt threatened by it.[217]

The Quakers took the Biblical injunction against swearing so literally that they would not swear allegiance to the Crown, an act of defiance that was interpreted as disloyalty or even treason. They also refused to pay tithes to the Church of England.

Excluded from other professions, they went into banking, and they eventually came to dominate that business in England. Lloyds and the founding families of Barclays were Quakers. Most of the country banks were also Quaker-owned and Quaker-run.[218]

Driven by persecution, the Quakers soon began to migrate to America; but they were not accepted in Massachusetts either. They wished to have a colony of their own.[219] This wish was fulfilled when William Penn, the most prominent Quaker in England, was granted the land that would become Pennsylvania in payment of a debt owed by the King to his father.

Penn was a leader of a sort rarely seen today. In 1904, H. W. Elson wrote of him in his *History of the United States of America*:

> It is difficult to find a man, especially one whose life is spent in the midst of political turmoil and governmental strife, so utterly incorruptible as was William Penn. . . . He founded a government and based it on the eternal principle of equal human rights, with its sole object as the freedom and happiness of its people.[220]

Penn drew up a government that gave the whole power of lawmaking to the people. The people were represented by a council that originated all the laws and an assembly that approved them. He also made a treaty with the Indians and vowed to live in harmony with them.

Pennsylvania grew more rapidly than the other colonies, and Philadelphia soon became the chief city in colonial America. Later it would be the birthplace of independence, and of the Constitution of the United States. Half the population of Pennsylvania were Scots-Presbyterians, who had occupied northern Ireland for two or three generations before coming to America. Like the Quakers, they were attracted by the liberal, humane government inaugurated by William Penn.[221]

The colony also attracted the most famous figure in colonial America, Benjamin Franklin. Franklin has been called "the father of paper money." He did not actually invent it or the public banking system that worked so well in his adopted colony, but he wrote about these innovations and extolled their virtues, popularizing them in the Middle Colonies.

Redefining Money

The idea of a paper currency was suggested as far back as 1650, in an anonymous British pamphlet titled "The Key to Wealth, or, a New Way for Improving of Trade: Lawfull, Easie, Safe and Effectual." But the currency proposed by the pamphleteer was modeled on the receipts issued by London goldsmiths and silversmiths for the precious metals left in their vaults for safekeeping. The colonists needed a payment system that was based on something besides gold, which was scarce in the colonies. They had to use foreign coins to conduct trade; and since they imported more than they exported, the coins were continually being drained off to England and other countries, leaving the colonists without enough money for their own internal needs.

What they came up with in place of foreign currency was a payment system based simply on credit—the "credit of the whole Country," said Cotton Mather, the most famous minister in New England. When confidence in the new paper money waned, Mather argued:

> Is a Bond or Bill-of-Exchange for £1000, other than paper? And yet is it not as valuable as so much Silver or Gold, supposing the security of Payment is sufficient? Now what is the security of your Paper-money less than the Credit of the whole Country?[222]

Mather had redefined money. What it represented was not a sum of gold or silver but simply the credit of the nation. A paper bill of credit was the government's IOU or promise to pay, an acknowledgment by the community of a debt owed and due, redeemable by the members of the community in goods and services.

Funding Local Government with Credit

The first local government to issue its own paper money was the province of Massachusetts. The year was 1691, three years before the charter of the Bank of England. Massachusetts' buccaneer governor had led a daring assault on Quebec in an attempt to drive the French out of Canada, but the assault had failed. Militiamen and widows needed to be paid. The local merchants were approached but had declined, saying they had other demands on their money.[223]

The innovative Massachusetts Assembly then came up with the idea of paying with paper money. Just as the banker's banknotes were promissory notes or IOUs of the banks, the provincial governments' "bill of credit" represented the "bond" or IOU of the government—its promise to pay tomorrow on a debt incurred today.

Other colonies followed suit with their own issues of paper money. Some were considered government IOUs, redeemable later in "hard" currency (silver or gold). Other issues were "legal tender" in themselves—money that must legally be accepted in the payment of debts. Legal tender was "as good as gold" in trade, without bearing debt or an obligation to redeem the notes in some other form of money later.[224]

Turning Prosperity Tomorrow into "Ready Money" Today

It was into this experimental cauldron that Benjamin Franklin stepped at the age of 17, arriving from Boston in 1723. Six years later, in 1729, he wrote a pamphlet called "A Modest Enquiry into the Nature and Necessity of a Paper-Currency," which was circulated throughout the colonies. It became very popular, earning him contracts to print paper money for New Jersey, Pennsylvania, and Delaware.[225]

Franklin wrote his pamphlet after observing the remarkable effects paper currency had had in stimulating the economy in Pennsylvania. He said, "Experience, more prevalent than all the logic in the World, has fully convinced us all, that [paper money] has been, and is now of the greatest advantages to the country."

Paper currency secured against future tax revenues, he said, turned prosperity tomorrow into "ready money" today. The government did not need gold to issue this currency, and it did not need to go into debt to the banks. In America, the land of opportunity, ready money would allow even the poor to get ahead. Franklin wrote, "Many that understand . . . Business very well, but have not a Stock sufficient of their own, will be encouraged to borrow Money; to trade with, when they have it at a moderate interest."

He also said, "The riches of a country are to be valued by the quantity of labor its inhabitants are able to purchase and not by the quantity of gold and silver they possess."[226] When gold was the medium of exchange, money determined production rather than production determining the money supply. When gold was plentiful, things got produced. When it was scarce, men were out of work and people knew want. The virtue of government-issued paper scrip was that it could grow along with productivity, allowing potential wealth to become real wealth. The government could pay for services with paper receipts that were basically community credits. In this way, the community actually created supply and demand at the same time. The farmer would not farm, the teacher would not teach, the miner would not mine, unless the funds were available to compensate them for their labors. Paper "scrip" underwrote the production of goods and services that would not otherwise have been on the market. Anything for which there was a buyer and a producer could be produced and traded. If A had what B wanted, B had what C wanted, and C had what A wanted, they could all get together and trade. They did not need the moneylenders' gold, which could be hoarded, manipulated, or lent only at usurious interest rates.

The colonists' new paper money financed a period of prosperity that was considered remarkable for isolated colonies lacking their own silver and gold. Edward Burke, speaking in the British House of Commons in 1774, would say of the American colonies:

> Nothing in the history of mankind, is like their progress. For my part, I never cast an eye on their commerce, and their cultivated and commodious life, but they seem to me rather nations grown to perfection through a long series of fortunate events, and a train of successful industry accumulating wealth in many centuries, than the colonies of yesterday; than a set of miserable outcasts, a few years ago, not so much sent as thrown on the bleak and barren shore of a desolate wilderness, three thousand miles from all civilized intercourse.[227]

The wilderness had been transformed into abundance using a medium of exchange that economist David Hume called "representative money" and Benjamin Franklin called "bills of credit" or "ready money." It was money backed, not by gold, but by the goods and services for which it was traded by the issuing government.

Funding Local Government on Credit

It was an era of monetary experimentation, and some of these colonial experiments were more sustainable than others. In the middle colonies—Pennsylvania, Delaware, New York and New Jersey—the colonial governments managed to finance their operations in a way that reduced or avoided the need to tax the people; and they did it by going into the banking business.

Alvin Rabushka, a senior fellow at the Hoover Institution at Stanford University, traced this development in a 2002 article called "Representation Without Taxation." He wrote that there were two main ways the colonies issued paper money. Most colonies used both, in varying proportions.[228]

One was a direct issue of notes, usually called "bills of credit" or "treasury notes." These were promissory notes or IOUs of the government backed by specific future taxes. Although taxation was involved, the payback was deferred well into the future, and sometimes the funds never got returned to the treasury at all.

The advantage of this system of note issuance over the British bankers' gold was that the funds were not owed back to private foreign lenders, and no interest was due on them. They were just credits issued and spent into the economy on goods and services. The problem with the system of print-and-spend without drawing the money back to the issuer was that it tended to inflate the money supply and devalue the currency.

The inflation problem was solved when a second method of issue was devised. Colonial assemblies discovered that provincial loan offices could generate a steady stream of revenue in the form of interest, *by taking on the lending functions of banks.* In the sustainable system of the middle colonies, a government loan office called a "land bank" would issue paper money and lend it to residents (usually farmers) at low rates of interest. This money would come back to the loan office on a regular payment schedule, preventing the money supply from over-inflating and keeping the value of the loan-office bills stable in terms of English sterling. The loans were secured by mortgages on real property, silver plate, and other hard assets. Benjamin Franklin wrote, "Bills issued upon Land are in Effect Coined Land." The interest paid on the loans went into the public coffers, funding the government in place of taxes.

Pennsylvania's Model Public Bank

The most celebrated of these loan offices was in Pennsylvania, where the Quakers applied their banking expertise to the problem of designing a sustainable monetary system. The Pennsylvania model demonstrated that it was quite possible for the government to issue new money in place of taxes, without inflating prices. The loan office was the province's chief source of revenue. Except for import duties on liquor, the provincial government collected no taxes at all.[229]

During this period, which lasted from 1723 into the 1750s, Pennsylvania wholesale prices remained stable. The currency depreciated by 21 percent against English sterling, but Rabushka states that this was due to external trade relations rather than to changes in the quantity of currency in circulation.[230] In 1938, Dr. Richard A. Lester, an economist at Princeton University, wrote, *"The price level during the 52 years prior to the American Revolution and while Pennsylvania was on a paper standard was more stable than the American price level has been during any succeeding fifty-year period."*[231]

In 1776, Adam Smith wrote in *The Wealth of Nations*:

> The government of Pennsylvania, without amassing any treasure [gold or silver], invented a method of lending, not money indeed, but what is equivalent to money to its subjects. By advancing to private people at interest . . . paper bills of credit . . . made transferable from hand to hand like bank notes, and declared by act of assembly to be legal tender in all payments from one inhabitant to another, it raised a moderate revenue which went a considerable way toward defraying . . . the whole ordinary expense of that frugal and orderly government. . . . *[This] paper currency . . . is said never to have sunk below the value*

of gold and silver which was current in the colony before the issue of paper money.

Franklin said the money system of Pennsylvania was the reason that it "has so greatly increased in inhabitants," having replaced "the inconvenient method of barter" and given "new life to business [and] promoted greatly the settlement of new lands (by lending small sums to beginners on easy interest)."

The Pennsylvania land bank was not lending gold or the money of its depositors, and it was not drawing from a pool of "reserves." It was not bound by capital requirements, reserve requirements, or the need for "liquidity." It was just issuing credit—paper bills representing the credit of the community. British banknotes had to be borrowed at 8 percent interest, and they were scarce. The Pennsylvania scrip was lent at 5 percent interest, and there was enough of this credit for every creditworthy borrower who wanted it. Yet it did not over-inflate the money supply. The loans-plus-interest recycled back to the government, which spent and lent the money back into the economy in a sustainable way. It was a bold model that produced remarkable results, a model that would be repeated and proven in other countries later.

The Pennsylvania experiment was brought to an end not because it was unsuccessful but because it was too successful in making the colonists economically independent. Government-issued money competed with the monopoly of the Bank of England.

King George Bans the Colonial Scrip

Paper currency was stable in Pennsylvania, but this was not true in some of the other provinces. In the New England colonies— Massachusetts, Rhode Island, Connecticut and New Hampshire— paper currencies were issued in excessive quantities, both as bills of credit and as loans, and they did not maintain their value. They also suffered from a lack of common regulations and standards. Some paid interest; others did not. Some could be used only for purchase and not in the repayment of debt. Some could be used for public debts but not for private transactions. The result for trade was chaos and confusion.

Although these paper currencies helped to finance development in New England that would not otherwise have occurred, their rapid depreciation threatened the investments of British merchants and financiers who were doing business with the colonies, and they leaned on Parliament to prohibit the practice. In 1751, King George II enacted a ban on the issue of new paper money in New England, although existing issues could be still renewed. This ban was continued under King George III, who succeeded his father in 1760.

In 1764, Benjamin Franklin went to London to petition Parliament to lift the ban. He recounted the many benefits of colonial scrip for the citizens of Pennsylvania, and assured his listeners that "New York and New Jersey have also increased greatly during the same period, with the use of paper money; so that it does not appear to be of the ruinous nature ascribed to it."

Rather than pacifying Parliament, however, the petition only alarmed British banking interests. Giving the government the benefit of money creation was a complete reversal of the established British school of economics, in which the government had to borrow from private bankers at interest. The bankers viciously opposed Franklin's appeal.

Parliament wound up passing a Currency Act that was actually stricter than the earlier prohibition, banning not only new issues but the reissue of existing currency.[232] The bill declared that "no act, order, resolution, or vote of assembly, in any of his Majesty's colonies or plantations in America, shall be made, for creating or issuing any paper bills, or bills of credit of any kind or denomination whatsoever, declaring such paper bills, or bills of credit, to be legal tender . . . ."[233]

The colonists were forced to pay all future taxes to Britain in silver or gold, or in the Bank of England banknotes that were supposedly backed by those precious metals. Since the colonists lacked mines of their own, that meant they had to go into debt to the British bankers. When they could not issue their own currency, the money supply suddenly shrank, leaving widespread unemployment, hunger and poverty in its wake.

"The Corner Stone of the Revolution"

The oppressed colonists finally ignored the ban and went back to issuing their own paper money. Stephen Zarlenga quotes historian Alexander Del Mar, writing in 1895:

> [T]he creation and circulation of bills of credit by revolutionary assemblies . . . coming as they did upon the heels of the strenuous efforts made by the Crown to suppress paper money in America [were] acts of defiance so contemptuous and insulting to the Crown that forgiveness was thereafter impossible . . . [T] here was but one course for the Crown to pursue and that was to suppress and punish these acts of rebellion . . . . Thus the Bills of Credit of this era, which ignorance and prejudice have attempted to belittle into the mere instruments of a reckless financial policy were really the standards of the Revolution. They were more than this: they were the Revolution itself![234]

This version of the events leading up to the Revolution was echoed by Peter Cooper, founder of Cooper Union College and a former colleague of Treasury Secretary Albert Gallatin. Cooper wrote in his 1883 book *Ideas for a Science of Good Government*:

> After Franklin had explained . . . to the British Government as to the real cause of prosperity, they immediately passed laws, forbidding the payment of taxes in that money. This produced such great inconvenience and misery to the people, that it was the principal cause of the Revolution. A far greater reason for a general uprising, than the Tea and Stamp Act, was the taking away of the paper money.

Like Massachusetts nearly a century earlier, the colonists suddenly found themselves at war and without the means to pay for it. The first act of the new Continental Congress was to issue its own paper scrip. Popularly called the Continental, it allowed the colonists to do something that had never been done before: they financed a war against a major power, with virtually no "hard" currency of their own. It was a bold stroke, which evoked the wonder and admiration of foreign observers. Franklin wrote that "the whole is a mystery even to the politicians, how we could pay with paper that had no previously fixed fund appropriated specifically to redeem it. This currency as we manage it is a wonderful machine."

Thomas Paine called it a "corner stone" of the Revolution:

> Every stone in the Bridge, that has carried us over, seems to have claim upon our esteem. But this was a corner stone, and its usefulness cannot be forgotten.[235]

Economic Warfare: The Bankers Counterattack

The British retaliated with their own form of economic warfare: they attacked their competitor's currency and drove down its value. In the 1770s, when paper money was easy to duplicate, its value could be diluted by physically flooding the market with counterfeit money.

The British shipped in counterfeit Continentals by the boatload. They could be purchased in any amount, essentially for the cost of the paper on which they were printed. Thomas Jefferson estimated that counterfeiting added $200 million to the money supply, effectively doubling it; and later historians thought this figure was low.

Zarlenga cites historian J. W. Schuckers, who wrote, "The English Government which seems to have a mania for counterfeiting the paper money of its enemies entered into competition with private criminals." Schuckers quoted a confidential letter from an English general to his superiors, stating that "the experiments suggested by your Lordships have been tried, no assistance that could be drawn from the power of gold or the arts of counterfeiting have been left untried; but still the currency . . . has not failed." [236]

What could not be achieved by counterfeiting was finally achieved by speculation. Northeastern bankers, stockbrokers and businessmen bought up the scrip at a fraction of its value, after convincing the soldiers and suppliers who had been paid with it that it would be worthless after the war. The Continental also had to compete with other currencies, making it vulnerable to speculative attack. The British bankers' gold and silver coins were regarded as far more valuable than the paper promises of a revolutionary government that might not prevail. The Continental also had to compete with the paper notes of the States, which had the taxation power to back them.

The problem might have been avoided by making the Continental the sole official currency, but the Continental Congress did not yet have the power to enforce that sort of order. It had no courts, no police, and no authority to collect taxes to redeem the notes or contract the money supply. The colonies had just rebelled against taxation by the British and were not ready to commit to that burden from the new Congress.[237] Speculators took advantage of these weaknesses by buying up Continentals at a deeper and deeper discount until they became virtually worthless, giving rise to the expression "not worth a Continental."

The colonists won the war, but the paper currency that had funded it wound up completely discredited. The new government was faced with the challenge of finding some other means of paying the debts of the nation and jumpstarting the economy.

Chapter 11

HAMILTON AND THE FIRST U.S. BANK: FUNDING THE ECONOMY ON CREDIT

"He smote the rock of the national resources, and abundant streams of revenue gushed forth. He touched the dead corpse of Public Credit, and it sprung upon its feet."

– Daniel Webster's speech on Alexander Hamilton (1831)

The colonists won the Revolutionary War but lost the power to issue their own paper money, leaving the country heavily in debt. Alexander Hamilton, the first U.S. Treasury Secretary, turned the situation around by making the national debt itself the basis of the money supply. The securities representing debt became the capital of a national bank, which leveraged it into credit for the country. Although the First U.S. Bank remains controversial, it succeeded in getting the economy up and running.

By the end of the Revolutionary War, rampant counterfeiting and speculation had so thoroughly collapsed the value of the Continental that the new country's leaders had completely lost faith in what they called "unfunded paper." Hamilton summed up the majority view at the Constitutional Convention, when he said:

To emit an unfunded paper as the sign of value ought not to continue a formal part of the Constitution, nor ever hereafter to be employed; being, in its nature, repugnant with abuses and liable to be made the engine of imposition and fraud.[238]

The Founding Fathers were so disillusioned with paper money that they simply omitted it from the Constitution. Congress was given the power only to "coin money, regulate the value thereof," and "to borrow money on the credit of the United States . . . ."

An enormous loophole was thus left in the law. Creating and issuing money had long been considered the prerogative of governments, but the Constitution failed to define exactly what "money" was. Was "to coin money" an eighteenth-century way of saying "to create money"? Did this include creating paper money? If not, who *did* have the power to create paper money? Congress was authorized to "borrow" money, but did that include borrowing paper money or just gold?

Hamilton Turns the National Debt into Money

While the Founding Fathers were pledging their faith in gold and silver as the only "sound" money, those metals were quickly proving inadequate to fund the new country's expanding economy. The national war debt had reached $42 million, with insufficient silver and gold available to pay it off. Much of the paper money issued by the revolutionary government and the states had taken the form of promissory notes to be redeemed in coinage after the war.[239]

It was a debt that might have been avoided if the notes had been issued as legal tender in the first place—something on the tally stick model, redeemable in the payment of taxes. As Thomas Edison reasonably observed in an interview reported in *The New York Times* in 1921:

> If our nation can issue a dollar bond, it can issue a dollar bill. The element that makes the bond good, makes the bill good, also. The difference between the bond and the bill is that the bond lets money brokers collect twice the amount of the bond and an additional 20 percent, whereas the currency pays nobody but those who contribute directly in some useful way.

But the promissory notes of the revolutionary government had been issued as debt, and the debt had now come due. The creditors expected their gold, and the gold was not to be had.

Meanwhile, tightening the money supply by limiting it to precious metal had quickly precipitated another depression. Since the colonists' paper scrip was no longer available, debts had to be repaid in the "hard" coin of the British bankers, or in the paper banknotes that were ostensibly backed by it. Both were scarce, leaving an insufficient supply of money to conduct trade; and farmers were losing their farms to foreclosure. Visions of anarchy heightened the sense of urgency in creating both a strong central government and an expandable money supply.

Treasury Secretary Hamilton's innovative solution was to "monetize" the national debt. He said the government's bonds, or promises to pay, could be turned into a source of money for the country, trading as if they were money.[240] Hamilton wrote in his *First Report on Public Credit* in 1789:

> It is a well known fact, that in countries in which the national debt is properly funded, and an object of established confidence, *it answers most of the purposes of money*. Transfers of stock or public debt are there equivalent to payments in specie [precious metal currency] . . . . The benefits of this are various and obvious. . . . Trade is extended by it, because there is a larger capital to carry it on . . . .[241]

The money supply could be expanded in another way—by fractional reserve lending. Hamilton said in his *Report on a National Bank* in 1790:

> It is a well established fact, that Banks in good credit can circulate a far greater sum, than the actual quantum of their capital in Gold and Silver.
> . . . [I]t is one of the properties of Banks to increase the active capital of a country. . . .The money of one individual, while he is waiting for an opportunity to employ it . . . is in a condition to administer to the wants of others, without being put out of his own reach.

If you lend your money to a neighbor, you cannot use it until the neighbor gives it back. But if you put it in a bank, the bank can lend it and you can still have access to it when needed. The system works because the bank pools its deposits, and most people leave their money in the bank. The bank is not really lending "your" money but is just issuing bank credit and drawing on a fungible pool of money to cover withdrawals. The effective result is to double the money in the circulating money supply. Hamilton wrote:

> This . . . faculty of a bank to lend and circulate a greater sum than the amount of its stock in coin, are all to the purposes of trade and industry, an absolute increase of capital. Purchases and undertakings, in general, can be carried on by any given sum of bank paper or credit, as effectually as by an equal sum of gold and silver. And thus by contributing to enlarge the mass of industrious and commercial enterprise, *banks become nurseries of national wealth.*

An expanding trade needed an expanding money supply, and extending "bank credit" could achieve that result. Private banks did this routinely. But Hamilton stressed that *"such a bank is not a mere matter of private property, but a political machine of the greatest importance to the State."*[242] The nursery of national wealth he had in mind was a public one.

It would not do, however, to just pump credit into the economy. It had to be pulled back out in some way. The "true secret for rendering public credit immortal," said Hamilton, was that *"the creation of debt should always be accompanied with the means of extinguishment."*[243]

How to extinguish the debt? One obvious way would be through taxes. Another was the self-liquidating loan. Credit could be advanced and the loan paid off through fees and tolls charged to users of the goods produced (transportation, power, water, etc.). Loans can also pay for themselves by adding jobs, education, and services that improve overall economic performance, increasing the tax base and federal revenues. This proposition would be proved after World War II with the G.I. Bill, which paid for itself seven times over. (See Chapter 14.)

Opening the Door to Privatization

Hamilton's plan killed two birds with one stone: it increased the circulating money supply while disposing of the government's crippling debts. It did this by allowing the creditors to trade their government securities, or promissory notes, for interest-bearing stock in the new national bank. (Today this is called a debt for equity swap.) The problem with that arrangement was that it opened the door to private ownership and control of the bank.

The charter for the new bank fixed its total initial capitalization at $10 million. Eight million were to come from private stockholders and two million from the government. But the government did not actually have $2 million, so the bank (which was now a chartered lending institution) lent the government the money at interest. The bank, of course, did not have the money either. The whole thing was sleight of hand.[244]

The rest of the bank's shares were sold to the public, who bought some in hard cash and some in the securities that had been issued by the revolutionary government during the war. The federal government paid six percent interest annually on all the securities now held by the bank—those exchanged for the "loan" of the government's own money, plus the bonds accepted by the bank from the public.

The new banking scheme was hailed as a brilliant solution to the nation's economic straits. If the fledgling Congress had simply printed its own paper money, speculators would have challenged the currency's worth and driven down its value, just as they had during the Revolution. To maintain public confidence in the national currency and establish its stability, the new Republic needed the *illusion* that its dollars were backed by the bankers' gold; and Hamilton's bank successfully met that challenge. The federal central bank would handle the government's enormous war debt and create a standard form of currency. The scheme would dispose of an oppressive national debt, stabilize the economy, fund the government's budget, and create confidence in the new paper dollars. But it left the bank largely in private hands, and the government ended up in debt for money it could have generated itself—money it actually *should* have generated itself under a reasonable reading of the Constitution.

The bank's shareholders were supposed to pay one-fourth the cost of their shares in gold; but only the first installment was actually paid in hard money, totaling $675,000. The rest was paid in paper banknotes. Some came from the Bank of Boston and the Bank of New York; but most of this paper money was issued by the new U.S. Bank itself and lent back to its new shareholders, through the magic of fractional reserve lending.

Within five years, the government had borrowed $8.2 million from the bank. The additional money was obviously created out of thin air, just as it would have been if the government had printed the money itself; but the government now owed principal and interest back to the bank.

To reduce its debt to the bank, the government was eventually forced to sell its shares, largely to British financiers. Hamilton, to his credit, opposed these sales; but they went through, and the first Bank of the United States wound up largely under foreign ownership.[245]

A Revolution in Economic Growth: Funding Business and Development with National Credit

Although much of the stock of the bank was owned by foreigners, they did not control it, since they were prohibited from electing directors; and their participation served the useful purpose of contributing a substantial pool of capital, which the bank was able to leverage into the credit needed to get the economy up and running without specie (money in the form of metal coins rather than notes). Alexander Hamilton reiterated in his *Report on Public Credit of 1795* that "public credit" worked virtually as well for money as specie:

> Public Credit . . . is among the principal engines of useful enterprise and internal improvement. As a substitute for capital, it is little less useful than gold or silver . . . One man wishes to take up and cultivate a piece of land; he purchases upon credit, and, in time, pays the purchase money out of the produce of the soil improved by his labor. Another sets up in trade; in the credit founded upon a fair character, he seeks, and often finds, the means of becoming, at length, a wealthy merchant. A third commences business as manufacturer or

mechanic, with skill, but without money. It is by credit that he is enabled to procure the tools, the materials, and even the subsistence of which he stands in need, until his industry has supplied him with capital; and, even then, he derives, from an established and increased credit, the means of extending his undertakings.

In a July 2012 research paper on the First and Second U.S. Banks titled "Nicholas Biddle and the 2nd Bank of the United States," Michael Kirsch observes that the Bank's notes had a value set by the amount of specie in the Bank and could be redeemed for specie if desired, "payable on demand, in gold and silver coin." But the system was designed to prevent such redemption. A circulating currency was created that was proportional to the active capital of the country (manufactures, agriculture, etc.), without having to trade it in for the specie that would otherwise be needed to exchange goods and pay taxes. Kirsch notes:

> Had all taxes been demanded in gold and silver, it would have been highly oppressive in 1790, not only because there were no mines or mint in the United States, but because such a law would demand that much of the active capital of the nation be traded for the coin to make the payments, draining the capability to conduct foreign commerce, as well as creating a non-dependable source of revenue for the government.
>
> Likewise, in the settlements of new land, it required years before the land was developed and a surplus of production would be obtained for the market, and when it was finally generated, it was exchanged for the continued necessities of development. An even longer time would be necessary for a whole community to part with its resources for the purposes of a circulating medium of coin, and had settlers been forced to buy a metallic currency by selling their surplus, all progress would have ground to a halt.
>
> In general, between 1790 and 1811, the Bank of the United States and state banks would keep one-third of the whole currency in specie in their vaults to meet any settlements required, meaning a saving of two thirds of the capital required to create a currency.[246]

The ability to fund future productivity on credit is taken for granted today, but in the early 19th century, it was a revolutionary innovation. Kirsch quotes Michel Chevalier, a Frenchman who toured the United States in 1834. Contrasting the innovative U.S. system with that prevailing in Europe, Chevalier wrote:

> The great extension of credit, which resulted from the great number of banks, and from the absence of all restraint on their proceedings, has been beneficial to all classes, to the farmers and mechanics not less than to the merchants. The banks have served the Americans as a lever to transfer to their soil, to the general profit, the agriculture and manufactures of Europe, and to cover their country with roads, canals, factories, schools, churches, and, in a word, with every thing that goes to make up civilization. Without the banks, the cultivator could not have had the first advances, nor the implements necessary for the cultivation of his farm. . . . The credit system has . . . also enabled him, although indirectly, to buy at the rate of one, two, or three dollars an acre, and to cultivate lands, which are now, in his hands, worth tenfold or a hundred fold their first cost. The mechanics . . . owe to it that growth of manufacturing industry, which has raised their wages from one dollar to two dollars a day. . . . [I]t furnishes the means by which many of their number raise themselves to competence or wealth; for in this country every enterprising man, of a respectable character, is sure of obtaining credit, and thenceforth his fortune depends upon his own exertions.

In Europe, noblemen were generally unwilling to lend their capital for productive use, and tended to accumulate it as stores of metal currency; but in America, anyone who wanted to be industrious could get a loan. Kirsch writes:

> The ability to have an entire economy operating on the basis of accepting future payment for productive investment was, and still is, revolutionary. It allowed an increasingly large amount of surplus productivity to be immediately absorbed into further productive investment . . . . Thus, the domestic economy was able to grow in relation to its productive power, on credit, rather than by artificial controls.

This was quite different from the old European money system then prevailing in France. Quoting Michel Chevalier again:

> In France . . . It would be difficult to teach them to look upon a scrap of paper, although redeemable at sight with coin, as equivalent to the metals. A metallic currency, has, in our notions, a superiority to any other representative of value, which to an American . . . is quite incomprehensible; to our peasants, it is the object of a mysterious feeling, a real worship; and, in this respect we are all of us more or less peasants.
>
> The Americans, on the other hand, have a firm faith in paper; and it is not a blind faith. . . . [T]hey have had their continental money, and they need not go far back in their history to find a record of the failure of the banks in a body. Their confidence is founded in reason, their courage is a matter of reflexion. . . . [I]t will be a long time before we shall be in a condition, in France, to enjoy such a system of credit as exists in the United States or England; in this respect we are yet in a state of barbarism.[247]

A Victim of Politics

Despite these revolutionary contributions to an economy lacking in precious metals, both the First U.S. Bank and the Second U.S. Bank would remain controversial. When the twenty-year charter of the First U.S. Bank expired in 1811, it was not renewed. According to *The Economic History Association Encyclopedia*, this was largely due to politics:

> The opponents charged that because three-fourths of the ownership of the stock was held by foreigners, that the Bank was under their direct influence. The charge was false, as foreigners were prohibited from electing directors. The opposition also charged that the Bank was concealing profits, operating in a mysterious fashion, unconstitutional, and simply a tool for loaning money to the Government.
>
> . . . The reason the Bank lost its charter had precious little to do with banking. When the charter renewal debate transpired

in 1811 banking on the whole was flourishing. The Bank was born, lived, and eventually died a victim of politics. The Bank has been remembered not for what occurred during its operation—stimulating business, infusing safe paper money into the economy, supporting the credit of the country and national government, and with the Treasury department regulating the financial arena—but rather for what occurred during the stormy debates at its birth and death. The death of the Bank was another chapter in an ongoing debate between the early leaders of the country who were split between those who preferred a weak central government on the one hand and those who desired a strong central government on the other.[248]

Those who preferred a strong central government, a strong central bank and a single uniform national currency included Alexander Hamilton, Henry Clay and Abraham Lincoln. Those who preferred a weak central government, a circulating currency largely dependent on specie, and a banking system that was left to state-chartered banks issuing their own paper banknotes included Andrew Jackson and Martin Van Buren. President Jackson made it his mission to kill the national bank, and President Lincoln made it his mission to restore it.

Chapter 12

THE SECOND U.S. BANK, THE NATIONAL BANK ACT, AND THE STATE BANKING SYSTEM

"It is assumed that . . . nobody labors unless somebody else, owning capital [money to invest and lend], somehow by the use of it induces him to labor. . . . Labor is prior to and independent of capital. Capital is only the fruit of labor, and could never have existed if labor had not first existed. Labor is the superior of capital, and deserves much the higher consideration."

-- President Abraham Lincoln,
First Annual Address to Congress,
December 3, 1861

If eighteenth-century America was an experimental laboratory for government-issued paper currencies, nineteenth-century America was an experimental laboratory for competing systems of bank-created credit and private "hard money" interests. The Second U.S. Bank, while both extolled and condemned, coincided with a period of expansion and prosperity; and so did Lincoln's government-issued Greenbacks.

No sooner had the charter for the first U.S. Bank expired in 1811 than the government found itself in need of money to fund another war. In this case, it was the War of 1812 with Britain. Rumor had it that the war was instigated by British banking interests bent on recapturing their former colony by debt.[249] Whatever prompted it, the government was indeed thrust heavily into debt, compelling President James Madison to sign legislation in 1816 for the Second Bank of the United States.

The Second U.S. Bank was a public-private partnership controlled by a board of twenty directors, fifteen of whom were elected by the private stockholders and five appointed by the U.S. president.[250] Critics accused the Bank of corruption and of serving foreign interests, but the two decades of its charter were years of widespread prosperity and growth. In *Andrew Jackson and the Bank War* (1967), Robert Remini wrote, "the Bank became a valuable ally to business just as the country moved into a new period of expansion and economic thrust. Providing the necessary capital for this expansion, *the bank helped to advance a decade of hitherto unparalleled prosperity.*"

According to the website of the Philadelphia Federal Reserve, the Second U.S. Bank under Nicholas Biddle was instrumental in aiding the country's westward expansion and economic growth. Its branches took in revenues from the sale of federal land, and customs duties collected from foreign trade; provided credit to businesses and farmers; and helped move deposits to other parts of the nation. The Bank's notes, backed by substantial gold reserves, gave the country a more stable national currency. And by holding the notes of the state banks, the Second U.S. Bank increased the state banks' reserves and allowed them to issue more banknotes in the form of loans. In that respect it was similar to the current U.S. Federal Reserve; but the Second U.S. Bank also made commercial loans, competing with the state banks.[251]

Despite its record of achievements, this was the bank on which President Andrew Jackson famously declared war. "The Bank is trying to kill me," he said, "but I will kill it!" And he did. In 1834, Jackson removed all federal funds from the Bank and deposited them in state-chartered banks. He later pulled federal funds out of the banking system altogether and created a system of "sub-treasuries" that continued until 1913.[252]

Jackson's complaint against the Bank evidently began when he was nearly bankrupted in a land sale more than two decades earlier. His buyers had paid in paper notes and then went bankrupt themselves, rendering the notes worthless. Jackson never trusted paper notes again. He distrusted the bankers' whole system of paper credits, and he believed that people should not borrow money to pay their bills. He thought that only specie – silver or gold coins – qualified as an acceptable medium for transactions. He also felt that the Second U.S. Bank put too much power in the hands of a few private citizens, power that could be used to the detriment of the government and the people.[253]

As the Second U.S. Bank wound up its operations following Jackson's veto, the economy at first experienced a boom. The state-chartered banks in the West and South relaxed their lending standards and expanded credit on minimal reserves, increasing the money in circulation by 50 percent. But the result of this sudden influx of private banknotes was to create serious price inflation.

To curb the inflation, Jackson issued the Specie Circular of 1836, mandating that Western lands be purchased only with gold and silver coin. For this and other reasons, the economy then crashed; and Martin Van Buren, who followed Jackson as president in 1837, refused to intervene to address the crisis. He said that the people and their state governments were in debt because they had spent too much money, and that they must now live within their means. A long period of depression followed.[254]

State Banks and "Real Bills"

For nearly three decades after the charter of the Second U.S. Bank expired in 1836, the country was left without a federal banking system; but it was not without banks. State-chartered banks, including some owned outright by the states, also issued paper money.

In the industrial states of the North and East, what allowed these notes to retain their value was that they were backed by invoices called "real bills" representing a claim on real goods and services.[255] Real bills were short-term bills of exchange that traded among merchants as if they were money, passing from hand to hand until they came due. Like the bills of exchange of the medieval Italian merchants, they served as a secondary form of money that allowed the money supply to expand in a sound, honest way without depreciating in value.[256] Unlike the paper banknotes backed by only a fraction of their face value in gold, real bills could not be multiplied by "fractional reserve" lending. One invoice was redeemable for only one particular set of goods, which the last signatory on the note was entitled to claim. The paper bills expanded only as the goods backing them expanded.

The *real bills doctrine* was postulated by Adam Smith in *The Wealth of Nations* in 1776. It held that money would not lose its value if issued for assets of equal value, no matter how much money was issued. If the issuer took in $100 worth of silver and issued $100 worth of paper money in exchange, the money would obviously hold its value, since it could be cashed in for the silver. If the issuer took IOUs for $100 worth of corn in the future and issued $100 worth of paper money in exchange, the money would also hold its value, since the issuer could sell the corn in the market and get the money back. The issuer would simply have "monetized" the asset, or turned it into a form of money that was fungible and could be traded in the marketplace.

Real bills were an independent form of currency that were often traded in the market without a bank even being involved. The bank came into the picture only when the merchant wanted payment before the 90-day delivery period was up. The merchant would then take the bill to the bank and cash it for a sum that was discounted by some percentage, depending on how close the goods were to delivery.

The real bills doctrine was relied on to defend the U.S. Treasury Notes or "Greenbacks" issued by President Lincoln during the Civil War. The Greenbacks were government-issued paper money similar to the paper scrip issued by the American colonists and the tallies issued by medieval kings. By paying with Greenbacks, Lincoln's government was able to avoid a usurious war debt to British bankers. But critics charged that this government-issued paper currency would hyperinflate the money supply. Proponents countered that the notes would retain their value so long as the government issued them in exchange for labor that produced an equivalent value in goods and services. Like the medieval tallies, the Greenbacks were simply receipts for goods and services delivered, tradable by the bearer for their equivalent in goods and services. When the supply of goods and services increased, the number of money tokens needed to increase just to keep prices stable.[257]

Because their banknotes were secured with real bills, the state-chartered banks of the industrial states were relatively sound. But in the non-industrial states of the West and South, this form of business invoice was not available to back the notes of the state-chartered banks. They therefore relied instead on fractional reserve lending, counting on a low demand for redemption in specie to keep their doors open. Holders of this kind of paper currency could redeem it only at the bank's branch office. The difficulty lay in judging the ability of an issuing bank to promptly redeem its currency for gold or silver on demand. This made it difficult for paper currency to serve as a means of exchange between those regions.[258]

The "Free Banking" Era

In the "free banking" era that followed the expiration of the Second U.S. Bank's charter, the private issue of banknotes by individual banks created a competitive free-for-all in privately-issued currencies.[259] This was the era of the "wildcat banks," a term thought to have come from a failed bank in Michigan that issued banknotes with the image of a wildcat on them. Wildcat banks recklessly issued far more banknotes than they had gold to back them. The banks were often short-lived; and when they collapsed, fortunes collapsed with them.

Even the bank notes of the sounder banks were unstable, however, since they lost value the further the bearer traveled from the bank. As economist Gary Gorton explained in a 2010 interview:

> [A] bank note issued by a New Haven bank as a $10 note might only be worth $9.50 at a store in New York City, for example. Such discounts from par reflected the risk that the issuing bank might not have the $10—redeemable in gold or silver coins—by the time the holder took the note back to New Haven from New York. . . . [Y]ou can see the problem of trying to buy your lunch when the cook has to figure out the discount. It was simply hard to buy and sell things in such a world.[260]

A merchant engaged in interstate commerce would have to resort to a money broker to exchange his depreciated currency for funds in another currency. And since state banknotes were less trusted outside that state or region, the merchant would have to allow a discount. He would then pass this expense on to the farmers. As a result, the brokers were taxing trade at a cost that was 10 percent to 20 percent higher than it had been when done through the Bank of the United States.[261]

To insure depositors against loss, banks started backing their banknotes with state bonds; but the state bonds themselves were risky, since the states might not be able to pay. The country needed a more stable, dependable yardstick for measuring value and engaging in trade.

Lincoln Battles the London-allied Bankers

Abraham Lincoln's fight to restore the U.S. Bank and a single uniform national currency began in the Illinois state legislature in 1839, when he saw the pioneering construction of some 2,000 miles of railway lines collapse along with the credit system underwritten by the Second U.S. Bank. Progressively, industrial development was taking a back seat to the southern slave system. According to Anton Chaitkin in a 1986 article titled "Abraham Lincoln's 'Bank War'":

> Lincoln was forced to watch his country fall under the complete control of the free-trade faction. Instead of government-fostered industrial development edging out the slave plantation system, plantation cotton, supported by anti-industrial bankers in New York and London, spread westward and dominated national politics. The banking system itself was an unregulated, chaotic swindle. Each bank printed its own notes, redeeming what it would. There was no national currency. Bank-fed speculation exploded in 1857, collapsing much of the factory system.

Chaitkin wrote that it was Lincoln's election as president in 1860 that prompted the anti-nationalists to launch secession and civil war:

> It was a two-front war, militarily in the South . . . and politically against the London-allied Northern bankers, only recently the main brokers of slave cotton. . . .
>
> The Eastern banks had agreed to a $150 million government loan package just after the Civil War commenced in 1861. They

would resell U.S. bonds in England . . . putting the United States at the mercy of the British aristocracy.[262]

Lincoln's response was to issue $150 million in U.S. Notes or Greenbacks through the U.S. Treasury. The Legal Tender Act of 1862 mandated that this paper money be accepted in lieu of gold and silver coins.

Predictably, however, the bankers fought this invasion of their monopoly on the issue of paper money. According to Lynn Wheeler in *Triumphant Plutocracy: The Story of American Public Life from 1870 to 1920* (1922), bankers in New York sent the following circular to every bank in the United States:

> Dear Sir: It is advisable to do all in your power to sustain such prominent daily and weekly newspapers, especially the agricultural and religious press, as will oppose the issuing of greenback paper money, and that you also withhold patronage or favors from all applicants who are not willing to oppose the Government issue of money. *Let the Government issue the coin and the banks issue the paper money of the country,* for then we can better protect each other. . . . *[T]o restore to circulation the Government issue of money, will be to provide the people with money, and will therefore seriously affect your individual profit as bankers and lenders.* See your Congressman at once, and engage him to support our interests so we may control legislation.[263]

The campaign to limit the government to issuing coins was so effective that today, the *only* money the Treasury issues are coins. The vast majority of the circulating money supply is now created as credit or debt on bank balance sheets.

Stabilizing the System with a National Currency: Intended and Unintended Consequences

The monopoly of private chartered banks over the national paper currency was formalized in the National Bank Acts of 1863 and 1864. Originally known as the National Currency Act, the stated purpose of the National Bank Act was to stabilize the banking system. It aimed to eradicate the problem of notes issued by multiple banks circulating at the same time, by creating a single banker-issued national currency. To do this it established chartered national banks, which would issue notes backed by the U.S. Treasury, in a quantity proportional to the bank's level of capital deposited with the Comptroller of the Currency. In order to standardize the currency, non-federally issued paper was pushed out of circulation. The notes issued by state and local banks were heavily taxed, and the Greenbacks were quickly phased out after the Civil War as a temporary war measure.[264]

Gary Gorton states, "That was the first time in American history that money traded at par," meaning a dollar was actually worth a dollar.

The National Bank Act was responsible for some other notable firsts:

(1) It was the beginning of our debt-based national currency. Economist John Kenneth Galbraith wrote in 1975:

> In numerous years following the [civil] war, the Federal Government ran a heavy surplus. [But] it could not pay off its debt, retire its securities, because to do so meant there would be no bonds to back the national bank notes. *To pay off the debt was to destroy the money supply.*[265]

(2) The National Bank Act spawned the "dual banking system" —state and federal. State-chartered banks that were regulated by local governments and served local communities had to compete with federally-chartered banks dominated by Wall Street. This competition continues today, as tightened regulations squeeze the balance sheets of local state-chartered banks, forcing many community banks to sell out to large, out-of-state, federally-chartered conglomerates.

(3) The National Bank Act spawned the first U.S. "shadow" banking system, a system designed to get around the rules. In this case, the rule circumvented was the banknote tax, and the innovation devised to get around it was "checkable money."

The Birth of "Checkbook Money"

To coerce state banks to submit to federal supervision, the National Bank Act taxed the banknotes of state banks at a standard rate of 10 percent.[266] Many state banks succumbed to these pressure tactics and became federally-chartered national banks, but other local banks avoided the tax through a creative device known as the "demand deposit account" or "checking account." Credits and debits were created and traded in bank ledgers, without physical money trading hands except when depositors withdrew their funds in cash. Since this ledger-entry money did not take the form of physical banknotes, it was not taxable.

Checkbook money is now so widely accepted that it is included in "M1," the part of the money supply we usually think of as money— coins, paper bills, and assets that can quickly be converted to currency. But in the late 19th century, according to Gorton, academics were still writing articles in major economics journals with titles like "Are Checks Money?"[267]

The debate was not just an academic one. The checkbook business quickly grew to enormous size, allowing banks to issue bank credit for far more money than they kept as cash in their vaults. They did this simply by opening deposit accounts in the names of their borrowers. In effect, they were creating money out of thin air, just as banks had done when they printed their own paper banknotes.

The result was repeated liquidity crises whenever there was a greater demand for withdrawals in physical money than the bankers could satisfy at one time. Banks could usually meet the demand by borrowing from each other; but when other banks would not lend, or when they could not collectively satisfy their customers' demands, there would be runs on the banks and bank panics. Loans would be called, the money supply would shrink, and farmers and factory workers would suffer the consequences. The people demanded a more stable money supply, one issued and controlled by the people themselves.

Chapter 13

FROM THE POPULIST MOVEMENT TO THE FEDERAL RESERVE

"The Farmers should raise less corn and more hell."

--attributed to Mary Ellen Lease,
a Populist leader of the 1890s

The populists of the late 19th century fought for a return of government-issued money. In 1913, the Federal Reserve Act purported to give it to them, while giving them something else. Today, virtually the entire circulating money supply is created by financial institutions when they make loans.

During the Civil War, President Lincoln had the Treasury issue U.S. Notes or Greenbacks on the model of the colonists' paper scrip in order to avoid being trapped in debt to London bankers and their Wall Street counterparts, a feature of war that has historically allowed bankers to lock both sides in debt for years afterwards. The Greenbacks helped the North win the war, but they were phased out after Lincoln's assassination; and in 1873, silver was "demonetized," leaving gold alone to back the dollar. The contraction in the money supply created a depression nearly as severe as the Great Depression of the 1930s.

Populist money reformers called it "the Crime of '73."

The response of debt-stricken farmers and laid-off factory workers was a grassroots movement for monetary reform. Among their proposed reforms was that banking should be a public utility, operated by government employees as a public service. Monetary reform was a chief political issue for decades after the Civil War.

An early leader in this Populist movement was a Kansas housewife and mother of four named Mary Ellen Lease. In *The Fantasy Tradition in American Literature* (1980), Brian Attebery called her the prototype for Dorothy in *The Wizard of Oz*, a populist allegory written by Frank Baum in the 1890s. Mary Ellen took up the study of law after her husband lost his farm to the bank. She is said to have studied by pinning her papers to the clothesline in front of the washboard while doing her laundry. A fiery orator, she went around the country speaking on monetary reform. In a speech given around 1890 that could have been written today, she said:

> *Wall Street owns the country.* It is no longer a government of the people, by the people, and for the people, but a government of Wall Street, by Wall Street, and for Wall Street. The great common people of this country are slaves, and monopoly is the master. . . . Money rules . . . . Our laws are the output of a system which clothes rascals in robes and honesty in rags. The parties lie to us and the political speakers mislead us.
>
> We were told two years ago to go to work and raise a big crop, that was all we needed. We went to work and plowed and planted; the rains fell, the sun shone, nature smiled, and we raised the big crop that they told us to; and what came of it? Eight-cent corn, ten-cent oats, two-cent beef and no price at all for butter and eggs—that's what came of it. The politicians said we suffered from overproduction. Overproduction, when 10,000 little children, so statistics tell us, starve to death every year in the United States, and over 100,000 shopgirls in New York are forced to sell their virtue for the bread their niggardly wages deny them. . . .
>
> We want money, land and transportation. *We want the abolition of the National Banks, and we want the power to make loans direct from the government. We want the foreclosure system wiped*

out . . . . We will stand by our homes and stay by our fireside by force if necessary, and we will not pay our debts to the loan-shark companies until the government pays its debts to us. The people are at bay; let the bloodhounds of money who dogged us thus far beware.

In a July 2008 article in the *Wall Street Journal* titled "Why No Outrage?", James Grant quoted Mary Ellen Lease and asked why we were not seeing that sort of outrage now. (This was before the collapse of Lehman Brothers in September 2008 and the Occupy Wall Street movement in 2010.) Grant suggested that it may have been because the old 19th century Populists had won:

> This is their financial system. They had demanded paper money, federally insured bank deposits and a heavy governmental hand in the distribution of credit, and now they have them. The Populist Party might have lost the elections in the hard times of the 1890s. But it won the future. . . . They got their government-controlled money (the Federal Reserve opened for business in 1914), and their government-directed credit [Fannie Mae and Freddie Mac]. In 1971, they got their pure paper dollar. So today, the Fed can print all the dollars it deems expedient and the unwell federal mortgage giants, Fannie Mae and Freddie Mac, combine [to] dominate the business of mortgage origination . . . .

That was the popular perception: the Populists got what they wanted. But what the American people actually got was not at all what the Populists had fought for, or what their leader William Jennings Bryan thought he was approving when he voted for the Federal Reserve Act in 1913. In the stirring speech that won him the Democratic nomination for President in 1896, Bryan insisted:

> [We] believe that the right to coin money and issue money is a function of government. . . . Those who are opposed to this proposition tell us that the issue of paper money is a function of the bank and that the government ought to go out of the banking business. I stand with Jefferson . . . and tell them, as he did, that *the issue of money is a function of the government and that the banks should go out of the governing business.*

He concluded with this famous outcry against the restrictive gold standard:

> You shall not press down upon the brow of labor this crown of thorns, you shall not crucify mankind upon a cross of gold.

What Bryan and the Populists sought was a national currency issued by the government, on the model of Lincoln's Greenbacks. What the American people got was a money supply created by private banks as credit (or debt) at interest.

At the time, however, even Bryan was seduced into thinking the Populists had won.

The Deceptive Federal Reserve Act

After he lost the presidential elections of 1896 and 1900, Bryan went on to lead the Congressional opposition to the bill that would become the Federal Reserve Act. Originally called the Aldrich Plan, it was pushed through in 1913 by a group of Wall Street bankers led by J. P. Morgan and John D. Rockefeller. What prompted the bill was a major bank panic. Later, the panic was rumored to have been initiated by Morgan himself. Robert Owens, a co-author of the Federal Reserve Act, testified before Congress that the banking industry had conspired to create a series of financial panics in order to rouse the people to demand "reforms" that served the interests of the financiers.[268]

The Aldrich Plan would have delivered control of the banking system to Wall Street moneyed interests; but the alert opposition saw through it and soundly defeated it. Bryan said he would not support any bill that resulted in private money being issued by *private* banks. Federal Reserve Notes must be *Treasury* currency, issued and guaranteed by the government.

To get their bill past the opposition in Congress, the Wall Street faction then changed its name to the Federal Reserve Act and brought it three days before Christmas, when Congress was preoccupied with departure for the holidays. The bill was so obscurely worded that few really understood its provisions.

Its sponsors knew it would not pass without Bryan's support, so in a spirit of apparent compromise, they made a show of acquiescing to his demands. The ruse worked, and Bryan was won over. He declared happily, "The right of the government to issue money is *not* surrendered to the banks; the control over the money so issued is *not* relinquished by the government . . . ."

That is what he thought; but while the national money supply would be *printed* by the U.S. Bureau of Engraving and Printing, it would be *issued* by the "bankers' bank," the Federal Reserve. The Fed is composed of twelve branches, all of which are 100 percent owned by the banks in their districts. Until 1935, these branches could each independently issue paper dollars that cost only pennies to print. The dollars would then be *lent* to the government and the banks. Originally, the Fed lent to the government by a direct interest-bearing loan to the Treasury. But in 1935, legislation was passed requiring the sale of U.S. Treasuries to go through private middleman bond dealers, largely Wall Street banks. The Fed could no longer lend its newly-issued dollars to the government directly but had to buy government securities on the open market.

Marriner Eccles, governor of the Federal Reserve Board from 1934 to 1948, thought that this was an unnecessary cost and supported a bill in 1947 to eliminate the banker middlemen. He said, "Those who inserted this proviso were motivated by the mistaken theory that it would help to prevent deficit financing." He noted that the Federal Reserve had been purchasing securities directly from the government from its inception in 1914 until the Banking Act of 1935. Nothing constructive would be accomplished by requiring the bonds to be purchased in the open market. It just meant a commission had to be paid to the bond dealers.[269] But the bill Eccles supported did not pass, and today the government still sells its bonds through private bond dealers rather than funding its budget directly through its own central bank.

Wright Patman Strong-arms the Fed into Returning the Interest to the Government

For half a century, the Federal Reserve continued to pocket the interest on the currency it issued and lent to the government. Then in the 1960s, Wright Patman, Chairman of the House Banking and Currency Committee, pushed to have the Fed nationalized. To avoid that result, the Fed quietly agreed to rebate its profits to the U.S. Treasury. What went on behind the scenes was revealed by Congressman Jerry Voorhis in *The Strange Case of Richard Milhous Nixon*, published in 1973. He wrote:

> As a direct result of logical and relentless agitation by members of Congress, led by Congressman Wright Patman as well as by other competent monetary experts, the Federal Reserve began to pay to the U.S. Treasury a considerable part of its earnings from interest on government securities. This was done without public notice and few people, even today, know that it is being done. It was done, quite obviously, as acknowledgment that *the Federal Reserve Banks were acting on the one hand as a national bank of issue, creating the nation's money, but on the other hand charging the nation interest on its own credit*—which no true national bank of issue could conceivably, or with any show of justice, dare to do.

Rebating the central bank's profits to the Treasury was a step in the right direction, but the central bank did not actually fund much of the federal debt. Commercial banks held a large chunk of it; and as Voorhis observed, "[w]here the commercial banks are concerned, there is no such repayment of the people's money." Commercial banks did not rebate the interest they collected to the government, said Voorhis, although they also "'buy' the bonds with newly created demand deposit entries on their books—nothing more."

Today, the proportion of the federal debt held by the Federal Reserve has shot up due to repeated rounds of "quantitative easing." (More on this later.) But the majority of the debt is still funded privately at interest, and most of this money originates as "bank credit" entered on the books of private banks.

The Treasury's website reports the amount of interest paid on the national debt each year, going back 24 years.[270] In 2011, the total for the previous 24 years came to $8.2 trillion, on a federal debt of $15 trillion. If the government had been borrowing from its own central bank interest-free during that period, *the debt would have been reduced by more than half.*

The Federal Reserve Act Ends the "Fractional Reserve" System—Or Does It?

Among other functions for which the Federal Reserve was established was to serve as a clearing house between banks, to make sure that checks were honored and paid. In successive bank panics, banks had refused to honor each other's checks because they did not trust the other banks to have the gold necessary to redeem them. After 13 banking panics over a period of 80 years, with the worst in 1907, Congress finally decided to eliminate the sort of "wildcat banking" in which banks could issue paper money worth far more than the gold in their vaults.

According to economist J. W. Smith, it was a seismic change in banking. The system brought to an end the sort of fractional reserve lending in which banks could issue and lend ten times as many banknotes as they had gold without anyone being the wiser, as they had for centuries under the goldsmith theory of banking. Not only could member banks no longer print and lend their own banknotes, but they now had to clear their checks and balance their books. That meant showing as much money coming into the bank as going out.[271]

The new system did not prevent banks from creating money as bank credit and entering it in their borrowers' accounts; but in order for the borrowers' checks to clear, an equivalent sum in "base money" had to move from the issuing bank's reserve account into the receiving bank's reserve account at the Fed. "Base money," or the "monetary base," consists of Federal Reserve notes, coins, and Federal Reserve bank credit—money only the central bank or the Treasury can create.

For commercial banks, the effective result was that all money lent had to be borrowed—not before advancing it as credit on their books, but by the time the outgoing checks cleared. Preferably, the bank would borrow from the reserve pool created by its own depositors, at minimal cost to itself. But if its incoming deposits fell short of its outgoing checks, it would need to borrow the reserves of another bank or find some other cheap source of funds to clear its negative reserve balance.

The new system put the brakes on wildcat banking, and that was obviously a good thing; but it also had the negative effect of restricting the free flow of credit. Banks were transformed from credit machines into borrowing machines, vacuuming up cheap credit and lending it out at substantially higher rates. Quoting again from British money reformer Ann Pettifor:

> The banking system was invented in 14th century Florence, 16th Century London, and 17th century Amsterdam—to create and disburse credit. We learned nearly five hundred years ago that a sound banking system could do just that, stimulating trade and other forms of economic activity. The effortless and almost costless creation of credit by both central and commercial banks creates deposits and savings—and not the other way around.
>
> ... Today, ... thanks to the persistence of archaic, neo-liberal economic theories of finance, the banking system has frozen lending and been turned on its head. Instead of lending into the economy, bankers are borrowing from the real economy.[272]

Then How Does the Money Supply Expand?

If every outgoing check must be cleared by drawing from base money created by the Fed and held in the commercial bank's reserve account, how does the circulating money supply expand? Why do private banks still seem to be creating the vast majority of the money supply today?

In part, the answer has to do with how the money supply is officially tallied up. The figure called "M2" is an attempt to quantify the amount of money in the circulating money supply. It consists of currency in circulation (notes and coins) plus demand deposits, savings deposits, time deposits, and money market deposit accounts for individuals.[273] A deposit is created by double-entry bookkeeping whenever a loan is taken out. The borrower's promise to pay (his mortgage or other promissory note) is entered on the asset side of the balance sheet, and the sum advanced as a deposit is entered on the liability side. That means increasing deposits increases M2. *Thus the very act of borrowing from a bank increases the official money supply.*

The checks written on these new deposit accounts still need to be cleared in the bank's reserve account, but checks fly back and forth between banks all day, and most of them are netted out. Only the deficit in the reserve account at the end of the day has to be cleared by borrowing from somewhere else. That is typically done overnight and the money is paid back the next day.

Consider this example: Bank A issues a loan for $100, which becomes a deposit, which becomes a check, which is written to a customer at Bank B, who deposits it in Bank B. Bank B, meanwhile, issues a loan for $100 to another customer, which becomes a deposit, which becomes a check, which is written to a customer who deposits it in Bank A. The two checks net out, so there is no need for either bank to borrow reserves to cover the checks at the end of the day. But two new deposits of $100 each have been created, increasing the money supply by $200; and two depositors each have $100 more to spend into the economy.

If there are insufficient reserves within the banking system as a whole to match the checks flying daily between accounts, notes Smith, the Federal Reserve will simply create more. The Fed was set up to backstop the banks; and it will create all the base money needed to protect their virtual-monopoly system.[274]

1929: The Fed Triggers the Worst Bank Run in History

The new system was supposed to prevent bank runs, but it clearly failed in that endeavor. In 1929, the United States experienced the worst bank run in its history. What went wrong?

While individual banks could no longer issue their own banknotes or add credits without accounting for debits, the twelve individual Federal Reserve Banks were allowed to issue Federal Reserve Notes independently for their regions. From 1926 to 1929, the New York Fed poured newly-created money into New York banks, which then lent it to stock speculators. When the New York Fed heard that the Federal Reserve Board of Governors had held an all-night meeting discussing this risky situation, the flood of speculative funding was retracted, precipitating the stock market crash of 1929.

At that time, paper dollars were freely exchangeable for gold, but banks were required to keep sufficient gold to cover only 40 percent of their deposits. Panicked bank customers rushed to cash in their dollars for gold, and gold reserves shrank. Loans then had to be recalled to maintain the 40 percent requirement, collapsing the money supply. To stop the bleeding, in 1933 Roosevelt finally applied the controversial tourniquet of taking the dollar off the gold standard within the United States.[275]

The result of the collapse of the money supply was massive unemployment, loss of homes and savings, and widespread devastation. In a scathing indictment before Congress in 1934, Representative Louis McFadden blamed the Federal Reserve. He said:

> Mr. Chairman, we have in this Country one of the most corrupt institutions the world has ever known. I refer to the Federal Reserve Board and the Federal Reserve Banks, hereinafter called the Fed. . . . The depredations and iniquities of the Fed has cost enough money to pay the National debt several times over.
>
> This evil institution has impoverished and ruined the people of these United States, has bankrupted itself, and has practically bankrupted our Government. . . .
>
> Some people think that the Federal Reserve Banks are United States Government institutions. They are private monopolies which prey upon the people of these United States for the benefit of themselves and their foreign customers; foreign and domestic speculators and swindlers; and rich and predatory money lenders. . . .
>
> These twelve private credit monopolies were deceitfully and disloyally foisted upon this Country by the bankers who came here from Europe and repaid us our hospitality by undermining our American institutions.[276]

That was the conspiratorial view, but others saw the Crash and Depression simply as an experiment gone wrong. In 1935 and 1936, laws were enacted under President Franklin D. Roosevelt placing the entire money-creating power under the authority of the Board of Governors of the Federal Reserve. Except for coins, which are minted by the Treasury, all new money creation since then has been by the Federal Reserve Board. For several decades, some banks remained outside the Federal Reserve system; but in 1980, the Monetary Control Act brought all U.S. deposit institutions within its purview.[277]

What finally made banks safe for depositors, and checks safe as a medium of exchange, was not the Federal Reserve but the federal government itself, forced by popular demand. In 1933, the government set up an independent agency called the Federal Deposit Insurance Corporation (FDIC) to guarantee deposits. The funds for the agency were provided in the same way as those for a private insurance company, but on a larger scale. Premiums were paid by all participating institutions.[278] The losses of the riskier banks were thus borne by other banks, which had to pay hefty premiums to belong to the FDIC system; and the whole arrangement was underwritten by the taxpayers.[279] Again it was the public that was providing security to the banks rather than the banks providing security for the public. Then as now, the government was the ultimate guarantor.

Freed from the Bankers' "Cross of Gold"

Roosevelt's radical move to take the dollar off the gold standard was highly controversial. The gold standard had prevailed since the founding of the country. Critics viewed the move as a crime; but proponents saw it as finally allowing the country to be economically sovereign.

The latter, more benign view was taken by Beardsley Ruml, Chairman of the Federal Reserve Bank of New York, in a presentation before the American Bar Association in 1945. He said the government was now at liberty to spend as needed to meet its budget, drawing on credit issued by its own central bank. It could do this until price inflation indicated a weakened purchasing power of the currency. Then, and only then, would the government need to levy taxes—not to fund the budget but to counteract inflation by contracting the money supply. The principal purpose of taxes, said Ruml, was "the maintenance of a dollar which has stable purchasing power over the years. Sometimes this purpose is stated as 'the avoidance of inflation.'"[280]

It was a remarkable realization. The government could be funded without taxes, by drawing on credit from its own central bank. Since there was no longer a need for gold to cover the loan, the central bank would not have to borrow. It could just create the money on its books. Only when prices rose across the board, signaling an excess of money in the money supply, would the government need to tax—not to fund the government, but simply to keep supply (goods and services) in balance with demand (money).

As British economist John Maynard Keynes pointed out, adding money to the money supply would not in itself create price inflation. So long as workers were idle and materials were available, an increase in demand would put workers to work creating more supply. The shoe salesman with more customers demanding shoes would put in more orders for shoes, and the shoe factory would hire more laborers to fill the orders. Supply would rise along with demand, keeping prices stable. Only when the economy hit full productive capacity would taxes need to be levied, not to fund the federal budget but to prevent price inflation.

Ruml's vision is echoed today in the school of economic thought called Modern Monetary Theory (MMT). (See Chapter 30.) But after Roosevelt's demise, it was not pursued. The U.S. government continued to fund itself with taxes; and when it failed to recover enough to pay its bills, it continued to borrow, putting itself in debt. The crises of depression and war did clear the way for a number of other creative experiments in government financing, however, both in the United States and abroad.

Section III.

PUBLIC BANKING MODELS SPAWNED BY DEPRESSION AND WAR

Chapter 14

THE RECONSTRUCTION FINANCE CORPORATION:
THE LITTLE-KNOWN PUBLIC FINANCIAL INSTITUTION THAT REVERSED THE DEPRESSION AND FUNDED WORLD WAR II

"[I]t became apparent almost immediately, to many Congressmen and Senators, that here was a device which would enable them to provide for activities that they favored for which government funds would be required, but without any apparent increase in appropriations. . . . [T]here need be no more appropriations and its activities could be enlarged indefinitely, as they were, almost to fantastic proportions."

-- Chester Morrill, former Secretary of the Board of Governors of the Federal Reserve, on the RFC[281]

In the 1930s and 1940s, the Reconstruction Finance Corporation was America's largest corporation and the world's largest banking organization. It was a remarkable credit machine that allowed the government to fund the New Deal and World War II without turning to Congress or the taxpayers for appropriations. It generated massive infrastructure and development all across the country, while returning a profit to the government. Yet this stellar model for what might be done is rarely mentioned in the media today.

Congress did not take the advice of Eccles or Ruml to borrow directly from its own central bank, but President Roosevelt had a funding mechanism that worked nearly as well. The Reconstruction Finance Corporation (RFC) was not a commercial bank and did not issue loans against deposits. It operated more like the BNDES (the Brazilian development bank discussed in Chapter 4), funding its loans with bonds. The bonds soaked up money sitting idle in the economy and put it to work building infrastructure and creating jobs, *and it did this without tapping into the federal budget or raising taxes*. The bonds were paid off with the proceeds from the projects funded by the loans (called "self-funding" loans). The RFC funded the rebuilding of the country while at the same time turning a profit for the government.

The RFC was first instituted in 1932 by President Herbert Hoover; but he used it only to make loans to banks, railroads and insurance companies. He was wary of government intervention in the marketplace. He saw the primary purpose of the RFC as bailing out the banks so they could start making loans again. The theory was that this would allow the private sector to initiate its own recovery.

That was the theory, but it wasn't working. As the financial crisis deepened, the RFC's powers were extended. The Emergency Relief and Reconstruction Act of 1932 authorized the RFC to make loans directly to farmers, states, and public works projects. But to avoid competing with private lenders, the loans were issued at high interest rates, and the collateral requirements were high.[282]

Franklin D. Roosevelt was inaugurated as president in 1933. He had none of Hoover's reservations about mixing government with business. Roosevelt continually enlarged and modified the RFC's mission to meet the crisis of the times. The semi-independent status of the RFC let him work around Congress and work quickly, allowing New Deal agencies to be financed as the need arose. The Federal Emergency Relief Administration was modeled on the RFC's state grant program, and the Public Works Administration was spun off its public works division.

The RFC Act of 1932 provided the RFC with capital stock of $500 million, "subscribed by the United States of America." With its government-owned stock, it had the authority to extend credit up to $1.5 billion. This was subsequently increased to $3 billion, a substantial sum at the time, since in 1932 the entire budget of the U.S. government was only $4.66 billion. Beyond the initial $500 million, the RFC raised capital by issuing its own debentures, a form of bond.[283]

Former Federal Reserve Board secretary Chester Morrill said that when Congress realized the potential of the RFC to fund the government's programs without increasing appropriations, those projects were enlarged "almost to fantastic proportions." How fantastic was indicated in a Treasury report titled *Final Report of the Reconstruction Finance Corporation* (Government Printing Office, 1959), stating that from 1932 to 1957 (the years of its operation), the RFC loaned or invested more than $40 billion. By some estimates, the sum was about $50 billion. A small part of this came from its initial capitalization. The rest was borrowed from the Treasury and the public. The RFC ended up borrowing a total of $51.3 billion from the Treasury and $3.1 billion from the public. These loans did not cost the government but actually produced a profit, earning a total net income of $690,017,232 on the RFC's "normal" lending functions (omitting such things as extraordinary grants for wartime). The RFC generated the funds for roads, bridges, dams, post offices, universities, electrical power, mortgages, farms, and much more; and it funded all this while actually making money for the government.[284]

The Remarkable Story of the RFC as Told by Its Chairman

Roosevelt gave the RFC the green light, but its stellar achievements were due chiefly to the vision and dedication of its chairman, Jesse Jones. Jones detailed the RFC's trials and triumphs in a book that is now out of print, titled *Fifty Billion Dollars: My Thirteen Years with the RFC, 1932-1945* (Macmillan, 1951). He wrote:

> In January, 1932, the Reconstruction Finance Corporation was created to combat the ravishing elements of deflation and despair in our own country. Farm products had fallen to a starvation level, and the stocks of many banks, railroads, and industrial corporations had dropped to less than 10 percent of their previous market value; some as low as 1 percent. Eight years later, with the coming of the war, the immense

resources and well trained capacities of the RFC were turned to strengthening America's arsenal and military might.

In these two roles, as a corporate combatant, the RFC loaned and spent, invested, and gave away a total of more than thirty-five billion dollars ($35,000,000,000) and authorized many billions more that were not finally used. *It grew to be America's largest corporation and the world's biggest and most varied banking organization. . . .*

In the struggle against the depression the Corporation used approximately ten and one-half billion dollars ($10,500,000,000) *without loss to the taxpayers.* To the contrary, that money was all returned to the Federal Treasury with approximately $500,000,000 profits, after paying the Corporation's operating expenses and a fair rate of interest on the money which it borrowed to finance this phase of its operations.

The RFC was America's largest corporation and the world's biggest banking organization – yet it is virtually unknown today. Why? Perhaps it is kept out of the limelight by the media (which have interlocking directorships with large banks) because it showed what could be done with a public lending institution. It broke the private banking monopoly. Private bankers did not own it, had no control over it, and could not extract profits from it. In a mere seven year period, when the economy was at its lowest ebb ever, the government funded the remarkable achievements of the New Deal and World War II by circumventing the banks and using its own public financial institution. The RFC set a formidable precedent, one that private banking interests had good reason to suppress when they later recaptured the lending market and the media.

Unlike the loans of the Federal Reserve to the banks, the loans of the RFC were made directly to farmers, homeowners and small businessmen. About $1.5 billion dollars were lent to farmers, and most of these loans were repaid with no loss to the taxpayers. The RFC advanced $500 million to the RFC Mortgage Company and the Federal National Mortgage Association in order to thaw the frozen market for real estate mortgages. With the return of better times, these loans too were repaid. Jones wrote:

Government credit, much of it supplied through the RFC, saved from foreclosure a million urban homes and half a million farms. It built several hundred thousand new homes and repaired and modernized a million and a half other dwellings throughout the land.[285]

The RFC established a special bank to promote exports, a corporation to aid victims of natural disasters, and a rural electrification agency. It extended credit not only to individuals but to cities and states. It also extended more than nine thousand loans to the small businesses that were the backbone of the economy. The loans ranged from $500 and $10,000 and collectively totaled about $500 billion dollars.

Self-Liquidating Loans

A unique funding feature of the RFC was that its portfolio consisted of loans that were largely "self-liquidating." They paid for themselves by securing the future income streams of the assets created by the loans.[286] For bridge and tunnel projects, tolls were sufficient to repay the loans. For aqueducts or power plants, a small fee would be added per gallon of water or kilowatt of power to repay the cost of construction. Originally authorized by Congress to provide employment, these loans not only succeeded in funding much-needed infrastructure without taxing the people, but they significantly lowered the costs of transportation, energy, and water for businesses and consumers.

The long list of projects involving self-liquidating loans included the San Francisco Bay Bridge, the California Aqueduct, three bridges over the Mississippi river, the Pennsylvania turnpike, and other large and small local projects too numerous to name. Jones wrote:

> For each grandiose enterprise which required millions, often many millions, to build, there were scores of small-town improvements arranged on a pay-for-itself basis that called for only a few thousand dollars; just enough, in some cases, to provide a village with a pump, a water tank and some pipe, or to replace its outdoor privies with indoor sanitation.
>
> In size, the loans ranged from the $208,500,000 required to funnel the Colorado's water to Los Angeles down to the $500

that was sufficient to put up a canning "factory" in a little
school district near Yoakum, Texas. With few exceptions the
small enterprises, like the large, have paid for their way in
the manner anticipated when the loans were made.

. . . Our self-liquidating loans not only provided hundreds
of thousands of jobs but acted as a nation-wide stimulant to
business, since each contractor had to buy materials from
many sources as well as hire labor on the task itself.

. . . We approved more than $145,000,000 in loans to
drainage, levee, and irrigation districts. We undertook
to reduce and refinance the outstanding indebtedness of
hundreds of drainage, levee, and irrigation districts which had
over-optimistically sprouted in many of the agricultural states
during the boom seasons of the 1920's.

. . . Our country is dotted today with thousands of
public works – bridges, aqueducts, tunnels, dormitories, toll
highways, recreation centers, water and sewer systems, and
sundry other improvements – which were financed by the
RFC during the depths of the depression as self liquidating
work projects. These constructions provided tens of thousands
of jobs on the projects themselves, while indirectly creating
employment in the supplying and transportation companies
which manufactured the required materials or moved them to
sites chosen for their utilization.

The majority of these loans turned a profit. Jones wrote:

The New Orleans bridge was but one of many projects whose
bonds we were able to sell to the public at a profit through
investment houses, and with no recourse whatsoever on the
[RFC]. On the bonds of the San Francisco to Oakland Bay
Bridge, for which we loaned $73,000,000, we made several
millions. . . .

The San Francisco to Oakland Bay Bridge . . . was . . .
enthusiastically supported as a project by the forward-looking
businessmen of the San Francisco Bay area. . . .

The engineers estimated that it would require a toll of
65 cents for automobiles to meet the interest and principal
payments on the loan. . . . It began earning so well that we

soon allowed a toll reduction; first I think to 50 cents, then to 35. Today the toll is 25 cents, the bridge is making money, and the traffic is so thick that plans for a second bridge across the Bay are being evolved and its location debated.

But that was then. Contrast the highly favorable interest rates available to the RFC—the government's own finance institution—with those burdening local governments today. The price tag for the new East span of the San Francisco-Oakland Bay Bridge jumped from an estimated $1.3 billion in 1996, to $6.3 billion in 2009, to an estimated final price of over $12 billion, due largely to interest on bond debt and other Wall Street finance charges. Commuters will be paying this debt off until at least 2049.[287] Tolls have also shot up, to $6 during rush hours for regular vehicles and $35 for some trucks.[288] *Debt servicing now eats up 55.2 percent of toll revenue.*[289]

New Deal Triumphs and Tribulations

The four years after 1933 proved to be the biggest cyclical boom in U.S. economic history. Real GDP grew at a 12 percent rate and nominal GDP grew at a 14 percent rate.[290]

But in 1935, a retreat in New Deal programs was forced by the Supreme Court, then as now the defender of corporate profits over the interests of the struggling masses. The conservative majority on the Supreme Court invalidated several major reform initiatives, arguing that they represented an unconstitutional extension of federal authority.

To protect his programs from further meddling, in 1937 President Roosevelt announced a plan to add enough liberal justices to the Court to neutralize the "obstructionist" conservatives. The move was legal, since there was no constitutional limit on the number of justices on the Court; but it looked bad, and it did substantial public relations damage to the Administration.

When the economy seemed to be recovering, the president was leaned on to reduce public investment. The economy then slipped back into a recession. Despite this seeming vindication of New Deal policies, however, Roosevelt found it difficult to enact any new programs.[291] As Nobel Prize winner Frederick Soddy cynically observed in 1926:

The old extreme *laissez-faire* policy of individualistic economics jealously denied to the State the right of competing in any way with individuals in the ownership of productive enterprise, out of which monetary interest or profit can be made.[292]

Economic Stimulus from War—or from Deficit Spending?

Congress was spurred to open the money spigots once again only by the emergency of another World War. Money advanced for war is a less efficient use of funds than money advanced for infrastructure, since the expenditures produce few societal goods; but the war machine at least keeps the money pump going. Economist John Maynard Keynes observed:

> Pyramid-building, earthquakes, even wars may serve to increase wealth, if the education of our statesmen on the principles of the classical economics stands in the way of anything better.[293]

War was the economic stimulus of last resort when politicians were so entrenched in the outmoded principles of classical economics that they would not allow the government to go into debt except for national emergencies; and in those cases, the war stimulus worked quite well to push the economy into overdrive. Jones wrote:

> In the June week of 1940, when France fell and the world of free men stood dazed and full of dread, Congress, with a grant of perhaps the broadest powers ever conferred upon a single government agency, authorized the RFC to help the United States gird itself for whatever military perils might befall. *Under this almost limitless power the RFC could do practically anything the defense and war-making authorities thought best for the nation's safety and the prosecution of the war.* The Corporation set up subsidiaries to devote themselves exclusively, first, to strengthening the country's ramparts and, after Pearl Harbor, to the waging of total war. The law provided that these wide powers should be exercised in each instance only upon my

request, as Federal Loan Administrator, with the approval of the President. . . .

On the day the United States was bombed into the Second World War, the RFC and its subsidiaries were already conducting the most gigantic single business enterprise, or series of enterprises, the world has ever known. We were engaged in literally hundreds of separate businesses which, individually and collectively, affected the entire economy of our nation and stimulated the economy of many foreign countries in which we were making purchases of materials or helping to establish plants or mines.

Wartime loans and investments by the Corporation helped bring a 10 per cent increase in the country's steel-making capacity. They helped to build airplanes by the tens of thousands and to fuel them with billions of dollars' worth of gasoline. They constructed and operated pipe lines for gasoline and petroleum transportation. They brought about enormous expansion in the production of magnesium and aluminum, and set up competition in both of those formerly monopolistic industries.

While the Corporation's spectacular plant investments and material purchases, running into the billions, attracted public notice, its directors during the war quietly made nearly thirteen thousand loans to small businesses and industries, mostly to enable them to engage in war work as subcontractors, or feeders, to the big war plants. These small business loans in wartime aggregated almost $2,000,000,000, with local banks participating in many of the transactions, encouraged by a take-out agreement by the RFC.

What made all this possible was again the full cooperation of the government. Jones wrote:

Throughout that entire period we received in a manner probably unique in the history of federal agencies the complete cooperation and confidence of each successive Congress. Not a single request that I made of Congress during those thirteen years was refused. On the other hand, Congress increased and broadened our powers from year to year.

The RFC was a powerful tool, but its proper use clearly depended on the honesty and good judgment of the man in charge. The fact that Congress supported Jones without question was a testament to his own honesty and good judgment. Economist Hyman Minsky said of Jones, "He spent the public's money as though it were his own."[294] Jones himself wrote:

> Running day and night under forced draft and dealing in hundreds of thousands, millions, and billions, the Corporation's bookkeeping was simple but accurate. There were no irregularities. Although at the peak the Corporation's personnel exceeded twelve thousand men and women, there was not a single instance of fraud in the entire organization from its inception in 1932 until I left in 1945.

How different from our own era, with its Wall Street scandals and massive unaccounted-for military expenditures! War now justifies unlimited spending, for purposes to which we are not privy, serviced by private contractors notorious for exploiting the public purse, concealing their dark dealings in the hallowed name of "national security."

There are obviously more constructive ways to stimulate an economy than by war. Keynes said workers could be paid to dig ditches and fill them back up and it would stimulate the economy. What was needed was simply *demand* (available purchasing power). Demand would then stimulate businesses to produce more supply, creating jobs and driving productivity. The key was that demand had to come *first*.

Paying to dig ditches and fill them back up could get money in workers' pockets, but a more cost-effective solution would be for the government to pay for work that actually improved the standard of living of the people. The roads, bridges, dams, universities and libraries built with RFC funding attest to the success of the New Deal in achieving that goal; and it was done without taking money from the federal budget. Credit was just advanced through a publicly-owned institution for productive projects that ultimately paid for themselves, extinguishing the debt.

Phased Out Too Soon?

In 1952, Dwight D. Eisenhower was elected president. As memories faded of the Great Depression, the New Deal, and even World War II, the idea of keeping government and business separate regained popularity. In 1953, the RFC was abolished by act of Congress as an independent agency, and in 1957 it was totally disbanded. The very success of the RFC—America's largest corporation and the world's largest banking organization—may have been its nemesis. Without the emergencies of depression and war, it was a too-powerful competitor of private business.

Although the RFC seemed to have outlived its usefulness, there was still much to be done to improve the standard of living of the people. Roosevelt underscored this need in his last inaugural address in 1944, when he called for a Second Bill of Rights. He said:

> This Republic had its beginning, and grew to its present strength, under the protection of certain inalienable political rights . . . . They were our rights to life and liberty.
>
> As our nation has grown in size and stature, however—as our industrial economy expanded—these political rights proved inadequate to assure us equality in the pursuit of happiness.

The economic rights that he thought should be added included:

> The right to a job;
>
> The right to earn enough to pay for food and clothing;
>
> The right of businessmen to be free of unfair competition and domination by monopolies;
>
> The right to a decent home;
>
> The right to adequate medical care and the opportunity to enjoy good health;
>
> The right to adequate protection from the economic fears of old age, sickness, accident, and unemployment;
>
> The right to a good education.[295]

Roosevelt's Economic Bill of Rights was never implemented, but the G.I. Bill demonstrated the possibilities. It provided free technical training and educational support for nearly 16 million returning servicemen, along with government-subsidized loans and unemployment benefits. It made higher education accessible to all and created a nation of homeowners, new technology, new products, and new companies, with the Veterans Administration guaranteeing an estimated 53,000 business loans. Like the RFC, the G.I. Bill not only paid for itself but returned a substantial profit. Economists have determined that for every 1944 dollar invested, *the country received approximately $7 in return,* through increased economic productivity, consumer spending, and tax revenues.[296]

The G.I. Bill showed that improving the lot of the people can be a very good investment. But demonstrating the full potential of funding the government with public credit would be left to other countries, including Australia, New Zealand, Canada, Germany and Japan.

Chapter 15

THE COMMONWEALTH BANK OF AUSTRALIA: TURNING THE CREDIT OF THE NATION INTO MONEY

"The whole of the resources of Australia are at the back of this bank, and so strong as this continent is, so strong is the Commonwealth Bank. Whatever the Australian people can intelligently conceive in their minds and will loyally support, that can be done."

-- *Denison Miller, first governor of the Commonwealth Bank of Australia, quoted in the Australian Press in 1921*

> While the United States was setting up a banker-controlled central bank on the model of the Bank of England, Australia was taking the bold step of establishing a government-controlled central bank that issued the credit of Australia for the benefit of Australians. The model worked remarkably well – again, perhaps too well . . . .

As in the United States, the collapse of the banking system in the 1890s triggered a devastating depression in Australia; and there was no deposit insurance, no social security, no unemployment insurance to soften the blow. People who thought they were well off suddenly found they had nothing. They could not withdraw their funds, write checks on their accounts, or sell their products or their homes, because no money was available to buy them. Desperate Australians were leaping from bridges or throwing themselves in front of trains.

The private banking system had failed, and something had to be done. The Labor Party decided the country needed a publicly-owned national bank backed by the assets of the government, one that could maintain the banking system in times of financial stress and guarantee that money could be found for home building and other needs.[297]

In 1911, the Labor government passed a bill establishing the Commonwealth Bank of Australia on a radical new model: *the bank would simply lend the nation's credit, unbacked by either silver or gold*. It was a bold move at a time when the world was still on the gold standard. The Commonwealth Bank operated successfully in competition with private banks for most of the 20th century, conducting both savings business and general bank business.

In a 2001 article titled "How Money Is Created in Australia," David Kidd described the Bank's early accomplishments:

> At a time when private banks were demanding 6 percent interest for loans, the Commonwealth Bank financed Australia's first world war effort from 1914 to 1919 with a loan of $700,000,000 at an interest rate of a fraction of 1 percent, thus saving Australians some $12 million in bank charges. In 1916 it made funds available in London to purchase 15 cargo steamers to support Australia's growing export trade. Until 1924 the benefits conferred upon the people of Australia by their Bank flowed steadily on. It financed jam and fruit pools to the extent of $3 million, it found $8 million for Australian homes, while to local government bodies, for construction of roads, tramways, harbours, gasworks, electric power plants, etc., it lent $18.72 million. It paid $6.194 million to the Commonwealth Government between December, 1920 and June, 1923—the profits of its Note Issue Department—while by 1924 it had made on its other business a profit of $9 million, available for redemption of debt. The bank's independently-minded Governor, Sir Denison Miller, used the bank's credit power after

the First World War to save Australians from the depression conditions being imposed in other countries. . . . By 1931 amalgamations with other banks made the Commonwealth Bank the largest savings institution in Australia, capturing 60 percent of the nation's savings.[298]

Harnessing the Power to Create Money for the Public Interest

The inside story of the Commonwealth Bank was told by an Australian politician named Jack Lang in a revealing book called *The Great Bust: The Depression of the Thirties* (McNamara's Books, Katoomba, 1962). Lang was Australia's Treasurer in the Labor government of 1920-21 and Premier of New South Wales during the Great Depression of the 1930s. A controversial figure, he was relieved of his official duties after he repudiated loans owed by the Australian government to London bankers—a precedent followed more recently by such countries as Iceland, Argentina and Ecuador. *The Great Bust* is now out of print and is quoted here at length by permission of the publisher. (Thanks to Peter Myers for making portions of it available on the Internet.)

Lang attributed the remarkable success of the Commonwealth Bank to two men: Denison Miller, its first governor; and King O'Malley, its first and most ardent proponent. Both had been bankers themselves and knew the great secret of banking: that banks create the money they lend simply by writing accounting entries into the deposit accounts of borrowers. What was extraordinary was that they turned this insight to the advantage of the public. Lang wrote of O'Malley:

> Chief advocate of the cause of a Commonwealth Bank was King O'Malley, a colorful Canadian-American . . . . Before coming to Australia, he had worked in a small New York bank, owned by an uncle. . . . He had been much impressed by the way that his uncle had created credit. *A bank could create the credit, and at the same time manufacture the debit to balance it. That was the big discovery of O'Malley's banking career.* A born showman, he itched to try it out on a grand scale. He started his political career in South Australia by advocating a State Commercial

Bank. In 1901 he went into the first Federal Parliament as a one-man pressure group to establish a Commonwealth Bank, and joined the Labor Party for that purpose.

O'Malley's big discovery—that a bank could create positive money on one side of its ledger simply by balancing it with a negative sum on the other—was later confirmed by a number of Australian and British insiders. Ralph Hawtrey, Assistant Under Secretary to the British Treasury in the 1930s, wrote in *Trade Depression and the Way Out*, "When a bank lends, it creates money out of nothing."[299] He called it "the mystical power of creating the means of payment out of nothing." In *The Art of Central Banking*, Hawtrey wrote:

> When a bank lends, it creates credit. Against the advance which it enters amongst its assets, there is a deposit entered in its liabilities. But other lenders have not the mystical power of creating the means of payment out of nothing. What they lend must be money that they have acquired through their economic activities.[300]

Dr. H. C. Coombs, the first Governor of the Reserve Bank of Australia, confirmed this bit of magic in an address at Queensland University in 1954. He said:

> [W]hen money is lent by a bank it passes into the hands of the person who borrows it without anybody having less. Whenever a bank lends money there is therefore, an increase in the total amount of money available.[301]

The Right Honorable Reginald McKenna, former British Chancellor of the Exchequer, also confirmed it, telling shareholders of the Midland Bank in 1924:

> I am afraid the ordinary citizen will not like to be told that the banks can, and do, create and destroy money. The amount of money in existence varies only with the action of the banks in increasing or decreasing deposits and bank purchases. We know how this is effected. *Every loan, overdraft or bank purchase creates a deposit, and every repayment of a loan, overdraft or bank sale destroys a deposit.*[302]

It was this "mystical power of creating the means of payment out of nothing" that the Commonwealth Bank's far-sighted founders harnessed in the service of the Australian people.

Led by the Vision of a Renegade Banker

Denison Miller, the Bank's first governor, built on the groundwork laid by O'Malley in the legislature. Ironically, it was the other bankers who had gotten Miller appointed, fearing competition from a publicly-owned bank. They thought that by getting one of their own men in as governor, they could keep the bank in line. But they had not reckoned on their independent appointee, who knew how banking worked and saw the opportunity a government-backed bank presented to the struggling Australian economy. Miller set out to make the new national bank the finest institution the country had ever known.

His first bold stroke was to start the bank virtually without capital. He was wary of going to the politicians for money, locking the government in debt; and he was convinced that the bank could get by without capital. (This was before capital requirements were imposed by the Bank for International Settlements, the central banker's central bank in Switzerland, of which more shortly.) Lang wrote:

> Miller was the [bank's] only employee. He found a small office . . . and asked the Treasury for an advance of £10,000. That was probably the first and last time that the Commonwealth lent the Bank any money. From then on, it was all in the reverse direction.
>
> . . . By January, 1913 he had completed arrangements to open a bank in each State of the Commonwealth, and also an agency in London. . . . [O]n January 20th, 1913 he made a speech declaring the new Commonwealth Bank open for business. He said:
>
> "This bank is being started without capital, as none is required at the present time, but it is backed by the entire wealth and credit of the whole of Australia."
>
> In those few simple words was the charter of the Bank, and the creed of Denison Miller, which he never tired of reciting. He promised to provide facilities to expand the natural resources

of the country, and it would at all times be a people's bank. "There is little doubt that in time it will be classed as one of the great banks of the world," he added prophetically.

. . . Slowly it began to dawn on the private banks that they may have harbored a viper. They had been so intent on the risks of having to contend with bank socialisation that they didn't realize they had much more to fear from competition by an orthodox banker, with the resources of the country behind him.

Miller proceeded to advance massive sums, simply "on the credit of the nation." Lang wrote:

One of the first demonstrations of his vigor came when the Melbourne Board of Works went on the market for money to redeem old loans, and also to raise new money. Up to that time, apart from Treasury Bills and advances by their own Savings Banks, Governments had depended on overseas loans from London. . . .

They then decided to approach Denison Miller, who had promised to provide special terms for such bodies. He immediately offered to lend them £3 millions at . . . 4 per cent. They immediately clinched the deal. Asked where his very juvenile bank had raised all that money, Miller replied, "On the credit of the nation. It is unlimited."

An even greater test of Miller's leadership came in 1914, with the First World War:

The first reaction was the risk that people might start rushing to the banks to withdraw their money. The banks realized that they were still vulnerable if that happened. They were still afraid of another Black Friday.

There was a hurried meeting of the principal bankers. Some reported that there were signs that a run was already starting. Denison Miller then said that the Commonwealth Bank on behalf of the Commonwealth would support any bank in difficulties. . . . That was the end of the panic.

It was a dramatic demonstration of the power of government to stabilize the financial system. Banks did not need "capital" or "reserves" or "liquidity." They just needed the government's guarantee. A bank panic could be stopped overnight, simply through the government's agreement to guarantee the banks' loans. Miller could have created the bailout money with accounting entries if he had needed to, but it wasn't necessary. Just the assurance of the government's guarantee was sufficient to satisfy the depositors.

Lang went on:

> [I]t put Miller on the box seat. Now, for the first time, the Commonwealth Bank was taking the lead. It was giving, not taking, orders. . . .
>
> Denison Miller . . . was virtually in control of the financing of the war. The Government didn't know how it was going to be achieved. Miller did.

The City of London Responds: The Birth of "Central Banking"

Miller and his bank were a brilliant success—perhaps too brilliant. Like the American colonists' paper scrip, the ready credit issued at will by the Commonwealth Bank threatened the hegemony of the London bankers. Lang wrote:

> London capital had always dominated Australian finance and business. Despite Federation the Colonial system had remained intact. Tribute was levied by way of interest on Government loans and dividends from pastoral, mining, banking, insurance and industrial investments, as well as from imports. . . .
>
> It was the City of London that had established what was known as the Mercantile System out of the Industrial Revolution. The Victorian Era had been one of great commercial expansion. With that rare genius for political invention, Gladstone, Disraeli and other British statesmen sought a substitute for the old system of Crown Colonies. They found it in the British Empire. *Their formula was to hand to the colonies the right to govern themselves, providing they did not break the financial nexus with the City of London.*

The City of London provided all the capital required for the development of the colonies. The City controlled the ships, the wool and wheat exchanges, the insurance houses and all the other machinery of trade and commerce. *Self government for the colonies did not mean financial independence. . . .The Old Lady of Threadneedle Street, as they called the bank of England, presided over the financial dynasty of the Empire. . . .*

All our railways, our power plants, our school buildings and even our police courts and gaols [jails] had been built with money supplied by the City of London. We were a debtor nation. The bondholders never permitted us to forget it.

Australia had been a debtor nation dependent on the Motherland until the First World War. Then it had demonstrated its independence by financing its participation in the war with its own government-owned bank. Worse from the perspective of the London bankers, it had used its own bank to fund the Commonwealth Shipping Line, a rival poised to smash the City's shipping monopoly. Lang wrote:

Denison Miller had gone to London after the war had finished and had thrown a great fright into the banking world by calmly telling a big bankers' dinner that the wealth of Australia represented six times the amount of money that had been borrowed, and that the bank could meet every demand because it had the entire capital of the country behind it. The bank had found £350 million for war purposes.

A deputation of unemployed waited on him after he arrived back from London at the head office of the Commonwealth Bank in Martin Place, Sydney. He was asked whether his bank would be prepared to raise another £350 million for productive purposes. He replied that not only was his bank able to do it, but would be happy to do it.

Such statements as these caused a near panic in the City of London. If the Dominions were going to become independent of the City of London, then the entire financial structure would collapse. The urgent problem was to find ways and means of re-establishing the financial supremacy that had been lost during the war.

. . . If London was to retain the monopoly of finance, it had to deal with such upstart competition as that threatened by

Denison Miller. Canada, South Africa and other Dominions were causing a similar amount of concern.

Basically it was a problem of banking. Some formula had to be devised which would enable such local institutions as the Commonwealth Bank of Australia to be drawn into the City of London's net. The financial experts studied the problem deeply. *Out of their deliberations emerged the plan to centralize the control of all banking throughout the Empire by channeling it directly into the supervision of the Bank of England.*

The Bank of England was to become the super Bankers' Bank. The Commonwealth Bank of Australia was to be responsible for the local administration of Bank of England policy. It was to be the junior Bankers' Bank.

And thus was born the modern system of central banking, controlled in a hierarchical structure headed by a super-central bank in London. Later, the head office would move to the Bank for International Settlements in Basel, Switzerland. The central banks of the now-freed colonies might be owned by their governments, but they would have to march in lockstep with this super-governing power structure abroad. Lang wrote:

> If . . . the Bank of England could control the Commonwealth Bank of Australia, there should be no impediment in the way of controlling the Government of the country as well. The Genoa Economic Conference in 1922 took up the idea of this grand form of central banking, and extended its approval. . . .
>
> The quickest way to control credit in Australia was through the Commonwealth Bank. Why not make it into a central bank on the bank of England model: Why not hand over to it control of credit and currency? . . . But it had to have the right kind of control.
>
> The quickest way to ensure the right kind of policy in the Commonwealth bank was to set up a Commonwealth bank Board. . . . On the Board would be placed the right kind of managers—men who understood the Conservative philosophy and who would tune in to London.
>
> . . . The Labor Party . . . immediately pointed out that they were altering the entire conception of the Commonwealth

Bank. It had started out as a People's Bank. The Bruce-Page Government was converting it into a Banker's Bank.

Australian Resistance

That was the plan, but the Australian people and the Labor government of James Scullin were not so easily subdued. In 1931, Scullin came into conflict with the board of the Commonwealth Bank. The Bank's chairman refused to expand credit unless the government cut pensions, and Scullin refused to comply. The conflict led to demands from Labor for reform of the Bank and for more direct government control over monetary policy.

The Commonwealth Bank's powers were broadened in emergency legislation passed during World War II. At the end of the war, the Bank used this power to begin a dramatic expansion of the economy. In just five years, it opened hundreds of branches throughout Australia.

In 1958 and 1959, the government split the Bank. The central bank function was given to the Reserve Bank of Australia, while the commercial banking functions were retained by the Commonwealth Bank. But both banks remained publicly-owned.

The Commonwealth Bank was widely perceived to be an insurance policy against abuse by private banks. It eventually had branches or agencies in every town and suburb, in every post office or country store, and in the bush. As the largest bank in the country, it set the rates and set policy. The other banks had to fall in line or lose their customers. The Commonwealth Bank ensured that everyone had access to equitable banking.

It functioned as a wholly owned state bank until the 1990s, when it finally succumbed to privatization. The focus then changed to maximization of profits. The results were steady, massive branch and agency closures; staff layoffs; and reduced access to Automated Teller Machines and to cash from supermarket checkouts. At one time, the Commonwealth Bank was the lifeblood of the country. But critics say it has now become just another part of the banking cartel.

The central banks of Canada and New Zealand have followed suit; but they too were once publicly-owned sources of freely-flowing credit for the nation. How those institutions evolved and then succumbed to a private banking empire headed by the Bank for International Settlements (BIS) will be explored shortly. First, a look at the BIS itself, where it came from, and how it grew.

Chapter 16

THE BANKERS' COUP:
THE BANK OF ENGLAND PASSES
THE BATON TO THE BANK FOR
INTERNATIONAL SETTLEMENTS

"I have no use for politicians," says Fritz Leutwiler, head of the Bank for International Settlements. "They lack the judgment of central bankers."

-- *Quoted by Edward Jay Epstein in Harper's Magazine, November 1983*[303]

The modern global central banking system originated in the City of London, with the Bank of England at its apex; but when World War I exhausted England's financial resources, the apex moved to the Bank for International Settlements in Basel. The central bankers at its helm grew from a group of four, to seven, to ten. The BIS currently has 60 members; but the real leaders are a much smaller group.

In 1923, at the age of 63, Denison Miller died unexpectedly of heart disease. Management of the Commonwealth Bank of Australia was then delivered to a Committee that the Bank of England could control. In 1924, the power to issue the national currency was transferred from

---

the Australian Treasury to a central bank that could be directed by bankers in London. Jack Lang wrote:

> The Note Issue [the power to issue the national currency] was the key to central bank control. . . . The 1924 Act provided that the Note Issue should be handed over to the new Commonwealth Bank Board. That was in accordance with the plan drafted in London. . . . No longer could the Bank Governor promise to find money for public works as Denison Miller had found it. Had the Commonwealth Bank Board been in existence from the beginning there would have been no Transcontinental Railway Line and no Commonwealth Shipping Line.

Under Dennison Miller's leadership, the Commonwealth Bank had helped to save Australians from the ravages of the 1890s depression. Under the London-controlled Committee, said Lang, the Bank made the 1930s depression worse. Credit was tightened and austerity was imposed:

> The Committee had recommended a reduction in the amount of credit. It urged a form of deflation. It had intimated that Government borrowing should cease at the earliest possible moment. It said that credit expansion was threatening Britain's national solvency. Cheap money and the increase in the note issue were undermining the commercial fabric of the country. They said . . . the gold reserve should be used as a basis for the note issue. That was the plan as approved in London.

Credit expansion was threatening the national solvency, not of Australia, but of Britain, which was losing its economic grip on its former colonies. Returning Australia to a system in which the currency was backed by gold put control back in the hands of the keepers of the gold, the private banks that were now to be stacked in hierarchal formation under the City of London. Lang wrote:

> The Bank of England took up the idea of Empire control most enthusiastically. It was even decided to aim at a World Bank, to be run by the League of Nations, which would control the credit of the world. The grand idea was that one single Board of Directors would make the decisions which would determine the economic policy of the world. The bankers were to be the

supreme rulers. Naturally, the Governor of the bank of England expected to be at the apex of the system.

In 1930, the government of Australia received a visit from a director of the Bank of England named Sir Otto Niemeyer, who would go on to become chairman of the Bank for International Settlements. As the visit is described in *Wikipedia*, summarizing sources:

> He was critical of Australia's overconfidence and essentially said that Australia was *"living beyond its means"*, that it had become prosperous through "mistakes" and that in order to become economically viable Australians would have to *"accept a lower standard of living"*. The report continued to suggest that Australia should continue to exist only as a means to supply Britain with goods, and that its protectionist attitude was deviating Australia from its true purpose. The protectionism employed by the Australian Government at the time was very beneficial to Australia, but not to Britain, and therefore Niemeyer viewed that it was detrimental to British interests.[304]

In *The Power of Economic Ideas: The Origins of Macroeconomic Management in Australia, 1929-39* (2010), A. J. Millmow states that Niemeyer's draconian advice brought "the house of English orthodox economics down on Australia's head." Neimeyer attacked the prosperous Australian standard of living, which he considered unsustainable. He said wages needed to be cut and tariffs needed to be lifted. When asked by the speaker of the federal parliament if his mission were proceeding satisfactorily, he replied, "That depends on whether you do as you are told."[305]

In 1937, Sir Niemeyer went on to head the BIS, the institution later identified by Dr. Carroll Quigley as the apex of a private central banking scheme for dominating governments globally.

Carroll Quigley and the BIS

Dr. Quigley was a professor of history at Georgetown University, where he was President Bill Clinton's mentor. Quigley identified himself as an insider groomed by the powerful clique he called "the international bankers." His credibility is heightened by the fact that he actually espoused their goals. In *Tragedy and Hope: A History of the World in Our Time* (1966), he wrote:

> I know of the operations of this network because I have studied it for twenty years and was permitted for two years, in the early 1960's, to examine its papers and secret records. I have no aversion to it or to most of its aims and have, for much of my life, been close to it and to many of its instruments. . . . In general my chief difference of opinion is that it wishes to remain unknown, and I believe its role in history is significant enough to be known.

He wrote of this international banking network:

> [T]he powers of financial capitalism had another far-reaching aim, nothing less than to create a world system of financial control in private hands able to dominate the political system of each country and the economy of the world as a whole. This system was to be controlled in a feudalist fashion by the central banks of the world acting in concert, by secret agreements arrived at in frequent private meetings and conferences. *The apex of the system was to be the Bank for International Settlements in Basel, Switzerland, a private bank owned and controlled by the world's central banks which were themselves private corporations.*

The key to their success, said Quigley, was that *the international bankers would control and manipulate the money system of a nation while letting it appear to be controlled by the government.* The economic and political systems of nations would be controlled not by citizens but by bankers, for the benefit of bankers.

The goal was to establish an "independent" central bank in every country—meaning one that was independent of government and subject to the control of private banking interests. Today, this goal has largely been achieved. Central banks have the authority to issue the national currency in their respective countries, and it is from these banks that governments must borrow money to pay their debts and fund their operations. The result is a global economy in which not only industry but government itself runs on credit (or debt) created by a banking monopoly headed by a network of central banks that are independent of the dictates of government; and the top of this network is located at the BIS, the "central bank of central banks" in Basel.

Behind the Mask of an International Clearing House

The BIS was set up in 1929 to handle German war reparations, after Germany defaulted on its war debts under the Treaty of Versailles in 1923. The Dawes Plan was then set up to allow Germany to borrow money from America, so that Germany could repay its war debts to England and France. In 1929, the Young Committee restructured the Dawes loans and created the BIS to act as trustee for the loans. Germany made installment payments to America, giving American bankers a vested interest in German industry so that Germany could repay the loans.[306]

The plan for the BIS was agreed to at a conference at the Hague in August 1929, just two months before the Wall Street stock market crash of that year. A charter for the bank was drafted at the International Bankers Conference at Baden Baden in November and was adopted at a second Hague Conference on January 20, 1930.

Although the stated purpose of the BIS was to handle reparations, Quigley said that its primary purpose was to allow central bankers to maintain collective control over world finance without London remaining the sole dominating financial power, Britain having ceded much of that power to America with the economic burdens of World War I.[307] Quigley wrote:

> The BIS is generally regarded as the apex of the structure of financial capitalism whose remote origins go back to the creation of the Bank of England in 1694 and the Bank of France in 1803. As a matter of fact its establishment in 1929 was rather an indication that the centralized financial system of 1914 was in decline. It was set up rather to remedy the decline of London as the world's financial center by providing a mechanism by which a world with three chief financial centers in London, New York, and Paris could still operate as one. . . . It was intended to be the world cartel of ever-growing national financial powers by assembling the nominal heads of these national financial centers.

Quigley named London, New York, and Paris; but Germany also played a major role. The prime movers in establishing the BIS were Montague Norman, then governor of the Bank of England, and his German colleague Hjalmar Schacht, president of the Reichsbank. In *Trading with the Enemy* (1983), Charles Higham wrote that by the late 1930s, the BIS had assumed an openly pro-Nazi bias, a theme that was expanded on in a BBC Timewatch film titled "Banking with Hitler" broadcast in 1998.[308]

Schacht's character is suggested by the fact that even Hitler did not trust him. According to the BBC film, Hitler said of Schacht:

> It was his consummate skill at swindling other people which made him indispensable at the time. After all, seeing that the whole gang of financials are a bunch of crooks, what possible point was there in being scrupulously honest with them. . . .
>
> In spite of his abilities, I could never trust Schacht, for I had often seen how his face lit up when he succeeded in swindling someone out of a hundred mark note.

The BIS has been called "the most exclusive, secretive, and powerful supranational club in the world." The fact that the world was at war did not largely concern these central bankers. Their concern was to keep the money flowing. According to the BBC film, the BIS operated as a congenial bankers' club, neutral and above the fray of war and international conflict. Its purpose was to allow bankers to make money no matter what, and to continue exercising their vast powers, including making agreements on "the economic future of the chief areas of the globe."[309]

Higham wrote that the BIS functioned as the "[i]nstitution that would retain channels of communication and collusion between the world's financial leaders even in the event of an international conflict. It was written into the Bank's charter, concurred in by the respective governments, that the BIS should be immune from seizure, closure or censure, whether or not its owners were at war." Although it had "acquired a pro-Nazi bias", "its continuing existence was approved by Great Britain even after that country went to war with Germany, and the British director Sir Otto Niemeyer, and chairman Montagu Norman, remained in office throughout the war."

In 1944, the American government backed a resolution at the Bretton-Woods Conference calling for the liquidation of the BIS, following Czech accusations that it was laundering gold stolen by the Nazis from occupied Europe. But the central bankers succeeded in killing the American resolution.[310] According to Edward Jay Epstein in a 1983 *Harper's* article titled "Ruling the World of Money":

> The naive idea was that the settlement and monetary-clearing functions [that the BIS] provided could be taken over by the new International Monetary Fund. What could not be replaced, however, was what existed behind the mask of an international clearing house: a supranational organization for setting and implementing global monetary strategy, which could not be accomplished by a democratic, United Nations-like international agency. The central bankers, not about to let their club be taken from them, quietly snuffed out the American resolution.[311]

For many years the BIS kept a very low profile, operating behind the scenes in an abandoned hotel. It was here, according to Epstein, that decisions were reached to devalue or defend currencies, fix the price of gold, regulate offshore banking, and raise or lower short-term interest rates. In 1977, however, the BIS gave up its anonymity in exchange for more efficient headquarters. Epstein called the new building "an eighteen story-high circular skyscraper that rises above the medieval city like some misplaced nuclear reactor." It quickly became known as the "Tower of Basel." Today the BIS has governmental immunity, pays no taxes, and has its own private police force.[312] It is, as its founders envisioned, above the law.

Although the BIS is now composed of 60 nations, control is with a much smaller group. Epstein wrote in 1983 that the club was so secretive that information was not readily available, but that the real business got done in "a sort of inner club made up of the half dozen or so powerful central bankers who find themselves more or less in the same monetary boat" – those from Germany, the United States, Switzerland, Italy, Japan and England:

> The prime value, which also seems to demarcate the inner club from the rest of the BIS members, is the firm belief that *central banks should act independently of their home governments.*

> . . . A second and closely related belief of the inner club is that politicians should not be trusted to decide the fate of the international monetary system.

In 1974, the Basel Committee on Banking Supervision was created by the central bank Governors of the Group of Ten nations (now expanded to include 27 members). The BIS provides the twelve-member Secretariat for the Committee, which sets the rules for banking globally, including capital requirements and reserve controls. In an article titled "The Bank for International Settlements Calls for Global Currency," Joan Veon wrote in 2003:

> The BIS is where all of the world's central banks meet to analyze the global economy and determine what course of action they will take next to put more money in their pockets, since they control the amount of money in circulation and how much interest they are going to charge governments and banks for borrowing from them. . . .
>
> When you understand that the BIS pulls the strings of the world's monetary system, you then understand that they have the ability to create a financial boom or bust in a country. If that country is not doing what the money lenders want, then all they have to do is sell its currency.[313]

That is the shady history of the BIS, but it not clear where or what the inner circle is today. According to Steve Waddell, Executive Director of Global Action Network Net, the BIS is arguably the most important and least recognized of all the organizations of what he calls the "Global Finance System;" but it is only one of many overlapping and interlocking organizations and committees. (See Figure 7.) The BIS may have sprung from a "grand design" in the World War II era along with the founding of the World Bank and the International Monetary Fund, but it has grown in an ad hoc manner since.

Today, says Waddell, the BIS serves as a critical forum for information exchange, social network development, research, workshops and seminars, and a range of banking services for central banks. It has an expanded representation in the G20 group of developed countries, but it is controlled by the central banks of the G10 group.

The global coordinating organization for the Global Finance System is now the Financial Stability Board, which brings together representatives from many organizations. The Financial Stability Board grew out of two crises. The first was the Asian crisis in the late 1990s, which produced the Global Stability Forum (GSF). (Figure 6 below.) The second was the 2008 crisis that began on Wall Street and transformed the GSF, a merely advisory body into the all-powerful Financial Stability Board. (More on this in Chapter 28.) Waddell writes:

> As a product of the most recent crisis, in April 2009 [the GSF] was renamed the Financial Stability Board with expanded G20 membership, and its role was enhanced to address vulnerabilities and to develop and implement strong regulatory, supervisory and other policies in the interest of financial stability.[314]

Financial Stability Forum (FSF)
Participant Value Network: Only Tangible Transactions

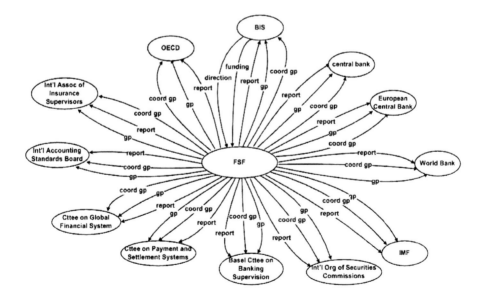

Figure 6.

Source: Steve Waddell, Global Action Network Net[315]

The problem is that "financial stability" has been limited to preserving the private financial system itself. The BIS, its staff and its offspring do not see beyond their computer models and economic indices to the environment, poverty and social stresses, the sorts of things Waddell's networks are working to address. If the Global Finance System is to survive, they maintain, it will need to widen its lens to include the public interest.

But more on all that later. There is a great deal of history to cover first, going back to the 1930s.

Bank for International Settlements (BIS) Participant Value Network: Only Tangible Transactions

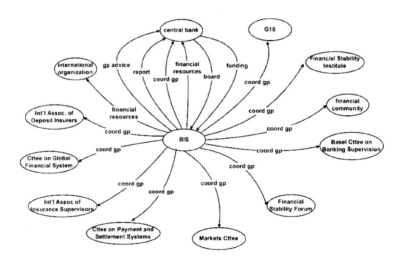

Figure 7.

Source: Steve Waddell, Global Action Network Net [316]

Chapter 17

THE CANADIAN MOVEMENT FOR MONETARY SOVEREIGNTY: RISE AND FALL

"Once a nation parts with the control of its currency and credit, it matters not who makes the nation's laws. Usury, once in control, will wreck any nation."

-- *William Lyon Mackenzie King,*
Prime Minister of Canada, 1935

> The government of Canada devised its innovative system of state-bank-created credit in the 1930s, and drew freely from it for nearly four decades of unusual prosperity, growth and development. Then in the 1970s, Canada joined the Basel Committee of G10 countries at the BIS. A change in economic policy followed, which cut the government off from its own state bank funding, subjecting it to the skyrocketing interest rates of private international credit markets. Canada is now struggling with debt and deficits along with most of the rest of the Western world.

While Australia's innovative central bank was being reined in by the City of London in the 1930s, Canada's was just getting started. Before 1935, the Canadian government did not have a central bank. It had to borrow from private banks that issued their own banknotes, with the country's largest private bank, the Bank of Montreal, serving as the government's de facto banker.[317] But in the throes of the Great Depression, this private system had failed. The money supply had collapsed, forcing businesses to close and unemployment to soar. The banks were blamed for making conditions worse by failing to extend loans; and for the government, a national debt to private banks meant a mounting interest burden.

By the eve of the depression, interest on Canada's public debt had reached an alarming one-third of government expenditures. Many officials believed that the government needed a central bank to generate its own money. In 1933, a Royal Commission was put together to look into creating such a bank. A major debate then ensued over whether it should be public or private.

William Lyon Mackenzie King was elected prime minister in 1935. He thought the bank should be public. He admonished:

> Until the control of the issue of currency and credit is restored to government and recognized as its most conspicuous and sacred responsibility, all talk of the sovereignty of Parliament and of democracy is idle and futile.[318]

Imagine a Canadian prime minister or U.S. president saying that today!

Gerald McGeer and the Model of Guernsey

Another zealous advocate for a public central bank was a Canadian mayor and Member of Parliament named Gerald Gratton McGeer. In *The Conquest of Poverty* (1936), McGeer wrote:

> Ever since the passage of The English Bank Act of 1844, the creation, issuance, and the regulation of the circulation of the current medium of exchange, though being duties that constitute the most conspicuous and sacred responsibilities of government, have been in large measure delegated in blind faith and absolute confidence to bankers and financiers.
>
> The complete collapse of the economic structure under banker management . . . proves that the private control of credit is fundamentally unsound. . . .

Necessity now compels all to recognize that the creation and issuance of the medium of exchange, the monetization of public credit, the circulation of the medium of exchange, and the general supervision of the monetary system must be restored to government.

McGeer made lengthy presentations to the Ottawa Common Banking Committee, clarifying for bankers, economists and legislators how well a national currency issued by a publicly-owned bank could work. For a model, he cited the British Channel Island state of Guernsey, which had been issuing its own currency to pay for public works since 1820.

New Zealand researcher Kerry Bolton summarized the Guernsey experience in an August 2011 article like this:

Guernsey's banking system was prompted by dire need, the island being in serious financial trouble from the beginning of the 19th Century. Guernsey's town was undeveloped, the roads were cart-tracks, and there was no prospect for employment... [I]t was the need to upgrade the Public Market that prompted a committee to report back with a solution in 1816 to issue £6000 worth of States Notes. The committee also recommended that the States Notes be used not only for the new market, but also for Torteval Church, road construction, and other State expenses. The notes' issue was started in 1820, and was followed by other issues, until by 1837 £55,000 of the Notes were in circulation, debt-free and having created prosperity and development, which in turn stimulated visitors to the island.[319]

It was all going well, says Bolton, until two local banks flooded Guernsey with their own notes to undermine the State Notes. The Island responded by agreeing to limit the issue of its own Notes. But with the outbreak of war in 1914, the State Notes were restarted; and they continued to circulate alongside British Pounds Sterling thereafter. Despite that influx of new money, writes Bolton, "there has never been inflation, and the prosperity of the island continues as it has since 1820, operating on minimal taxation."

What a Nationalized Central Bank Can Do

The Bank of Canada opened in 1935 under private ownership; but in 1938, the Bank Act was amended to make it a publicly-owned institution. According to William Krehm in *A Power Unto Itself: The Bank of Canada*, the 1938 nationalization allowed the central bank to create the money to finance federal projects on a nearly interest-free basis. The bank could also lend to the provinces. The interest it collected went back to the federal treasury.[320]

In creating the credit to finance federal, provincial, and municipal projects, the Bank of Canada was doing what private banks do every day; but it was doing this in the public interest. In parliamentary hearings in 1939, Graham Towers, the first governor of the Bank of Canada, confirmed that banks routinely create credit with accounting entries. When asked by Gerald McGeer whether banks create the medium of exchange, Towers replied:

> That is right. That is what they are there for. . . . That is the banking business, just in the way that a steel plant makes steel. The manufacturing process consists of making a pen-and-ink or typewriter entry on a card in a book. That is all.[321]

In another interesting exchange, McGeer asked Towers:

> Q: Would you admit that anything physically possible and desirable can be made financially possible?
>
> A: Certainly.
>
> Q: Will you tell me why the government with power to create money should give that power away to a private monopoly and then borrow that which Parliament can create itself, back at interest?
>
> A: Now, if Parliament wants to change the form of operating the bank system, then certainly that is within the power of Parliament.[322]

For over three decades, the Bank of Canada used its lucrative credit-creating tools for the benefit of the public. The Canadian government funded infrastructure and social programs simply by advancing the credit needed to accomplish them. William Krehm writes:

In the years 1935 to 1945, Canada's monetary base – that is, the supply of legal tender – was increased from $259 million to $2,017 million. M1 – all currency and non-interest-bearing deposits – rose from $742 million to $2,956 million. Because the central bank created most of the money itself and lent it to the government in the form of treasury bills at rates as low as .37 percent, the bank was able to keep the interest paid on Canada Savings Bonds bought by the public to 3 percent or less. Without the low-rate financing provided by the central banks, the Allied powers could not have won the war.[323]

According to the late Will Abram in *Money: The Canadian Experience with the Bank of Canada Act of 1934* (2009), the Canadian government first showed what it could do with its own central bank during World War II, when Canada ranked fourth among the Allies for production of war goods. Under the Returning Veterans Rehabilitation Act of 1945, some 54,000 returning vets were given financial aid to attend university. The Department of Veterans Affairs provided another 80,000 vets with vocational training, and the Veterans' Land Act helped 33,000 vets buy farmland.

After the war, the Industrial Development Bank, a subsidiary of the Bank of Canada, was formed to boost Canadian businesses by offering loans at low interest rates. The Bank of Canada also funded many infrastructure projects and social programs directly. Under the Trans-Canada Highway Act passed in 1949, Canada built the world's longest road and the world's longest inland waterway (a joint venture with the United States), as well as the 28-mile Welland Canal. Senior citizens, regardless of income or assets, received a modest allowance from the government under the Old Age Security Act; and children under 15 got one as well.[324]

In 1957, funding from the Bank of Canada helped launch the Canadian federal health care system. A Hospital Act was passed under which the federal government agreed to pay half its citizens' bills at most hospitals, and a Diagnostic Services Act gave all Canadians free acute hospital care, as well as lab and radiology work. In 1966, the Hospital Act was expanded to cover physician services. In 1984, the Canada Health Act ensured that no medically-necessary care would include private fees or a charge to citizens.[325]

Bad Economic Policy Kills the
Canadian Golden Goose

From 1939 to 1974, Canada financed these projects largely through its government-owned central bank, without sparking price inflation or driving up the federal debt. (See Figure 9 below.) From 1935 to 1939, the Bank of Canada issued most of the nation's credit, and it issued 62 percent of the credit during the last years of World War II. Until the mid-1970s, the Canadian government continued to create enough new state money to monetize 20 percent to 30 percent of the national deficit. It advanced money at low interest, forcing commercial banks to keep interest rates low in order to compete.[326]

This four-decade run of prosperity came to an end, however, when Canada abandoned its successful experiment in self-funding and began borrowing heavily on the private market. This change in policies occurred when the Basel Committee was established by the central-bank Governors of the Group of Ten countries of the Bank for International Settlements in 1974, and Canada joined it.[327] A key objective of the Committee was and is to maintain "monetary and financial stability." To achieve that goal, the Committee discouraged governments from borrowing from their own central banks interest-free and encouraged them to borrow instead from private creditors, including large international banks.[328]

The proffered justification for the policy was that borrowing from a nation's own central bank, which had the power to create money on its books, would inflate the money supply and prices, while borrowing from private creditors would not. Overlooked or concealed was that private banks create the money they lend just as public banks do. The difference is that a publicly-owned bank returns the interest to the government and the community, while a privately-owned bank siphons it into private accounts, progressively drawing money out of the productive economy.

The change in government borrowing policies was justified as being necessary to fight "stagflation"—rising prices accompanied by high unemployment—which had set in during the late 1960s. Under the sway of the classical monetarist theories promoted by U.S. economist Milton Friedman, the phenomenon was blamed on governments either issuing money too freely or borrowing too freely from their own central banks. Overlooked was that the stagflation was global, and that Canadian prices had remained stable and the national debt had been low for decades, although the Bank of Canada had been steadily increasing the monetary base. Paul Hellyer, former Defense Minister of Canada and founder of the Canadian Action Party, maintains that elevated prices in the 1970s were the result not of government money creation but of "cost-push" inflation, triggered by big labor unions, big government, and big corporations negotiating top dollar for their contracts.[329]

According to William Engdahl in *The Gods of Money* (2009), there was another cause of cost-push inflation in the early 1970s, and this one was intentionally engineered: the skyrocketing cost of oil. When Nixon took the U.S. dollar off the gold standard in 1971, the dollar dropped precipitously in international markets. U.S. Secretary of State Henry Kissinger and President Nixon then held a clandestine meeting in 1972 with the Shah of Iran, who was offered any weapons he wanted from the U.S. arsenal except nuclear bombs. He would need vastly greater income to pay for them, but the revenue was soon provided.

Engdahl cites evidence that in 1973, a group of powerful financiers and politicians met secretly in Sweden to discuss how the dollar might effectively be "backed" by oil. An arrangement was then finalized in which the oil-producing countries of OPEC would sell their oil only in U.S. dollars, and the dollars would wind up in Wall Street and London banks, where they would fund the burgeoning U.S. debt. For the OPEC countries, the *quid pro quo* was military protection, along with windfall profits from a dramatic boost in oil prices.

In 1974, according to plan, an oil embargo caused the price of oil to quadruple, forcing countries without sufficient dollar reserves to borrow from Wall Street and London banks to buy the oil they needed. Increased costs then drove up prices worldwide.[330]

In *Demon Money* (2013), James Cumes points to yet another factor driving up prices: the rising cost of money itself. The monetarist prescription for combatting price inflation was to raise interest rates, making credit more expensive and reducing its supply. That was the theory, but raising interest rates actually had the opposite effect: prices *rose*. (See Figure 8.)

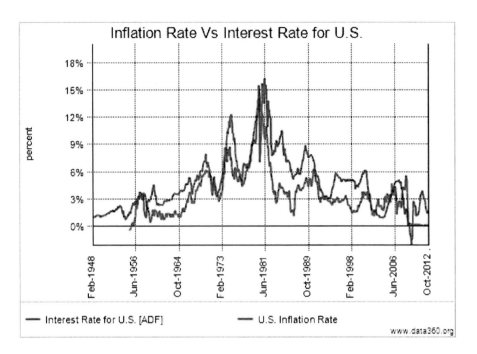

Figure 8. U.S. inflation rate tracks interest rate, 1948-2012

President Richard Nixon began raising interest rates proactively in 1969, before prices had really begun to rise. They were just expected to rise due to the Vietnam War and other large government expenditures.[331] Interest rates rose steadily thereafter, peaking in Canada at a staggering 22 percent in 1981. Prices rose right along with them. The reason is not hard to see: businesses have to recoup their interest charges by raising their prices; and businesses that cannot afford to borrow at the higher rates decrease production, reducing supply relative to demand, driving prices up.[332]

The debt curve that began its exponential rise in 1974 tilted toward the vertical in 1981, when interest rates were raised by the U.S. Federal Reserve to 20 percent, and Canadian rates went as high as 22 percent. At 20 percent compounded annually, debt doubles in less than four years. (See Figure 9.)

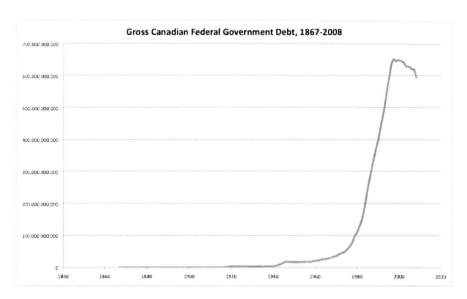

Figure 9. Canadian federal debt, 1867-2008.
Source: Statistics Canada, CANSIM using CHASS, v151537 Canada[333]

From Sustainable to Unsustainable Debt

The Canadian Auditor General is the accountant who reviews the government's books. In his 1993 annual report he acknowledged that *most of the government's debt consisted of interest charges*:

> [The] cost of borrowing and its compounding effect have a significant impact on Canada's annual deficits. From Confederation up to 1991-92, the federal government accumulated a net debt of $423 billion. Of this, *$37 billion represents the accumulated shortfall* in meeting the cost of government programs since Confederation. *The remainder, $386 billion, represents the amount the government has borrowed to service the debt created by previous annual shortfalls.*[334]

Thus in 1993, *91 percent of the debt consisted of interest charges*. Without those charges, the government would have had a debt of only C$37 billion—very low and sustainable, just as it was before 1974.

By 2012, the government had paid C$1 trillion in interest—*twice its national debt.*[335] Interest on the debt is now the government's single largest budget expenditure—larger than health care, senior entitlements or national defense.[336]

Today, the Bank of Canada monetizes only 7.5 percent of the state deficit. The Canadian money supply increases by C$22 billion annually, but the Bank of Canada creates less than 2 percent of that increase. If the Canadian government had continued to fund itself as it had before the mid-1970s, estimates are that Canada would now be operating with a surplus of C$13 billion.[337]

In March 2012, the Canadian House of Commons passed the federal government's latest round of budget cuts and austerity measures, including cutting 19,200 public sector jobs, slashing federal programs by C$5.2 billion per year, and raising the retirement age for millions of Canadians from 65 to 67. The justification for these austerity measures was a massive federal debt exceeding C$ 581 billion, or 84 percent of GDP. It is a debt that might have been avoided if the government had continued to borrow heavily from its own central bank, as it did between 1939 and 1974.

Taking It to Court

In December 2011, William Krehm, along with Ann Emmett and COMER (the Committee for Monetary and Economic Reform), brought suit in Canadian federal court "to restore the use of the Bank of Canada to its original purpose, including making interest-free loans to municipal/provincial/federal governments for 'human capital' expenditures (education, health, other social services) and/or infrastructure expenditures." According to a press release:

> The Plaintiffs state that since 1974 there has been a gradual but sure slide into the reality that the Bank of Canada and Canada's monetary and financial policy are dictated by private foreign banks and financial interests contrary to the Bank of Canada Act.
>
> The Plaintiffs state that the Bank of International Settlements (BIS), the Financial Stability Forum (FSF) and the International Monetary Fund (IMF) were all created with the cognizant intent of keeping poorer nations in their place which has now expanded to all nations in *that these financial institutions*

largely succeed in over-riding governments and constitutional orders in countries such as Canada over which they exert financial control. The Plaintiffs state that the meetings of the BIS and Financial Stability Board (FSB) (successor of FSF), their minutes, their discussions and deliberations are secret and not available nor accountable to Parliament, the executive, nor the Canadian public notwithstanding that the Bank of Canada policies directly emanate from these meetings. These organizations are essentially private, foreign entities controlling Canada's banking system and socio-economic policies.

The story of the secretive foreign influence of the BIS and the Financial Stability Board will be picked up shortly. While we're on the subject of Canada, we'll look first at another Canadian public banking innovation of the 1930s, the Alberta Treasury Branches.

Chapter 18

THE ALBERTA EXPERIMENT WITH SOCIAL CREDIT

"[Y]ou have an enormous vested interest possessing the most powerful monopoly that the whole history of the world has ever known, the monopoly, as we call it, of credit, the monopoly of the creation of and dealing in money, a monopoly against which any other monopoly pales into insignificance – and it is determined to use every weapon to retain this monopoly."

-- C. H. Douglas, "Money and the Price System," speech to the king and government of Norway, 1935

The depression years of the 1930s were fertile ones for experimenting with new economic theories, and one of these experiments involved the "Social Credit" approach of Major C. H. Douglas. While the Social Credit Party was in power in Alberta for 35 years, however, it never actually succeeded in implementing his policies. What it did succeed in creating was a highly successful publicly-owned financial institution called the Alberta Treasury Branches, which at least in its early years effectively turned credit into a public utility. Douglas's theories will be explored at length here because they also had a major impact in New Zealand and Japan, where they came into conflict with the independent central banking empire that was being fostered at the same time.

While Canada's federal government was experimenting with public credit issued on a national scale, the Canadian province of Alberta was engaged in an experiment of its own. Hit particularly hard by the Great Depression, Albertans decided they needed a change from the current political party, the United Farmers of Alberta. In 1935, they voted for a radical new group called the Social Credit Party, which promised a new way to run society, including payment of a monthly dividend for each citizen, regulated and fair prices, and protection for debtors during hard times. It called on democratically-elected governments to take monetary control of the system away from privately-owned "debt-creating" banks.

The thought leader of this movement was Major Clifford Hugh (C. H.) Douglas, a Scottish engineer who published a popular book called *Social Credit* in 1924. Douglas formed his initial insights working as an engineer for international companies immediately after the First World War. According to the Social Credit website:

> . . . Douglas had observed that, in the case of any individual project, there was only ever one problem which could not be overcome, and that was lack of finance. If a project was considered desirable for a local community, it was always possible to find the tools, the machinery, the skills, the materials, the workers and all essential resources. But if the finance was not forthcoming, the project was invariably scrapped, or put on hold until the finance was available. In other words, policies were being determined by the availability of finance.
>
> . . . Douglas observed . . . that finance flows into the economic system as bank-created debt. Firms use the debt-created finance to pay their costs of production. The wages, salaries and dividends paid out by firms form incomes to households. With their incomes, households can purchase the stream of goods and services coming onto the market. As the modern economic system has developed, it has created a massive bureaucracy. Behind that bureaucracy, obscured by the very complexity of the system, financial speculation, profiteering, marketing, advertising and a whole range of growth-driven economic activities are making human existence increasingly

precarious. In Douglas' view, this is not a necessary state of human affairs.[338]

Douglas saw that the economy routinely produces more goods and services than consumers have the money to purchase, because workers collectively do not get paid enough to cover the costs of the things they make. Businesses first pay out their costs to workers, suppliers, and creditors. Since the purpose of the business is to make a profit, they then set their prices at cost plus profit; but they do not collectively pay enough money into the circulating money supply to cover this profit. Moreover, the wages they do pay are not all spent, since people like to save some of their money and watch it "grow." The result is an inevitable gap between supply and demand

Douglas saw this simply as a mathematical problem: the solution was to fill the gap by getting more money into the pockets of consumers. He proposed to do this with a government-issued dividend for everyone, an entitlement by "grace" rather than "works," something that was necessary just to raise purchasing power enough to cover the cost of the products on the market. The dividend would not be funded through taxes or debt but would simply be issued by the government as "social credit"—a credit against the collective productivity of the nation.

That is not, however, what is done today. Social Credit proponents point out that the "gap" is now filled in other ways—ways that are ultimately unsustainable:

(a) Consumers rely on borrowed money, leading to a spiraling pyramid of debt.

(b) Businesses seek additional markets abroad, pitting nation against nation and leading to economic warfare that often intensifies into military warfare.

(c) Some businesses must go bankrupt or operate at a loss to create the excess for the profits of other businesses.

(d) Governments finance war, involving products such as bombs that do not compete in the marketplace but are designed to be destroyed.[339]

In China, workers are paid to build high-rises for which there is little market. This is similar to Keynes' proposition that workers could be paid to dig ditches and fill them back up, and it would serve to create the demand necessary to stimulate the economy. But simply paying people a social dividend, as Douglas proposed, would work just as well and would save a lot of unnecessary use of labor and materials.

Thwarted by Politics and the Banks

Douglas' innovative ideas resonated with the beleaguered farmers of Alberta, who voted the Social Credit Party into power and kept it there for 35 years—the longest any political party retained a majority in Alberta.[340] Yet the revolutionary policies Douglas proposed never actually got implemented. According to Frances Hutchinson in *Understanding the Financial System: Social Credit Rediscovered* (2010), politicians elected on a Social Credit platform wound up rejecting Douglas' teachings and pursuing Social Credit policies in name only. Political interests dominated by conventional banking thwarted his policies at every turn.[341]

Douglas anticipated all this. He wrote in 1935:

> Since the application of Social Credit principles involves the use of financial credit for the benefit of the general population rather than the banking system, it is certain that the new Government will meet with all opposition that can be provided by International Finance.[342]

Expanding on this point in 1937, he wrote:

> . . . I am convinced that in the case of the ring of international financiers who control the system, the conscious objective is to keep the great mass of the population in fear of poverty and loss of social position; by which I do not necessarily mean in lack of physical necessities, but I do mean that it is intended that they should be kept in constant insecurity and under the threat of grinding toil, even though such toil is not demanded by anything realistic in the situation. In the main this is accomplished by immense misdirection of production

effort—redundant factories, "Public Works", "Fashions", etc.—anything but wanted consumers' goods.

This objective of the financiers could be demonstrated, Douglas said, from the following simple propositions:

(A) Modern life and work cannot be carried on without the use of money;

(B) All money comes into existence as a debt from the community to the money-creating agencies;

(C) The debtor is the servant of the lender until his debt is paid;

(D) The debts owed by the community to the money-lending agencies are increasing in geometrical ratio, and can never possibly be paid off, since the amount of money in existence at any time in the possession of the community is only a microscopic fraction of the debts held against them by the money-lending agencies.

The good news, said Douglas, was that "money" was not "wealth." The crisis of scarcity and debt was an artificial one. "The debts owed by the community to the money-lending agencies are assuming astronomical proportion," yet "they are quite small in comparison with the real wealth of the community measured in the same units."[343]

Once the mathematical flaw in the monetary scheme was understood and the system was set right, Douglas foresaw a new Age of Leisure. The real wealth of the community had increased enormously with mechanization, and industrialized production would soon require only a fraction of the available work force. But for most people, the Age of Leisure Douglas envisioned has not yet arrived. The dividends from mechanization and other technological advances have not been shared among the populace but have been expropriated by the financial rentiers Douglas sought to expose.

The Alberta Experience: Confusion in the Ranks

It was one thing to talk theory; quite another to get it implemented. Douglas's policies were up against not only what he saw as intentional attempts to thwart them, but the failure of even his followers to thoroughly understand them. His vision was for the government to create the money needed to fill the gap in demand by issuing social credit directly, essentially by just printing it. William Aberhart, the charismatic leader of the Social Credit Party, thought that paying a national dividend required either raising taxes or adding to the public debt, something the province could not afford.[344]

Insights into the challenges of the day come from Derryl Hermanutz, a native Albertan who encountered Douglas's writings during the post-1982 Alberta recession and, after intensive study, became deeply impressed with the straightforward arithmetic logic of Social Credit monetary thinking. He explains the political developments of that period like this:

> In 1935 Alberta elected a nominally Social Credit provincial government, but Premier William Aberhart either didn't understand the basis of social credit as a fundamentally different monetary system, or he thought he could get its benefits without first having to win a battle against the bankers. Banking (the creation and allocation of credit money) is a federal jurisdiction in Canada, and Aberhart's social credit legislation was legally challenged, blocked, and ultimately ruled ultra vires (unconstitutional) with the support of the federal Mackenzie King government. Aberhart's government did issue two "dividend checks" to Albertans, but issuing money is a "banking" function and Aberhart was ultimately forced to accept orthodox bankster finance. So Alberta never actually implemented a social credit system.
>
> The central Canadian shills for the Bay Street bankers derided social credit "funny money," and emotionally powerful slogans like that are far more effective moulders of public opinion than is reasoned argument. There is a long history of animosity between Alberta and Ottawa, as the federal government has historically represented the central Canadian money and corporate interests who exploited Alberta (and the West generally) in a colonial fashion. "Political" colonialism may no longer be in vogue in the 21st century, but "financial" and "industrial" colonialism, which has always been the driver

and objective of political colonialism, is alive and flourishing as never before.

. . . The tried and true response is, "If you can't beat 'em, join 'em." Nothing is stopping governments from starting their own banks, funding socially useful and desirable projects, and paying the interest to themselves instead of to Wall Street bankers. Where monetary reform fails, public banking can succeed. That's what Alberta ended up doing after its efforts to implement social credit were thwarted by the banker friendly Canadian Federal government.[345]

If You Can't Beat 'Em, Join 'Em:
The Alberta Treasury Branches

When the resourceful Social Credit government was blocked from advancing "social credit" outright, it did the next best thing: it formed a financial institution that created money as credit on its books, as all banks do. The Alberta Treasury Branches (ATB) were actually part of the Alberta Treasury, a department of the provincial government. According to an ATB publication called "Albertans Investing in Alberta, 1938-1998," the goal of the ATB was to "provide the people with alternative facilities for gaining access to their credit resources."[346]

The private banking community scoffed at this attempt by the government to compete, but the ATB proved to be an overnight success. Albertans rushed to deposit their meager savings in the Treasury Branches, hoping that this new system would help solve their economic woes. The ATB grew from six branches in 1938 to more than 150 branches and agencies by the end of World War II. Deposits grew from C$763,000 in 1939 to more than C$24 million in 1946. By the mid-1940s, the temporary Treasury Branches had become an important part of Alberta's economy.

The services the ATB provided were at first simple ones. There were no loans. Branches just accepted deposits into current accounts or term savings accounts, paying 1.5 percent to 3 percent interest, depending on the term. The ATB also sold automobile, hunting and fishing licenses, and hail and crop insurance.

In a ploy reminiscent of the medieval bankers' transfers "in bank," the ATB encouraged Albertans to use NonNegotiable Transfer Vouchers as an alternative to bank checks for transferring credits. A penalty of 2 percent was charged for cash withdrawals. In this way, the money supply was expanded without either "printing" or "coining" money, and with little need to borrow additional hard currency from outside the ATB system.

Civil servants were paid mainly in Transfer Vouchers, and they were encouraged to deal with the Treasury Branches instead of the banks. The vouchers were good only at the ATB, and customers got a 3 percent bonus if they used them to buy products that were at least 33 percent made in Alberta. The slogan was, "What Alberta Makes, Makes Alberta." The Treasury Branches promoted Alberta-made goods in order to create local employment, increase local purchasing power and provide wider markets for Alberta's agricultural products. The bonuses rewarded loyal customers for their faith in the program, and the Transfer Vouchers expanded the local money supply, just as community currencies do today. Nearly C$500,000 were paid out as bonuses and Transfer Vouchers before the program ended in 1945.

Like the Commonwealth Bank of Australia, the ATB boldly competed with Alberta's private commercial banks. According to an Alberta government publication entitled "These Are the Facts: An Authentic Record of Alberta's Progress, 1935-1948":

> The Treasury Branch system enables the people to pool their financial resources and to use these resources for their mutual benefit thereby enabling them to progressively free themselves from the stranglehold of the existing financial monopoly. These Treasury Branches provide effective competition for chartered banks thereby ensuring banking services at reasonable rates. At some points the Treasury Branches provide the *only* service available to the public.[347]

By 1950, the Treasury Branches had captured about a tenth of Alberta's loans, something they achieved by charging an interest rate that was 1 percent lower than the private banks.' Loans grew from C$7 million in 1947 to just over C$28 million in 1959. ATB set itself apart by offering financial services in areas that private banks did not consider profitable, and by delivering government services and information to remote parts of the sprawling province.

Subverted by Politics, Big Business and Oil

The political scene changed in 1943, when Aberhart died unexpectedly and was succeeded by his former disciple Ernest Manning. Manning gradually transformed the government into a right-wing party that was opposed more to "socialism" than to the banks. He abandoned further ambitions of instituting Social Credit and committed instead to restoring the province's credit rating. By 1945, all foreign debt had been repaid; and by 1949, all domestic debt had been repaid. When oil was discovered at Leduc in 1947, Manning invited American investors to exploit the province's abundant oil and gas reserves. Pipelines began moving Alberta's oil and gas to distant markets.[348]

Still cautious from the hard times of the 1930s, the ATB's administrators continued to operate the Treasury Branches conservatively, and they made steady profits. Deposits more than doubled, increasing from C$26 million in 1947 to more than C$58 million in 1959.

By 1969, the ATB was the dominant lending institution outside the major cities. It returned its profits to the Alberta government, averaging more than C$1 million a year during this period. Profits topped out at over C$2.6 million in 1972-73.

In 1977, the Treasury Branches had more than C$1 billion on deposit, and in 1979 they made an unprecedented C$17 million in profits on gross assets of C$1.5 billion. Returns to the Alberta Treasury were spectacular: more than C$2.5 million in 1974, C$4.5 million in 1975, C$6 million in 1976, C$6.1 million in 1977, C$5 million in 1978 and over C$10 million in 1979.[349]

In 1971, the Social Credit Party was finally ousted from its 35-year reign by the Conservative Party. As Derryl Hermanutz cynically describes this coup, "The Alberta Treasury Branches were basically taken out of 'public service' and converted into bankster replicas."

The Conservative Provincial Cabinet pressured the Treasury Branches to make unwise loans to companies that were affiliated with politicians. In the late 1980s, ATB was the subject of scandal when some major clients defaulted on loans that had been granted for political reasons.

In the 1990s, the government reformed ATB so that it was a competitive financial institution with an independent board of directors. Critics today complain that it is too independent, operating at arms' length from the government while retaining its government privileges, including its tax-free status and government guarantees.[350]

In its heyday, however, the government-owned ATB was an innovative mechanism for providing banking and credit facilities to struggling farmers and small businessmen at affordable interest. It has been called the most significant surviving remnant of social credit economic policies in Alberta.[351] For several decades, at least, the ATB succeeded in turning credit into a public utility.

Chapter 19

THE RESERVE BANK OF NEW ZEALAND AND KIWIBANK

"The banks do create money. They have been doing it for a long time, but they didn't realise it, and they did not admit it. . . . [I]n the intervening years . . . there has been a development of thought, until today I doubt very much whether you would get many prominent bankers to attempt to deny that banks create it."

— H. W. White, Chairman of the Associated Banks of New Zealand, to the New Zealand Monetary Commission, 1955

The Social Credit proposals of C. H. Douglas never got implemented in Alberta, but they did take root in New Zealand. Like the Commonwealth Bank of Australia, the Reserve Bank of New Zealand later got captured by the central bank system overseen by the Bank of England. But in its early years, it was able to do remarkable things simply by issuing credit backed by the productivity of the country. More recently, the New Zealand government has engaged in another experiment in public banking with its national postal bank, Kiwibank.

Like the Bank of Canada, the Reserve Bank of New Zealand (RBNZ) was privately owned when it was first established in 1934. It was launched following a visit from the same Sir Otto Niemeyer who brought the Commonwealth Bank of Australia into the British central bank empire. He intended for the RBNZ to fall in line as well, but a strong populist Social Credit movement thwarted the plan.

In a controversial tract called *All These Things* (1936), New Zealand journalist A. N. Field described the events following the visit of Sir Niemeyer and Professor Theodor Emanuel Gugenheim Gregory in 1930. In a follow-up report, Niemeyer urged the government to establish a private corporation to control the volume of currency and credit in the country. He advised that:

> [T]his privately owned central reserve bank should be given a permanent monopoly of all the Government's "money, remittance, exchange and banking transactions." He further proposed that the Government should find a million sterling for the working capital of the bank, in respect of which sum it would hold no shares and have no voice in the management; and that half a million should be obtained by the issue of shares to the public, the holders of such shares to be the owners of the bank. In the original Bill as introduced it was left open to foreigners to own the bank, though only shareholders who were British subjects resident in New Zealand had votes at bank meetings. Furthermore, the share list was not open to inspection and ownership of the institution was thus secret.

Field traced this very banker-friendly proposal to the same 1922 conference in Genoa, Italy, referred to by Jack Lang. In attendance, according to Field, were Bank of England Governor Montagu Norman, the Governor of the Bank of France, the Governor of the Federal Reserve Bank of New York, and other international bankers. Field wrote:

> This conference resolved that central reserve banks should be set up in all countries where they were not already in existence. This work was thereafter steadily proceeded with and such banks have been established throughout almost the whole world.
>
> . . . Mr. Einzig, conductor of London's "Financial Review," proceeds to tell us that: "Another condition on which Mr. Norman and his collaborators insisted was that the central banks should be independent of their governments." . . . Sir Otto Niemeyer in his report said we ought to have a reserve

bank to co-operate with the reserve banks of other countries as these banks had "no single point of contact in New Zealand."

. . . A message from Basle, Switzerland, published in the London "Times" of April 9, 1934, in reporting a meeting of [the Bank for International Settlements], said: "The newly-established [Reserve] Bank of Canada and Bank of New Zealand are empowered by their Governments to buy B.I.S. shares and to make deposits at the bank as soon as the stabilization of the respective currencies will allow."

"This shows," said Field, "that these reserve banks were established as part of the network of an international money trust."

The plan was for the RBNZ to be a private banking corporation issuing and controlling the national currency and credit, hooked into a network of similar corporations globally. But as in Australia, the people had other ideas.

In 1935, New Zealand elected its first Labor Government, led by Michael Joseph Savage. Considered New Zealand's most popular prime minister ever, Savage was a Social Credit sympathizer. He was the architect of free education and health care, pensions, free milk in schools, and other popular social programs. In 1936, he nationalized the central bank that Niemeyer had intended to bring into the private global banking hierarchy. According to New Zealand journalist Dr. Kerry Bolton, writing in 2011:

> [W]ith a popular electoral mandate, financial orthodoxy and the rule of the Bank of England were thrown out during the 1934 General Election and in 1936 *the First Labour Government was able to reduce unemployment by 75 percent by the one act of issuing Reserve Bank credit at 1 percent and 1.5 percent to fund state housing.*[352]

Bolton says the election of a Labor Government largely centered on its platform of nationalizing the Reserve Bank and issuing "state credit." This platform was a response to popular demand, following a lecture tour by C.H. Douglas in 1934. But as is typical with election promises, Savage and his finance minister Walter Nash were dragging their feet in fulfilling them. The real driver behind the Social Credit program, says Bolton, was the flamboyant, one armed war veteran John A. Lee, who kept up a continuous agitation for it.[353]

Lee actually pressed for more radical reforms than Douglas would have approved himself. He wanted the "immediate control by the State of the entire banking system," including the "state issue of credit for production and distribution of commodities." Conventional Social Credit theory was opposed to bank nationalization, but Lee wrote pragmatically:

> A planned economy will be of little use if the Government has not the power to carry its plans into effect. Such power will require the control of credit which, if it remains in private hands, can be used to thwart the will of the Government.

In 1936, the "independent" central bank launched on the Bank of England model was bought by the government from its private stockholders, netting them a tidy profit. The Bank came under state control, and the board of directors became "the direct servant of the Government of the day," obliged to fulfill the policies of the government, subject to removal if it did not. The Bank's function as set out in an Amendment Bill was to "regulate and control credit and currency in New Zealand" for the "economic and social welfare of New Zealand."

In 1937, according to Bolton:

> Lee stated that the Government's powers had been used cautiously, but that state credit was being provided to the dairy industry account, . . . and hence there was a guaranteed price for farmers. The Reserve Bank issued the dairy industry state credit, at minor profit, where hitherto the private banks had gained through interest, with the additional factor that the profits that were made by the State on these advances were placed back into a Consolidated Fund. *The aim was to eventually reduce the amount of interest to a charge for costs.*

These achievements were revolutionary as far as they went, but the government was still caught in the debt trap:

> The Government was still borrowing from overseas moneylenders, a matter that was never resolved. Lee warned that unless the State assumed sole responsibility for creating and issuing credit, "the debt will be compounded forever" and that "at some future date the Capitalist bailiff will liquidate New

Zealand's social experiment." That is precisely what happened, ironically, when a "free market revolution" proceeded decades later under a Labour Government, in a typical example of socialists playing lackey to international finance. New Zealand is still in the process of divesting itself of what few state assets remain to pay off debt.[354]

The State Housing Project: "The Most Important Factor in Housing Costs Is the Price of Money"

According to Lee's 1937 report, the State Housing Project was the only program for which the State had actually issued its own money as of that date. The project was detailed in a 1949 publication by the New Zealand Ministry of Works titled *State Housing in New Zealand*. It said:

> To finance its comprehensive proposals, the Government adopted the somewhat unusual course of using Reserve Bank credit, thus recognizing that *the most important factor in housing costs is the price of money* – interest is the heaviest portion in the composition of ordinary rent. The newly created Department was able therefore to obtain the use of funds at the lowest possible rate of interest, the rate being 1 percent for the first £10 million advanced, and one and a half percent on further advances. *The sums advanced by the Reserve Bank were not subscribed or underwritten by other financial institutions. This action shaped the Government's intention to demonstrate that it is possible for the State to use the country's credit in creating new assets for the country.*[355]

Recall the research of Dr. Margrit Kennedy discussed in Chapter 1, showing the average cost of interest to be about 77 percent for public housing, and 35 percent to 40 percent for all public projects.[356] That means infrastructure projects that might not appear to be cost-effective, such as low cost housing, alternative energy development, and public transportation, could be not only self-sustaining but quite profitable if funded interest-free through the government's own bank.

In *The Modern Universal Paradigm* (2007), Rodney Shakespeare and Tarek El-Diwany give the example of the Humber Bridge, which was built in the UK at a cost of £98 million. Every year since the bridge opened in 1981, it turned an operating profit; that is, its running costs (basically repair, maintenance and staff salaries) were exceeded by the fees it received from travelers crossing the River Humber. But by the time the bridge opened in 1981, interest charges had driven its cost up to £151 million; and by 1992, only 10 years later, the debt had shot up to a breath-taking £439 million. The UK government was forced to intervene with sizeable grants and writeoffs to save the local residents from bearing the brunt of these costs. If the bridge had been financed with interest-free government-issued money, these costs could have been avoided and the bridge could have funded itself.[357]

The New Zealand public housing project was a win-win-win: the people got low-cost housing, the government got a producing asset, and the unemployed got jobs—enough to reduce unemployment by 75 percent. In a 2004 article on the State Housing Project in New Zealand's *Guardian Political Review*, Stan Fitchett wrote that he had confirmed with banking experts that this approach would not be inflationary if attempted today. The RBNZ could create 100 million New Zealand dollars for new houses without noticeably impacting the money supply, since the sum was only one-half of one percent of what was already being added annually by private commercial banks.[358] In 2004, the money supply increased by 18.5 billion New Zealand dollars, or 16.8 percent; and 97 percent of this increase came from commercial bank lending.

In funding the State Housing Project, the New Zealand central bank was doing something similar to the "quantitative easing" (QE) engaged in by central banks today, but with this difference: the housing project actually got money into the circulating money supply. The problem with QE as currently practiced by central bankers is that the money gets no further than the reserve accounts of banks. (More on this in Chapter 35.)

How the RBNZ Used Its Credit Power, and Why It Stopped

According to New Zealand money reformer John Rawson, it was not only low-cost housing for which the RBNZ issued national currency directly. The dairy industry, other farm industries, and the government itself were allowed to borrow at low interest directly from the RBNZ, in a way that actually increased the money supply. He cites *The Report of the Royal Commission on Monetary, Banking and Credit Systems* (NZ) 1956, Section 157 (c), stating that the volume of money is increased:

> . . . *When the Reserve Bank makes a loan to the Government or marketing authorities.* At first the borrower's deposits at the Reserve Bank are increased, and when the money is spent the recipients may lodge part of it in their accounts at the trading banks and retain part of it in circulation in the form of notes and coins.

John Rawson described in private correspondence how the RBNZ came to embark on this practice, and why it was abandoned:

> The first Labour Government, elected in 1935, had about a third of its Members of Parliament who were monetary reformers. Not all Social Crediters, but with very similar views.
>
> That government used Reserve Bank credit to finance road building, etc., building of state rental houses, financing some local bodies and also the dairy industry with loans at 1 percent. The dairy industry was very important to general agriculture then, even more than now. New Zealand also came out of World War II with no overseas debt, although we also had about the highest proportion of men in the armed forces overseas of any Allied nation.
>
> People like the late Prof. John Hotson acknowledged that New Zealand helped lead the world out of recession by these policies.
>
> *Then the Bank of England threatened the government with dire consequences if they continued these "silly policies."* Minister of finance Walter Nash, more or less leader of the party's Socialist faction, capitulated and the Party was split, the Socialists kicking out the monetary reformers by one vote.

Nash was later involved in the Bretton Woods agreement, setting up the World Bank and IMF. He came back to New Zealand with his head completely "turned," stating he "belonged to the world" rather than New Zealand. He was later Prime Minister.

In 1984 the then Labour Government brought in draconian monetarist policies, more extreme than our supposed "right wing" party would have, and by abandoning their own people and capturing a lot of votes from the "right," got a second term to wreck things still further. We are still suffering from shortages of skilled people resulting from cuts about that time, among other results.

Bob Beresford, another money reformer native to New Zealand, adds that many soldiers were settled on their own new farms after World War II with loans that were at 1 percent interest and had long payment terms. But the Savage government, swayed by misguided fears of inflation planted by finance minister Nash, made loans through the central bank rather than issuing money outright, as C. H. Douglas had recommended. Loans even at low interest must be repaid and therefore do not solve the problem of the "gap" – the difference between collective wages and the collective price of the products on the market. To correct that problem, according to Social Credit theory, money must actually be added to the money supply.

The Deficit Hawks, Privatization, and the IMF Protection Racket

Today, little money is created by the RBNZ. Both the government and the banks must borrow offshore, which always involves more money going out than coming in. The effect is to shrink the money supply, leaving insufficient money to pay down debts and conduct trade, propelling the economy into debt deflation and austerity. In New Zealand as elsewhere, the international lenders are now in charge. The role of austerity police once played by Otto Niemeyer and the Bank of England is now being played by such organizations as the International Monetary Fund and the Bank for International Settlements.

In a revealing February 2011 article titled "The IMF Protection Racket," Dr. Stuart Jeanne Bramhall, another New Zealander, compared the IMF to the mafia. The IMF demands government cutbacks and privatization of public assets, she says, not just for loans but for "protection"—in this case, against the draconian axe of the privately-owned rating agencies. Downgrades can destroy a currency or a country, as was recently demonstrated in the Eurozone. Dr. Bramhall says the IMF pressured New Zealand in this way, although the nation's debt was quite low:

> The IMF came knocking on our door in April 2010, issuing a warning that our public debt was too high and that we needed to (further) reduce public spending on education, health care and social services . . . .
>
> Given New Zealand's low debt to GDP ratio (currently 20 percent, in contrast to a U.S. debt to GDP ratio of 86 percent), many Kiwi economists were surprised by the IMF "warning" our country received. . . . Prior to the global economic collapse, New Zealand had both a budget surplus and a debt to GDP ratio of 6 percent. A second world country in many respects, New Zealand was one of the few industrialized countries that didn't implement economic bail-outs for banks or a rescue package for jobless workers or families losing their homes. Moreover at the time the IMF issued their warning, our government had already laid off 1500 public service workers.
>
> At the same time, the ominous implications of the warning were clear—if we failed to implement more spending cuts, the international credit ratings agencies would downgrade our AA+ credit rating to BBB- (like Iceland and Greece) and private lenders would jack up our interest rates and either bankrupt us or force us to borrow from the IMF (like Greece and Ireland) and agree to draconian "austerity" cuts in health care, education and other public services.
>
> In the end, New Zealand declined to end subsidized GP [doctor] visits and student loan rebates, as the IMF demanded. The response of our National-led (conservative) government was to (predictably) lower income taxes for the wealthy, increase the sales tax (which covers everything) from 12 to

15 percent and to continue to fire public sector workers. They have also signaled their intention to make substantial cuts (which will seriously cripple education and health care) in July 2011. . . . [T]hey also plan to raise money by selling off (privatizing) state-owned utilities and possibly the post office and our government-owned Kiwi-bank. [359]

Why, asked Dr. Bramhall, do governments borrow from the IMF at all? She wrote:

Since the 2008 economic collapse, all industrialized countries have been running large deficits. And because it's political suicide to raise taxes on the rich, they borrow the money they need to run government services from Wall Street investment banks.

But this puts governments at the mercy of the creditors:

With a low credit rating, Goldman Sachs can jack your interest rate as high as 8 percent, and your country goes broke trying to make the interest payments.

When the private credit market fails, the IMF steps in, not to "rescue" the country but to impose "conditionalities" designed to privatize public assets and open the country to purchase by foreign interests:

There is an immediate demand for your government to slash public spending – on education, health care, social services and basic needs, such as clean drinking water. Forcing a country to privatize their public water services immediately creates a market for a multinational water monopoly to move in. Likewise forcing them to privatize health services (all industrialized countries, except for the US, have national health systems) creates more favorable markets for drug and health insurance companies.

The obvious alternative is for governments either to issue the money they need directly or to borrow from their own central banks interest-free. But in New Zealand, as in Canada, that option has largely been abandoned. New Zealanders, like Albertans, have therefore done the next best thing—opened a chain of local, publicly-owned banks.

Kiwibank:
An Innovative Experiment in Postal Banking

Kiwibank is a public postal bank launched in 2002 to compete with the large foreign banks dominating the banking industry in New Zealand. Australian banks control at least 80 percent of the country's retail banking, with interest and profits winding up in foreign bank accounts, shrinking the money supply in New Zealand. In order to maximize their profits, these large foreign banks closed their less profitable branches, especially in rural areas, creating hardships for many New Zealand families and small businesses.

Responding to that need, in 2002 the New Zealand government launched its own state-owned bank. They named it Kiwibank after the national symbol, the kiwi bird. To keep costs low while still providing services in communities throughout New Zealand, Kiwibank was established as a subsidiary of the government-owned New Zealand Post. Bank branches were opened in the national post offices already dotting the countryside. This was not a new idea, since a post office savings bank branch had once been in every post office.

A promotional description on the Kiwibank website states:

> Back in 2002, we launched with a thought: New Zealand needs a better banking alternative—a bank that provides real value for money, that has Kiwi values at heart, and that keeps Kiwi money where it belongs—right here, in New Zealand.
>
> So we set up shop in PostShops throughout the country, putting us in more locations than any other bank in New Zealand literally overnight (without wasting millions on new premises!).[360]

When New Zealanders suddenly had a choice in banking, they voted with their feet. In an early "move your money" campaign, in its first five years Kiwibank drew 500,000 customers away from the big banks, an impressive number in an island nation of only 4 million people. Kiwibank consistently earns the nation's highest customer satisfaction ratings, forcing the Australian-owned banks to improve their service in order to compete. Prime Minister John Key had to promise repeatedly to voters that Kiwibank would not be sold, a testament both to its popularity and to the pressure being levied by big foreign banks to remove this competitive thorn from their sides.[361]

In its early years, Kiwibank borrowed from its own depositors and serviced its own loans. But with a change of governments in 2008, according to Bob Beresford, it is now borrowing heavily abroad and delegating loan servicing to American giant GE Capital. The postal bank remains competitive, however, and it continues to service local markets. How the United States might save its own bankrupt post office by expanding into postal banking services is explored in Chapter 34.

Chapter 20

JAPAN AND GERMANY BREAK THE SHACKLES OF INTEREST – AND PAY THE PRICE

"[It is] a war of financiers and fools, though most people, on the Allied side at any rate, do not yet see very clearly how financiers come into it."

-- Hasting W. S. Russell, Duke of Bedford, ca. 1939[362]

Germany and Japan have been heavily stigmatized for the aggressions of World War II, but there are two sides to every story. In the 1930s, both countries funded their economies with interest-free national credit rather than borrowing from international banks. Thus freed from the debt trap, they became economic powerhouses. Some historians of the period say they threatened international banking interests. They were not members of the British Commonwealth, so more was needed than just the friendly visit from the Mafia boss to bring them around. . . .

It was not just Canada and New Zealand that were influenced in the 1930s by the innovative approach to finance of Major C. H. Douglas. The Japanese also took to his logical mathematical theories. They used these insights, however, in a way of which he disapproved. He declared in a speech in Sydney, Australia, in 1934:

> There is a very completely instructed population, or section of the population, in Japan; I know it because they pirated my books. There is very little doubt that the tremendous advance in Japanese export trade which amounted to an increase of 53 percent in one year – such an increase as has never been known in the history of industry – is an example of working the Douglas Scheme upside down, *subsidizing exports for sale much below the cost and making up the difference to the manufacturer out of the national credit. We know for a fact that the same thing is happening in China.* My books have been translated into both Chinese and Japanese.[363]

The part of the Douglas Scheme that the Japanese had so enthusiastically adopted was the transfer of the money-creating power to the government. Japanese products could be sold below market and the government could make up the difference, simply by advancing credit on its books. In Douglas' Social Credit philosophy, goods were to be locally produced for local consumption as far as possible; but the Japanese were using the state's money-creating power to subsidize exports and for other national purposes, eventually including the finance of war.

This Japanese version of social credit was explored by Stephen M. Goodson, a former director of the South African Reserve Bank, in a November 2008 article titled "The Real Reason the Japanese Attacked Pearl Harbor." He wrote that during the 1930s, Japan rapidly expanded its industrial production, while most of the rest of the world stagnated. By 1941, it had become the leading economic power in East Asia, and its exports were steadily replacing those of America and England. Goodson linked this feat to the 1929 lecture tour of Major C. H. Douglas:

> Douglas's economic theory advocated the transfer of the money creation process from private banks, which create money out of nothing as an interest-bearing debt, to the state.
>
> This government-created money he termed social credit. He also favored the payment of a basic income or national dividend to each citizen. This dividend would provide consumers with

the additional buying power necessary to absorb all the current production of goods in a non-inflationary manner.

Douglas's financial proposals for an honest money system, based on government creating the nation's money and credit on an interest-free basis, were enthusiastically received by Japanese industry and government. All Douglas's books and pamphlets were translated into Japanese, and more copies were sold in that country than in all the rest of the world put together.[364]

The effects on the Japanese economy, says Goodson, were dramatic:

Once the shackles of usury had been removed, sustained improvement took place in the Japanese economy. During the 1931-41 period manufacturing output and industrial production increased by 140 percent and 136 percent respectively, while national income and Gross National Product (GNP) were up by 241 percent and 259 percent respectively. These remarkable increases exceeded by a wide margin the economic growth of the rest of the industrialized world. In the labor market unemployment declined from 5.3 percent in 1930 to 3.0 percent in 1938.

In 1932, the privately-owned Bank of Japan (Nippon Ginko) was reorganized as a state bank, administered exclusively for the accomplishment of national interests. The reform was completed in 1942 with the Bank of Japan Law, which was modeled on the 1939 Reichsbank Act of Germany. Goodson writes:

The bank was "to assume the task of controlling currency and finance and supporting and promoting the credit system in conformity with policies of the state to ensure the full use of the nation's potential.". . . As for the functions of the bank, the law abolished the old principle of priority for commercial finance, empowering it to supervise facilities for industrial finance. The law also authorized the bank to make unlimited advances to the government without security, and to subscribe for and to absorb government bonds.

Germany in the 1930s:
Looking Beyond the Propaganda

Meanwhile, the German economy was also achieving extraordinary things. Germany had been through a crushing defeat in World War I, followed by massive hyperinflation that bankrupted the country. Yet while the rest of the world was struggling with crippling depression, it managed in a mere four years, from 1933 to 1937, to become the strongest country in Europe. How was this achieved?

Germany was following banking policies similar to Japan's, but they did not come from C. H. Douglas. They originated with a German military lecturer named Gottfried Feder, who formed the Fighting League Against Interest Slavery in 1917. In his *Manifesto for the Breaking of the Bondage of Interest,* published in 1918, Feder maintained that the international banking system got its power from "the effortless and infinite multiplication of wealth which is created by interest." He argued that money "is not and must not be anything but an exchange for labor," and that it must not be given, "through interest, a supernatural power to reproduce itself at the cost of productive labor."[365]

Kerry Bolton, the New Zealand researcher cited earlier, notes that most people have been dissuaded by propaganda and political labels from looking at the German economic model, which was actually quite resourceful. He quotes from Hitler's speech to the Reichstag on January 30, 1939, explaining that Germany had not actually withdrawn from world trade but had bypassed the international financial system by means of barter. Hitler said:

> If ever need makes humans see clearly it has made the German people do so. Under the compulsion of this need we have learned in the first place to take full account of *the most essential capital of a nation, namely, its capacity to work.* All thoughts of gold reserves and foreign exchange fade before the industry and efficiency of well-planned national productive resources.[366]

The concept echoes Abraham Lincoln's assertion that "labor is prior to and independent of capital." If the workers and materials are available, lack of "money" need not limit the government's ability to carry out the work. Money is just a system of credits and debits, a tracking of goods and services delivered and due. The work can be paid for with "Greenbacks" or "state credits," which serve as money in the community.

Bolton cites European correspondent Bertram D. Colonna, writing in the Labor-oriented New Zealand *Mirror* in 1938. DeColonna said that because capital and gold reserves were not available, the German government had decided to issue and assume control of currency and credit. One million marks of state credit were issued to finance public works, including state housing. "The bankers prophesied speedy bankruptcy. Those prophecies proved utterly wrong . . ." State credit was issued by newly created state banks. "The new money backed by the credit of the nation was gradually absorbed by the open money market," greatly increasing state revenue without the need to increase taxation. Private banks were placed under state supervision and the rate of interest was limited by law.[367] Writes Bolton:

> De Colonna pointed out that *the state money was in no way inflationary* (a frequent objection against such schemes by orthodox economists). The issue of credit and new money "is based upon the actual production of real wealth," through greater industrial output. De Colonna stated that after five years of pursuing this policy it had proven its worth in keeping money in constant circulation; "after all that is the only use of money – to circulate and exchange the wealth produced by the nation."

The result, according to British historian Prof. A.J.P. Taylor, was "to give Germany practically a monopoly of trade with south-eastern Europe; and similar plans were being prepared for the economic conquest of South America when the outbreak of war interrupted them."[368]

Bolton also cites Hasting W. S. Russell, Marquis of Tavistock and later 12th Duke of Bedford, writing at the beginning of World War II. A pacifist and money reformer, he saw the impetus for the war in the threat Germany posed to the "financial racket" of the international bankers. He said:

> Financiers . . . desired war as a means of overthrowing their rivals and consolidating still further their immense power. . . . Hitler not only engaged in barter trade which meant no discount profits for bankers arranging bills of exchange, but

he even went so far as to declare that a country's real wealth consisted in its ability to produce goods; nor, when men and material were available, would he ever allow lack of money to be an obstacle in the way of any project which he considered to be in his country's interests. *This was rank heresy in the eyes of the financiers of Britain and America, a heresy which, if allowed to spread, would blow the gaff on the whole financial racket.*[369]

Goodson agrees with this version of events. He writes:

> Both the Bank of Japan and the German Reichsbank, with their systems of state creation of the money supply at zero interest, and the inevitability that those systems of finance would be replicated by other countries, in particular those of the proposed Greater East Asian Co-prosperity Sphere, posed such a serious threat to the private investors of the U.S. Federal Reserve, that a world war was deemed to be the only means of countering it.[370]

And that, says Goodson, was the real reason the Japanese were blockaded into war:

> In July 1939 the United States unilaterally abrogated the Treaty of Commerce of 1911, thereby restricting Japan's ability to import essential raw materials. . . . By means of the economic blockade, a noose was being placed around Japan's neck. . . .
>
> After numerous diplomatic initiatives, including the offer of a summit on August 8, 1941 had failed, Japan was forced into attacking America in order to maintain her prosperity and secure her existence as a sovereign state.

From Hawk to Dove

Germany and Japan went down to defeat; and in 1947, a new Japanese Constitution was signed. Sometimes referred to as the "Peace Constitution," it expressly forbade the government to go to war, and denied Japan the right to have anything beyond purely defensive military forces. Article 9 of the Japanese Constitution states that "the Japanese people forever renounce war as a sovereign right and the threat of use of force as means of settling disputes," and that offensive armed forces "will never be maintained."[371]

Overt defiance of the international bankers was obviously not a prudent policy. But that did not necessarily mean the Japanese would give up their successful economic policies. They just needed to go about them more discreetly. They had to play by international banking rules, or appear to be playing by them. Goodson writes:

> One of the first acts of the U.S. occupation forces in Japan in September 1945 was to restructure the Japanese banking system so as to make it compliant with the norms of the international bankers, i.e. usury. The unrestricted financing of the state by the Bank of Japan was abolished and the large industrial combines, the zaibatsus, were dismantled.[372]

The Japanese government could no longer use its central bank to create money and credit directly. Like Alberta and New Zealand, it therefore did the next best thing: it turned to its publicly-owned banks to create money as credit on their books.

Chapter 21

JAPAN POST BANK AND THE "SECOND BUDGET": TURNING THE PEOPLE'S SAVINGS INTO PUBLIC REVENUE

"The reality is we issue a massive amount of Japan government bonds and we need someone to buy them—we should be thankful the Post Office is willing to buy."

-- Financial Services Minister Shizuka Kamei, defending his decision in 2010 not to privatize Japan Post Bank[373]

When the Japanese government was restricted from issuing money directly, it did the next best thing: it borrowed from its own bank, which created the money as credit on its books. But the bank the government used for this purpose was not its "independent" central bank, the Bank of Japan, which was in a decades-long struggle with the government for power. Rather, it was Japan Post, the national postal bank. The struggle for control continues to this day, with Japan Post caught in the middle.

The use of the Japanese Postal Savings System (JPB) to fund the government without taxing the people is similar to President Franklin Roosevelt's use of the Reconstruction Finance Corporation for that purpose. But in the Japanese version, the government-owned financing entity is actually a bank, having the powers of a bank to advance credit by double-entry bookkeeping. No bonds need to be sold to outsiders. The whole operation occurs in-house, using the deposited savings of the Japanese people.

According to a University of Leipzig discussion paper called "Behold the 'Behemoth'—The Privatization of Japan Post Bank," Japan's public banking sector was already fully developed by the end of World War II. It had a postal banking system that went back to 1875. The postal banks were a popular place for the Japanese people to park their savings, and they had built up a massive deposit base. This pool of funds formed the basis of a unique and opaque system of borrowing and lending sometimes referred to as "Japan's second budget." [374]

The postal savings banks competed with private savings banks, which paid higher interest rates but were considered less safe than the government's banks. Postal savings banks specialized in offering small accounts for low-income households. They were attractive to savers because they offered special time deposits on quite favorable terms. The result was a massive accumulation of publicly-held household savings, which were channeled by the government to wherever the money was needed. The funding arrangement was formalized after the Second World War as a system called FILP (Fiscal Investment and Loan Plan), which turned postal services into a huge, opaque pool for funding local governments, government-affiliated public companies, and specialized government lending institutions. Lending was guided by the Ministry of Finance (MoF), the government body in charge of public finance and monetary affairs. *Funds allocated to FILP did not place a burden on the taxpayers, and they did not require parliamentary approval.*

The depositors' savings remained available to the depositors on short notice without penalty, even when they had at the same time been lent out. The system worked because most people left their money in the bank, so there was always plenty to shift around in the pool. People's savings remained very liquid, and interest-rate risks were reduced. What distinguished the system from the creation of credit by private banks was that this credit was directly accessible by the government for public use. Many countries have government-sponsored loan programs, but the Japanese program was remarkable for its size. By 2001, the FILP program involved over 400 trillion yen, *a sum equal to 82 percent of Japan's GDP. Nearly half the government's spending was funded by borrowing from the savings accounts of the Japanese people themselves.*

Attack of the Vulture Capitalists

Like Germany, which managed to arise Phoenix-like from the ashes of both World War I and World War II, Japan had risen to become an economic powerhouse by the late 1980s. To many observers, it seemed poised to take over the world. Japan's exports of vehicles, consumer electronics and other goods had achieved global dominance. The Japanese used their export earnings to buy Midwest farmland, Pebble Beach, and Rockefeller Center. Americans feared they might soon be working for Japanese companies or run out of business by them. Even more threatening to international interests, Japan was the world's largest creditor country, a position it retains today despite its later vicissitudes.[375]

In 1988, the Japanese economy then suddenly took a dive. Housing was in a major bubble, and the Bank for International Settlements supplied the pin, issuing a "Basel Accord" that raised bank capital requirements from 6 percent to 8 percent.[376] Japan's banks were less well capitalized than other banks, and the higher capital requirement forced them to cut back on lending. As credit collapsed, so did the housing market, creating a property-led recession in Japan like the one that would follow in the United States two decades later. (The U.S. recession has also been traced to a Basel Accord. More on this in Chapter 28.)

In 1990, Japan's soaring stock market dropped by 32 percent, and it continued its downward slide through the decade. The squeeze on Japanese banks caused property prices to fall and loans to go into default, as the security for them shriveled up. A downward spiral followed, ending with the insolvency of the banks—or their apparent insolvency. The banking system was actually rescued by the government, and the banks were nationalized; but that word was avoided, in order to prevent arousing criticism.[377]

In the opinion of some critical observers, the squeeze on the Japanese banks by the BIS was an intentional move to cut them down to size.[378] The Bank of Japan, one of the Group of Ten central banks that formed the original Basel Committee on Banking Supervision in 1974, may also have played a role.

The MOF Versus the BOJ: A Decades-long Struggle for Power

Prof. Richard Werner, Director of International Development at the University of Southampton in the UK, advised the Japanese in the 1990s. He maintains that the BOJ has long been at war with the Ministry of Finance for control of the economy. According to a synopsis of his revealing book *Princes of the Yen: Japan's Central Bankers and the Transformation of the Economy* (East Gate Book 2003):

> The post-war disappearance of the military triggered a power struggle between the Ministry of Finance and the Bank of Japan for control over the economy. While the Ministry strove to maintain the controlled economic system that created Japan's post-war economic miracle, the central bank plotted to break free from the Ministry by reverting to the free markets of the 1920s.
>
> . . . The U.S. Occupation had put the central bank insiders into their positions. But they misused them to create a small elite within the central bank that had power over life and death of companies, whole industries, and even the economy. And they had no scruples about using it. They handpicked and groomed their successors early on and called them "Princes." Hiding behind the smoke screen of traditional interest rate policies, the five Princes that ruled post-war Japan remained unaccountable to anyone—neither the prime minister, nor the ministry of finance nor their own governor.
>
> The Princes wanted nothing less than a revolution. They reckoned that the wartime economic system and the vast legal powers of the Ministry of Finance could only be overthrown if there was a large crisis—one that would be blamed on the ministry. While observers assumed that all policy-makers have been trying their best to kick-start Japan's economy over the past decade, the surprising truth is that one key institution

did not try hard at all. To the contrary, the Bank of Japan consistently sabotaged government attempts at creating a recovery during the 1990s.

Not only did the BOJ block recovery in the 1990s, says Werner, but it may have been instrumental in creating the problem in the 1980s:

> [T]hose central bankers who were in charge of the policies that prolonged the recession were the very same people who were responsible for the creation of the bubble. As tape-recorded eyewitness testimonials reveal, the Princes at the Bank of Japan had ordered the banks to expand their lending aggressively during the 1980s. In 1989, the Princes suddenly tightened their credit controls, thus bringing down the house of cards that they had built up before. . . .
>
> With banks paralysed by bad debts, the central bank held the key to a recovery: only it could step in and create more credit. It failed to do so, and hence the recession continued for years. Thanks to the long recession, the Ministry of Finance was broken up and lost its powers. The Bank of Japan became independent and its power has now become legal.[379]

The Battle Over Japan Post

This decades-long power struggle between warring factions helps explain the battle over Japan Post, the source of independent financing for the MOF. Japan Post has long been targeted for privatization, yet it is still in the hands of the government. To bring down the MOF, the BOJ would need to bring down the publicly-owned bank that funds it..

By 2001, the economic woes of the 1990s had allowed Western financial interests to penetrate Japanese markets that were previously closed to them. The merger-and-acquisition market was used to acquire Japanese companies by some of the same financial interests that had helped to cripple these companies. Major public utilities were targeted and were partially or wholly privatized, including the railway, telegraph and telephone companies.[380]

Japan Post was also on the target list. In 2001, it was formed as an independent public corporation, as a first step to privatizing it and selling it off to investors. But it continued to be owned by the government, and employees retained their status as public servants. Government agencies that had relied on FILP loans were encouraged to issue their own securities, and FILP agencies no longer had automatic access to postal savings funds; but Japan Post bought the securities issued by the government agencies, keeping the flow of funds largely unchanged.

That Japan Post Bank has so far refused to go down may be explained by its strategic importance to the Japanese economy. By 2007, it was the largest holder of personal savings in the world, and the largest employer in Japan. It was also the holder of one-fifth of the Japanese national debt in the form of government bonds.[381]

Today, fully 95 percent of Japan's national debt is held domestically by the Japanese themselves, either individually or through their banks.[382] That helps explain how Japan has managed to retain not only its credit rating but its status as the world's third largest economy and largest creditor, *while carrying the largest debt-to-GDP ratio in the world.* In a *CIA Factbook* list of debt-to-GDP ratios of 132 countries in 2010, Japan topped the list at 226 percent, passing even Zimbabwe at 149 percent.[383] Greece and Iceland were fifth and sixth, at 144 percent and 124 percent. Yet Japan's credit rating was still AA, while Greece and Iceland were in the BBB category.[384] Japan has remained impervious to the speculative attacks crippling other countries, because it has not fallen into the trap of dependence on foreign financing. According to Joe Weisenthal, writing in *Business Insider* in February 2010:

> Because Japan's enormous public debt is largely held by its own citizens, the country doesn't have to worry about foreign investors losing confidence.
>
> If there's going to be a run on government debt, it will have to be the result of its own citizens not wanting to fund it anymore. And since many Japanese fund the government via accounts held at the Japan Post Bank—which in turn buys government debt—that institution would be the conduit for a shift to occur.[385]

The Japanese government can afford its enormous debt because the interest it pays to its own banks and its own people is very low.[386] But politicians are under heavy pressure to privatize Japan Post Bank;

and if it is sold off, interest rates are liable to rise. The government could then be plunged into an international debt trap that so far it has largely escaped.

A Tool for Corruption or for Funding without Taxes?

The push to privatize Japan Post was described by Christian Caryl in a March 2011 article in *Foreign Affairs*, a publication of the neoliberal Council on Foreign Relations (CFR). Writing from that perspective, Caryl saw privatization as a good thing:

> Under the Liberal Democratic Party (LDP)—the party whose cadres ruled Japan almost continuously from the party's formation in 1955 to its defeat in a general election two years ago—politicians, bureaucrats, and corporate leaders developed a powerful web of patronage and interconnected interests, which ended up funneling taxpayer money into public works projects of dubious justification.
>
> But . . . Japan's political culture began to change ten years ago, when Junichiro Koizumi, then LDP's leader, won a remarkable election victory by vowing to dismantle his party's entrenched establishment and the vested interests that propped it up. (On the eve of the election, Koizumi famously declared that he would "destroy the LDP.") He pushed through a vital restructuring and privatization of Japan Post, which is not only Japan's postal service but the world's biggest savings bank by assets and the source of much of the funding for public works.[387]

Koizumi tried, at least, to push through the privatization of Japan Post; but as of the start of 2013, its stock is still owned by the government.[388] Privatizing Japan Post would mean eliminating much of the funding for public works. Caryl calls it "funneling taxpayer money into public works," but the money furnished by Japan Post does not come from taxes. It comes from a bank that generates credit from the deposits of Japanese savers, deposits that at the same time remain available for the depositors' own use. The credit is "created out of thin air," just as it was under the more blatant social credit program engaged in by Japan in the 1930s. It allows the government to fund its budget and public programs without turning to the taxpayers, the BOJ, or the private banking system. The MOF has just had to be more discreet about its methods.

Since the FILP shadow budget is "dark," it does pose the risk of patronage and corruption, as Caryl observes. But that problem could be eliminated by making Japan's shadow banking system wholly transparent and accountable, subject to the will of elected parliamentary representatives. With the invention of the Internet, total transparency and public access to information are realistic possibilities today.

"A Mouthwatering Target for Investors"

The FILP system was a major innovation in finance, allowing the government to generate the credit to fund public projects without taxing the people. But that was not the agenda being pursued by Prime Minister Koizumi. When his efforts to privatize Japan Post met with resistance, he vowed to "discipline" opponents. In 2004, he shuffled his Cabinet and appointed reform-minded people as new ministers. He created a new position for Postal Privatization Minister and appointed Heizo Takenaka to the post.[389]

When the Upper House of the Japanese Diet did not pass Koizumi's bills, he dissolved the Lower House and called for a general election. A few weeks later, his postal privatization plan did pass both chambers of the Diet. According to a March 2006 article in *Highbeam Business*:

> By privatizing Japan Post, [Koizumi] aims to break the stranglehold that politicians and bureaucrats have long exercised over the allocation of financial resources in Japan and to inject fresh competition into the country's financial services industry. *His plan also will create a potentially mouthwatering target for domestic and international investors*: Japan Post's savings bank and insurance arms boast combined assets of more than ¥380 trillion ($3.2 trillion) . . . .[390]

A mouthwatering target indeed. To break this $3 trillion asset pool free for investors, the postal savings division was separated from the post office's other arms in a 2007 reorganization, turning Japan Post

Bank into a full-fledged bank. According to an October 2007 article in *The Economist*:

> The newly created Japan Post Bank will be free to concentrate on banking, and its new status will enable it to diversify into fresh areas of business such as mortgage lending and credit cards. To some degree, this diversification will also be forced upon the new bank. Some of the special treatment afforded to its predecessor will be revoked, obliging Japan Post Bank to invest more adventurously in order to retain depositors—and, ultimately, to attract investors once it lists on the stock market.[391]

That was the plan; but as with the Commonwealth Bank of Australia, the investors may have simply unleashed a giant public sector competitor, turning Japan Post into what is now the world's largest depository bank. A March 2007 article in *USA Today* warned, "The government-nurtured colossus could leverage its size to crush rivals, foreign and domestic."[392]

Keeping Japan's Debt Out of the Hands of Foreign Creditors

The plan to privatize Japan Post was moving ahead until the Democratic Party of Japan (DPJ) came to power in 2009. The DPJ appointed Shizuka Kamei, the leader of a junior coalition party called People's New Party, as the minister responsible for the post office; and Mr. Kamei proceeded to freeze the postal privatization.

He freely acknowledged that he was doing it to keep Japan's public debt out of the hands of foreign creditors. He said, "The reality is we issue a massive amount of Japan government bonds and we need someone to buy them—we should be thankful the Post Office is willing to buy."[393]

In an April 2010 article in *The Australian*, Peter Alford called Kamei "the man who masterminded a major change to Japan's public finance arrangements in the guise of restructuring postal services." Alford wrote:

The irascible 73-year-old Financial Services Minister proposed—well, demanded, actually—that Japan Post Bank's individual deposit limit be raised to ¥20 million ($230,000) and Japan Post Insurance's maximum policy coverage rise to ¥25m.

In doing so, *he has significantly expanded Japan Post's capacity to use those savings and premiums to finance public debt.*

As of March 31 last year, 74 per cent of the postal bank and postal insurer's combined assets of ¥303 trillion (that's right, $3480 billion) were held in Japan government bonds (JGBs) and another 4 per cent in local government bonds.[394]

Michiyo Nakamoto wrote in *The Financial Times* in September 2009:

Mr. Kamei . . . has been particularly vocal about the need to reverse course on postal privatization. . . .

The minister has also been vocal on the need to support struggling small- and medium-sized companies, fuelling concerns that the government would adopt a socialist approach to the private sector.

Of particular alarm to some critics have been Mr. Kamei's remarks suggesting that the government would shelter SMEs [small and medium-sized enterprises] facing financial problems via a temporary moratorium on loan repayments.

"When the lender is in trouble, we will rescue them with taxes and when the borrower is in trouble, we will grant them a reprieve [on their loans]. That is the natural thing to do," Mr. Kamei told the Nikkei business daily at the weekend.[395]

The Outcry from Competitors

Giving distressed borrowers a break might be the natural thing to do, but it was not a model private competitors wanted to see tested. A coalition of organizations representing American, Canadian and European business interests objected that the expansion of the Post Bank was "anti-competitive." It disregarded "international best practices to ensure equal competitive conditions" and raised "new and serious questions regarding Japan's commitment to fulfilling its international GATT obligations." [396] (GATT is the acronym for the General Agreement on Tariffs and Trade.)

Michiyo Nakamoto wrote in the May 2010 *Financial Times*:

> The private sector banks are fuming at the government's decision to raise the maximum that can be held in an account at the postal bank from Y10m ($112,000) to ¥20m and allow the lender into a wider range of businesses than it has been permitted to engage in so far.
>
> They argue that the government's stake, which is currently at 100 per cent, gives the postal bank almost a state guarantee that will encourage depositors to shift their savings out of private banks into the post bank. They are also worried that the post bank, the country's biggest bank by deposits, will encroach on the few profitable areas of banking business in Japan's sluggish economy. [397]

From the point of view of depositors, the government's guarantee is a good thing, ensuring the safety of their money. But competitors cry, "Unfair!" The very strengths of a public bank are considered its defects, because competitors cannot compete with them.

The consolidated Post Bank has now grown to enormous size, passing up Citigroup as the world's largest commercial financial institution. [398] In December 2010, sources said the Post Bank was considering opening its first overseas office in London, "aiming to obtain the latest financial information there to help diversify its asset management schemes." The world's largest commercial bank was moving to diversify away from low-interest government bonds into more lucrative international investments. [399] The "government-nurtured colossus" did indeed appear to be "leveraging its size to crush rivals, foreign and domestic."

But that was before the March 2011 tsunami that devastated Japan, triggering a nuclear disaster. Talk then reverted to the neoliberal model of selling off public assets to find the funds to rebuild. [400] Christian Caryl commented in *Foreign Affairs*:

> As horrible as it is, the devastation of the earthquake presents Japan and its political class with the chance to push through the many reforms that the DPJ has long promised and the country so desperately needs. [401]

In other words, a chance for investors to finally get their hands on Japan's prized publicly-owned bank and the massive deposit base that has so far protected the economy from the attacks of foreign financial predators.

Whether they will succeed remains to be seen. The Japanese are intensely patriotic, and they are not likely to submit quietly to domination by foreigners. Moreover, their economy may not be as weak as it appears.

The Japanese banking system will be the subject of one more chapter, because it has led the way for the development of an Asian model of financing the economy, government, and social services that is not only out-performing the Western model but may hold the key to escaping our current financial doldrums. That doesn't mean we need to "go Asian." We just need to remember our roots and return to them. The American colonists devised a sustainable public banking system in the 18th century; and the Japanese took their inspiration, at least in part, from the Scotsman C. H. Douglas.

Section IV.

PUBLIC BANKING MODELS, HYBRIDS AND RIVALS AFTER WORLD WAR II

Chapter 22

BEYOND CAPITALISM AND SOCIALISM: THE JAPANESE STATE-GUIDED MODEL AND THE "ASIAN TIGERS"

"After a long period of prewar and wartime experimentation, Japan's state-guided but privately-owned economic system was the primary agent responsible for Japan's spectacular, if unexpected, post-World War II advance to the rank of the world's second most productive economy. . . . Japan's economic achievement was not unique; its main principles and institutions were being duplicated in South Korea and Taiwan with equally impressive results."

-- Chalmers Johnson, Japan Policy Research Institute, 2001[402]

Despite its apparent economic problems, Japan continues to dominate as the world's largest creditor and largest exporter of high-tech manufacturing. It has achieved all this while purporting to play by Western capitalist rules. But there is a key feature of its system that is different, a feature that was recognized and imitated by Korea, Taiwan, and even China. That feature is public control of the banking system.

The Japanese had seen what could happen when they displayed their power. They invited boycotts, mafia-like tactics, and war. In *In the Jaws of the Dragon*, Eamonn Fingleton maintains that the Japanese have long exaggerated their country's weaknesses and understated its strengths, in order to stay out of Washington's sights. In a 2004 review, Dr. Robert Locke agreed, writing:

> Contrary to popular belief, Japan has been doing very well lately, despite the interests that wish to depict her as an economic mess. The illusion of her failure is used by globalists and other neoliberals to discourage Westerners, particularly Americans, from even caring about Japan's economic policies, let alone learning from them. It has been encouraged by the Japanese government as a way to get foreigners to stop pressing for changes in its neo-mercantilist trade policies.[403]

Mercantilism means supporting and protecting one's own industries, keeping competitors out. It was how the U.K. and the U.S. nurtured their fledgling industries until they became colonial powers. But the world has room for only so many colonial powers. Protectionism by smaller nations trying to support their own industries is now frowned on by the major world powers, as they seek to pry open global markets.

Locke maintains that the response of the Japanese to this sort of prying has been to pull a veil over their economic success. He notes the following anomalous facts, among others:

- Japan's net exports for the decade of the 1990s, when the country was supposedly in decline, were 240 percent of its exports in the decade of the 1980s, when everyone admitted the country was booming. How was this possible if its economy was falling apart? In an export-centered economy, exports cannot be booming while the economy as a whole is failing. IMF figures indicate that Japan's foreign assets nearly quadrupled in the 11 years to 2000, an inevitable consequence of its relentless trade surpluses.
- Western press reports about the supposed crisis in the Japanese banking system are based on the assumption that Japan's banks are similar to banks in the United States and Europe. They are not. Because of their complex structural relationships to Japanese industry and government, they have sources of

stability to tide them over temporary difficulties that Western banks do not, and their rare failures cause far less disruption.[404]

The Japanese economy has been called "stagnant," but Locke says it has simply stabilized at an elevated plateau. The Japanese are aiming less for growth than for sustainability and a high standard of living. They have replaced quantity of goods with quality of life and a secure economic future.

Economist Hazel Henderson concurs. She says Japan's debt appears to be twice its GDP only because of an anomaly in how economists calculate GDP. They count only "sales" and omit government-provided services. If these services were included, Japan's GDP would be much higher, and its debt to GDP ratio would be more in line with other countries.[405] Investments in education, health care, and social security improve both the standard of living of the people and national productivity. Businesses that have to pay less for health care can be more profitable and competitive internationally; and families that have to save less to put their children through college can spend on better housing, more vacations, and other consumer items.

The Power Struggle Between the MOF and the BOJ

While those authorities feel the Japanese economy is quietly thriving, Richard Werner, another expert on the subject, has reservations. He invented the term "quantitative easing" when he was advising the Japanese in the 1990s. He says the economy could be doing far better if the Bank of Japan had taken his advice and implemented what he intended by the term—credit creation that got money into the real economy for productive purposes. The BOJ adopted the term, but for two decades its brand of quantitative easing has simply padded the reserve accounts of banks; and other central banks, including the U.S. Fed, have followed suit with their own quantitative easing programs. Today, says Werner:

> [A]ll QE is doing is to help banks increase the liquidity of their portfolios by getting rid of longer-dated slightly less liquid

assets and raising cash. . . . Reserve expansion is a standard monetarist policy and required no new label.[406]

As noted in the last chapter, Werner attributes the BOJ's resistance to real solutions to an ongoing power struggle between the BOJ and MOF. The BOJ precipitated a long recession that finally broke the power of the MOF, allowing the BOJ to act independently of the government.[407]

That power struggle puts the challenge to the BOJ of the new administration of Shinzo Abe in a different light. According to a January 2013 article in *Business Week*:

> Shinzo Abe and the Liberal Democratic Party swept back into power in mid-December by promising a high-octane mix of monetary and fiscal policies to pull Japan out of its two-decade run of economic misery. *To get there, Prime Minister Abe is threatening a hostile takeover of the Bank of Japan, the nation's central bank.* The terms of surrender may go something like this: Unless the BOJ agrees to a 2 percent inflation target and expands its current government bond-buying operation, the ruling LDP might push a new central bank charter through the Japanese Diet. That charter would greatly diminish the BOJ's independence to set monetary policy and allow the prime minister to sack its governor.[408]

A hostile takeover of the independent central bank—times may indeed be changing!

Forging a New Economic Model

Fingleton sheds light on the power struggle between the MOF and BOJ by tracing it to events before World War II. The Japanese economy was then controlled by the owners of large industrial conglomerates called *zaibatsu*, who formed a wealthy plutocratic class bent on controlling the economy for their own ends.

The modern Japanese model, says Fingleton, was developed in the economic laboratory of Manchuria, a Japanese colony that was relatively free from capitalist private interests. In the 1930s, there were no Manchurian plutocrats to get in the way, so the planners had a free hand. They wanted something more efficient than conventional capitalism, which left the economy to the whims of privateers pursuing their own interests. They developed the rudiments of a system in Manchuria that produced sustainable growth at rates two to three times those possible under Western capitalism.

After World War II, Japan's military government handed the reins of power over to civilian agencies; and the most important of these was the Ministry of Finance (MOF), which boasted the brightest and most ambitious graduates of Japan's best universities. The MOF bureaucrats then set out to implement the Manchurian system in postwar Japan.

The first step was to eliminate large concentrations of private wealth and power that might interfere with their plan. To do this, they convinced U.S. General MacArthur that the *zaibatsu* owners were responsible for the Japanese militarism that caused the war and that the *zaibatsu* should be dismantled. The MOF forced the *zaibatsu* to be sold in exchange for non-negotiable bonds, which were then quickly made worthless by a short burst of hyperinflation. At a stroke, says Fingleton, the *zaibatsu* fortunes were wiped out and the dream of the Manchurian military planners was realized.[409]

With the removal of the *zaibatsu* plutocrats from their controlling position in the Japanese economy, the road was cleared for the MOF to proceed with its plans. The MOF's next move was to revive the *zaibatsu* in a new cooperative form known as *keiretsu*. These cooperative units were not owned by plutocrats but were largely *self-owned*, similar to cooperatives in the West.

In the *keiretsu* system, the main banks are no longer under the private control of rich families but are controlled by the Ministry of Finance. Banks are embedded in networks of companies that preferentially trade among themselves and have family-like commitments to each other. At the apex of each *keiretsu* pyramid is its bank, which allocates capital. The MOF keeps tight control over these banks. It does not try to micro-manage, as in the old Soviet-style central planning, but it sets the agenda, directing the banks in a way that implements the government's plans for economic development.[410]

Japan's Hybrid Economic Model

In achieving all this after World War II, Japan purported to play by Western capitalist rules; but its model is actually a hybrid.

Classical socialism emphasized the need to control the economy's "commanding heights." This was taken to mean the major industries — steel, coal, and the like. But the Japanese leaders recognized that it is not those industries that command the economy. Rather, it is the banking sector, which supplies capital to business. They understood, says Locke, that:

> [I]t is possible to manipulate an economy that is 99 percent capitalist into being, essentially, a centrally-planned economy if the state controls the right 1 percent. And this "right 1 percent" is the allocation of capital, especially big capital. The MOF uses its stranglehold on the allocation of capital to make the banks into willing servants of its mission to control the Japanese economy.

The Japanese model is called "state-guided capitalism." The government is at the helm, directing the economy in a way that serves the public interest.

The cooperative corporate groupings called *keiretsu* are both more egalitarian and more economically efficient than either the plutocratic *zaibatsu* or their Western capitalist competitors. Locke explains the *keiretsu* cooperatives like this:

> [T]heir system is designed so that corporations, in essence, largely own themselves. Even when there are nominal outside owners, corporations are managed so that the bulk of the wealth generated by the corporation flows either to the incomes of present workers or to investment in the future competitive strength of the company, making the workers and the company itself the de facto or beneficiary owners.
>
> Most corporate capital in Japan is owned by banks, and the banks are principally owned not by shareholders, but by other companies in the same keiretsu or industrial group. And who owns these companies? Although there are some outside shareholders, majority control is in the hands of the keiretsu's bank and the other companies in the group. So in essence, the

whole thing is circular and private ownership of the means of production has basically been put into the back seat.[411]

Businesses in the *keiretsu* have cheap credit lines with their own cooperatively-owned banks. This gives them an obvious competitive edge over businesses forced to borrow at usurious rates from private banks bent on extracting as much "rent" for the use of the bank's credit as the market will bear.

The *keiretsu* add an element of cooperation and integration to the Japanese economy. Businesses remain very competitive, but they compete as a team. They are less concerned with short-term gain than with market share, improving production techniques, and maintaining employment. They can take the long view because their funding comes from their own banks rather than from shareholders whose chief interest is quarterly profit.

Japan proved the model by rocketing from a per capita GDP of $610 in 1962 to $38,500 in 2006, a *63-fold* increase in GDP.[412] Its industries now lead the world in high-tech manufacturing, due to its lead in production techniques, electronic miniaturization, robotics, aerospace, and other technological advances. The fact that Japan might be doing better without the obstructive tactics of the BOJ makes its actual achievements all the more remarkable. Behind the façade of the "lost decade," Japan has evidently managed to amass extraordinary wealth; and this wealth is distributed in an egalitarian way. Fingleton calls Japan one of the most egalitarian societies on earth. The top fifth of the population have incomes that are only 2.9 times those of the bottom fifth, compared to a spread of 9 to 1 in the United States.

Korea Test-Flies the Japanese Model and Breaks the Sound Barrier

While Japan's growth potential was being slowed by a decades-old struggle with the BOJ for power, its neighbors were busy proving the state-guided model. Japan's impressive growth quickly attracted the attention of two of its former colonies, Korea and Taiwan.

In 1961, South Korea's per capita GDP stood at $103, making it one of the poorest countries in the world—poorer even than North Korea. By 1989, its per capita GDP had skyrocketed to $5,438. By 2007, it was

$20,000; and by 2010, it was $30,000, placing it solidly in the club of wealthy first-world nations.[413]

South Korea's achievements were all the more impressive considering the country's rocky start after World War II. President Syngman Rhee was a staunch anti-communist, educated in the United States, who followed American economic prescriptions. The nation's banks had been government-owned under Japanese colonial rule (1910-1945), but under Rhee they were privatized.[414] The economy suffered runaway inflation, highly unfavorable trade balances, and mass unemployment; and it was dependent on U.S. foreign aid. South Korea's war with North Korea in the early 1950s was one of the bloodiest in human history, claiming four million lives and destroying half of Korean industry.

The corrupt authoritarian Rhee regime was finally toppled by a student uprising in 1960; and in 1961, General Park Chung Hee seized power in a military coup. Educated at the Imperial Japanese Army Academy in Tokyo before serving in the Imperial Japanese Army in Manchuria, Park was well aware of Japan's successful experiment and its rapid economic progress in the 1950s. He instituted Japanese-style state-guided planning and development in South Korea, including nationalization of the banks. Fingleton writes:

> In a critical preparatory move that paved the way for the coming economic revolution, he renationalized the Korean banking system, thus establishing at a stroke the sort of fingertip control over the nation's savings flows that Japanese officials already enjoyed via a nominally private, but in reality tightly state-controlled, banking system.

South Korea faithfully replicated the Japanese model. It adopted a similar system of economic planning, industrial conglomerates (called *chaebol*), life-time jobs and export assistance, and close copies of the Japanese Ministry of Finance, Ministry of Trade and Industry, and Development Bank of Japan. In 1965, Korea normalized relations with Japan and received massive Japanese financial and technical aid. It used state-owned enterprises (SOEs) extensively and was highly protectionist, including controlling foreign currency and investment.

According to Cambridge economist Ha-Joon Chang in *Bad Samaritans: The Myth of Free Trade and the Secret History of Capitalism* (2008):

> The neo-liberal establishment would have us believe that, during its miracle years between the 1960s and the 1980s, Korea pursued a neo-liberal development strategy. The reality, though, was very different indeed. What Korea actually did during these decades was to nurture certain new industries, selected by the government in consultation with the private sector, through tariff protection, subsidies, and other forms of government support . . . until they "grew up" enough to withstand international competition. *The government owned all the banks, so it could direct the life-blood of business – credit.*[415]

South Korea's version of the Japanese model was a stellar success. Fingleton observes:

> Even as early as 1978, per-capita income had already increased nearly twenty-fold – a performance that surely was not overlooked by Chinese leaders as they searched for ways to boost China's economic performance.[416]

The Taiwanese Miracle

Taiwan, too, emulated Japan's impressive growth model on gaining independence. Between 1952 and 2007—a period of more than fifty years—Taiwan's average growth was an astonishing 7.8 percent annually, raising the per capita GDP from $97 to almost $7,000 over that period.

Taiwan was Japan's first overseas colony, and much effort had been put into making it a showpiece "model colony" by improving the island's economy, industry, public works and culture. But in the 1950s, it was still basically a third world country. By the 1990s, however, it had become one of the "Asian tigers," enjoying world leadership in many economic sectors. It achieved this remarkable success by setting out on a strongly state-guided, export-driven mercantilist program, and by taking control of the economy's true commanding heights, its banking system. Nearly all banks in Taiwan are wholly or partially owned by the state, and the lending activities of all Taiwanese financial institutions are under strict state supervision.[417]

The Taiwanese bureaucrats did not have to battle their plutocrats. They started out with an economy that was already largely state-owned, having inherited a tradition of strong central government control from the Japanese militarists. Fingleton writes:

> They took good care to retain state control as they launched the Taiwanese miracle and repeatedly resisted considerable American pressure to privatize the Taiwanese corporate sector. *Crucially, virtually the entire Taiwanese banking industry remains to this day subject to extremely detailed back-seat driving from the Taipei Finance Ministry.* State-owned enterprises were to form the backbone of the economy in Taiwan's years of fastest growth in the 1960s and 1970s.[418]

The Taiwan government was able to guide the economy, support exports, and keep unemployment low because it owned its banks. Its strong public banking sector made the banking environment very competitive, keeping costs low. Like Japan and Korea, Taiwan has been under foreign pressure to privatize its banks, but the domestic political resistance is high. The country was able to weather the 1997 Asian financial crisis relatively unscathed, thanks to the resilience of its public banks.[419]

The remarkable successes of Japan, Korea and Taiwan also attracted the attention of the Chinese, who implemented their own adaptation of the model, called a "socialist market economy." Its stellar results were detailed in Chapter 6.

Chapter 23

PUBLIC BANKING IN GERMANY: AN OVERLOOKED KEY TO ITS ECONOMIC STRENGTH

> *"[S]avings banks appear to provide a 'European Advantage' over the United States and other countries without these institutions. . . . [S]avings banks retained a significant comparative advantage in terms of organizational network and lending discretion that was critical for ushering small and medium enterprises through economic downturns."*
>
> *--- Kurt von Mettenheim, et al., Government Banking: New Perspectives on Sustainable Development and Social Inclusion from Europe and South America (2008)*[420]

Germany, like Japan, managed to rise phoenix-like from the ashes of war. Industrial development in both cases was undergirded by a strong tradition of public and cooperative banks. Today, EU rules are stripping the large German public banks of some of their traditional strengths; but the local public and cooperative banks are still going strong.

Less than ten years after World War II, people were already talking about a German economic miracle. The war had left the country with a collapsed economy that had degenerated into barter. In 1947,

German industrial output was only one-third its 1938 level, and a large percentage of its working-age men were dead. Twenty years later, the German economy was the envy of most of the world. In the second half of the twentieth century, Germany went on to become Europe's economic powerhouse.[421]

By 2003, a country half the size of Texas had become the world's leading exporter, producing high quality automobiles, machinery, electrical equipment, and chemicals. Only in 2009 was Germany surpassed in exports by China, which has a population of over 1.3 billion to Germany's 82 million. In 2010, while much of the world was still reeling from the 2008 financial collapse, Germany reported 3.6 percent economic growth. Today, it is the largest and most robust economy in the Eurozone.[422] Manufacturing contributes 25 percent of Germany's GDP, more than twice that in the UK.

Germany's dramatic comeback has been variously attributed to debt forgiveness by the Allies, currency reform, the elimination of price controls, and the reduction of tax rates.[423] But while those factors may have freed the country from its economic shackles, they do not fully explain its phenomenal rise from a war-torn battlefield to world leader in manufacturing and trade.

An overlooked springboard to Germany's recovery is its vast network of public and cooperative banks, including the publicly-owned banking groups called *Landesbanken* and the municipally-supervised, cooperatively-owned savings banks called *Sparkassen* (singular *Sparkasse*). After the war, these public and cooperative banks helped family-run provincial companies get a foothold in world markets. As the system was described by Peter Dorman in 2011:

> [The Landesbanken] are publicly owned entities that rest on top of a pyramid of thousands of municipally owned savings banks. If you add in the specialized publicly owned real estate lenders, about half the total assets of the German banking system are in the public sector. (Another substantial chunk is in cooperative savings banks.) They are key tools of German industrial policy, specializing in loans to the Mittelstand, the small-to-medium size businesses that are at the core of that country's export engine. *Because of the landesbanken, small firms in Germany have as much access to capital as large firms*; there are

no economies of scale in finance. This also means that workers in the small business sector earn the same wages as those in big corporations, have the same skills and training, and are just as productive.[424]

Public, private, and cooperative banks compose the "three pillars" of the German banking system, with fierce competition among them. Big international private banks serve the big enterprises, while public banks serve the regional enterprises and SMEs (small and medium-sized enterprises). The German economy is 90 percent SMEs, and public and cooperative banks are essential to their efficient operation. Cooperatives also serve most SMEs, as well as their own members. By 1999, public and cooperative banks dominated German domestic lending. Private banks accounted for less than 20 percent of the market, compared to more than 40 percent in France, Spain, the Nordic countries, and Benelux.[425]

The Profitability of Philanthropy

In a June 2011 paper titled "Alternative Banking: Competitive Advantage and Social Inclusion," Kurt von Mettenheim and Olivier Butzbach trace the origins of the public and cooperative banks to the charitable pawnshops developed five centuries ago. While modern banking was emerging from the transformation of money lenders into merchant banks in 16th century Europe, Catholic orders and monarchies in Italy and Spain were encouraging the creation of pawnshops to reduce usury and the power of urban money lenders, as well as to expand the supply of money available in the marketplace. Public and cooperative banks were thus already in competition with the "usury banks" in the late Middle Ages. They sprang up at the local level but soon had a significant share of the market. The authors write:

> Instead of profit maximization, early alternative banks were founded by religious orders, public concession or philanthropists with the mission of consolidating a capital base and endowment able to cover the budgets of charitable institutions. The accumulation of deposits and endowments was such that several decades after founding, alternative

banks generally emerged to gain significant market share of domestic banking.[426]

These banks wound up financing governments:

The Monti di pietà, or elaborate pawnshops, emerged during the 16th and 17th century with large capital reserves and a patrimony that became essential to finance crown and court, especially for war and to repress rebellions. The Monti soon set up their own banks. Those banks were public in nature and performed banking activities that were already quite distinct from the burgeoning merchant bank business.

As early as 1572, this public banking model was being exported to Northern European monarchs. More than two centuries later, savings banks emerged in Northern Europe, followed in the mid-nineteenth century by cooperative banks. They all competed with the private, for-profit banks, forcing down interest rates and providing affordable credit.

Although they sprang up at the grassroots level, they were aided by government from the top. Authorizations granted by government allowed the alternative banks to extend their activities into a territory usually controlled by the usury bankers, quickly making them dominant in the market.[427]

The German Sparkassen – Local Savings Banks

The local German savings banks grew from this cooperative philanthropic model. The first German savings bank was set up by academics and philanthropically-minded merchants in Hamburg in 1778, and the first municipal savings bank with a local government guarantor was founded in Goettingen in 1801. The municipal savings banks were so effective and popular that they spread rapidly, increasing from 630 in 1850 to 2,834 in 1903. Today the savings banks have over 15,600 branches and offices and employ over 250,000 people, and they have a strong record of investing wisely in local businesses.[428]

Germany's public and cooperative banking sector now includes seven publicly-owned Landesbanken (regional banking groups) and 420 cooperatively-owned Sparkassen (municipally supervised savings banks). The Landesbanken function as "universal banks" operating in all sectors of the financial services market, but the system is not one of top-down hierarchical control. Rather, the local Sparkassen are autonomous and have jurisdiction over the larger regional Landesbanken. The alternative German banks emerged as local and regional associations that then linked to form regional, national and international networks. These networks allowed them to compete when banking was opened to globalization and trade liberalization in the 1990s, achieving economies of scale while retaining their core principles. Contrary to the predictions of liberal economists, they were not squeezed out but maintained or increased their market share across Europe.

In 2009, the Sparkasse system (including the Landesbanken) had total assets of 2,364 billion euros, or 35.5 percent of the German banking sector's total assets. That made the system the third largest banking group in the world, behind the French BNP and UK's RBS. It held 38.7 percent of the German market in bank deposits and 28.1 percent of the lending market. Similarly, in Spain in the late 2000s, the Spanish savings banks, called Cajas de Ahorro, held 39 percent of domestic bank assets, 50 percent of deposits, and 46.9 percent of Spanish loans.[429]

Richard Werner contrasts the German system to that in the UK, where five Highstreet banks make up 95 percent of the banking system and lend largely for financial speculation. In Germany, large nation-wide banks make up only about 13 percent of the banking system, which is overwhelmingly locally based, supporting the small and medium sized enterprises that provide 80 percent of employment in any economy. Seventy percent of banks are locally-owned and controlled (42.9 percent savings banks and 26.6 percent cooperative banks). These banks are legally required to invest locally, and they do not lend for speculation but lend to productive firms that add to real GDP. To grow and prosper, they must do so in partnership with the local productive economy. The system is not extractive but is supportive and sustainable.[430]

European savings banks are also required by law to contribute to social improvements. German savings banks direct part of their revenues to foundations active in culture, social assistance and philanthropy. French savings banks must reserve half their dividends to fund social responsibility programs. Spanish savings banks are required to channel all after-tax profits that are not used to build reserves into activities fulfilling their social mandate, or Obra Social.[431]

These social services have not hurt profitability. To the contrary, write von Mettenheim and Butzbach, alternative banks have *outperformed* private, for-profit banks, not just in market share but in profitability and efficiency. Several recent studies have shown at least slightly higher cost efficiencies with savings and cooperative banks than with private banks.[432]

Targeted for Privatization

Public and cooperative banks continue to be the most profitable and stable sector of the German banking system, but the reputation and standing of the Landesbanken began to be challenged starting in the mid-nineties, when they emerged as competitors in international markets. The privately-owned banks, led by Deutsche Bank AG, enlisted the EU in the attack. Peter Dorman writes:

> [T]he EU doesn't like the landesbanken. They denounce the explicit and implicit public subsidies that state ownership entails, saying they violate the rules of competition policy. For over a decade they have fought to have the system privatized. In the end, the dispute is simply ideological: if you think that public ownership should only be an exception, narrowly crafted to address specific market failures, you want to see the landesbanken put on the auction block. If you think an economy should be organized to meet socially defined needs, you would want a large part of capital allocation to be responsive to public input, and you'd fight to keep the landesbanken the way they are. (There is a movement afoot in the U.S. to promote public banking.)

The slings and arrows aimed at German public banking in the last decade were tracked in a July 2011 article by Ralph Niemeyer, editor-in-chief of *EUchronicle*, titled "Commission's Dirty Task: WESTLB Devoured by Private Banks."[433] He noted that after 1999, the major private banks left sustainable traditional banking to gamble in collateralized debt obligations, credit default swaps, and derivatives.

Private German banks accumulated an estimated €600 billion in toxic assets through their investment banking branches—assets for which German taxpayers wound up providing guarantees. Deutsche Bank AG was amassing its record profits almost exclusively through its investment banking division, which made a fortune trading credit default swaps on Greek state obligations. This investment eventually turned sour, and the German government was forced to bail out the financial institution into which Deutsche Bank AG had dumped these toxic assets.

While the large private banks were betting in the ephemeral casino of the financial markets, lending to the physical, productive economy was left to the locally-owned savings banks. The Sparkassen were more efficient in serving average citizens and local business than the private, for-profit banks, because they were not stock companies that had to satisfy shareholders' hunger for ever-larger dividends.

Niemeyer maintains that the private banks wanted to break up the market dominance of the public banks to get a bigger piece of the pie. In 2011, the slice of the German pie held by private banks was only 28.4 percent. Deutsche Bank AG, which dominated the segment, had a mere 7 percent market share, leaving it well behind the public banks owned by municipalities and communities.

According to Niemeyer, the German private banks used the European Commission to achieve their ends. Ever since the early 1990s, the Commission had been lobbied by these banks, and by Deutsche Bank AG in particular, to attack the German government over the country's "inflexible" public banking sector. The IMF, too, had long been demanding that any competing public monopolies in the German banking market be broken up, citing their market "inefficiencies."

When the Landesbanken resisted turning to investment banking with its skyrocketing profits, they were branded as bureaucratic and "unsexy." Pressured to increase their returns on behalf of their government owners, they got sucked into the derivatives, collateralized debt obligations (CDOs), and mortgage-backed securities (MBS) being peddled largely by American banks, which misrepresented them as triple A. (This was mentioned in Michael Lewis' *The Big Short:Inside the Doomsday Machine*. A trader shorting the mortgage market asks: "Who's on the other side, who's the idiot?" The answer is: "Düsseldorf.

Stupid Germans. They take ratings agencies seriously. They play by the rules."[434])

The Landesbanken lost billions in what Niemeyer calls "the Goldman Sachs, Deutsche Bank and Lehman Brothers Ponzi schemes." But the extent to which they became involved in highly speculative transactions, he says, was "laughable in comparison with the damage done by private banks, for whom taxpayers are now providing guarantees."

It was the Landesbanken and Sparkassen that had supplied the local economy with liquidity when the private banks withdrew to bet in the financial casino. Yet it was their failings rather than the private banks' on which the media focused their attention. Why? Niemeyer observes that the large private banks largely control the media. He writes:

> In order to win back this important market share, it has become a prerogative to destroy public banking in Germany completely. This unpopular move could never come from the German government itself, so that's why the [European] Commission is being employed for this dirty job.

The Price of Success

In their heyday, the Landesbanken were stable and secure banks that were able to lend at low interest rates because they had the full faith and credit of the government and the public behind them. By eliminating the profit motive, focusing on the public interest, and relying on government guarantees, they succeeded in turning bank credit into a public utility.

Today, however, their public legs are being knocked out from under them. In 2001, the European Commission ruled that the Landesbanken would be deprived of their explicit state credit guarantees, forcing them to compete on the same terms as private banks. They still had an implied government guarantee, but the European Banking Authority is now refusing to count that, too, in the banks' "stress tests" for banking solvency. Meanwhile, the large private-sector banks have acquired implicit state guarantees themselves, on the theory that they are "too big to fail."

The German example demonstrates that success itself is no guarantee, in the face of a relentless onslaught of propaganda by large privately-owned banks driven to increase the profit share of their management, shareholders and wealthy clients. Peering behind the propaganda, however, the public banking model that helped underwrite Germany's economic success may be the fast track to a financial system that serves the local economy rather than international high finance.

While the internationally competitive Landesbanken have been under attack, the locally-based Sparkassen have emerged relatively unscathed and continue to flourish. Since they are local savings banks with a surplus of deposits over loans, they do not need money from international financial markets or state guarantees. They do not have guarantees at all but are self-insured. They have a wide deposit base and prudent lending practices, and they are not dependent on foreign ratings agencies to attract creditors and investors. If they are forced into a European banking union that imposes the losses of profligate foreign banks on the more prudent members, however, they may yet be brought down.

Bowing to Brussels

In August 2012, the European Commission insisted that the 6,000 banks in the euro area be centrally supervised to prevent future financial crises. Objections came chiefly from the Germans. According to *The New York Times*:

> [S]ome Germans are highly sensitive about giving up authority over their large public banking system, which is partly controlled by states, districts and cities, and that has cast some doubts over the goal of turning the proposal into European law by the year's end.
>
> Klaus-Peter Flosbach, finance policy spokesman for the parliamentary group of the ruling party in Germany, the Christian Democrats, told the daily newspaper Süddeutsche Zeitung that it was "completely wrong" for the European Central Bank to regulate the hundreds of German savings banks, called Sparkassen. Germany's regional banks, or

Landesbanken, were severely hit by the financial crisis in 2008 and 2009.

Writing in *The Financial Times*, the German finance minister, Wolfgang Schäuble, said supervision should focus only on those banks that could pose a threat to the entire European financial system, while some central policy makers at Germany's central bank, the Bundesbank, have expressed wariness about expanding the European bank's powers.[435]

Despite these objections, in December 2012 a deal was struck to establish a Single Supervisory Mechanism, with the European Central Bank at its center. According to *Bruegel*:

From press reports, the ECB will directly supervise all banks above €30 billion in total assets, as well as some smaller banks, and will have some form of backseat authority on all other smaller ones. . . . This covers not only large banks but also medium-sized ones, in total probably somewhere between 75 and 85 percent of the system's total assets. . . . The exclusion of small banks is not really justifiable from a technical or analytical perspective. But it was also arguably unavoidable given Germany's central role in the decision process and its unique political and banking structures, which grant enormous political influence to the savings banks.[436]

An accord was finalized in March 2013 that would give the ECB powers to supervise Eurozone banks from mid-2014. According to *RTÉ News*:

The deal envisages that banks with assets of €30 billion, or larger than one-fifth of their country's economic output, are supervised by the ECB rather than national supervisors.

The next pillar of a banking union should be the creation of a central system and fund to close troubled banks, rather than leaving it to individual countries such as Cyprus or Ireland to have to manage alone.

However the reluctance of Germany and other economically strong countries to underpin such a fund means it will be hard to set up.[437]

According to a release from the Luxembourg Bankers' Association:

The SSM constitutes the first block of the Banking Union, which encompasses also a single EU Deposit Guarantee Scheme and a single EU Resolution Scheme set up under the control of a EU Resolution Authority, and a single set of rules (the single rulebook). The motivation for creating the Banking Union is to restore confidence in the Euro-zone's capacity to overcome the current crisis, paving the way towards a more complete fiscal, economic and political integration. [438]

"Paving the way toward a more complete fiscal, economic and political integration": skeptical observers say that was the goal of the Eurozone all along . . . .

Chapter 24

EUROLAND AND THE ECB: A BANKING MODEL THAT FAILED

"In retrospect it is now clear that the main source of trouble is that the member states of the euro have surrendered to the European Central Bank their rights to create fiat money."

— *George Soros, remarks at the Festival of Economics, Trento, Italy, June 2012*

At one end of the banking spectrum, the BRICs have demonstrated what can be done when credit becomes a public utility and is allowed to flow freely through the economy. At the other end, the Eurozone is demonstrating what happens when countries are blocked from issuing their own money and credit or borrowing from their own central banks.

When the European Union (EU) was established in 1993, it was ostensibly for political reasons. Germany had been through two devastating world wars with its neighbors and an even more devastating hyperinflation, and no one wanted to risk a repeat performance. That was how the union was sold, but its effect was to take from the Eurozone nations the right to issue their own currencies or borrow interest-free from their own central banks. From a competitive standpoint, it also eliminated the German deutsche mark as an independent currency, one that in the 1960s through 1980s functioned alongside the dollar as a rival currency for international commerce.[439]

The EU evolved from a trade union into a currency union in 1999, with 17 signatories to the 1993 Maastricht Treaty qualifying to join the pact. The Eurozone countries turned the power to issue their own national currencies over to the European Central Bank (ECB), which alone can issue euros. Under the terms of the Treaty, the ECB cannot lend to governments but can lend only to banks.

Financial analyst Cullen Roche calls the euro system the modern equivalent of the gold standard.[440] Both are systems in which multiple nations share a single currency. Countries on these restrictive systems cannot expand their revenues, because there is nowhere to get the money. Eurozone countries cannot get more euros except by borrowing from each other or from private banks, and all the member countries are in debt. More is always owed back on loans than was lent out, due to interest; but there is nowhere to get the interest except by driving their neighbors further into debt. Euros can get shuffled around to keep the game going; but like drowning swimmers clinging together, in the end they must pull each other down.

In a draconian effort to prevent inflation at all costs, Eurozone members pledged to keep their budget deficits below 3 percent of GDP; but by June 2010, 26 of 27 EU countries—all but Luxembourg—were on the "debt watch list" for exceeding the 3 percent cap. Even Germany, the economic leader, has not been able to preserve the cap. The result has been repeated credit rating downgrades, driving interest rates to cripplingly high levels.

Yet public debt itself is not the problem. We've seen that Japan has managed to retain an AA or A+ credit rating despite a debt to GDP ratio of nearly 230 percent. The difference is that Japan issues its own currency and owes its national debt to its own people and its own banks. The problem for Eurozone countries is that their debts are owed to someone else, in a currency over which they have no control.

Unable to escape the spiraling debt trap, Eurozone countries have had to turn to the EU and IMF for bailouts; and to get them, they have had to agree to "structural readjustments" including harsh austerity measures, government cutbacks, privatization, and the disempowerment of national central banks. The latter has now officially been achieved in Eurozone countries, which are dependent on the ECB both for euros and as lender of last resort.

Critics warn that the Eurozone countries are turning their sovereignty over to an elite group of "Eurocrat" bankers. Paul Craig Roberts, former Assistant Secretary of the U.S. Treasury, wrote in November 2011:

> The European Union, just like everything else, is merely another scheme to concentrate wealth in a few hands at the expense of European citizens, who are destined, like Americans, to be the serfs of the 21st century.[441]

Bailout Contagion

The first country to need a bailout was Greece. Its rescue in 2010 was supposed to be an isolated case, a test of the EU's ability to quarantine an infected member and prevent it from spreading "debt contagion."

But that was before Ireland failed. Ireland was the poster child for how to conduct a successful austerity program.[442] Unlike the Greeks, who were considered profligate spendthrifts, the Irish did everything their creditors asked. The people sacrificed to pay for the excesses of their banks, but still the effort failed. In December 2010, Ireland's reward for voting to accept the "rescue package" offered by their creditors was a five-notch credit *downgrade* by Moody Investors Service, from AA2 to BAA1. There were warnings that further downgrades could follow.[443] By November 2012, there had been six bailouts—three for Greece and one each for Ireland, Portugal, and Spain.[444]

The burgeoning debts of Eurozone countries have been blamed on their large welfare states, but their social systems were set up before the 1970s, well before European governments were crippled with national debt. What caused their debts to shoot up was not that they overspent on social services but that they switched bankers.

Before the 1970s, European governments routinely borrowed from their own central banks. That made the money effectively interest-free, since they owned the banks and got the profits back as dividends. After the European Monetary Union was established, member countries had to borrow from private banks at interest—often substantial interest.

In *Money and Sustainability: The Missing Link* (2012), Bernard Lietaer and Christian Asperger, et al., cite the example of France.[445] From 1946 to 1973, the French government borrowed interest-free from the nationalized Banque de France. The law then changed to forbid this practice, requiring the Treasury to borrow instead from the private sector. The authors include the chart reproduced below, comparing what did happen to what would have happened if the French government had continued to borrow interest-free. Rather than dropping from 21 percent to 8.6 percent of GDP, the debt shot up to 78 percent of GDP.[446] (Figure 10 below.) That means that without the burden of interest, *France might have virtually no federal debt today.*

"No 'spendthrift government' can be blamed in this case," write the authors. "Compound interest explains it all!"

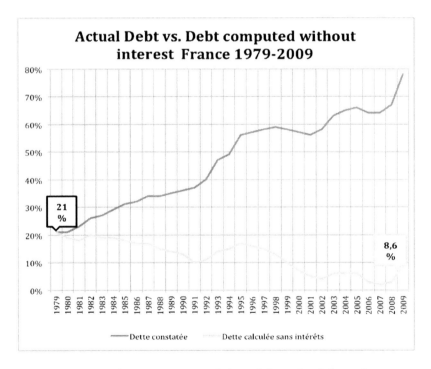

Figure 10. **French government debt with and without interest.** From *Money and Sustainability: The Missing Link* (2012)[447]

What Is Needed Is Not "Quantitative Easing" but "Deficit Easing"

The late Richard Douthwaite was co-founder of an Irish-based think tank called FEASTA (the Foundation for the Economics of Sustainability). Writing in 2011, he noted that the collective deficit of Eurozone countries was a very acceptable 1.9 percent of GDP in 2008. It shot up to 6.3 percent, exceeding the 3 percent cap, only in 2009. *This spike was due, he said, not to a sudden surge in government spending, but to the international financial crisis, which decreased the money supply globally by decreasing credit.* A shrinking money supply means shrinking profits in corporate accounts and fewer taxes paid. When taxes go down, revenues go down, but budgets don't.[448]

The obvious solution is to re-inflate the money supply, but the Eurozone framework prevents this. Governments without the flexibility to expand their money supplies to meet economic needs are reduced to trying to balance their budgets through brutal cuts to government programs and personnel, and sales of public assets at fire sale prices. As Douthwaite explained in November 2011:

> [I]ndividual eurozone countries [cannot] create money out of nothing by quantitative easing. Only the European Central Bank has that power but it has not yet used it to inject money into the system without withdrawing an equal amount. Consequently, *every cent in use in eurozone economies has to have been borrowed by someone somewhere*, at home or overseas. As a result, while countries with their own currencies can handle a debt-to-GDP ratio of over 100 percent because they have the tools to do so (Japan's is approaching 200 percent), countries using a shared currency must keep well below that figure unless they can agree that their shared central bank should use its interest rate, exchange rate and money creation tools in the way that a single country would.

In a November 2010 article in *The UK Guardian* called "There Is Another Way for Bullied Ireland," Mark Weisbrot observed that Ireland could fix its budget problem with a temporary fiscal stimulus, using deficit spending to kick-start the economy. But that was not the agenda being pursued:

Instead, the European authorities are trying what the IMF . . . calls an "internal devaluation". This is a process of shrinking the economy and creating so much unemployment that wages fall dramatically, and the Irish economy becomes more competitive internationally on the basis of lower unit labour costs. . . .

Aside from huge social costs and economic waste involved in such a strategy, it's tough to think of examples where it has actually worked. . . .

If you want to see how rightwing and 19th-century-brutal the European authorities are being, just compare them to Ben Bernanke, the Republican chair of the U.S. Federal Reserve. He recently initiated a second round of "quantitative easing", or creating money—another $600bn dollars over the next six months. And . . . he made it clear that the purpose of such money creation was so that the federal government could use it for another round of fiscal stimulus. The ECB could do something similar—if not for its rightist ideology and politics.[449]

It soon became evident, however, that the Fed's quantitative easing was not working either. As with Herbert Hoover's use of the RFC just to bail out the banks, the money was not getting into the pockets of consumers.[450] There was no Jesse Jones aiming the firehose of public credit at homeowners, businesses and consumers.

Douthwaite's solution was what he called "deficit easing." He distinguished it from quantitative easing like this:

Both approaches involve central banks creating money. With quantitative easing, the new money is generally used to buy securities from the banking system, thus providing the banks with more money to lend. Unfortunately that is where problems have been arising in the U.S. and the U.K. Because the public has been unwilling to borrow, or the banks have been unwilling to lend, quantitative easing has not increased the supply of money in circulation in the US, where M3 began to decline in the second half of 2009 and was still falling a year later. . . .

Deficit-easing avoids this "won't-borrow-won't-lend" bottleneck by giving the new money to governments to spend into use, or to pass on to their citizens to reduce their own debts or to invest in approved ways . . . .

The neatest solution would be for the European Central Bank to create money and to give it (rather than lend it) to governments in proportion to their populations. This would allow further public spending cuts to be avoided and, in countries with relatively small budget deficits, national debts to be reduced.

Like C. H. Douglas' "social credit," it was a commonsense solution to what was basically a mathematical problem: the money wasn't there to pay principal plus interest and costs plus profits in a system in which the money supply was fixed and was chiefly borrowed into existence through private banks.

The ECB Fiddles While Rome Burns

Even the limited form of money creation pursued by the Federal Reserve, however, was further than the ECB was prepared to go in 2011. Jack Ewing wrote in *The New York Times* in November of that year:

To some people, the European Central Bank seems like a fire department that is letting the house burn down to teach the children not to play with matches. . . .

The ECB has a fire hose — its ability to print money. But the bank is refusing to train it on the euro zone's debt crisis.

The flames climbed higher . . . after the Italian Treasury had to pay an interest rate of 6.5 percent on a new issue of six-month bills . . . the highest interest rate Italy has had to pay to sell such debt since August 1997 . . . .

But there is no sign the ECB plans a major response, like buying large quantities of the country's bonds to bring down its borrowing costs.

Why not? According to an article in *The Wall Street Journal*, "The ECB has long worried that buying government bonds in big enough amounts to bring down countries' borrowing costs *would make it easier for national politicians to delay the budget austerity and economic overhauls that are needed.*"[451]

The ECB was evidently engaging in a deliberate political ruse to extort concessions from vassal states. Relief was being withheld simply to twist the arms of member governments.[452] Twist their arms for what? According to *The Wall Street Journal*:

> *Euro-zone leaders are negotiating a potentially groundbreaking fiscal pact . . . [that] would make budget discipline legally binding and enforceable by European authorities.* . . . European officials hope a new agreement, which would aim to shrink the excessive public debt that helped spark the crisis, would persuade the European Central Bank to undertake more drastic action to reverse the recent selloff in euro-zone debt markets.[453]

The goal was to "make budget discipline legally binding and enforceable by European authorities." Which European authorities? It seems they were not actually elected officials. They were the banking technicians called "Eurocrats." The "potentially groundbreaking fiscal pact" was a permanent rescue funding program called the European Stability Mechanism (ESM), which would impose an open-ended debt on EU member governments, putting taxpayers on the hook for whatever the ESM's Eurocrat overseers demanded. According to the terms of the pact, its governing council and directorate would enjoy lifelong immunity without accountability.[454]

Critics said the ESM would turn the Eurozone into a dictatorship serving the interests of the banks. Some said that that was the original intent. When the euro was born, it was evident that a currency union could not function without political union. The euro was the leverage that would force member nations into such a union.[455]

Whatever the motive, the ESM was passed in the dead of night in January 2012, with barely even a mention in the press.[456] Ratification was calendared for July 1, 2012. Two days before that deadline, again in the dead of night, *the agreement was modified to make the permanent bailout fund cover the bailout of private banks.*[457] It was a bankers' dream—a permanent, mandated bailout of private banks by governments.

The ESM was cheered by Eurozone governments, their creditors, and "the market" alike, because it meant investors would keep buying sovereign debt. All was sacrificed to the demands of the creditors, because where else could the money be had to float the crippling debts of the Eurozone governments?

Changes at the European Central Bank

In November 2011, also without fanfare, former Goldman Sachs executive Mario Draghi replaced Jean-Claude Trichet as head of the ECB. Draghi wasted no time doing for the banks what the ECB refused to do for its member governments—lavish money on them at very cheap rates. French commentator Simon Thorpe observed:

> On the 21st of December, the ECB "lent" 489 billion euros to European Banks at the extremely generous rate of just 1 percent over 3 years. I say "lent", but in reality, they just ran the printing presses. The ECB doesn't have the money to lend. It's Quantitative Easing again.
>
> The money was gobbled up virtually instantaneously by a total of 523 banks. It's complete madness. The ECB hopes that the banks will do something useful with it—like lending the money to the Greeks, who are currently paying 18 percent to the bond markets to get money. But there are absolutely no strings attached. If the banks decide to pay bonuses with the money, that's fine. Or they might just shift all the money to tax havens.[458]

At the 18 percent interest rate being paid by the Greeks, debt doubles in just four years. It was this sort of onerous interest burden, more than the debt itself, that was crippling Greece and other Eurozone debtors.[459] By March 2012, the interest rate on Greek debt had shot up to *over 30 percent*. Thorpe asked:

> Why not lend the money to the Greek government directly? Or to the Portuguese government, currently having to borrow money at 11.9 percent? Or the Hungarian government, currently paying 8.53 percent? Or the Irish government, currently paying 8.51 percent? Or the Italian government, who are having to pay 7.06 percent?

That question was answered in an interview by Jens Eidmann, President of the Bundesbank and a member of the ECB Governing Council, like this:

The eurosystem is a lender of last resort for solvent but illiquid banks. *It must not be a lender of last resort for sovereigns because this would violate Article 123 of the EU treaty.*[460]

The ECB cannot lend to governments because there is a rule against it. But rules are just agreements, and they can be modified by agreement—as they have often been to save the banks. Thorpe wrote:

My understanding is that Article 123 is there to prevent elected governments from abusing Central Banks by ordering them to print money to finance excessive spending. That, we are told, is why the ECB has to be independent from governments. OK. But what we have now is a million times worse. The ECB is now completely in the hands of the banking sector. "We want half a billion of really cheap money!!" they say. OK, no problem. Mario is here to fix that. And no need to consult anyone. By the time the ECB makes the announcement, the money has already disappeared.

Despite the rule against it, Draghi told the European Parliament in September 2012 that the ECB was, after all, going to need to intervene in the bond markets to buy government debt, in order to regain control of interest rates and ensure the survival of the euro. The ECB was finally going to come to the aid of member governments, or so it seemed. But there was a catch: onerous strings were attached. The borrowing government would have to agree to "conditionalities," including "fiscal and structural reforms." That meant further fiscal austerity to pay off the banks. Whatever sovereignty the country had left would be turned over to the Eurocrat bankers.

Iceland Defies the Model

It was left to tiny Iceland to stand up to the banks and say no to the bankers' attempt to impose their debts on the backs of the people. The Icelanders let their too-big-to-fail banks fail, and their economy came out the better for it. In an interview of Iceland's president Olafur Grimson at the Davos conference in January 2013, he was asked why Iceland had survived when Europe had failed. He replied:

I think it surprises a lot of people that a year ago we were accepted by the world as a failed financial system, but now we are back on recovery with economic growth and very little unemployment, and I think the primary reason is that . . . we didn't follow the traditional prevailing orthodoxies of the Western world in the last 30 years. We introduced currency controls; we let the banks fail; we provided support for the poor; we didn't introduce austerity measures of the scale you are seeing here in Europe. And the end result four years later is that Iceland is enjoying progress and recovery very different from the other countries that suffered from the financial crisis.

In January 2013, Iceland won a four-year court battle over its refusal to compensate UK and Dutch depositors in the Icelandic bank Icesave that failed in 2008. It was a sweeping victory for Iceland, and a landmark precedent for countries inclined to follow suit.[461]

Iceland's bold move set a precedent for Europe, but it was not the first country to walk away from its debts. Argentina had done so very successfully nearly a decade earlier. Other Latin American countries were also quietly going their own way . . . .

Chapter 25

LATIN AMERICA: BREAKING THE TABOOS OF THE NEOLIBERAL AGENDA

"The issues are much too important for the Chilean voters to be left to decide for themselves."

-- Henry Kissinger, justifying the U.S. overthrow of Chile's elected leader Allende

> Latin America in the 20th century was battered and bruised by invasions, hyperinflations, and bloody coups. Disillusioned with neoliberal dogma, some Latin American countries have been ignoring the old rules and experimenting with models that make strong use of government banks, with quite successful results.

The international debt spider was active in Latin America in the late 20th century, spreading debt, IMF austerity and inflation throughout the region. Rapid privatization of banking in the 1980s and 1990s led to disastrous results in Mexico, Chile, and other Latin American countries.[462] Adding to the skepticism of U.S. propaganda was political repression, including the U.S. overthrow of socialist government in Chile, military takeovers and disappearances in Brazil and Argentina, and 30,000 killed in Nicaragua.

Latin America also got hit with some of the worst hyperinflations in history. According to economist Michael Hudson, hyperinflation—the kind that goes into triple digits and beyond—is not caused by domestic spending but is virtually always a foreign debt problem. He writes, "Every hyperinflation in history has been caused by foreign debt service collapsing the exchange rate."[463]

In the typical syndrome, short sellers speculate against the distressed currency, shrinking its value on foreign exchange markets. The currency buys less and less, until wheelbarrows are needed to get it to market to buy groceries, as in the notorious German Weimar hyperinflation of the 1920s.[464]

In the last century, Latin American countries have suffered hyperinflations as high as 20,000 percent. They have also seen some dramatic economic recoveries, not from paying off their debts (which is usually impossible) but from defying their foreign creditors and walking away, turning their resources instead to developing their own industries and feeding their own people.

The Latin American response to repeated onslaughts to their economic and political institutions has been a new wave of self-reliance, solidarity, and rejection of foreign hegemony. They are taking control of their own economies and forming new alliances, both among themselves, with regional development banks and trade pacts, and with other countries. They are selling more to China in trade partnerships, and are borrowing from China rather than from international agencies and U.S. banks. They are willing to do this even when interest rates are higher, because China does not impose invasive and onerous loan conditions or treat its trading partners like economic colonies.

Today in Latin America, the trend is to reject both the "free market" prescriptions of the Washington consensus on the radical right and the radical socialism of the left. Many Latin American countries have adopted a mixed "coordinated capitalism" approach. They respect private property and encourage private businesses, but they do it under a government umbrella that makes strong use of public banks. Like China, these countries are showing less concern for the color of the cat and more for catching mice.

In a 2008 book titled *Government Banking: New Perspectives on Sustainable Development and Social Inclusion from Europe and South*

America, Dr. Kurt von Mettenheim and co-authors describe a Latin America that is patterning itself less on the Washington consensus and more on the European model of socially-oriented banking. The trend is away from the excessive bank privatization and liberalization pushed in the 1980s and 1990s, toward an increased market share for public banks:

> Government banks . . . far from being doomed to being replaced by financial markets, appear instead still to be central agents of growth. . . . [S]avings banks and microfinance policies are capable of steering domestic financial systems toward better income distribution, social inclusion, political development, and democratization. . . .
>
> On the level of policy, this implies a return to traditional ideas from Europe about savings banks and local communities. Instead of radically reforming public banking sectors through privatization and liberalization, the experiences . . . from Europe and South America involve the reform, modernization, and integration of traditional public banking institutions such as savings banks.[465]

By 2000, neoliberal policies had reduced the number of public sector banks all across Latin America; but public banks still play a key role, remaining strong in major countries. The governments of Venezuela, Brazil, and Argentina retain control of 52 percent, 43 percent, and 30 percent of domestic bank assets respectively, with public and private banks in healthy competition for market share. Private banks do not have a monopoly and must keep their profits modest to remain competitive and retain their customer base.

Venezuela: Banking as a Public Service

In Venezuela, the government began an aggressive campaign to nationalize its banks after they were exposed as systemically weak and corrupt following the banking crisis of 2009-10. Some banks were engaged in questionable business practices. Others were seriously undercapitalized. Others were apparently lending top executives large sums of money. At least one financier could not prove where he got the money to buy the banks he owned.[466]

Unlike in the United States, the government did not bail out these corrupt, insolvent banks but simply took them over. In 2009, it nationalized seven Venezuelan banks, accounting for around 12 percent of the bank deposits in the country. In 2010, more were taken over. The government arrested at least 16 bankers and issued more than 40 corruption-related arrest warrants for others who had fled the country. These interventions followed government takeovers of eight small private banks, after a scandal involving fraud in the country's banking sector in late 2009. Four of these banks were liquidated, and the other four were nationalized and merged with the state-owned bank Banfoandes. The result was a new public investment bank called Banco Bicentenario. Ten bankers and public functionaries were arrested.[467]

By the end of March 2011, only 37 banks were left in the country, down from 59 at the end of November 2009. State-owned institutions took a larger role, holding 35 percent of assets as of March 2011, while foreign institutions held just 13.2 percent of assets.

Analysts say the banking system is now financially sound.[468] As of March 2011, the largest bank in Venezuela is the state-owned Banco de Venezuela, with 14.1 percent of banking sector assets. This bank was acquired by the government in 2009 from Spain's Banco Santander, one of the largest banks in the world. Venezuela's second-largest bank, Banco Bicentenario, is also state-owned and held 12.5 percent of banking assets in March 2011.[469]

In 2010, over the howls of the media, the late President Hugo Chavez took the bold step of passing legislation defining the banking industry as one of "public service." The legislation specified that 5 percent of the banks' net profits must go towards funding community council projects, designed and implemented by communities for the benefit of communities.

The Venezuelan government has increasingly become involved in the operations of private financial institutions, directing the allocation of bank credit to preferred sectors of the economy. By law, nearly half the lending portfolios of Venezuelan banks must be directed to these particular mandated sectors, including small business and agriculture.

In an April 2012 article titled "Venezuela Increases Banks' Obligatory Social Contributions, U.S. and Europe Do Not," Rachael Boothroyd wrote that the government has required Venezuelan banks to give back. The new legislation increases the percentage of net profits that banks must grant in credit to national social programs. Housing in Venezuela has been declared a constitutional right, and Venezuelan banks are obliged to contribute 15 percent of their yearly earnings to securing housing for the population. The government's Great Housing Mission aims to build 2.7 million free houses for low-income families before 2019. It is all part of a government drive to create a social banking system that contributes to the development of society rather than simply siphoning off its wealth. Boothroyd writes:

> It is not that Venezuelan financial speculators and bankers care more about the wellbeing of the national population, but rather that Venezuelans are in the fortunate position of having a national government which prioritizes their life quality, wellbeing and development over the health of bankers' and lobbyists' pay checks. If the 2009 financial crisis demonstrated anything, it was that capitalism is quite simply incapable of regulating itself, and that is precisely where progressive governments and progressive government legislation needs to step in.
>
> . . . [T]hrough restructuring the banking system, the [Venezuelan] government is attempting to "orientate the use and investment" of the banking system's funds towards the "public interest," in order to "really create a social state of law and justice." The Law of the National Financial System also outlines the legal framework through which the Venezuelan people can "participate and supervise the management" of the country's financial system through "social control" of the sector.
>
> . . . Venezuela has proved that, despite the globalised nature of the banking system, these changes can be implemented when the government is on the side of the people and not the financial institutions.[470]

Governments on the Right: Mexico and Chile

A strong public banking sector is to be expected in countries such as Venezuela on the political left, but public banking is also strong in parts of Latin America leaning to the political right.

Mexico has a right-leaning president, but it also has a publicly-owned development bank and a publicly-owned bank for the military, called Banjercito—the National Bank of the Army, Air Force and Navy.[471] Chile also has a right-leaning president, yet it has a strong tradition of public savings banks that goes back over 150 years.

Banking in Chile is dominated by the giant publicly-owned Banco Estado, which boasts over $20.5 billion in assets as well as Chile's largest network of bank branches and ATM machines, half of its savings accounts, two-thirds of its mortgages, 60 percent of payments, 45 percent of the micro-business bank market, and 80 percent of public sector banking. Banco Estado has a strong record of serving the public. It mobilizes household savings to finance sustainable economic and social development, provides equal access to banking and finance, and increases competition in the banking sector. It has a mandate to promote entrepreneurship, invest in human capital and culture, lead infrastructure investment, finance social spending, and contribute to financial stability, public confidence and national development.[472]

These contributions to national and social well-being have not hurt the bank's profitably. To the contrary, from 2000 to 2005 Banco Estado posted solid growth, with annual loans growing an average of 9.1 percent, and before-tax earnings rising an average of 4.6 percent. In 2005, Banco Estado and its subsidiaries obtained before-tax earnings of $192.7 million and generated a before-tax return on equity (ROE) of 24.4 percent, outperforming the rest of the banking system.[473]

The bank's profitability was also not hurt by the credit crisis that hit globally in 2008-09. To the contrary, Banco Estado made more loans in that period than any other bank in Latin America and the Caribbean. Based on figures reported by the Economic Commission for Latin America and the Caribbean (ECLAC), the Chilean state-owned bank increased its loans by 20 percent between December 2008 and September 2009; and its profitability was reported at 22.2 percent, exceeding 2008 figures. State-owned banks in Colombia and Brazil also increased their lending, by 18.6 percent and 17.1 percent respectively.

Chilean private banks reduced their lending by 3.6 percent during the same period.[474]

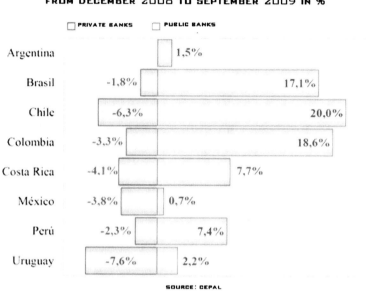

CREDIT FROM PUBLIC AND PRIVATE BANKS
FROM DECEMBER 2008 TO SEPTEMBER 2009 IN %

☐ PRIVATE BANKS   ☐ PUBLIC BANKS

Country	Private Banks	Public Banks
Argentina		1,5%
Brasil	-1,8%	17,1%
Chile	-6,3%	20,0%
Colombia	-3,3%	18,6%
Costa Rica	-4,1%	7,7%
México	-3,8%	0,7%
Perú	-2,3%	7,4%
Uruguay	-7,6%	2,2%

SOURCE: CEPAL

Figure 11. **Countercyclical lending of Latin American public banks in the post-2008 downturn.**
Source: CEPAL - Comisión Económica para América Latina y el Caribe

Ecuador: Central Banking in the Public Interest

Ecuador is another Latin American country that suffered less than other countries during the banking crisis of 2008–09. It did this despite—or perhaps because of—having defaulted on $3.2 billion in foreign bonds. President Rafael Correa claimed that the securities were illegitimate and illegal. Critics said the move would shut Ecuador out of international credit markets; but by mid-2011, its bonds were rewarding investors with the best performance in Latin America, as Chinese loans and higher oil prices boosted confidence in the country's ability to repay its debts.[475] Ecuador is one of those countries choosing to get development loans from China rather than the IMF, because

China does not attach "conditionalities" to them. Ecuador came out of the recession after only three quarters of declining GDP; and by 2012, its poverty and unemployment levels were well below pre-crisis levels.

A study reported in May 2012 by the Center for Economic and Policy Research in Washington suggested that Ecuador has fared so well because it did not go along with the neoliberal model. The country is "dollarized," meaning its national currency is the U.S. dollar; but it engages in activities that would be frowned on by Washington and the European Central Bank. Petroleum exports have not been privatized as in other countries. Instead, profits from the nationalized oil company PetroEcuador are funneled into central bank reserves. During difficult economic times, this money has been used to fund economic stimulus.[476]

The government not only owns its own oil company but uses the profits as the reserves for its publicly-owned central bank, which are used to fund public economic stimulus. The approach is radical, innovative, and eminently sensible. Why isn't it followed elsewhere? Perhaps, as Frederick Soddy said in the 1920s, it is simply because laissez faire capitalism jealously denies to the state "the right of competing in any way with individuals in the ownership of productive enterprise, out of which monetary interest or profit can be made."[477]

Ecuador, like China, has preserved the ideal of a "national" central bank—one serving the interests of the nation. The central bank serves the government and the economy rather than the other way around, and so does the nation's oil wealth.

Bill Black is associate professor of economics and law at the University of Missouri-Kansas City. In a February 2013 article titled "Correa's and Ecuador's Success Drive *The Economist* Nuts," he wrote:

> In 2009, *The Economist* practically licked its lips in eager anticipation of what it hoped would become Corea's (and Ecuador's) failure due to "the country's acute financial problems." . . . The problem is that Correa, and Ecuador, refuse to fail. Indeed, the most popular elected head of state in the Americas is Correa—by a considerable margin.

The *Economist* article Black was discussing was dated February 2013 and was titled, "Ecuador's Election: The Man with the Mighty

Microphone." It began, "Having mixed the good, the bad and the ugly during six years in power, Rafael Correa is heading for another term." The author was hard-pressed, however, to identify much that was bad or ugly about Correa's presidency. He conceded:

> Mr Correa appears to be uncorrupt. The giant increase in public spending he has overseen (it rose by 71 percent last year) has resulted in new schools and hospitals. Testing of teachers, with pay linked to results, has been introduced. When talking to an educated audience, Mr Correa stresses the need to improve the country's economic competitiveness.
>
> ... Mr Correa raised the government's share of oil and other taxes as well. The result is that government revenues have almost tripled since 2006, with oil accounting for about half of the rise. Opportunistically, Mr Correa scrapped previous fiscal rules that required part of windfall revenues to be saved, and defaulted on $3.2 billion in foreign bonds.
>
> He has lavished all this cash on public spending. The public-sector payroll has risen by a quarter; the cabinet has swollen to 40 members; and the mandarins use 34,500 official cars. But Mr Correa has also shown political skill in ramping up social spending in a country where provision was inadequate and poverty reached 64 percent in 2000 (it is now 27 percent). Many Ecuadoreans sense that the oil wealth has at last trickled down to them. And Mr Correa has largely eschewed the expropriations of private companies and the smothering economic controls practised by Mr Chávez.[478]

Contrary to the insinuations of *The Economist*, it seems that Ecuadoreans knew what they were doing in re-electing this very popular and successful president.

Uruguay

Like Ecuador and other Latin American countries, Uruguay is thriving after rejecting the neo-liberal agenda. The economy expanded by 8.5 percent in 2010 and continued its high growth in 2011. Unemployment has been low, at 6.6 percent in early 2011 and 6.7 percent in 2010.[479] As of December 2008, only two of Uruguay's 14 banks were state-owned.[480]

But these two banks (República and BHU) dominated the sector, representing about 50 percent of assets as of the end of 2007.[481]

Across the political spectrum, Latin American countries have asserted their independence by taking a pragmatic path that transcends ideologies in an effort to create better lives for their citizens. The possibilities and pitfalls of pursuing that independent path are particularly evident in Argentina, a complex case that deserves a chapter of its own.

Chapter 26

ARGENTINA: THE WAGES OF DEFYING THE IMF AND AGRO-ELITE

"Some pictures will be coming down from the bank's hall of fame, beginning with Milton Friedman."

-- Mercedes Marcó del Pont, appointed Argentine central bank president in 2010[482]

Argentina dutifully followed the dictates of the IMF in the 1990s— and wound up with a severe banking crisis in 1995 and national bankruptcy in 2001-2002. The government finally walked away from its foreign debts and printed its own currency. The result was a remarkable flourishing of the economy, and a government that retained its popularity for many years. Yet in late 2012, that government was suddenly facing riots. Why? The answer is complicated, but pushback from a right-wing media monopoly is suspected as a major factor.

What Ecuador did in 2008-09, Argentina did six years earlier: it defied the bankers and walked away from its debts. The Argentine government did not have much choice. The country had been in full-scale depression since 1998 and was bankrupt. Banks had closed, depriving millions of depositors of their savings. Unemployment reached over 25 percent, and in many working-class neighborhoods it was over 50 percent. By the end of 2002, hundreds of bankrupt factories had been occupied by workers—literally taken over and run by them.

When Nestor Kirchner was elected president in early 2003, he rejected efforts to repress these popular movements or to force debt repayment on the people. Instead, he inaugurated a series of emergency public works programs and authorized payments to unemployed workers that were sufficient to meet the basic needs of nearly half the labor force. He used the economic catastrophe as an opportunity to curtail the power of the military and to channel state revenues toward employment programs, productive investments and nontraditional exports.[483]

In 2007, Cristina Fernandez de Kirchner became president, following her husband Nestor, who passed away in 2010. Argentina's second woman president after Eva Peron, she retained her husband's strong popular mandate, and in October 2012, she won a landslide re-election victory at the polls.

Yet in December 2012, only two months later, she faced riots in the streets. How could her popularity have fallen so far so fast? Professor James Petras asserts that the riots were an orchestrated coup intended to stamp out the politically-dangerous precedent set by the revolutionary and very popular Kirchner/Fernandez leadership.[484]

The Disasters Wrought by IMF Policy

How revolutionary the transformations brought about by this dynamic duo were is evident from a look at the long history of political ineptitude and brutality that preceded them. Petras writes:

> Between 1966 and 2002, Argentina suffered brutal military dictatorships culminating in the genocidal generals who murdered 30,000 Argentines from 1976 to 1982. From 1983 to 1989 Argentina suffered under a neo-liberal regime (Raul Alfonsin) which failed to deal with the dictatorial legacy and which presided over triple digit hyper-inflation. From 1989-1999 under President Carlos Menem Argentina witnessed the biggest sell-off of its most lucrative public firms, natural resources (petrol included), banks, highways, zoos and public

toilets to foreign investors and kleptocratic cronies for bargain basement prices.

Last but not least, Fernando De la Rua (2000–2001) promised change and proceeded to deepen the recession that led to the final catastrophic crash of December 2001 and the closing of the banks, the bankruptcy of 10,000 firms and the collapse of the economy.

The neoliberal push from abroad to privatize public enterprises began in 1989. Between 1990 and 1999, privatization brought the nations of Latin America and the Caribbean a combined total of $177.8 billion in revenues; but little of this money filtered down to the public. Most of it was acquired by wealthy elites and sent to overseas banks.[485]

Worse for Argentina, it was targeted by international lenders for massive petrodollar loans. When the rocketing interest rates of the 1980s made the loans impossible to pay back, concessions were required that put it at the mercy of the IMF. Under a new government in the 1990s, Argentina dutifully tightened its belt and tried to follow the IMF's dictates.

The result was a series of crippling currency devaluations. To curb them, a "currency board" was imposed in 1991 that maintained a strict one-to-one peg between the Argentine peso and the U.S. dollar. The Argentine government and its central bank were prohibited by law from printing their own pesos unless fully backed by dollars held as foreign reserves.[486]

The maneuver worked to prevent currency devaluations, but the country lost the flexibility it needed to compete in international markets. The money supply was fixed, limited and inflexible. The result of obediently adopting all the policies mandated by the IMF was an overvalued peso, massive economic contraction, and collapse of the financial system.

Innovative Response:
Community and Local Government Currencies

In 1995, in the wake of Mexico's devaluation of its currency, Argentina suffered a major banking crisis. International investors, fearing the same in Argentina, caused a sharp fall in debt prices, leading to lack of confidence in the peso, capital flight, and a full-scale run on the banks. People rushed to their banks to withdraw their life savings, since there was no deposit insurance. Deposits in the Argentine banking system fell 19 percent between December 1994 and May 1995. The banks' doors closed; and in the ensuing recession, money for commerce became unavailable.[487]

Lacking the national currency, the people responded by creating their own. At the local level, community currencies evolved. One environmental group held a massive yard sale, where people brought what they had to sell and received tickets representing money in exchange. The tickets were then used to barter the purchase of other goods. This system of paper receipts for goods and services developed into the Global Exchange Network (*Red Global de Trueque* or RGT), which went on to become the largest national community currency network in the world. The model spread throughout Central and South America, growing to seven million members and a circulation valued at millions of U.S. dollars per year.

At the local government level, provinces short of the national currency resorted to issuing their own. They paid their employees with paper receipts called "Debt-Cancelling Bonds" that were in currency units equivalent to the Argentine Peso. These notes were similar to "negotiable bonds" (bonds that are legally transferable and negotiable as currency) except that they did not pay interest. The bonds canceled the provinces' debts to their employees and could be spent in the community. The Argentine provinces had actually "monetized" their debts, turning their bonds, or promises to pay, into legal tender.[488]

Although these various measures increased the currency in circulation, prices did not inflate. To the contrary, studies found that in provinces in which the national money supply was supplemented with local currencies, prices actually declined compared to other Argentine provinces. Local exchange systems allowed goods and services to be traded that would not otherwise have been on the market. Supply and demand thus increased together. But the system had some flaws, including a lack of adequate controls against counterfeiting. Large amounts of inventory were stolen with counterfeit scrip, and by the summer of 2002, the RGT had shrunk to 70,000 members. It nevertheless remains a remarkable testament to what can be done at a grassroots level when neighbors get together to trade with their own locally-grown currency.

National Bankruptcy

The banking crisis of 2001-02, like that in 1995, was largely the result of "adjustment policies" (today called "austerity measures") prescribed by the IMF. Unemployment soared, and so did the poverty rate. In the face of dire predictions that the economy would collapse without foreign credit, in 2001 the government simply walked away from its debts, and used its scant resources to stimulate internal production and consumption. Creditors were told to get in line with everyone else.

As critics had warned, foreign capital flows to Argentina ceased almost completely. Yet by the fall of 2004, three years after a record default on a debt of more than $100 billion, the country was well on the road to recovery; and it achieved this feat without foreign help. President Kirchner re-nationalized several privatized firms and pension funds, intervened in the banks, doubled social spending, expanded public investment in production, and increased popular consumption. By the end of 2003, Argentina had turned from negative to 8 percent positive growth.[489] The economy grew by that amount the next year as well. Exports increased, the currency was stable, investors were returning, and unemployment had eased.

"This is a remarkable historical event, one that challenges 25 years of failed policies," said Mark Weisbrot in an interview quoted in *The New York Times*. "While other countries are just limping along, Argentina is experiencing very healthy growth with no sign that it is unsustainable, and they've done it without having to make any concessions to get foreign capital inflows."[490]

Most of Argentina's debt was later restructured at 35 to 60 percent of what was originally owed. But the IMF debt, totaling 9.81 billion U.S. dollars, was paid in full. To Kirchner, it was worth the price to get out from under the thumb of the IMF, which he said had been "a source of demands and more demands," forcing "policies which provoked poverty and pain among Argentine people."[491]

Where did he get the dollars to pay this debt? The Argentine central bank had been routinely "issuing" pesos to buy dollars in order to keep the dollar price of the peso from dropping. Apparently the bank was just printing them (or creating them on a computer screen). The bank accumulated over 27 billion U.S. dollars in this way before 2006.[492] Kirchner negotiated with the bank to get a third of these dollar reserves, which were then used in January 2006 to pay the IMF debt.[493]

As with the local issuance of currencies, this large government issue of pesos did not inflate prices as long as it was accompanied by new products and services. According to a December 2006 article in *The Economist*, the new pesos just stimulated the economy, providing the liquidity sorely needed by Argentina's money-starved businesses.[494] By 2004, however, spare production had been used up, and price inflation became a problem. President Kirchner then stepped in to control it by imposing price controls and export bans. Critics warned that these measures would halt investment, but according to *The Economist*:

> So far they have been wrong. Argentina does lack foreign investment. But its own smaller companies have moved quickly to expand capacity in response to demand. . . . Overall, investment has almost doubled as a percentage of GDP since 2002, from 11 percent to 21.4 percent, enough to sustain growth of 4 percent a year.

The Fastest Growth in the Western Hemisphere

The banking sector in Argentina is now dominated by state-owned banks, and the government has considerable control over financial activities. The country's largest bank, Banco de la Nación Argentina, is state-owned and may be the sole financial institution in some areas.

During the deep recession of 2008-09, the United States economy declined by 8% annually. Argentina's economy, meanwhile, expanded by about 1 percent in 2009 and by a healthy 8 percent in 2010-11. By the end of 2011, it had enjoyed eight straight years of economic growth, averaging nearly 8 percent annually.[495] For the years 2002-2011, according to the IMF, *Argentina had real GDP growth of about 94 percent—* over three times the growth of the U.S. economy, and the fastest in the Western hemisphere.

The benefits from this growth were not siphoned off by the wealthy but were shared with the populace. By 2011, poverty and extreme poverty in Argentina had been reduced by about two-thirds from their peak in 2002, and employment had increased to record levels. Social spending by the government had nearly tripled, and inequality had been substantially reduced.[496] From 2001 to 2011, the percentage of poor Argentines declined from over 50 percent to less than 15 percent. In the United States, poverty *increased* by nearly 50 percent in the same period. During that decade, the incomes of wage and salaried workers in Argentina increased in real terms by over 50 percent, while declining by nearly 10 percent in the United States.[497] James Petras observes that income disparity is now greater in the United States than in any other member of the Organization for Economic Cooperation and Development (OECD). One percent of the U.S. population controls 40 percent of wealth, up from 30 percent in less than a decade. In Argentina, by contrast, inequality actually declined by about half during that period.

A Quiet Revolution in Monetary Policy

IIn 2010, the administration of President Cristina Fernandez took another bold step, when it subordinated the formerly independent central bank under its authority. Mercedes Marcó del Pont (another woman) was appointed to be central bank president.[498] (Note that neither the U.S. presidency nor the chairmanship of the U.S. central bank has *ever* gone to a woman.)

According to Rick Rowden, writing in *Foreign Policy* in July 2012, these two women have fired the first shot in a quiet revolution in monetary policy, adopting reforms that could threaten to overturn 25 years of conservative central bank policies long considered best practice by the IMF and central banks around the world.[499]

The Presidentas are no longer buying the neoliberal taboos against the government issuing its own money. They have seen in the last dozen years what government-issued pesos can do to turn a collapsed economy around. Nor are they issuing money just to fill bank reserve accounts with "sterilized" paper, as is being done with the "quantitative easing" of the U.S., U.K. and Japan. According to Rowden, they are aiming the nation's credit power at the physical productive economy, with the goal of promoting job creation and more equitable development.

Other reforms include giving the central bank an increased role in supervising the financial system by regulating domestic credit conditions, including loan maturities, interest rates, and commissions; preventing excessive risk-taking; and increasing central bank aid to the government for financing domestic banks and institutions involved in job creation and productive investments. Rowden writes:

> *The changes break a host of taboos in the dominant school of monetarism in neoclassical economics and conservative policy circles*—a bold effort to show that central banks can play more proactive roles by providing credit to promote productive investment and job creation, and doing so with an eye to ensuring greater socioeconomic equality.

Although the Argentine Presidentas are breaking with the dominant monetarism of the last 40 years, Rowden observes that in earlier eras, central banks in both industrialized and developing countries routinely worked with their governments to provide credit as needed to support government programs. A number of successful economic recoveries after World War II were based on this sort of collaboration, including those in South Korea, Taiwan, China, and India. Only in the Thatcher/Reagan era did central banks become "independent," working to maintain low inflation at all costs. Then, says Rowden:

> [L]ow inflation became the leading goal of monetary policy, regardless of what else might be happening in an economy, and any fiscal policy goals had to be constrained to accommodate it.

The Inflation Problem

It has been a bold experiment, but the monetarists maintain that it isn't working. They point to significant price inflation in Argentina—of 10 percent to 25 percent, depending on whose figures you believe.

As in India, however, it is not clear what has triggered the price rises. Mercedes Marcó del Pont blames supply-side shortages in a fast-growing economy and international conditions, rather than too much money in the system.

The low-double-digit price rises in fast-growing economies are a quite different phenomenon from the hyperinflations that Argentina suffered historically. In July 1989, the country saw 200 percent inflation for the month, peaking at 5,000 percent for the year. It reached a breathtaking high of 20,262.8 percent in March of 1990.[500]

Cambridge economist Ha-Joon Chang, cited earlier, notes that in countries experiencing miracle growth, price inflation is a common phenomenon. Higher inflation rates in those cases can actually have a favorable effect on growth and jobs. He cites Korea and Brazil as examples.

Mark Weisbrot of the Center for Economic and Policy Research agrees, writing:

> Inflation may be high in Argentina, but it is real growth and income distribution that matter with regard to the well-being of the mass majority of the population.[501]

And that seems to have been the attitude of Argentines themselves until recently. An October 2011 article in *The Washington Post* observed:

> [P]ublic outrage over inflation numbers has given way to giddy optimism as Argentina's red-hot economy continues to grow. That has won the loyalty of Argentines such as Veronica Mariño, 38, a state worker who contends that the higher inflation figures offered by private economic consultants are cooked up to tarnish the government.
>
> "The inflation issue, to be honest, does not worry many Argentines as long as there is work," Mariño said.[502]

Pushback and Protests

A year later, however, work was not so plentiful, and Argentines were not doing so well. The question was why. According to James Petras, the economy was being squeezed by the United States and the European Union. He wrote in a December 2012 article:

> The U.S. and E.U. increased pressure on Argentina by excluding it from international capital markets, questioning its credibility,

downgrading its ratings and promoting a virulently hostile anti-Fernandez mass media campaign in the financial press.[503]

Despite these foreign pressures, in October 2012 President Fernandez won a landslide re-election, receiving 54 percent of the vote – 37 percentage points higher than her nearest opponent. Her coalition also swept the congressional, senatorial, and gubernatorial elections, along with 135 of the 136 municipal councils of Greater Buenos Aires.

Only two months later, sentiment had suddenly changed to violent protests and riots in the streets. Why?

James Petras suggests that where the Fernandez government went too far was in moving to end the monopoly of the corporate media and the concessions given to the agro-export elite backing the earlier Argentine dictatorships. Legislation was passed restricting monopoly media ownership and promising to expand media licensing to local communities and diverse social groups. The right-wing mass media monopoly and powerful agrarian interests then struck back. According to Petras:

> The major media monopoly, Clarin, organized a virulent systematic propaganda campaign trumpeting the demands of the economic elite, fabricating stories of government corruption and refusing to comply with the new government legislation in hopes of staving off the dismantling of its huge media monopoly. . . .
>
> The destabilization campaign has been orchestrated by the same economic elites who supported the brutal seven-year military dictatorship during which an estimated 30,000 Argentines were murdered by the juntas. Elite opposition is rooted in reactionary social and economic demands, i.e. lower taxes on exports, deregulation of the dollar market, their monopoly of the mass media and a reversal of popular social legislation.

British commentator Dave Truman observes that the riots and looting are different from those of a decade earlier:

> Ten years ago, the supermarkets were certainly looted, but the perpetrators then were making off with basic foodstuffs. The recent looting has been of luxury goods, such as televisions

and computers. The mainstream Argentinean press has been quick to identify the looters as young people, who are neither educated nor employed.[504]

Truman maintains that looting is a sign of the times, which is dominated by materialism, consumerism and greed:

[L]arge sections of the population no longer have the wages to buy consumer goods; neither can they participate in the lifestyle images constantly dangled before their eyes by the corporate media. They are repeatedly being urged by today's not-so-hidden persuaders to buy, buy, buy, but they do not have the means to do so. Is it any wonder then that they take matters into their own hands?

Commenting on Petras' views of the Argentine situation, Truman writes:

James Petras considers the current Argentine government of Cristina Fernandez de Kirchner as being caught somewhere between a rock and a hard place. His view is that she is a populist and largely progressive President, who is finding it difficult to finance her worthy program of social reforms, largely because Argentina is being squeezed in the international money markets by EU and U.S. banking interests.

Even so, Petras does recognise that the Kirchner presidency has been keen to embrace neo-liberalism. He points out that Kirchner has opened up the country to foreign speculators and has relaxed the laws governing the spraying of toxic chemicals near agricultural communities. Ms. Kirchner, it would seem, is a great friend of Monsanto and their ilk.

... Kirchner is doing the bidding of international bankers and corporations in her policy of developing international agri-businesses and mining at the expense of locally-based manufacturing.

Petras, too, recognizes the legitimacy of many of the looters' demands. But he fears the rioters are being used by an agro-export elite to destabilize what has until now been a largely successful social-liberal democracy. He writes:

The "left opposition" includes a variety of movements including Marxist grouplets and trade unions who demand salary increases commensurate with "real inflation" as well as environmentalists demanding tighter controls over agro-chemical pollution, GM seeds and destructive mining operations. Many of these demands have legitimacy, however some of the Marxist and leftist groups have been participating in protests and strikes convoked by the rightwing parties and economic elites designed to destabilize and overthrow the government. . . .

This de-facto Right-Left alliance on the streets is led by the most rancid, authoritarian and neo-liberal elites who ultimately will be the prime beneficiary if the Fernandez regime is destabilized and toppled. . . . The left grouplets maintain that they are in favor of building a "worker state" as they march abreast with the rich and militarists. Objectively, their capacity to catalyze a revolution is nil and the real outcome of their "opportunism" will be a victory for the agro-export elite— mass media monopolies—US-EU alliance.

Staging a "leftist" workers' protest, says Petras, is mere window dressing for destabilizing a populist government that successfully overthrew an oppressive far-right regime. The protest will succeed only in helping to return that regime to power:

By joining in opportunist alliances to score some small victories today, they foreclose any possible role in the near future of forming progressive democratic leftist governments [and] are creating the basis for the seizure of state power by the military.[505]

"Spontaneous" grassroots uprisings of this sort, triggered by big money and foreign interests, have frequently been seen of late. According to some critical observers, the scenario Petras fears for Argentina has already played out in Libya . . . .

Chapter 27

LIBYA AND THE "ROGUE" STATES: A CLASH OF BANKING IDEOLOGIES?

"The US, the other G-8 countries, the World Bank, IMF, BIS, and multinational corporations do not look kindly on leaders who threaten their dominance over world currency markets or who appear to be moving away from the international banking system that favors the corporatocracy. Saddam Hussein had advocated policies similar to those expressed by Qaddafi shortly before the U.S. sent troops into Iraq."

— John Perkins, author of
Confessions of an Economic Hitman[506]

Most countries have been persuaded by economic means to join the central banking scheme overseen by the Bank for International Settlements, but a few have remained outside. These "rogue states" have been embroiled in undeclared wars popularly characterized as being about human rights. Less well known is that these wars also involve a clash of banking ideologies.

While the Argentine Presidentas were quietly sidestepping the international banking model, Libya's Muammar Gaddafi was defiantly shaking a fist at the world. He wound up in a civil war, with the United States and other Western countries supporting the rebels. Western media characterized this support as being about human rights violations by Gaddafi. But some non-Western commentators saw it differently.

According to a March 2011 Russian article titled "Bombing of Libya–Punishment for Gaddafi for His Attempt to Refuse U.S. Dollar," the Libyan president was primarily targeted for initiating a movement to refuse the dollar and the euro. He had called on Arab and African nations to use a new currency, the gold dinar; and he had sought to establish a united African continent, with its 200 million people using this single currency. The idea was approved by many Arab countries and most African countries, according to the article, with only the Republic of South Africa and the head of the League of Arab States opposed. The initiative was viewed negatively by the U.S. and E.U., with French president Nicolas Sarkozy calling Libya a threat to the financial security of mankind. But Gaddafi was not swayed and continued his push for the creation of a united Africa.[507]

Reports on the Libyan abuse of human rights also differed. According to a *Fox News* article on February 28, 2011:

> As the United Nations works feverishly to condemn Libyan leader Muammar al-Qaddafi for cracking down on protesters, the body's Human Rights Council is poised to adopt a report chock-full of praise for Libya's human rights record.
>
> The review commends Libya for improving educational opportunities, for making human rights a "priority" and for bettering its "constitutional" framework. Several countries, including Iran, Venezuela, North Korea, and Saudi Arabia but also Canada, give Libya positive marks for the legal protections afforded to its citizens—who are now revolting against the regime and facing bloody reprisal.[508]

A delegation of medical professionals from Russia, Ukraine and Belarus maintained that the international community had been misinformed. In an appeal to Russian President Medvedev and Prime Minister Putin, they wrote that after becoming acquainted with Libyan life, it was their view that in few nations did people live in such comfort:

> [Libyans] are entitled to free treatment, and their hospitals provide the best in the world of medical equipment. Education in Libya is free, capable young people have the opportunity to study abroad at government expense. When marrying, young couples receive 60,000 Libyan dinars (about 50,000 U.S. dollars) of financial assistance. Non-interest state loans, and as practice shows, undated. Due to government subsidies the price of cars is much lower than in Europe, and they are affordable for every family. Gasoline and bread cost a penny, no taxes for those who are engaged in agriculture. The Libyan people are quiet and peaceful, are not inclined to drink, and are very religious.[509]

There was no denying at least one very popular achievement of the Libyan government: it had brought water to the desert by building the largest and most expensive irrigation project in history, the $33 billion GMMR (Great Man-Made River) project. Even more than oil, water is crucial to life in Libya. The GMMR provides 70 percent of the population with water for drinking and irrigation, pumping it from Libya's vast underground Nubian Sandstone Aquifer System in the south to populated coastal areas 4,000 kilometers to the north. The Libyan government under Gaddafi had done at least some things right.[510]

There were other odd facts about the revolt. As rebellion was being fomented against Gaddafi in the spring of 2011, the rebels had taken the time to create their own central bank—this before they even had a government. Robert Wenzel wrote in *The Economic Policy Journal*:

> I have never before heard of a central bank being created in just a matter of weeks out of a popular uprising. This suggests we have a bit more than a rag tag bunch of rebels running around and that there are some pretty sophisticated influences.[511]

Alex Newman wrote in *The New American*:

> In a statement released last week, the rebels reported on the results of a meeting held on March 19. Among other things, the supposed rag-tag revolutionaries announced the "[d]esignation of the Central Bank of Benghazi as a monetary authority competent in monetary policies in Libya and appointment of a Governor to the Central Bank of Libya, with a temporary headquarters in Benghazi."[512]

Newman quoted CNBC senior editor John Carney, who asked, "Is this the first time a revolutionary group has created a central bank while it is still in the midst of fighting the entrenched political power? It certainly seems to indicate how extraordinarily powerful central bankers have become in our era."

Some critics said the assault on Libya was actually about oil, but that theory too was problematic. As noted in *The National Journal*, the country produces only about 2 percent of the world's oil. If Libyan oil were to disappear from the market, Saudi Arabia alone has enough spare capacity to make up the deficiency. And if it was all about oil, why the rush to set up a new central bank?[513]

Another provocative bit of data circulating on the Internet was a 2007 "Democracy Now" interview of U.S. General Wesley Clark (Ret.). In it he said that about 10 days after September 11, 2001, he was told by a general that the decision had been made to go to war with Iraq. Clark was surprised and asked why. "I don't know!" was the response. "I guess they don't know what else to do!" Later, the same general said they planned to take out seven countries in five years: Iraq, Syria, Lebanon, Libya, Somalia, Sudan, and Iran.[514]

What did these seven countries have in common? In the context of banking, one that sticks out is that none was listed among the member banks of the Bank for International Settlements.[515] That meant they were outside the long regulatory arm of the central bankers' central bank in Switzerland. Other countries later identified as "rogue states" that were also not members of the BIS included North Korea, Cuba, and Afghanistan.[516]

Iraq was the first of the seven targets to be "taken out." On *Examiner.com*, Kenneth Schortgen Jr. wrote that "[s]ix months before the U.S. moved into Iraq to take down Saddam Hussein, the oil nation had made the move to accept Euros instead of dollars for oil," and that "this became a threat to the global dominance of the dollar as the reserve currency, and its dominion as the petrodollar."[517]

In a March 2011 article posted on *Market Oracle*, Filipino money reformer Eric Encina posed a similar theory about Libya. He wrote:

> One seldom mentioned fact by western politicians and media pundits: the Central Bank of Libya is 100 percent State Owned.
> . . . Currently, the Libyan government creates its own money,

the Libyan Dinar, through the facilities of its own central bank. Few can argue that Libya is a sovereign nation with its own great resources, able to sustain its own economic destiny. One major problem for globalist banking cartels is that in order to do business with Libya, they must go through the Libyan Central Bank and its national currency, a place where they have absolutely zero dominion or power-broking ability. Hence, taking down the Central Bank of Libya (CBL) may not appear in the speeches of Obama, Cameron and Sarkozy but this is certainly at the top of the globalist agenda for absorbing Libya into its hive of compliant nations.[518]

Libya had its own oil and its own gold, and it issued its own currency and credit. In 2011, according to the IMF, the Libyan central bank had nearly 144 tons of gold in its vaults.[519] (That was then. The gold is now rumored to be sitting in London banks.[520]) The functions of the Central Bank of Libya included issuing and regulating banknotes and coins in Libya and managing and issuing all state loans. That means the nation's wholly state-owned bank could issue and lend the national currency for state purposes.[521] That might explain where Libya got the money to provide free education and medical care, and to issue young couples $50,000 in interest-free state loans. It could also help explain where the country found the $33 billion to build the Great Man-Made River project.

The real threat of Libya and other resource-rich "rogue" states may have been that they could show the world what was possible. They had their own oil, owned their own central banks, issued their own currencies and credit, and declined even to give lip service to the BIS and the Basel rules. Because they did not need to borrow U.S. dollars to buy oil, they were able to escape the debt trap of the international bankers. With energy, water, and ample credit to develop the infrastructure to access them, they could free themselves from the grip of foreign creditors and turn their resources to serving their own economies and their own people.

Most countries do not have their own copious oil reserves, but new technologies are being developed that could make non-oil-producing nations energy-independent, particularly if infrastructure costs were halved by borrowing from their own publicly-owned banks.[522]

Energy independence would free governments from the foreign bank domination that requires them to shift production from domestic to foreign markets to service foreign loans.

Needless to say, it all ended badly for Gaddafi. His violent end was capped by U.S. Secretary of State Hillary Clinton's notorious exclamation, "We came, we saw, he died!"[523]

Why Is Iran Still in the Cross-Hairs?

The seven countries targeted for take-down have something else in common. They are all Islamic countries, which means they all promote interest-free banking.

Iran is the leader in this relatively new banking concept. In 1979, it was established as an "Islamic Republic," designed to enforce the principles of the Koran not just morally or religiously but as a matter of state government policy. Afghanistan and Pakistan are also now Islamic Republics. The economic principles of the Koran include *sharia* banking, which forbids "usury"—defined in the Koran as charging not just excess interest but *any* interest.

Few Islamic banks existed before Iran became an Islamic Republic in 1979, but the concept is now spreading globally. Seven of the ten leading Islamic banks are in Iran. With the fall of the Iron Curtain in 1989, the model that threatens the global dominance of Western banks may no longer be Communism but an Islamic banking system that would eliminate the powerful economic weapon of compound interest.

The Islamic view of the evils of interest is captured in the following entry in *The World Guide Encyclopedia,* which is published in Uruguay and has a Third World/Islamic orientation:

> This "demon" [interest] governs current global relations, condemning most of the world population to living under the sign of debt: i.e., each person born in Latin America owes already $1,600 in foreign debt; each individual being conceived in Sub-Saharan Africa carries the burden of a $336 debt, for something that its ancestors have long ago paid-off. In 1980 the Southern countries' debt amounted to $567 billion; since then, they have paid $3,450 billion in interest and write-offs,

six times the original amount. In spite of this, that debt had quadrupled by the year 2000, reaching $2,070 billion.[524]

As with Libya, the justification for the U.S. push for war with Iran is problematic. According to the media, it is to deter an imminent threat of nuclear attack. But experts say Iran not only does not have nuclear weapons but has not even made the decision to develop them.[525] There is also the inconvenient inconsistency that India, Pakistan, and Israel are known or believed to have nuclear weapons already, yet they have not been targeted for aggressive action.[526]

Some commentators suspect that the push against Iran, as with Iraq, is really about oil. But many countries have oil, and we don't normally invade them to get their assets. Why go to war for something we can just buy from them?

Another theory says that the saber-rattling is about defending the dollar. Iran has now opened its own oil bourse (market) and is selling much of its oil in non-dollar currencies. Iran has broken the petrodollar stranglehold imposed in the 1970s, when OPEC entered into an agreement with the United States to sell oil only in U.S. dollars.[527] But Iran is not alone in dropping the dollar as its oil currency. And as William Engdahl pointed out in 2006, military aggression against Iran has been in the cards as part of the U.S. Greater Middle East strategy since the 1990s, long before Iran threatened to open its own oil bourse.[528]

Iran was targeted in the infamous policy paper titled "Rebuilding America's Defenses," published by the Project for a New American Century (PNAC) in 2000. In a May 2005 summary of the PNAC directive, Professor Michel Chossudovsky described PNAC as a neo-conservative think tank linked to the defense-intelligence establishment and the powerful Council on Foreign Relations (CFR), which plays an important role in the formulation of U.S. foreign policy. In its policy paper, PNAC called for "the direct imposition of U.S. 'forward bases' throughout Central Asia and the Middle East, with a view to ensuring economic domination of the world, while strangling any potential 'rival' or any viable alternative to America's vision of a 'free market' economy."[529]

"Any potential 'rival' or any viable alternative to America's vision of a 'free market economy'" is read by skeptics as meaning any alternative that threatens the right to extract profits globally in a "free market" economy. Declaring the powerful extractive tool known as interest illegal, as has been done in Islamic republics, could satisfy that definition.

To the disillusioned in developing countries, "America's vision of a free market economy" is seen as simply another form of exploitation—prying countries open to be plundered of their physical and human resources in return for loans of the dollars necessary to buy oil at inflated prices. Oil is the bait for ensnaring the world in the debt trap, and the "terrorism" that must be suppressed is the rebellion of any locals who will not be ensnared quietly. The weapon in this economic war is debt, and the bullets are compound interest, which has allowed a private global banking monopoly to control most of the resources of the world.

As noted earlier, the debt trap was set in 1974, when OPEC was induced to trade its oil only in U.S. dollars. The price of oil then suddenly quadrupled, and countries with insufficient dollars for their oil needs had to borrow them. In 1980, international interest rates shot up to 20 percent. At 20 percent interest compounded annually, $100 doubles in under 4 years. In 20 years, it becomes a breathtaking $3,834.[530]

The impact on Third World debtor nations has been devastating. President Obasanjo of Nigeria complained in 2000:

> All that we had borrowed up to 1985 was around $5 billion, and we have paid about $16 billion; yet we are still being told that we owe about $28 billion. That $28 billion came about because of the injustice in the foreign creditors' interest rates. If you ask me what is the worst thing in the world, I will say it is compound interest.[531]

Interest-free Banking and Public Banking

Although a viable interest-free banking system could be seen as a covert threat in the war-posturing against Iran, today that threat remains largely theoretical. Islamic scholars themselves have complained that most of what passes for *riba-free* (interest-free) banking amounts to interest-bearing loans by other names. They use terms such as "the usury of deception" and "the jurisprudence of legal tricks."[532]

Islamic banks typically charge "fees" on loans that are little different from interest. A common arrangement is to finance real estate purchases by buying property and selling it to clients at a higher price, to be paid in installments over time.

One problem for banks attempting to follow an interest-free model is that they are normally private institutions that have to make a profit for their owners, in competition with other private banks. Their owners have little incentive to engage in commercial lending if they are taking risks without earning a corresponding profit.

There might be other ways, however, to design a *sharia*-compliant banking system. The model is not set in stone, since few Islamic banks were even in existence before 1979. Like China, Islamic countries might have less concern for the color of the cat than whether it catches mice.

The religious objection to charging interest is that it involves unjust gains, generally through exploitation.[533] This unfair result could be avoided, however, without actually banning interest, just as it was in Sumer, the ancient forerunner of Iraq. Interest was collected but went to the temple, which then disbursed it to the community for the common good.

A similar model was created by Mohammad Yunus, a Muslim professor who founded the Grameen Bank of Bangladesh. The Grameen Bank charges interest, but at a lower rate than would otherwise be available to poor women lacking collateral; and the interest is returned to the bank, where it is used for the benefit of the women themselves as its shareholders.[534]

This sort of model was also successfully employed in colonial Pennsylvania. A public land bank collected interest and returned it to the provincial government, to be used in place of taxes for the benefit of the colony and its residents.

If interest-free lending were considered an essential requirement of ethical banking, however, it would be easier to achieve that result if the bank were owned by a government having the power to create and issue its own money. One function served by interest is to cover losses from default; but as was demonstrated in China, a government that does not need to worry about carrying a multi-trillion dollar federal debt can afford to carry a few private bad debts on its books without upsetting the economy.

A publicly-owned bank providing interest-free credit would just be a credit clearing agency, an intermediary that allowed people to "monetize" their own promises to repay. As in a community currency system, people would become sovereign issuers of their own money, not just collectively but individually.

To visualize how this might work, consider what happens when purchases are made with a credit card. Your signature turns the credit slip into a negotiable instrument, turning your promise to pay into money. The merchant accepts it in payment because the credit card company stands behind it and will pursue legal remedies if you don't pay when the bill comes due. The bank facilitates and guarantees the deal, but in effect you create the "money" yourself, in the same way that banks do. And if you pay your bill in full every month, you are creating money *interest-free*. It is not debt-free, since you have to pay it back; but you have to pay only what was advanced, not the bank royalty known as interest.

Credit could be extended interest-free for longer periods than a month on the same model. To assure that advances of the national credit got repaid, national banks would have the same remedies that lenders have now, including foreclosure on real estate and other collateral, garnishment of wages, and the threat of a bad credit rating for defaulters. Borrowers would also have the usual consumer protections, including filing for bankruptcy if they could not pay. They would just have an easier time meeting their obligations, since their interest-free loans would be far less onerous than the credit card charges of 16 percent or more that are prevalent today.

Whatever new models we wind up with, they will have to be cooperative ones that serve the economy and the people if they are to be sustainable. It is too late to suppress the global revolt against the extractive banking model that has dominated the world through debt. Iran is a far more formidable opponent than either Iraq or Libya.[535] And Russia, China and India are nuclear powers. They will have to be negotiated with, and the first step to forming a working relationship is to understand how their economies work. Rather than declaring war on their successful practices, a more sensible approach might be to assimilate some of them into our own. Just as they succeeded in competing with us by adopting our technologies, so we might be better able to compete with them by adopting some of their better banking practices.

The End of Empire

John Perkins, author of *Confessions of an Economic Hitman* (2004), is an insider who understands the exploitation and coercion of Third World countries by such institutions as the World Bank and IMF. He understands them because he served as one of their hitmen. Commenting on the plight of Libya in April 2011, he wrote:

> One definition of "empire" . . . states that an empire is a nation that dominates other nations by imposing its own currency on the lands under its control. The empire maintains a large standing military that is ready to protect the currency and the entire economic system that depends on it through extreme violence, if necessary. The ancient Romans did this. So did the Spanish and the British during their days of empire-building.
>
> Now, the U.S. or, more to the point, the corporatocracy, is doing it and is determined to punish any individual who tries to stop them. Qaddafi is but the latest example.
>
> Understanding the war against Quaddafi as a war in defense of empire is another step in the direction of helping us ask ourselves whether we want to continue along this path of empire-building. . . .
>
> History teaches that empires do not endure; they collapse or are overthrown. Wars ensue and another empire fills the vacuum. . . . We cannot afford to watch history repeat itself.[536]

And that brings us back to the clandestine global banking empire exposed by Carroll Quigley in the 1960s, for which the Bank for International Settlements was to be the apex. The next chapter will look at how close the BIS has come to achieving its goals. It has managed to become the apex of the system, but is it a system we want to continue to support? Or is it a banking dinosaur on the verge of collapse?

Chapter 28

THE TOWER OF BASEL: ANOTHER LOOK AT THE APEX OF THE SYSTEM

"One of the most powerful forces behind large system change comes with emphasizing contradictions between how a system claims to work as the basis of its legitimacy, and the way it actually works. In the physical sciences this gave rise to the term 'paradigm shift'; adapted in the social sciences and paired with the concept of erosion of legitimacy, emphasizing contradictions is behind the concept of 'revolutions' . . . ."

— Steve Waddell, "Global Finance and the Role of
Responsible Investors," in Responsible Investing in
Times of Turmoil (Springer Netherland 2011)

The Basel Committee on Banking Supervision, housed at the Bank for International Settlements, now sets banking standards globally. The stated purpose of these regulations is to preserve the stability of the global financial system, but they often do this at the expense of the economies the banks are supposed to be servicing. The result is to force national policies to serve the profit incentives of the banks rather than the needs of the people and local businesses.

Today, the clique of financiers Carroll Quigley called "the international bankers" has evidently reached its goals. The key to their success, he said, was that "the international bankers would control and manipulate the money system of a nation while letting it appear to be controlled by the government," and that has been achieved. The Bank for International Settlements is now the apex of a global banking hierarchy.

The Basel Committee on Banking Supervision, formed in 1974, demonstrated its power to make or break economies when it set the global standard for capital adequacy at 8 percent in 1988. Before that, banks were not subject to international capital requirements. Japan, as noted earlier, had emerged as the world's largest creditor; but its banks were less well capitalized than other major international banks. Raising the capital requirement forced them to cut back on lending, creating a recession in Japan like that triggered in the United States in 2008. A downward spiral followed, ending with the bankruptcy of the banks and their covert nationalization.[537]

In a May 2002 article in *The Asia Times* titled "Global Economy: The BIS vs. National Banks," economist Henry C. K. Liu observed that the Basel Accords have forced national banking systems "to march to the same tune, designed to serve the needs of highly sophisticated global financial markets, regardless of the developmental needs of their national economies." He wrote:

> [N]ational banking systems are suddenly thrown into the rigid arms of the Basel Capital Accord sponsored by the Bank of International Settlement (BIS), or to face the penalty of usurious risk premium in securing international interbank loans. . . . National policies suddenly are subjected to profit incentives of private financial institutions, all members of a hierarchical system controlled and directed from the money center banks in New York. *The result is to force national banking systems to privatize . . . .*
>
> *BIS regulations serve only the single purpose of strengthening the international private banking system, even at the peril of national economies. . . .* The IMF and the international banks regulated by the BIS are a team: the international banks lend recklessly to borrowers in emerging economies to create a foreign currency

debt crisis, the IMF arrives as a carrier of monetary virus in the name of sound monetary policy, then *the international banks come as vulture investors in the name of financial rescue to acquire national banks deemed capital inadequate and insolvent by the BIS.*

Among other collateral damage produced by the Basel Accords was a spate of suicides among Indian farmers unable to get loans. Similar complaints have come from small entrepreneurs in other countries. An article in the December 2008 *Korea Times* titled "BIS Calls Trigger Vicious Cycle" described how Korean entrepreneurs with good collateral could not get operational loans from Korean banks, at a time when the economic downturn required increased investment and easier credit:

> "The Bank of Korea has provided more than 35 trillion won to banks since September when the global financial crisis went full throttle," said a Seoul analyst, who declined to be named. "But the effect is not seen at all with the banks keeping the liquidity in their safes. They simply don't lend and *one of the biggest reasons is to keep the BIS ratio high enough to survive,*" he said. . . .
>
> Chang Ha-joon, an economics professor at Cambridge University, concurs with the analyst. *"What banks do for their own interests, or to improve the BIS ratio, is against the interests of the whole society.* This is a bad idea," Chang said in a recent telephone interview with *Korea Times.*

As John Perkins revealed in *Confessions of an Economic Hitman*, the trap for governments begins when they are induced to accept loans in foreign currencies, making them "debtor nations" subject to IMF and BIS regulation. They are forced to divert their production to exports, just to earn the foreign currency necessary to pay the interest on their loans.

According to Henry Liu, national banks deemed "capital inadequate" have to deal with strictures comparable to the "conditionalities" imposed by the IMF on debtor nations: escalating capital requirements, loan writeoffs, and restructuring through selloffs, layoffs, downsizing, cost-cutting, and freezes on capital spending. He writes:

Reversing the logic that a sound banking system should lead to full employment and developmental growth, BIS regulations demand high unemployment and developmental degradation in national economies as the fair price for a sound global private banking system.

Ironically, notes Liu, developing countries with their own natural resources do not actually need the foreign investment that has trapped them in debt to outsiders:

Applying the State Theory of Money [which assumes that a sovereign nation has the power to issue its own money], any government can fund with its own currency all its domestic developmental needs to maintain full employment without inflation.

The Last Domino to Fall

While banks in developing nations were being penalized for falling short of the BIS capital requirements, large international banks managed to skirt the rules, although they actually carried enormous risk because of their derivative exposure. The mega-banks took advantage of a loophole that allowed for lower charges against capital for "off-balance sheet activities." The banks got loans off their balance sheets by bundling them into securities and selling them off to investors, after separating the risk of default from the loans and selling it to yet other investors, using the form of derivative known as the credit default swap.

But it was evidently not in the game plan that U.S. banks should escape the regulatory net indefinitely. Complaints about the loopholes in Basel I prompted a new set of rules called Basel II, which based capital requirements for market risk on a "Value-at-Risk" accounting standard. The new rules were established in 2004, but they were not levied on U.S. banks until November 2007, the month after the Dow Industrial Average passed 14,000 to reach its then all-time high. On November 1, 2007, the Office of the Controller of the Currency approved a final rule implementing "advanced approaches of the Basel II Capital Accord."[538] On November 15, 2007, the Financial Accounting Standards

Board or FASB, a private organization that sets U.S. accounting rules for the private sector, adopted FAS 157, the rule called "mark-to-market accounting."[539] The effect was similar to that of Basel I on Japan: the market plunged, and U.S. banks found themselves struggling to survive.[540]

The mark-to-market rule requires banks to adjust the value of their marketable securities to the "market price" of the security.[541] Lenders that had been considered sufficiently well capitalized to make new loans suddenly found they were insolvent; or at least, they would have been if they had tried to sell their assets, an assumption required by the new rule. Financial analyst John Berlau complained in October 2008:

> Despite the credit crunch being described as the spread of the "American flu," the mark-to-market rules that are spreading it were hatched [as] part of the Basel II international rules for financial institutions. It's just that the U.S. jumped into the really icy water last November when our Securities and Exchange Commission and bank regulators implemented FASB's Financial Accounting Standard 157, which makes healthy banks and financial firms take a "loss" in the capital they can lend even if a loan on their books is still performing, even when the "market price" [of] an illiquid asset is that of the last fire sale by a highly leveraged bank. Late last month, similar rules went into effect in the Eurpoean Union, playing a similar role in accelerating financial failures. . . .
>
> The crisis is often called a "market failure," and the term "mark-to-market" seems to reinforce that. But the mark-to-market rules are profoundly anti-market and hinder the free-market function of price discovery. . . . In this case, the accounting rules fail to allow the market players to hold on to an asset if they don't like what the market is currently fetching, an important market action that affects price discovery in areas from agriculture to antiques.[542]

A post on the American Bankers Association website called "What People Are Saying About Fair Value Accounting" included these criticisms, among others:

Simon Ward:

"This kind of accounting is causing investors to see ghosts in banks' balance sheets which just don't exist. If we had suspended mark-to-market accounting a year ago, the current crisis may have been avoided." (*The Daily Telegraph*, October 8, 2008)

Joseph Grundfest:

". . . [M]ark-to market creates situations where you have to go out and raise physical capital in order to cover losses that as a practical matter were never really there." (*CFO.com*, May 6, 2008)

Mark Zandi:

"Current mark-to-market rules have exacerbated the crisis as financial institutions have been forced into a self-reinforcing negative cycle of asset price declines forcing write-downs and thus asset sales and further price declines." (*Knight Ridder*, September 28, 2008)

Steve Schwarzman:

"What they are trying to ask you to do is value your companies as if you're going to sell them at the bottom of a recession." (*Financial Times*, February 3, 2008)[543]

Imposing the mark-to-market rule on U.S. banks caused credit to freeze, triggering a domino effect that took down the economies not only of the United States but of countries worldwide. In early April 2009, the mark-to-market rule was finally softened by FASB; but critics said the modification did not go far enough, and it was done in response to pressure from politicians and bankers, not out of any fundamental change of heart or policies by the BIS or FASB. Indeed, the BIS was warned as early as 2001 that its Basel II proposal was "procyclical," meaning that in a downturn it would only serve to make matters worse. In a formal response to a Request for Comments by the Basel Committee for Banking Supervision, a group of economists stated:

Value-at-Risk can destabilise an economy and induce crashes *when they would not otherwise occur.* . . . Perhaps our most serious concern is that these proposals, taken altogether, will enhance both the procyclicality of regulation and the susceptibility of the financial system to systemic crises, thus negating the central purpose of the whole exercise. *Reconsider before it is too late.*[544]

But the Basel Committee did not reconsider, and there is no democratic mechanism for appeal. That feature of the global regulatory scheme is of particular concern with Basel III, which was ostensibly designed to prevent a repeat of the 2008 banking crisis but is having the effect of taking down the local community banks, forcing them to sell out to their big international competitors.

Crisis and Response: Global Regulation Is Achieved

In April 2009, the leaders of the G20 nations agreed to expand the powers of an advisory group called the Financial Stability Forum (FSF) into a new group called the Financial Stability Board (FSB). The old FSF was chaired by the General Manager of the BIS and was set up in 1999 by the finance ministers and central bank governors of the G7, the seven major industrialized nations. The FSB served in a merely advisory capacity for its members, which included about a dozen nations. The new FSB was expanded to include all G20 members (19 nations plus the EU); and it has real teeth, imposing "obligations" and "commitments" on its members. The secretariat is based at the BIS headquarters in Basel.

What particularly alarmed observers at the time the new board was announced was a vague parenthetical reference in a press release titled "Financial Stability Forum Re-established as the Financial Stability Board," issued by the BIS on April 3, 2009. It stated:

> "As obligations of membership, member countries and territories commit to . . . implement international financial standards (including the 12 key International Standards and Codes) . . . ."

This was no longer just friendly advice from an advisory board. It was a *commitment* to comply, so some detailed discussion would have been expected concerning what those standards entailed. But a search of the major media revealed virtually nothing. The 12 key International Standards and Codes were left undefined and undiscussed. The FSB website listed them but was vague. The Standards and Codes covered broad areas that were apparently subject to modification as the overseeing committees saw fit. They included:

Money and financial policy transparency
Fiscal policy transparency
Data dissemination
Insolvency
Corporate governance
Accounting
Auditing
Payment and settlement
Market integrity
Banking supervision
Securities regulation
Insurance supervision

Take "fiscal policy transparency" as an example. The "Code of Good Practices on Fiscal Transparency" was adopted by the IMF Interim Committee in 1998. The "synoptic description" says:

The code contains transparency requirements to provide assurances to the public and to capital markets that a sufficiently complete picture of the structure and finances of government is available so as to allow the soundness of fiscal policy to be reliably assessed.

Members are required to provide a "picture of the structure and finances of government" that is complete enough for an assessment of its "soundness"—but an assessment by whom, and what if a government fails the test? Is an unelected private committee appointed by the FSB allowed to evaluate the "structure and function" of a particular national government and, if that government is determined to have fiscal policies that are not "sound," to require them to be brought in line with the committee's mandates?

Consider this scenario: the new FSB rules precipitate a global depression the likes of which have never before been seen. XYZ country wakes up to the fact that all of this is unnecessary—that it could be creating its own money, freeing itself from the debt trap, rather than borrowing from bankers who create money on computer screens and charge interest for the privilege of borrowing it. But this realization comes too late. The FSB has ruled that for a government to issue money is an impermissible "merging of the public and private sectors" and an "unsound banking practice" forbidden under the "12 Key International Standards and Codes." XYZ is forced into line. National sovereignty has been abdicated to a private committee, with no say by the voters.

Marilyn Barnewall, called by *Forbes Magazine* the "dean of American private banking," wrote in an April 2009 article titled "What Happened to American Sovereignty at G-20?":

> It seems the world's bankers have executed a bloodless coup and now represent all of the people in the world. . . . President Obama agreed at the G20 meeting in London to create an international board with authority to intervene in U.S. corporations by dictating executive compensation and approving or disapproving business management decisions. Under the new Financial Stability Board, the United States has only one vote. In other words, the group will be largely controlled by European central bankers. My guess is, they will represent themselves, not you and not me and certainly not America.[545]

The G20 Summit has been called "a New Bretton Woods," referring to agreements entered into in 1944 establishing new rules for international trade. But Bretton Woods was adopted in the United States by Congressional Executive Agreement, requiring a majority vote of the legislature; and it probably should have been done by treaty, requiring a two-thirds vote of the Senate, since it was an international agreement binding on the nation. Adoption of the FSB was never voted on by the U.S. public, either individually or through their legislators.

What we have today is very close to what Quigley projected: an unelected private financial regulatory body operating behind closed doors to impose rules globally, rules serving the interests of the large international banks. The BIS has come full circle. The international bankers are now in control, sitting at the apex of a system in which they are indeed "able to dominate the political system of each country and the economy of the world as a whole."

Basel III:
Reining in the Public, Cooperative, and Community Banks

In September 2010, the Basel Committee on Banking Supervision issued heightened capital requirements with the stated purpose of preventing a repeat of the 2008 crisis.[546] The new regulations, called Basel III, raised the mandatory reserve known as Tier 1 capital from 4 percent to 4.5 percent by 2013, to reach 6 percent in 2019.

For Wall Street, it turned out not to be a problem. The megabanks, propped up by generous taxpayer bailouts, would have no trouble meeting the new capital requirements, which were lower than expected and would not be fully implemented until 2019. Only the local banks, the ones already struggling to meet capital requirements, would be seriously challenged by the new rules.

Critics complained that all Basel III really achieved was to shake down the smaller competitors of the big banks that triggered the crisis. "Indeed," observed one cynical commentator, "on the day Lehman Brothers collapsed, *they* would have been in compliance with the Basel III standards."[547]

The smaller local banks not only did not cause the crisis and did not get the bailout money but are the banks that make most of the loans to local businesses, which do most of the hiring and producing in the real economy. In Europe, publicly-owned banks would be particularly hard hit. As reported in *The Huffington Post* in September 2010:

> Bankers and analysts said new global rules could mean less money available to lend to businesses and consumers [and] European savings banks warned that the new capital requirements could affect their lending by unfairly penalizing small, part-publicly owned institutions.
>
> "We see the danger that German banks' ability to give credit could be significantly curtailed," said Karl-Heinz Boos, head of the Association of German Public Sector Banks.[548]

The smaller local banks that cannot meet the capital requirements imposed from abroad have been progressively sold to the international banks that can. The result has been to make the megabanks even larger and riskier—so large and risky that governments are now balking at further bank bailouts.

The response of the BIS and the Financial Stability Board has been the ultimate display, and the ultimate test, of their global power: the new "bail-in" policies directing critically undercapitalized international banks to convert the money of their creditors into bank equity, effectively confiscating depositor funds.

Chapter 29

THE ULTIMATE AFFRONT: BAIL-INS, DERIVATIVES AND FORCED AUSTERITY

"[W]hy do they consider the banks to be the holy churches of the modern economy? Why are private banks not, like airlines and telecommunications companies, allowed to go bankrupt if they have been conducted in an irresponsible way? The theory that you have to bail out banks is a theory about bankers enjoying for their own profit the success and then letting ordinary people bear the failure through taxes and austerity, and people in enlightened democracies are not going to accept that in the long run."

-- Iceland's President Olafur Grimson, January 2013[549]

The ultimate test of international bank sovereignty, and the ultimate affront to our own, are the new "bail in" policies first surfacing in Cyprus in March 2013. These policies are designed to keep highly leveraged and risky derivative banks alive through the legalized confiscation of the funds of creditors—a class that includes depositors. At risk are not just individual deposits but local government revenues and pension funds.

Shock waves went around the world in March 2013, when the IMF, the EU, and the ECB not only approved but mandated the confiscation of depositor funds to "bail in" two bankrupt banks in Cyprus. The EU had warned that it would withhold €10 billion in bailout loans, and the ECB had threatened to end emergency lending assistance for distressed Cypriot banks, unless depositors shared the cost of the rescue. A one-time levy on depositors would be required in return for a bailout of the banking system. Deposits below €100,000 would be subject to a 6.75 percent levy or "haircut," while those over €100,000 would be subject to a 9.99 percent "fine."[550]

The Cyprus national legislature, to its credit, overwhelmingly rejected the proposed levy. As Reuters quoted one 65-year-old pensioner, "The voice of the people was heard."[551] But while the insured depositors with under €100,000 in the bank were finally spared, it was at the expense of the uninsured depositors, who took a much larger hit, estimated at about 60 percent of their deposits.[552]

The new approach to megabank insolvency, called a "bail in," is a quantum leap beyond a "bail out." Bankers who cannot balance their books are no longer beheaded in front of their banks as in the Middle Ages. They can now legally take their depositors' money and call it their own. The banks are being instructed from on high to "recapitalize" themselves by confiscating the funds of their creditors, either with "haircuts" or by turning debt into equity (bank stock). And the "creditors" include the naïve customers who put their money in the bank thinking it was a secure place to store their savings.[553]

Few depositors realize it, but the bank legally owns their money as soon as it is deposited in the bank. The money becomes the bank's, and the depositor becomes an unsecured creditor holding an IOU or promise to pay.[554] That has been the law for over a century, although bankers have failed to point it out to their customers. No one has paid much attention until now, because banks have always been obligated to pay the money back in cash on demand; and if they ran short, FDIC deposit insurance would cover the losses. Today, however, derivative claims have "super-priority" in bankruptcy, meaning they are first in line to grab bank assets; and they could squeeze out not only the depositors but the FDIC itself. The giant international banks are considered simply too big to fail, even if it means that depositor funds must be confiscated to keep them alive.

The BIS Bail-In Template Goes Global

The Cyprus bail-in was not just a one-off emergency measure. It was consistent with similar policies already in the works for the US, UK, EU, Canada, New Zealand, Australia, Brazil, and other G20 countries. The original template grew out of an agreement drafted by a sub-committee of the BIS and endorsed at a G20 summit in 2011. The approach under consideration was presented in October 2011 in a paper published by the Financial Stability Board, called *Key Attributes of Effective Resolution Regimes for Financial Institutions.* It was endorsed at the Cannes G20 summit the following month.[555] This was followed by a consultative document in November 2012 called *Recovery and Resolution Planning: Making the Key Attributes Requirements Operational.*[556]

The template seems first to have gone public in New Zealand. A September 2011 article in the Bulletin of the Reserve Bank of New Zealand titled "A Primer on Open Bank Resolution" referenced recommendations made in 2010 and 2011 by the Basel Committee of the Bank for International Settlements, and said that similar plans had been in discussion since the 1997 Asian financial crisis.[557]

New Zealand's *Voxy* reported on March 19, 2013:

> The National Government [is] pushing a Cyprus-style solution to bank failure in New Zealand which will see small depositors lose some of their savings to fund big bank bailouts . . . .
>
> Open Bank Resolution (OBR) is Finance Minister Bill English's favoured option dealing with a major bank failure. *If a bank fails under OBR, all depositors will have their savings reduced overnight to fund the bank's bail out.*[558]

The stated purpose of the OBR is to deal with bank failures when they have become so expensive that governments are no longer willing to bail out the lenders. Among its primary objectives is to "ensure that, as far as possible, any losses are ultimately borne by the bank's shareholders and creditors . . . ."[559] The spectrum of "creditors" is defined to include depositors:

> At one end of the spectrum, there are large international financial institutions that invest in debt issued by the bank (commonly referred to as wholesale funding). At the other

end of the spectrum, are customers with cheque and savings accounts and term deposits.

The OBR justifies the creditor haircuts by stating that the creditors have all enjoyed a return on their investments and have freely accepted the risk. This could come as a surprise to most people. What return do you get from a bank these days on a deposit account? And when did you freely agree to accept the risk that your funds would be confiscated?

The bail-in template for the U.S. and U.K. was presented in a joint paper by the U.S. Federal Deposit Insurance Corporation and the Bank of England, dated December 10, 2012. The 15-page FDIC-BOE document is called *Resolving Globally Active, Systemically Important, Financial Institutions* (G-SIFIs). Like the New Zealand OBR, it is basically a plan for keeping insolvent international banks alive and profitable when the government and taxpayers have gone the way of Iceland and said no to further bailouts. The FDIC-BOE plan, however, is not to impose "haircuts." Rather, it is to turn deposits into stock in a debt-to-equity swap:

> An efficient path for returning the sound operations of the G-SIFI to the private sector would be provided by exchanging or converting a sufficient amount of the unsecured debt from the original creditors of the failed company [meaning the depositors] into equity [or stock]. In the US, *the new equity would become capital in one or more newly formed operating entities.* In the U.K., the same approach could be used, or *the equity could be used to recapitalize the failing financial company itself*—thus, the highest layer of surviving bailed-in creditors would become the owners of the resolved firm. In either country, *the new equity holders would take on the corresponding risk of being shareholders in a financial institution.*[560]

The directive does not explicitly refer to "depositors" but names only "unsecured creditors." But as John Butler pointed out in an April 2013 article in *Financial Sense*, the effective meaning of the term is belied by the fact that the FDIC has been put on the job. The FDIC has direct responsibility only for depositors, not for the bondholders who are wholesale non-depositor sources of bank credit. Butler comments:

Do you see the sleight-of-hand at work here? Under the guise of protecting taxpayers, depositors of failing institutions are to be arbitrarily, de-facto subordinated to interbank claims, when in fact they are legally senior to those claims!

... [C]onsider the brutal, unjust irony of the entire proposal. Remember, its stated purpose is to solve the problem revealed in 2008, namely the existence of insolvent TBTF institutions that were "highly leveraged and complex, with numerous and dispersed financial operations, extensive off-balance-sheet activities, and opaque financial statements." *Yet what is being proposed is a framework sacrificing depositors in order to maintain precisely this complex, opaque, leverage-laden financial edifice!*

If you believe that what has happened recently in Cyprus is unlikely to happen elsewhere, think again. Economic policy officials in the US, UK and other countries are preparing for it. Remember, someone has to pay. Will it be you? If you are a depositor, the answer is yes.[561]

The Real Threat: Derivatives Claimants Could Grab All the Collateral in Bankruptcy

The "interbank claims" that Butler says are made senior to depositor claims include the claims of derivatives counterparties; and today, these could be huge. Derivatives are sold as a kind of insurance for managing profits and risk; but as Satyajit Das points out in *Extreme Money: Masters of the Universe and the Cult of Risk* (2011), they actually increase risk to the system as a whole.

In the U.S. after the Glass-Steagall Act was implemented in 1933, a bank could not commingle its deposit business with its investment business; but in 1999, that barrier was removed. The biggest banks now have massive derivatives books; and in a major gambling fiasco, derivative claimants could take all the collateral, leaving other claimants, public and private, holding the bag.

Normally, the FDIC would have the power as trustee in receivership to protect a failed bank's collateral for payments made to depositors. But the FDIC's powers are overridden by the special status of derivatives in bankruptcy, another victory of bank lobbyists.[562]

Under the Bankruptcy Reform Act of 2005, derivatives counter-parties are given preference over all other creditors and customers of the bankrupt financial institution, including FDIC-insured depositors. According to Harvard Law Professor Mark Row:

> . . . [D]erivatives counterparties, . . . unlike most other secured creditors, can seize and immediately liquidate collateral, readily net out gains and losses in their dealings with the bankrupt, terminate their contracts with the bankrupt, and keep both preferential eve-of-bankruptcy payments and fraudulent conveyances they obtained from the debtor, all in ways that favor them over the bankrupt's other creditors.[563]

In *The New Financial Deal: Understanding the Dodd-Frank Act and Its (Unintended) Consequences,* David Skeel notes that Congress has made no attempt in the Dodd-Frank legislation to reduce the size of the big banks or to undermine the implicit subsidy provided by the knowledge that they will be bailed out in the event of trouble. Why? Skeel attributes it to "the Lehman myth" – the widely-held belief that the 2008 banking collapse was due to the decision to allow Lehman Brothers to fail. Skeel disputes that this was the cause of the collapse. He notes that the Lehman bankruptcy was orderly, and that the derivatives were unwound relatively quickly.[564]

Rather than preventing the Lehman collapse, the bankruptcy exemption for derivatives may have helped precipitate it. When the bank appeared to be on shaky ground, the derivatives players all rushed to put in their claims, in a run on the collateral before it ran out. As pointed out by financial analyst Yves Smith, Lehman failed over a weekend after JPMorgan grabbed collateral. She wrote in a March 2013 post:

> In the US, depositors have actually been put in a worse position than Cyprus deposit-holders, at least if they are at the big banks that play in the derivatives casino. The regulators have turned a blind eye as banks use their depositaries to fund derivatives exposures. And as bad as that is, the depositors, unlike their Cypriot confreres, aren't even senior creditors. Remember Lehman? When the investment bank failed, unsecured creditors (and remember, *depositors are unsecured creditors*) got eight cents on the dollar. One big reason was that derivatives

counterparties require collateral for any exposures, meaning they are secured creditors. The 2005 bankruptcy reforms made derivatives counterparties senior to unsecured lenders.[565]

Lehman had only two itty bitty banking subsidiaries, and to my knowledge, was not gathering retail deposits. But as readers may recall, Bank of America moved most of its derivatives from its Merrill Lynch operation to its depositary in late 2011.

Its "depositary" is the arm of the bank that takes deposits; and at Bank of America, that means over $1 trillion in deposits. The deposits are now subject to being wiped out by a major derivatives loss. How bad could that be? Smith cites OCC data showing that Bank of America's holding company held almost $75 trillion of derivatives the previous year. Similarly, JPMorgan had $79 trillion of notional derivatives, of which 99 percent were in its deposit-taking entity, JPMorgan Chase Bank NA.

Seventy-five and seventy-nine trillion dollars in derivatives! These two mega-banks hold more in notional derivatives *each* than the entire global GDP (at about $70 trillion). The "notional value" of derivatives is not the same as cash at risk, but according to a cross-post on Smith's site, in 2010 there was an estimated total of $12 trillion in cash actually at risk in derivatives.[566]

Twelve trillion dollars is close to the U.S. GDP; and JPMorgan is the largest player, with 30 percent of the market.[567] Smith writes:

> Remember the effect of the 2005 bankruptcy law revisions: derivatives counterparties are first in line, they get to grab assets first and leave everyone else to scramble for crumbs. . . .
>
> But it's even worse than that. During the savings & loan crisis, the FDIC did not have enough in deposit insurance receipts to pay for the Resolution Trust Corporation wind-down vehicle. It had to get more funding from Congress. This move paves the way for another TARP-style shakedown of taxpayers, this time to save depositors.

Perhaps, but Congress has already been burned and is liable to balk a second time. Section 716 of the Dodd-Frank Act now bans taxpayer bailouts of a large range of derivatives activities.[568]

How Reliable Is Deposit Insurance?

Before the Federal Deposit Insurance Corporation was instituted in 1934, depositors routinely lost their money when banks went bankrupt. Today, we think we are protected by FDIC insurance, at least up to the $250,000 limit. But insurance is only as good as the insurer's access to funds. How secure is the FDIC? Its insurance fund is mandated by law to keep a balance equivalent to only 1.15 percent of insured deposits. As of March 2013, it had only about $25 billion in its deposit insurance fund, as against $9,283 billion in total U.S. deposits.

In 2009, the FDIC fund went $8.2 billion in the hole as a result of the 2008 banking crisis; but depositors were assured that their money was protected by a hefty credit line with the Treasury.[569] However, the FDIC is funded with premiums from its member banks.[570] They had to replenish the fund, and the special assessment was crippling for the smaller banks. That was just to recover $8.2 billion. What happens when Bank of America or JPMorganChase, which have commingled their massive derivatives arms with their depositary arms, is propelled into bankruptcy by a major derivatives fiasco?

Bank of America Corporation moved its trillions in derivatives (mostly credit default swaps) from its Merrill Lynch unit to its banking subsidiary in 2011. It did not get regulatory approval for this move. It just acted at the request of frightened counterparties, following a downgrade by Moody's.[571] The FDIC opposed the move, reportedly protesting that the FDIC would be subjected to the risk of becoming insolvent if Bank of America were to file for bankruptcy.[572] But the Federal Reserve endorsed the measure as being necessary to give relief to the bank holding company.[573] (Professor Bill Black, a former regulator, says it was proof that the Fed is working for the banks and not for us. "Any competent regulator would have said: 'No, Hell NO!'"[574])

Drawing on the FDIC's credit line with the Treasury to cover a Bank of America or JPMorgan derivatives bust would be the equivalent of a taxpayer bailout, at least if the money were not paid back; and as noted, the Dodd-Frank Act now precludes that sort of derivatives bailout. The government won't pay, and the FDIC member banks cannot afford to pay. If they were forced into it, they would no doubt just pass the cost on to their depositors.

Bank of America is not the only bank threatening to wipe out the federal deposit insurance funds that most countries have. According to Willem Buiter, chief economist at Citigroup, most EU banks are zombies (insolvent).[575] Dutch Finance Minister Jeroen Dijsselbloem, who played a leading role in imposing the deposit confiscation plan on Cyprus, told reporters on March 13, 2013, that the Cyprus bail-in would be the template for any future European bank bailouts, and that "the aim is for the ESM never to have to be used."[576] Recall that the ESM (European Stability Mechanism) committed Eurozone countries to bail out failed banks.

Dijsselbloem's statement caused so much furor that he later retracted it, but there is little reason to believe it is not true; and Fed Chairman Ben Bernanke has not been reassuring either. When questioned, he would say no more than that "[t]he only way that [the Cyprus precedent] would create a problem would be if the runs became contagious in some sense, if depositors in other countries lost confidence;" and that in the U.S., the FDIC insures deposits.[577]

In February 2012, the Obama administration expressed concern about the FDIC's ability to meet its obligations, and in March 2012, Chairman Sheila Bair said the FDIC was on its way to becoming insolvent and that its job to insure bank deposits could be in danger.

All of which helps explain the impetus for the new "bail in" policies shifting the burden from the taxpayers to the creditors, including the depositors who constitute the banks' largest creditor class.

At Risk: Not Just Deposits but Public Revenues, Pension Funds, Brokerage Accounts, and More

Writing in *The Financial Times* in March 2009, Willem Buiter defended the bail-in approach as being better than the alternative. But he acknowledged that the "unsecured creditors" who would take the hit were chiefly "pensioners drawing their pensions from pension funds heavily invested in unsecured bank debt and owners of insurance policies with insurance companies holding unsecured bank debt," and that these unsecured creditors "would suffer a large decline in financial wealth and disposable income that would cause them to cut back sharply on consumption."[578]

The deposits of U.S. pension funds, too, are well over the insured limit of $250,000. They will get raided just as the pension funds did in Cyprus, and so will the insurance companies. Who else?

Most state and local governments keep far more on deposit than the insurance limit of $250,000, and they keep these revenues largely in G-SIFI (systemically important and systemically risky) banks. Community banks are not large enough to service the complicated banking needs of governments, and they are unwilling or unable to come up with the collateral that is required to secure public funds over the $250,000 FDIC limit.

The question is, how secure are public funds in the G-SIFI banks? Like the depositors who think FDIC insurance protects them, public officials assume their funds are protected by the collateral posted by their depository banks. But derivative claims are also secured with collateral, and they have super-priority over all other claimants, including other secured creditors. The vault may be empty by the time local government officials get to the teller's window. Main Street will again have been plundered by Wall Street.

Putting the Brakes on the Wall Street End Game

Survivors of major bank collapses say it can happen overnight. You wake up one morning to find your life savings wiped out. But where can they be kept in safety? The G-SIFI banks have commingled accounts in a web of debt that spreads globally. Stock brokerages put their money in G-SIFI banks in overnight sweeps. Credit unions may do the same with G-SIFI correspondent banks. Segregated accounts in commodities futures brokerages may be raided, as seen in the October 2011 bankruptcy of MF Global.[579] There are reports that even bank safety deposit boxes could be vulnerable to being raided by Homeland Security in a "national security crisis," which a major bank collapse no doubt would be.[580]

We need to take measures to block the Wall Street asset grab, and we need to take them quickly. But how? Here are some possibilities:

(1) Eliminate the super-priority status of derivatives in bankruptcy.

(2) Restore the portion of the Glass-Steagall Act separating depository banking from investment banking. See Rep. Marcy Kaptur's "Return to Prudent Banking Act of 2013" (H.R. 129).[581]

(3) Break up the giant derivatives banks. See Senator Bernie Sanders' "too big to jail" legislation.[582]

(4) Ban derivatives and unwind them. According to Paul Craig Roberts, former Assistant Treasury Secretary under President Reagan, "the only major effect of closing out or netting all the swaps (mostly over-the-counter contracts between counter-parties) would be to take $230 trillion of leveraged risk out of the financial system."[583]

(5) Impose a financial transactions tax on Wall Street. (This would probably have to be imposed selectively, to avoid crippling low-profit trades that are essential to the system.[584]) A pending bill to that effect is the Harkin-Whitehouse bill.[585]

(6) Nationalize failed international super-banks. More on this in Chapter 34.

(7) Establish postal savings banks as government-guaranteed depositories for individual savings. Many countries have public savings banks, which became particularly popular after savings in private banks were wiped out in the banking crisis of the late 1990s. (See Chapter 34.)

(8) Establish publicly-owned banks to be depositories of public monies, following the lead of North Dakota, the only state to completely escape the 2008 banking crisis. North Dakota does not keep its revenues in Wall Street banks but deposits them in the state-owned Bank of North Dakota by law. It has a mandate to serve the public, and it does not gamble in derivatives.

A motivated state legislature could set up a publicly-owned bank very quickly, allowing it to protect both the state's revenues and those of its citizens while generating the credit needed to support local businesses and restore prosperity to Main Street. That alternative will be explored in the next section, along with a number of others currently being proposed.

Section V

SOLUTIONS:
BANKING AS A PUBLIC UTILITY

Chapter 30

FIXES FOR A BROKEN SYSTEM: THE MONEY REFORMERS DEBATE

"He that will not apply new remedies must expect new evils; for time is the greatest innovator."

— Francis Bacon

The old model is obsolete. But what should replace it? This chapter will look at several popular money reform proposals and weigh their pros and cons.

The credit collapse of 2008 has had global ramifications, and it has become abundantly clear that the banking system needs to be overhauled. The debate today has focused on how this should be done. When the banks collapsed in the 1930s, some 2,000 schemes for monetary reform appeared out of the woodwork; and we're there again today. Everybody has an idea for how to fix the system. Groups are forming and vying with each other to have an impact.

The spectrum of alternatives ranges from all-gold currencies, to 100 percent reserves, to social credit, to community currencies, to publicly-owned banks. Proposals differ according to the perception of the problem. Some see it as governments creating too much money; others as banks creating too much; others as neither governments nor banks creating enough. Still others see it as the unsustainable debt burden created by compound interest, or as the creation of money and credit monopolized in private hands.

The Goldbugs

At one extreme are enthusiasts who would return to gold. "Goldbugs" see the problem as an out-of-control government that is spending the taxpayers into oblivion, in a system in which money is no longer tethered to a limited and relatively fixed supply of gold but is being irresponsibly expanded by government "fiat." They argue that gold has been "sound" money for thousands of years, and that only a return to that hard, inelastic currency will keep the money supply stable and politicians and bankers honest.

Critics of the goldbug approach counter that far from being stable, gold currencies have repeatedly been responsible for banking crises and depressions. Debts at compound interest grow exponentially; and when they are owed in a precious metal that is in fixed supply, the inevitable result is default and bankruptcy, not just for families and businesses but for whole economies.

In the best-selling *Lords of Finance: The Bankers Who Broke the World* (2009), former World Bank economist Liaquat Ahamed maintains that it was the rigid insistence on adhering to the gold standard that "broke the world" in the crash of 1929. The ensuing Great Depression was precipitated by four prominent central bankers – those of the Federal Reserve Bank of New York, the Bank of England, the Banque de France, and the Reichsbank of Germany (the four founders of the BIS). Tying the amount of currency in circulation to the amount of gold a country has in its vaults became a straitjacket which gave them little room to maneuver. There was not enough gold in existence to provide the capital needed to finance world trade.

Goldbugs contend that prices will adjust to the amount of gold in the system. If there is a shortage of gold, prices will drop. But the historical record disputes this, and the Great Depression is a prime example. Prices are "sticky." They cannot go down because costs do not go down. Mortgages, employment agreements, and other long-term contracts pervade commerce; there are laws setting minimum wages and Social Security deductions; suppliers cannot reduce their prices below cost. Companies faced with insufficient demand for their products do not lower their prices below cost. They lay workers off or close their doors.

The problem with a non-expandable money supply is evident today in the euro system, which has been called the equivalent of the gold standard. Eurozone countries are limited to a fixed supply of euros, which they cannot create on their own or through their own central banks. They must borrow from private and foreign creditors, who always demand more money back in principal and interest than they lend in principal alone. The result is a compounding debt burden that the money supply cannot expand to meet.

We've seen that historically, gold-backed currencies have been able to expand only through sleight of hand, in what was euphemistically called "fractional reserve" lending. Bankers discovered that they could lend many more notes than they had gold, since customers came for their gold only about 10 percent of the time. But the bankers were periodically found out in this shell game, triggering runs on the banks, bankrupting customers, contracting the money supply, and wreaking havoc on the local economy.

To eliminate the inherent fraud in a paper currency "backed" by gold, some goldbugs now advocate a currency consisting *only* of that precious metal.[586] But a 100 percent gold currency cannot expand at all, and critics even in the gold camp say it won't work.

Antal Fekete, a professor of mathematics and statistics in Newfoundland, Canada, calls a 100 percent gold currency a "pipe dream." He shows mathematically that the attempt to finance all of the stages of production by borrowing a nation's savings in gold would put a demand on gold supplies that simply could not be met.

Manufacturers all along the chain of production need to pay for workers and materials before the customer pays for the finished product, which can be 30 or 60 or 90 days after being invoiced. Their work is financed with credit lines or loans, which can add up to many times the final value of the product.

Dr. Fekete uses the example of a hypothetical drug that takes 91 days to produce and involves 90 firms, each one taking a day to do its work. Each adds $1 of value to the product, which ultimately sells for $100 a bottle. The first producer borrows $11 in gold for the raw materials. The second producer borrows $12 in gold to obtain the semi-finished product with the first producer's work added. The third producer borrows $13 to get the product from the second producer, and so forth. The total comes to $4,995, almost 50 times the retail value of the product. That means almost $5,000 worth of gold would be tied up for 91 days just to move one bottle of drug through the production process. Dr. Fekete maintains that the gold system worked historically only because the various stages of production were financed with bills of credit—paper credits that served as money in the economy.[587] (See Chapter 10.)

Gold enthusiast Jim Rickards would solve the problem of too little gold currency to meet the needs of trade by simply allowing the price of gold to rise. Until 1971, the gold price was fixed at $35 per ounce. Rickards says gold might need to go as high as $44,000 an ounce to adequately back today's global currency needs.[588] But $44,000 an ounce is clearly not the natural market price of gold. It is a manipulated price. If the goal is to limit a rise in prices by limiting the money supply, why not just determine the needs of trade and issue a fiat currency in a fixed sum to suit?

The 100 Percent Reserve Solution

That is the preferred alternative of the "100 percenters." They agree with the goldbugs that money creation should not be left to the whims of private banks, but they would shift that power to the government. To solve the problem of money creation by "fractional reserve" lending, they would require bank deposits to be backed not with 100 percent gold but with 100 percent "reserves."

Banks create money by double-entry bookkeeping. The bank creates a demand deposit in the borrower's name, and enters the sum as a liability on one side of its books. It then balances its books by entering the borrower's promise to pay as an asset on the other side of its books.

The reserve requirement is the percent of reserves relative to deposits that banks must have in their reserve accounts with the central bank. The reasoning of 100 percenters is that if the reserve requirement were raised to 100 percent for demand deposits, banks would not be able to create money by increasing the amount of demand deposits on their balance sheets without a corresponding inflow of reserves.

"Full reserve" banking proposals come in a variety of forms and complexities, but the basic idea is to force banks to lend only the existing money of customers who know it is being lent and are willing to part with it for the term of the loan. The lending arms of banks would effectively become mutual funds—pools of money from investors who had agreed to give up their claim to it for the term of the investment. Any expansion of the money supply would come from an independent federal agency, which would issue money and deliver it debt-free to the legislature. The money would then be dispensed according to political priorities—to increase spending, cut taxes, pay a social dividend, or pay down the national debt.[589]

Whether this money would wind up in "demand" accounts (transaction accounts) or "investment" accounts would be up to the individual recipients. As explained by Ben Dyson of Positive Money, a group promoting this approach in the UK:

> Individuals would . . . be faced with two choices with regards to where they could place their money:
> 1. In a "Transaction Account" (similar to a current account [or checking account] today). Although these accounts would be administered by commercial banks, they would be owned by the customer, with the funds in them held at the Bank of England [or other central bank]. They would therefore be 100 percent safe.
> 2. In an "Investment Account". These accounts would remain on the commercial banks' balance sheets, and would not be guaranteed by the government (i.e. they would be riskbearing). They would be non-transferable, and illiquid, with either maturity dates or minimum notice.[590]

In effect, the credit-creating function of banks would be eliminated. Either your money would be kept safe for your use only, or you would agree to give it up for a period of time and take the risk that it might be lost on bad loans. The question is, how many people would choose the time deposit option? We have that choice today, with mutual funds and certificates of deposit; yet most people keep their money in transaction accounts, because they want ready access to it. If the bank tells them that the time deposit will not be protected by deposit insurance and will put them at risk of losing their money altogether, they will be even less likely to take that option. That means the bank will have to pay substantially higher interest rates to get loan money, a cost that will no doubt be passed on to borrowers.

Professor Dirk Bezemer of the UK is sympathetic to the goals of the Positive Money group but thinks the full reserve solution won't work. In discussing it on Icelandic TV in April 2013, he said:

> [B]anks create money as debt and this has always been the case . . . . [T]he core idea of the Positive Money proposals, to separate money creation from lending, is not feasible, because *money creation and lending are the same thing.* . . . [T]he fact that banks create debt is good because it helps entrepreneurs who have good ideas but no money to get money from the bank as a loan to, whatever, build a factory, develop energy resources, invest in fishing or tourism, and if it's a good business plan it allows them to repay the debt, and meanwhile the economy is growing, jobs are being created, and so on.[591]

Bank credit must be advanced before workers can be paid to produce the products that create a thriving economy, allowing employers to pay off their loans. As Antal Fekete pointed out, it could take many times the market price of a product to fund its production through the development process. Where are sufficient "savers" going to be found to cover these loans, if it means tying up their money and risking its loss to defaulting borrowers?

Full reservers suggest that the lack of willing lenders could be circumvented by allowing banks short of lendable funds to borrow directly from the Treasury or other government agency given the money-creating function.[592] But that sounds very like the system we have now. Banks short of liquidity borrow at very low interest from other banks, the Federal Reserve, or the money market, then make loans to the public and the government at substantially higher interest. If banks can borrow from the money-creating agency at 0.75 percent, as they can now from the Federal Reserve, they will still have the ability to lend at extortionate interest rates to individuals and small businesses while giving favored loans to their cronies, or to engage in other abuses to which the system is now prone.

Even if the 100 percent reserve solution could prevent money creation by private banks, it would not eliminate the systemic risk that brought the economy low in 2008. We've seen that the crisis originated in the shadow banking system, which does not take deposits and is not bound by reserve requirements at all. That shadow system now generates "near-monies" in the form of liabilities that equal or exceed those created by the conventional banking system.[593] Until 2007, this near-money was reflected in the Fed's reported figures for M3. M3 is no longer reported, but the shadow money system not only is still there but continues to grow.

We've also seen that the shadow system arose, at least in part, from the need to free banking and credit from their strict regulatory limitations. Blocking commercial banks from creating money as credit on their books would just expand its private creation in this riskier, unregulated non-banking system. Transforming the banks into public utilities, fully accountable to and controlled by the public, would seem to be a safer, sounder, more functional solution.

Modern Monetary Theory

Proponents of Modern Monetary Theory (MMT) agree with the 100 percenters that government money-printing is not the villain but is rather where money *should* come from. But they do not advocate the 100 percent reserve solution, which they say is based on a misconception of how banking works.[594]

"How banking works" is at the heart of MMT, which is not a solution so much as simply an explanation of how things are – or how they could and should be – in a "fiat" money system. A fiat system is one in which the national currency is not constrained by precious metal backing, and the government has the sovereign right to issue it. The principles of MMT have been traced to the Chartalists and the "State Theory of Money" of German economist G. F. Knapp in the late 19th century. Today, MMT emanates from the University of Missouri-Kansas City and the Levy Economics Institute of Bard College in New York.[595]

A layperson's summary is presented by Dylan Matthews in a February 2012 article in the *Washington Post*. He writes:

In a "fiat money" system like the one in place in the United States, all money is ultimately created by the government, which prints it and puts it into circulation. Consequently, [MMT] thinking goes, the government can never run out of money. It can always make more.

But that does not mean taxes are unnecessary:

> [T]axes, in fact, are key to making the whole system work. The need to pay taxes compels people to use the currency printed by the government. Taxes are also sometimes necessary to prevent the economy from overheating. [596]

That the government "can never run out of money" may be an overstatement of the MMT position. MMTers say there is a limit to how much money the government can issue without creating significant price inflation, but that that limit has not yet been reached. The government funds its budget, according to MMT, not by drawing from taxes but simply by writing checks on its account with the Fed. Taxes become necessary only when prices go up across the board, indicating that demand (money in circulation) has outstripped supply. Taxes then need to be levied not to fund the government but rather to soak up the excess and prevent price inflation.

Matthews goes on:

> [I]f the theory is correct, there is no reason the amount of money the government takes in needs to match up with the amount it spends. Indeed, its followers call for massive tax cuts and deficit spending during recessions. . . .
>
> [They] concede that deficits can sometimes lead to inflation. But they argue that this can only happen when the economy is at full employment . . . .

MMTers are not opposed to private banks expanding the money supply with loans, but they propose regulations and modifications to keep the giant banks in check and to create a level playing field for the smaller local banks.

Warren Mosler is one of the founders of MMT and a banker himself. With boots-on-the-ground insight, he has made an innovative series of proposals for regulating the banks. [597] In October 2008, he suggested some proposals for solving the banking crisis that may be a bit inscrutable to non-bankers but are provocative for anyone wanting to do further research. They are:

(1) Normalize bank liquidity by allowing Fed member banks to borrow unsecured from the Fed in unlimited quantities.

(2) Have the Fed set term lending rates out to 3 months in addition to the Fed funds rate.

(3) Extend FDIC insurance to Fed deposits at member banks to keep any insolvency losses at the FDIC.

(4) Remove the cap on FDIC insurance to eliminate the need for money market funds.

(5) Declare a 'payroll tax holiday' and reduce social security and medicare payroll deduction rates to 0 percent until aggregate demand is sufficiently restored.[598]

MMT is an excellent resource for shedding light on how the banking system actually works. But as discussed in Chapter 2, merely regulating the banks has proven to be inadequate to fix the systemic flaws in the current system. Today, Wall Street effectively "owns" the government. Who will regulate the regulators? Other money reformers say the system itself needs to be overhauled.

Social Credit

While goldbugs and full reservers are trying to put a lid on the creation of money by banks, proponents of Social Credit are working to *expand* the money supply. Like MMTers, they feel the problem is *too little* money finding its way into the pockets of consumers. Unlike the MMTers, however, they do not call for full employment, which would not solve the problem of the "gap" between spendable income and overall prices.

As discussed earlier, Social Credit founder Major C. H. Douglas maintained that the economy routinely produces more goods and services than consumers have the money to purchase. This is because workers collectively do not get paid enough to cover the costs of the things they make, after factoring in various external costs including the interest paid to banks. Sellers set their prices at cost – including wages, materials and interest – plus profit. But they pay only the costs into the economy. The result is insufficient purchasing power to buy all the products that are for sale.

There is also the problem that people don't spend all of their incomes. Even if sellers were to set their prices at cost, the money would not all come back into the market to buy their products, since people like to save some of their money and invest it in money-making-money ventures. This is obviously true for the lavishly-rich one percent, but everyone does it who can afford it. That means much of the national income is not circulating in the real economy competing for goods and services. The result is a lack of demand.

To fill the gap between supply and demand (available purchasing power), Douglas recommended a national dividend for everyone, something bestowed by "grace" rather than "works" just to raise purchasing power enough to cover the products on the market.

In the 1930s and 1940s, critics of this idea called it "funny money" and said it would merely inflate the money supply. The critics prevailed, and the Social Credit solution has had little chance to be tested in the form Douglas recommended. The "quantitative easing" that has been tried in its place by central banks has not gotten money into the pockets of consumers but has gotten it only into the reserve accounts of banks. Quantitative easing has not hyperinflated the money supply as feared, but neither has it stimulated the economy as promised.[599] (More on this in Chapter 35.)

The Complementary Currency Solution

Other money reformers are working to expand the money supply and consumer purchasing power by developing "complementary" or "community" currencies that operate independently of banks. Credits and debits are generated by the members themselves as they trade with each other. Some complementary currency systems involve privately-printed paper money. Others are conducted online, without physical money at all.

A complementary currency system does not have to begin with a fund of capital or reserves, as is now required of private banking institutions; and members do not have to borrow from a pool of pre-existing money on which they pay interest to the pool's owners. They create their own credit, simply by debiting their own accounts and crediting someone else's. If Jane bakes cookies for Sue, Sue credits Jane's account with an agreed sum and debits her own. They have "created" money just as banks do. When Sue pays her debt by doing something for someone else, her balance goes back to zero. It is a zero-sum game.

Complementary systems are useful models for creating an organic money supply that expands and contracts naturally in response to the needs of trade. Their chief limitations are that they lack the enforcement tools of chartered banks backed by government agencies, and the currencies are not universally accepted. Only the products and services of the members are available for exchange. Because they do not involve the national currency, community currencies tend to be too limited for large-scale businesses and projects; and if they were to grow substantially larger, they could run up against the sort of exchange rate problems afflicting small countries today.

Community currencies are an excellent *complement*, however, to national and international money systems. They act counter-cyclically, lending when other banks are contracting credit; and they support local development. They create a market for goods that are sitting on shelves unsold, and for workers who are sitting idle because there is insufficient money in the system to pay them.

Many good books have been written on community currencies, including *People Money* by Margrit Kennedy, Bernard Lietaer and John Rogers (2012); *Creating Wealth: Growing Local Economies with Local Currencies* by Gwen Hallsmith and Bernard Lietaer; and *The End of Money and the Future of Civilization* by Tom Greco (2009).

Publicly-owned Banks

The solution explored at length here is an expandable credit mechanism using the *national* currency, a medium of exchange that is accepted as money everywhere. Banks do with the national currency what community currency systems do with locally-issued currencies: they turn personal IOUs, or promises to pay, into money. This much-maligned function of banks is actually good and necessary; but to ensure that the banking system serves the people, it needs to be owned and controlled by the people.

What differentiates publicly-owned banks from privately-owned banks is that the former operate in the public interest by law. That means supporting the real, wealth-producing economy rather than maximizing debt owed at compound interest to a private financial sector. Profits generated by the community are returned to the community.

One way for the federal government to acquire some banks is to nationalize banks that would otherwise need a bailout by the taxpayers. But nationalization, by definition, occurs only at the national level; and in the United States, the federal legislature is now gridlocked in civil war and unlikely to pursue that option any time soon.

Meanwhile, states, counties and cities could also own banks. The prototype for this arrangement was fine-tuned in the early American colony of Pennsylvania. Today, North Dakota is the only U.S. state to own its own depository bank; and until recently, the bank has kept a low profile. But the 2008 banking crisis brought it into the limelight, and the Bank of North Dakota has emerged as a beacon of what can be done.

Chapter 31

STATE SOLUTIONS: THE MODEL OF THE BANK OF NORTH DAKOTA

"The State of North Dakota does not have any funding issues at all. We in fact are dealing with the largest surplus we've ever had. . . . [R]eally where we take the most satisfaction is making sure we meet the needs of the state and finance those things that make our state go forward."

— Eric Hardemeyer, president of the
Bank of North Dakota (March 2009)[600]

States deposit their revenues in Wall Street banks at minimal interest, then borrow money at much higher rates; yet they have massive capital and deposit bases themselves. If they had their own banks, they could leverage this money into low-cost credit for local purposes. Most states are throwing this enormous credit power away. The exception is North Dakota, which has led the way with its landmark state-owned Bank of North Dakota.

Unlike the federal government, state and local governments cannot print their own money or borrow interest-free from their own central banks; and unlike private banks, they do not have nearly-free credit lines with each other. Like the Eurozone countries, they are

---

subject to the whims and vagaries of the private credit market. State governments that have never defaulted on their debts wind up paying far higher interest rates than the too-big-to-fail banks, which would have defaulted on hundreds of billions of dollars in debt if they had not been bailed out by the states and their citizens.

California's economy is the largest of any U.S. state and the eighth largest economy in the world. Yet in 2009, its credit rating was cut by Standard & Poor's to just above Greece's—the lowest of any state's—causing the interest rate on California's bonds to shoot up to 7.26 percent on 30-year taxable securities.[601]

Local governments have been forced to hoard funds in very inefficient ways, building excessive reserves and "rainy day" funds while slashing services, because they do not have the cheap and ready credit lines available to the private banking system. Incurring new debt requires voter approval, a process that is cumbersome, time-consuming and uncertain. Banks, on the other hand, need to keep only the slimmest of reserves, because they are backstopped by a central bank with the power to create reserves at will, along with Congress and the taxpayers themselves; and they can borrow from each other at the extremely low Federal funds rate of 0.25 percent.

State and local governments can, however, share in the perks enjoyed by Wall Street. They can do it by setting up their own banks. North Dakota, the only state that actually does this, is also the only state to be in continuous budget surplus every year since the banking crisis of 2008.[602] The Bank of North Dakota (BND) was formed in 1919 to free farmers and small businessmen from the clutches of out-of-state bankers and railroad men. Its stated mission is to deliver sound financial services that promote agriculture, commerce and industry in North Dakota. Today it is a major source of profit for the state, generating a whopping 25 percent return on equity even in 2008, when revenues in other states were plummeting.[603] North Dakota has the lowest foreclosure rate in the country, the lowest credit card default rate, and the lowest unemployment rate. It has no debt at all, and it has had no bank failures at least in the last decade.[604]

Not Just About Oil

The state's thriving economy and low unemployment rate have been attributed to an oil boom; but while oil is a factor, something else has put North Dakota over the top. Profiting from an oil boom requires more than just finding oil in the ground. Infrastructure is needed to get it to market. Oil companies do not build houses, hotels, or roads; and private banks in boom towns are reluctant to fund those projects, because the boom could be gone before the loans get repaid.

Alaska has roughly the same population as North Dakota and produces nearly twice as much oil.[605] Yet unemployment in Alaska in 2011 was running at 7.7 percent, compared to a low 3.3 percent in North Dakota.[606] Montana, South Dakota, and Wyoming have all benefited from a boom in energy prices, with Montana and Wyoming extracting much more oil than North Dakota has. The Bakken oil field stretches across not just North Dakota but Montana, where the greatest Bakken oil production comes from Elm Coulee Oil Field.[607] Yet Montana's unemployment rate, like Alaska's, was 7.7 percent percent in 2011. Montana and Alaska had 3 to 4 times the home foreclosure rates of North Dakota, along with other financial problems. Other mineral-rich states that were not initially affected by the economic downturn lost revenues with the later decline in oil prices, but not North Dakota. Its balance sheet remained so strong that in 2009, it was in the unique position of *reducing* individual income taxes and property taxes by a combined $400 million. In 2011, they were reduced by $500 million.[608]

The enabling factor that has fostered both a boom in oil and record profits from agriculture in North Dakota is ready access to credit; and that access has been facilitated by what is truly unique to the state, its state-owned bank.

In a June 2011 paper called "The Public Option: The Case for Parallel Public Banking Institutions," Professor Timothy Canova observed that California, like North Dakota, has copious resources, including agriculture and oil. But it has been unable to mobilize those resources effectively to create local infrastructure and investment, because unlike North Dakota, it lacks its own bank:

> . . . California is the largest state economy in the nation, yet without a state-owned bank, is unable to steer hundreds of billions of dollars in state revenues into productive investment

within the state. Instead, California deposits its many billions in tax revenues in large private banks which often lend the funds out-of-state, invest them in speculative trading strategies (including derivative bets against the state's own bonds), and do not remit any of their earnings back to the state treasury. Meanwhile, California suffers from constrained private credit conditions, high unemployment levels well above the national average, and the stagnation of state and local tax receipts. The state's only response has been to stumble from one budget crisis to another for the past three years, with each round of spending cuts further weakening its economy, tax base, and credit rating.[609]

Not so in North Dakota:

> The state deposits its tax revenues in the Bank [of North Dakota] which in turn ensures that a high portion of state funds are invested in the state economy. In addition, the Bank is able to remit a portion of its earnings back to the state treasury . . . .

Having its own bank allows North Dakota to fund projects without either raising taxes or incurring debt. Professor Canova comments:

> The dilemma facing governments today is how to pay for stimulus and jobs programs without incurring new debt. Public banking institutions should point the way, in part for their ability to expand lending on a revolving basis without raising taxes or even borrowing from bond markets.[610]

The BND Model

The Bank of North Dakota has a massive, captive deposit base, since all of the state's revenues are deposited in the bank by law. Most state agencies also must deposit with it. The BND does not compete with local banks for commercial deposits or loans. It takes some token individual deposits, but the vast majority of its deposits come from the state itself. Municipal government deposits are generally reserved for local community banks, which are able to use those funds to back loans because the BND provides letters of credit guaranteeing them.[611]

The BND also has a massive capital base. The bank was originally set up as "North Dakota doing business as the Bank of North Dakota." That means that technically, all of the assets of the state are assets of the bank. Beyond that technical pillar, the BND has built up a sizable capital fund. By the end of 2010, it had capital of $327 million. It had $4 billion in assets, of which $2.8 billion were loans; and it had deposits of $3 billion.

Like private banks, a publicly-owned bank has the ability to create money in the form of bank credit on its books, and it has access to very low interest rates. It differs from private banks in that their business model requires them to take advantage of the low rates to extract as much debt service from their customers as the market will bear. Private banks are legally bound to think first of the quarterly profits of their shareholders. The BND, by contrast, is obligated by its mission statement to serve the community. A public bank can pass low interest rates on to public agencies, local businesses, and residents.

The BND has a loan program called Flex PACE, which allows local communities to provide assistance to borrowers in areas of jobs retention, technology creation, retail, small business, and essential community services.[612]

For the state, infrastructure projects are effectively interest-free, since the bank returns interest to the state in the form of an annual dividend. The result is to reduce project costs by an average of 40 percent over the life of the loan. (See Chapter 1.)

The BND's revenues have been a major boost to the state budget. In the first decade of this century, it contributed over $300 million to state coffers, a substantial sum for a state with a population that is only about one-fifteenth the size of Los Angeles County. In April 2011, the BND reported annual profits of $62 million, setting a record for the seventh straight year.[613] *These profits belong to the citizens, and they are generated without taxation.* According to a study by the Center for State Innovation, the BND added nearly as much money to the state's general fund from 2007 to 2009 as oil and gas tax revenues did.[614]

Unlike the Federal Reserve, which is not authorized to lend directly to state and local governments except in very limited circumstances, the BND can help directly with local government funding. When North Dakota went over-budget one year, the BND acted as a rainy day fund for the state; and when a local town suffered a massive flood, it provided emergency credit lines.[615] Having a cheap and ready credit line with the state's own bank reduces the need for wasteful rainy-day funds invested at minimal interest in out-of-state banks.

While Wall Street banks were being bailed out by the taxpayers and were drastically cutting back on local lending, the BND was increasing local lending—and showing record profits. The Bank's loan portfolio has shown a steady, uninterrupted increase in North Dakota lending programs ever since 2006. In 2011, according to its annual report:

> BND continues to be financially strong, recording its eighth consecutive year of record profits; this year's profits were over $70 million. Standard & Poors (S&P) raised BND's credit rating in December. Its long-term issuer credit rating was raised to AAf- from A+ and its short-term issuer credit rating to A-1+ from A-1. This is significant when viewed in context of the ratings downgrades received by many financial institutions across the country.[616]

Every year from the 2008 banking crisis up through 2012, the BND has reported a return on investment of between 17 percent and 26 percent.[617] Compare that to California's pension funds—CalPERS and CalSTRS—the largest pension funds in the world. From a peak of $260 billion in 2007, CalPERS fell to $160 billion in March 2009, a 38 percent decline. CalSTRS peaked at $180 billion in October 2007 and dropped to $112 billion in the same period, a 34 percent decline. [618] They did better in 2011 and 2012, but they are still well below where they were before the crisis.[619] For their questionable performance in managing the CalPERS portfolio, Wall Street firms reported earning $1.1 billion in 2010.[620]

A Partner, Not a Competitor, with Local Banks

The BND is a boon not only to the government and local economy but to the local banking community. It acts as a mini-Fed for the state, providing correspondent banking services to virtually every financial institution in North Dakota. It offers a federal funds program that in 2011 provided secured and unsecured federal fund lines to 113 financial institutions, with combined lines of almost $400 million.

Federal fund sales averaged over $10 million per day, peaking at $41 million one day in July.[621] The BND also provides check-clearing, cash management and automated clearing house services.

Local banks are willing to take on more risk when the BND participates in their loans. Because it assists them with mortgages and guarantees their loans, local North Dakota banks have been able to keep mortgages on their books rather than selling them off to investors to meet capital requirements. As a result, they managed to avoid the subprime and securitization debacles.[622] By partnering with the BND, local banks can also take on local projects in which Wall Street has no interest, projects that might otherwise go unfunded.

Due to this amicable relationship, the North Dakota Bankers' Association endorses the BND as a partner rather than a competitor of the state's private banks. The BND may actually be helping to save local banks from extinction. A November 2012 report in *Fortune* predicted that the number of U.S. banks would shrink over the next decade from 7,000 to only a few hundred, with small banks taking the hit.[623] A major reason they are selling out to their larger competitors is that they cannot satisfy heightened regulatory requirements, something the BND helps local banks meet. That could explain why North Dakota now has more banks per capita than any other state.

Stepping Up to the Plate in Disasters: The Grand Forks Story

Another role the BND is in a unique position to play is in providing disaster relief. It has a mandate to serve the public interest and no shareholders other than the state itself, giving it wide-ranging flexibility in emergencies and allowing it to act quickly to coordinate resources and catalyze recovery. While disaster victims in other states wait for federal relief that is often too little too late or rely on insurance policies with obscure clauses that exclude coverage when most needed, North Dakota's state-owned bank is on the spot ready to serve.

The BND's emergency capabilities were demonstrated in 1997, when record flooding and fires devastated Grand Forks, North Dakota. The town and its sister city, East Grand Forks on the Minnesota side of the river, lay in ruins. Floodwaters covered virtually the entire city and took weeks to fully recede. Property losses topped $3.5 billion.

The response of the state-owned bank was immediate and comprehensive, demonstrating a financial flexibility and public generosity that no privately-owned bank could match. Soon after the floodwaters swept through Grand Forks, the BND was helping families and businesses recover. Led by then-president and CEO John Hoeven (future North Dakota governor and U.S. senator), the Bank quickly established nearly $70 million in credit lines – to the city, the state National Guard, the state Division of Emergency Management, the University of North Dakota in Grand Forks, and to individuals, businesses and farms. It also launched a Grand Forks disaster relief loan program and allocated $5 million to help other areas affected by the spring floods. Local financial institutions matched these funds, making a total of more than $70 million available.

Besides property damage, flooding swept away many jobs, leaving families without livelihoods. The BND coordinated with the U.S. Department of Education to ensure forbearance on student loans; worked closely with the Federal Housing Administration and Veterans Administration to gain forbearance on federally backed home loans; established a center where people could apply for federal/state housing assistance; and worked with the North Dakota Community Foundation to coordinate a disaster relief fund. The Bank served as the deposit base for this fund. It also reduced interest rates on existing Family Farm and Farm Operating programs. Families then used these low-interest loans to restructure debt and cover operating losses caused by wet conditions in their fields.

To help finance the disaster recovery, the BND obtained funds at reduced rates from the Federal Home Loan Bank. These savings were then passed on to flood-affected borrowers in the form of lower interest rates.

The city was quickly rebuilt and restored. As a result, Grand Forks lost only 3 percent of its population between the 1997 floods and 2000, while East Grand Forks, right across the river in Minnesota, lost 17 percent of its population.[624]

When serious floods struck again in North Dakota in 2011, the BND again came to the rescue. According to its 2011 annual report:

Floodwater and the havoc it created was headline news. It hampered the ability of farmers to plant their fields; nearly 30 percent of the land was not farmed. Residents of nine counties fled homes because of spring and summer flooding.

BND employees were excused from work to help North Dakota communities in their fight against the floods. Lending programs were designed to assist with recovery efforts: Rebuilder's Loan Program for homeowners, Business Disaster Relief Loan Program, and the Farm Disaster Relief Loan Program.

It was the sort of community effort that rarely makes headlines, and the BND has generally chosen to keep out of the headlines in any case. But when North Dakota and its state-owned bank pulled through the banking crisis with flying colors, legislators from other beleaguered states started to take notice . . . .

Chapter 32

THE STATE BANK MOVEMENT: GUIDELINES AND FAQS

> *"Each time a man stands up for an ideal, or acts to improve the lot of others, or strikes out against injustice, he sends forth a tiny ripple of hope . . . and crossing each other from a million different centers of energy and daring those ripples to build a current that can sweep down the mightiest walls of oppression and resistance."*
>
> —*Robert F. Kennedy*

Twenty U.S. states have now introduced bills of one sort or another to form state-owned banks. This chapter looks at what states can do with their own banks and suggests guidelines for getting them implemented, including where to find the money for startup capital.

Inspired by North Dakota's example, by the end of 2012 twenty states had introduced bills to form state-owned banks or study their feasibility, and more are on the way.[625] But politicians are inherently conservative. They are adept at finding reasons not to do a thing until they are faced either with overwhelming evidence in its favor or with an overwhelming popular demand for it; and if the people are to demand it, they first need to understand it themselves.

How effective a grassroots push can be was demonstrated in New Zealand in the 1930s, when a popular movement transformed the Reserve Bank of New Zealand from a privately-owned central bank that would take orders from the Bank of England into a vehicle for generating credit for the local economy. A similar movement was instrumental in establishing the Alberta Treasury Branches as a local public banking system. But such populist successes have usually been preceded by years of meeting in living rooms and neighborhood centers to learn, share and organize.

To persuade politicians, advocates need a firm grasp of the principles themselves, and of the objections likely to be raised. This chapter will look at some of those issues with respect to publicly-owned banks. More information can be found on the websites and FAQ pages of the Public Banking Institute, the Center for State Innovation, Demos, and the Pennsylvania Project, listed in the endnotes.[626]

Where to Find the Money: The Magic of Double-Entry Bookkeeping

One of the first objections likely to be raised to a state-owned bank is, "We don't have the money. We need our state revenues to meet our budget. We can't afford to lend them out." That objection has been heard from more than one state treasurer or his aides.

It may be presumptuous to try to instruct a state treasurer in how banking works, but he could politely be pointed to literature attesting that banks do not actually lend their deposits. The deposits at all times remain in the bank, available for withdrawal by the depositor—in this case the state. The deposits will be no less available to the state when deposited in its own state-owned bank than they are when deposited in Bank of America. In fact, they are more at risk in Bank of America, which gambles in derivatives and other questionable ventures that a transparent and accountable state-owned bank would avoid.

What does a bank lend, if not its deposits? It simply advances "bank credit" on its books. The bank needs the deposits to replenish its reserves when the checks leave the bank, but if it comes up short—if borrower and depositor come for their money at the same time—the bank can borrow the needed reserves.

A bank is a very different animal from the revolving funds through which governments normally lend money. In a revolving fund, the money has to be there first. Banks, on the other hand, are allowed to lend money *before* they have it in hand. They can acquire it later from the cheapest available source; and for a bank, that source can be very cheap indeed—as low as 0.25 percent on the Fed funds market. *That is one of the major benefits to the state of having its own bank: it can borrow extremely cheaply from other banks, the money market, the Federal Reserve or Federal Home Loan Board. It gets the sort of Wall Street perks not otherwise available to governments, businesses, or individuals.*

The textbook money multiplier model says that banks can lend a sum *equal to* their deposits, less the reserve requirement (typically 10 percent). But today, a bank with adequate capital will lend to any creditworthy borrower, without first checking its deposits or its reserves. If the bank has insufficient reserves, it can borrow from a variety of cheap sources of liquidity. Access to these funds is normally exclusive to the banking club, but local governments and communities can tap into them by owning their own banks.

Only banks are authorized to use leverage in their lending operations, and only banks are backstopped by the Federal Reserve system if they run short of funds. This is the "magic" which allows banks to be so profitable. It is also what makes a publicly-owned bank exceptionally useful at the state, county, and local levels of government.

Consider the Possibilities

The imaginations of local legislators can be stimulated by showing them some numbers, extrapolating from the time-tested model of the Bank of North Dakota. In 2010, the BND reported $3 billion in deposits, of which 93 percent were drawn from the state's own revenues. With a population of just over 672,000, that works out to about $4,500 in deposits per capita. The BND had over $4 billion in assets (loans, cash and securities), of which $2.8 billion were loans. That means it had about $4,200 in loans per capita.[627]

Consider the possibilities, for example, if those numbers were scaled up for California, which has 37 million people—more than 50 times the population of North Dakota. Multiplying its population by

$4,500, California might have amassed $166.5 billion in deposits if it had a state-owned bank that performed like the BND. Multiplying $4,200 (the loans per capita in North Dakota) by 37 million, the State Bank of California could, in theory, have generated $155.4 billion in credit for the state.

"But," our hypothetical government official is liable to object, "California does not have nearly $166.5 billion in demand deposits in banks!" According to the State Treasurer's Report for Fiscal Year 2010-11, the average daily balance in demand accounts was only about $2 billion.

True. But the report also stated that only enough money was kept in demand deposits to meet the state's demand for banking services. The rest was invested through the Treasurer's Investment Pool, which contained *$67 billion* in assets in 2010-11. In North Dakota, this money would have been run through the BND.

When state agencies find that they have excess funds at the end of the year, they have no obligation to return them to the taxpayers. Instead, they keep them in rainy day funds. State governments also have funds of this sort, along with various agency funds that they cannot legally spend on the state budget. Bond issues are approved for particular purposes; and when excess funds are collected, they are not handed over to the state toward next year's budget. This money, too, just sits idly in an earmarked fund drawing a very modest interest.

The Treasurer's Investment Pool consists of these rainy day funds and excess monies collected from around the state. The totals in the pool don't seem to have changed much over the last decade. The money is evidently just sitting there, out of reach of the state government budget because it is earmarked for other purposes. As such, it is a waste of taxpayer funds. In 2010-11, the Treasurer's Investment Pool was earning just 0.49 percent interest.[628] Deposited in a state-owned bank, this money could have been earning a competitive return for members of the pool (the BND pays a competitive rate on deposits[629]), *while at the same time earning 4 percent or so for the state itself on the loan portfolio backed by those deposits.*

The $67 billion in the California Treasurer's Investment Pool in 2010-11 was not all composed of state government revenues. It also included agency and other funds from around the state. But the BND's deposits are not all state revenues either. According to Standard &

Poor's 2010 credit rating report for the BND, the majority of the bank's deposits are "non-core deposits," meaning deposits that come from somewhere besides the bank's own "core depositors" (in this case, the state itself). The report gave the BND a rating of AA+, the same as the state itself. It stated:

> Noncore deposits provided the majority of BND's funding, as core deposits constituted roughly 28 percent of the funding base at that date. Because core deposits do not fully fund the loan portfolio, the loan-to-core deposits ratio (253 percent of core deposits at March 31) is high compared with other banks'. Noncore deposits primarily consisted of large certificates of deposits from local state agencies, which the law requires them to deposit at BND. When adding these state-sourced captive deposits to the core deposits, the loan leverage ratio improves materially to 122 percent. Although these deposits are not considered core based on our definition, we recognize their stickiness and therefore do not view these measures as negative rating factors for BND. Furthermore, the state provides certain guarantees to BND that support the rating.
>
> The duration of the captive deposit base is variable. Consequently, the bank may seek additional funding from Federal Home Loan Bank advances and borrow from the Federal Reserve discount window. Also, it can enter into a repurchase agreement using the securities in its investment portfolio as collateral.[630]

The BND's non-core deposits are thus the same sort of agency funds that the California treasurer keeps in his Investment Pool. They are not "hot money" ready to flee to the highest bidder, like the "brokered" (or borrowed) deposits considered unsafe by rating agencies. The treasurer himself has control over where the agency funds are invested, and he knows they aren't going anywhere. The State Bank of California could draw on non-core deposits of this type just as the BND does.

Cutting the Cost of Infrastructure Projects Nearly in Half

How could California's potential credit power be used? In November 2010, it had outstanding general obligation bonds and revenue bonds of $158 billion. Of that, *$70 billion were owed just for interest.*[631] If California had been funding its debt through its own bank, the state could have saved $70 billion on its bonded debt, enough to pay its budget deficit several times over.

If the rating agencies should frown on a state funding its own projects interest-free through its own bank, the same result could be achieved by buying municipal bonds with the state bank's credit power. Assume the bank invested in municipal bonds paying 4 percent interest, and the state was paying 4 percent interest on its own state bonds. Revenue from the municipal bonds would be sufficient to pay the interest on the state bonds, so the state's own debt would still effectively be interest-free. By depositing its revenues and investing its capital on Wall Street, the state is giving this potential income stream away.

Tom Hagan, who pays taxes in Maine, maintains that infrastructure costs could be slashed by this device risk-free.[632] In a December 2011 letter to the editor in the Portland *Press Herald*, he maintained that there is no need for a publicly-owned bank to invest in risky retail ventures. It could just buy safe state and municipal bonds. Using the example of a Maine turnpike project, he showed that this simple measure could cut the cost of local projects nearly in half:

> Improvements are funded by bonds issued by the Maine Turnpike Authority, which collects the principal amounts, then pays the bonds back with interest.
>
> Over time, interest payments add up to about the original principal, doubling the cost of turnpike improvements and the tolls that must be collected to pay for them. The interest money is shipped out of state to Wall Street banks.
>
> Why not keep the interest money here in Maine, to the benefit of all Mainers? This could be done by creating a state-owned bank. State funds now deposited in low- or no-interest checking accounts would instead be deposited in the state bank.

Those funds would be used to buy up the authority bonds and municipal bonds issued by the Maine Bond Bank. All of them. Since all interest payments would flow into the state treasury, we would end up paying half what we now pay for our roads, bridges and schools.

North Dakota has profited from a state-owned bank for 90 years. Why not Maine?

Publicly-owned banks are a way not only to recapture the interest on public projects but to return public funds to local investment. That point was stressed by Kyle Hence in a January 2012 article titled "Where Are R.I. Revenues Being Invested? Not locally." He wrote:

> According to a December Treasury report, only 10 percent of Rhode Island's short-term investments reside in truly local in-state banks, namely Washington Trust and BankRI. Meanwhile, 40 percent of these investments were placed with foreign-owned banks, including a British-government owned bank under investigation by the European Union.
>
> Further, millions have been invested by Rhode Island in a fund created by a global buyout firm . . . . From 2008 to mid-2010, the fund lost 10 percent of its value—more than $2 million. . . . Three of four of Rhode Island's representatives in Washington, D.C., count [this fund] amongst their top 25 political campaign donors . . . .

Hence asked:

> Are Rhode Islanders and the state economy being served well here? Is it not time for the state to more fully invest directly in Rhode Island, either through local banks more deeply rooted in the community or through the creation of a new state-owned bank?[633]

How to Capitalize the Bank Without Using Tax Dollars

Besides deposits, banks need capital to back their loans. "Capital" means the bank's own money (paid-in shareholder capital plus profits). How much capital? In 2009, according to Standard & Poor's, the worldwide average risk-adjusted capital ratio stood at 6.7 per cent of assets (loans). In response to the 2008 credit crisis, however, capital requirements have been raised. For local banks, a 10 percent ratio is now usually considered adequate.[634] That means $10 in capital can back $100 in loans.

The initial capital needed to start a bank also varies. In some states, $8 million in "Tier 1" capital is enough to charter a bank. Some consultants say $20 million is a good figure, but it depends on what the bank is designed to achieve. If the focus is to refinance the capital appreciation bonds for all school districts in California, for example, the bank will need $900 million in capital, since the principal outstanding on those bonds is about $9 billion. If the goal is simply to protect local government assets from a Cyprus-style "bail in," only the minimum capitalization necessary to satisfy state regulators will be sufficient for startup capital. The bank needs capital to make loans, not to take deposits. Requirements will go up only as loans are made. A state or municipal bank can start small and work up from there, adding accumulated profits to its capital base over time.

The "dba" Option

The possibilities for finding startup capital are also varied. One alternative is to make the bank a "dba" of the state. "Dba" is short for "doing business as." It means the state itself would be the bank, operating under a different name. The BND was set up as "North Dakota *doing business as* the Bank of North Dakota." In an article exploring this alternative at length, Michael Sauvante of the National Commonwealth Group notes that the effect is to make all of the assets of the state the assets of the bank.[635]

Take California again as an example. The eighth largest economy in the world, the state owns at least $200 billion in real estate, over $200 billion in pension funds, $67 billion in the Treasurer's Investment Pool as of 2010-11, and many other assets. That means it has at least $500 billion in assets, sufficient to capitalize a hypothetical loan portfolio of $5 trillion, or enough to embark on any program for which the state bank can otherwise meet the requirements. Recall the pronouncement of Denison Miller, governor of the Commonwealth Bank of Australia, who said nearly a century ago:

> The whole of the resources of Australia are at the back of this bank, and so strong as this continent is, so strong is the Commonwealth Bank. Whatever the Australian people can intelligently conceive in their minds and will loyally support, that can be done.

Recall, too, that before the 1980s, banks did not have capital requirements at all.[636] The requirement was imposed by the Bank for International Settlements, a foreign entity whose chief objective is to "maintain monetary and financial stability." The effective result is to prevent governments from printing their own money or borrowing from their own central banks. This maintains the dominance of the private banker-issued currency as against public competitors, but it does not necessarily serve the local economy. (See Chapter 28.) A state-owned bank has the incomparable advantage that when the BIS comes knocking at its door, it can point to all of the assets of the state as the source of its rock-like stability, just as Denison Miller did. It cannot be put out of business for lack of capital, something to which community banks and credit unions are highly vulnerable.

Setting the bank up as a dba of the state can be done quickly and inexpensively. The challenge will be persuading your legislators of its wisdom. Their concern will be that it will put state assets at risk.

In response, you might point out that the BND imperils neither the state's nor the taxpayers' funds when it makes loans. It has amassed a sizable capital fund of its own. Fully 50 percent of its loan portfolio is federally guaranteed, including VA and FHA loans and low-income subsidies. These safe and lucrative cash cows require more staff and facilities than are cost-effective for smaller banks, so the profits from them would have gone to larger out-of-state banks if the BND had not captured them. Guaranteed profits of this sort, along with those from nearly a century of prudent banking, have built up a comfortable cushion for the BND. If capital gets depleted from the occasional loan gone bad, it is these surplus funds that are used, without jeopardizing state or taxpayer money.

The Bond Alternative

Despite those reasonable arguments, legislators are liable to resist taking the *dba* approach. In that case, another readily available option is to issue bonds, something the BND also did initially to raise capital. Selling bonds to private parties does not involve dipping into taxpayer funds, and it is a good way to soak up investor money that is sitting idle on the sidelines. State bank bonds can be a safe, locally-friendly investment for people or businesses wanting to earn some interest while helping their local communities.

Digging into the CAFR Goldmine

Another option that is particularly promising for capitalizing a state bank is to tap into some of the surplus funds sitting idle in state and municipal government coffers. These funds are not counted in the state budget, but they can be seen in the Comprehensive Annual Financial Reports (CAFRs) that must be filed with the federal government by all local, county and state governments. The government is composed of thousands of different state, county, and local government entities across the country, including school districts, public authorities, and the like; and these entities all keep their financial assets in liquid investment funds, bond financing accounts and corporate stock portfolios. The only income that must be reported in government budgets is that from taxes, fines and fees; but the CAFRs show that virtually every U.S. city, county, and state has vast amounts of money stashed away in surplus funds of this sort.

The purpose and uses of these funds have been the source of much speculation on the Internet, with conjectures ranging from conspiracy to fraud. But local finance officers have a more mundane explanation. They say funds must be amassed because state and local governments don't have cheap and accessible credit lines of the sort available to banks. Local governments are required by law to balance their budgets; and if they come up short, public services and government payrolls may be frozen until the voters get around to approving a new bond issue. When this happens, local governments can be brought to a standstill. In emergencies, government officials may try to borrow short-term through "certificates of participation" or tax participation loans, but the interest rates are prohibitively high; and in today's tight credit market, finding willing lenders is difficult.

To avoid those unpredictable contingencies, municipal governments keep a cushion that is well beyond what their budgets actually require. This money is invested, but not necessarily lucratively. Interest on certificates of deposit and other conservative short-term investments can be a mere fraction of a percent today.

Clint Richardson is a concerned citizen who has laboriously studied California's 2011 CAFR. His figures show that *over $577 billion* in investment fund balances were buried in the state's books for that year.[637]

In 2010, the State of California was in the anomalous position of being $26 billion in the red and plunging toward bankruptcy, while the State Treasurer's Pooled Money Investment Account (PMIA) alone tallied in at over $70 billion.[638] This massive pool could not legally be used for the state budget. Some of it could be borrowed, but it had to be paid back.

When Governor Arnold Schwarzenegger tried to raid the Public Transportation Account one year for the budget, the California Transit Association took him to court and won. The Third District Court of Appeals ruled in 2009 that diversions from the Public Transportation Account to fill non-transit holes in the General Fund violated a series of statutory and constitutional amendments enacted by voters via four statewide initiatives dating back to 1990.[639]

The gold mine of untouchable funds revealed in the CAFR reports is either invested at very slender interest or, depending on the type of fund, turned over to Wall Street gambling. Recall the 38 percent and 34 percent drops in the California pension funds, CalPERS and CalSTRS, following the 2008 banking crisis. The same sort of Wall Street investment disasters have occurred in other states. In New York State, investment managers lost $40 billion for the state pension fund, while the (formerly) $155 billion fund spent just under $5 billion on actual pension outlays. The result was to leave the state with an "underfunded" pension fund of $110 billion.[640] Wall Street lost the money, and the taxpayers and local governments had to tighten their belts to bear the losses.

Investing these funds or even a portion of them in the state's own state-owned bank could be not only safer but more lucrative than these risky investments. If the state bank follows in the footsteps of the Bank of North Dakota, once it gets up to speed it might have a return on equity of 17 percent to 26 percent.

Investing a portion of the CAFR funds as capital in a state bank could require legislation, but that is what legislators are for – to legislate. Wall Street has routinely gotten rules relaxed, changed or withdrawn as needed to suit its purposes. States can and should modify their rules as appropriate to serve the interests of their constituents and local economies.

Studies and Surveys

The concerns of legislators can also be alleviated by presenting them with the results of well-crafted studies. A good resource is the Center for State Innovation (CSI), based in Madison, Wisconsin, which was commissioned by the states of Washington, Oregon and Maine to do detailed analyses of the possibilities posed by a bank on the model of the Bank of North Dakota. After extensive review, the CSI concluded in each case that the result would be a substantial positive impact on employment, new lending, and government revenue.[641]

Another well-researched report is one titled "Banking on America" by Heather McGhee and Jason Judd of Demos, posted in April 2011.[642] The report finds that "partnership banks" (meaning state-owned banks partnering with community banks on the BND model) could:

- **Generate new revenues for states** directly, through annual bank dividend payments, and indirectly by creating jobs and spurring local economic growth.
- **Lower debt costs** for local governments. Like the Bank of North Dakota, Partnership Banks can get access to low-cost funds from the regional Federal Home Loan Banks. The banks can pass savings on to local governments when they buy debt for infrastructure investments. The banks can also provide Letters of Credit for tax-exempt bonds at lower interest rates.
- **Strengthen local banks,** even out credit cycles, and preserve real competition in local credit markets. There have been no bank failures in North Dakota during the financial crisis. BND's charter is clear that its goal is to "be helpful to and to

assist in the development of [North Dakota banks] . . . and not, in any manner, to destroy or to be harmful to existing financial institutions." By purchasing local bank stock, partnering with them on large loans and providing other support, Partnership Banks would strengthen small banks in an era when federal policy encourages bank consolidation.

- **Build up small businesses**. Surveys by the Main Street Alliance in Oregon and Washington show at least 75 percent support among small business owners. In markets increasingly dominated by large corporations and the banks that fund them, Partnership Banks would increase lending capabilities at the smaller banks that provide the majority of small business loans in America.[643]

Some Other Issues and Responses

Here are a few other issues that state bank advocates have had to address. Others are in the Q and A sections of the websites cited earlier.

Issue: State ownership of a bank violates state constitutional provisions against lending the credit of the state.

Response: The state would not be lending its own credit. It would be depositing its revenues in a bank, just as it does when it deposits them in Bank of America. The bank then advances its own bank credit, again just as Bank of America does. States already advance their own credit in many ways, including through infrastructure banks and state revolving funds. If it is a violation of the state constitution to put the state's revenues in a state-owned bank, it is a violation to put those revenues in a Wall Street bank, or to advance them in an infrastructure bank or revolving fund.

Issue: "Bureaucrats make bad businessmen."

Response: A state bank is not run by bureaucrats. It is run by seasoned bankers like any other bank. BND bankers stress that they are not politicians, and that the BND is not a development agency inclined to make risky investments. It makes loans only to creditworthy borrowers, and it avoids speculation in derivatives and risky subprime loans. By partnering with local banks, the BND actually shields itself from risk, since the local bank takes the initial loss if the borrower fails to pay. The BND does not imperil either state funds or tax money when it makes loans. Rather, it uses its own built-up capital surplus to back its loan portfolio.

Issue: Moving the state's revenues into a state-owned bank would reduce the deposit base of the banks that are holding them now. The result would be to curtail local lending.

Response: Not true. The lion's share of state deposits and capital now go to Wall Street and other large out-of-state banks, which are doing little local lending. Moreover, the portion of state revenues deposited in local community banks has to be backed on a one-to-one basis with acceptable securities (usually government bonds), so this money does not expand local bank lending either. In North Dakota, the BND earmarks the deposits of municipal governments for local banks and then guarantees them. This relieves the local banks of the need to back the deposits with an equivalent sum in securities, allowing them to expand their loan portfolios by that amount.

Issue: Setting up a bank is a lengthy process. States need financial relief now.

Response: A bank could be set up very quickly by a motivated state legislature. An experienced attorney can organize the corporate entity and obtain a banking license from the State Department of Financial Institutions. The fastest route is to simply buy a bank. There are many for sale these days. An existing bank will have not only a charter but a building and a staff. The capital then needs to be found to capitalize it, but if the state is in a hurry—e.g., to avoid an impending Wall Street derivatives collapse—a bank could be set up as a DBA of the state, meeting the capital requirement instantly.

Issue: The BND is not FDIC-insured, putting state assets at risk.

Response: The recent expropriation of depositor funds in Cyprus, along with the bail-in policies being put in place in the US, UK, EU, Canada, New Zealand and Australia, puts this issue in a whole new light. For a state to put its assets into its own bank actually avoids the risk of the giant derivatives banks, which are favored now by local governments because they are large enough to handle the state's diverse banking needs.

Being self-insured actually avoids rather than incurs risk and unnecessary expense. The privately-funded FDIC could go bankrupt before the state does, and FDIC insurance would be of little use to a state which has far more in revenues than the $250,000 maximum deposit coverage.

FDIC insurance is also quite expensive, and it subjects members to FDIC regulation. The result would be to make the state subservient to a national banking association that is semi-private. Although the FDIC calls itself an independent agency of the federal government, it receives no congressional appropriations but is funded by premiums from banks and thrift institutions, along with the FDIC's earnings on investments in U.S. Treasury securities. The FDIC is dominated by large private Wall Street banks, and it could well end up dancing to the tune of the well-funded banks that pay the piper.

North Dakota prefers to maintain its financial independence, but other states setting up their own banks need not take that route. In fact, they may no longer have that option, since FDIC coverage is now required for newly-chartered banks. Arguably, a state-owned bank is in a different category and should be able to opt out of this new rule, since it is already a state agency guaranteed by the state and will be holding large institutional deposits well in excess of $250,000. But that regulatory wrinkle has not yet been tested.

Move Our Money

The recent campaign to "Move Your Money" has generated massive popular support. But what would have far more impact would be to "move our money"—move our collective public funds from Wall Street banks into the states' own publicly-owned banks. The urgency of this sort of move has become more compelling with the recent bail-in policies involving the confiscation of depositor funds. A state-owned bank on the model of the Bank of North Dakota can protect public revenues, while allowing the state to capitalize on the magic of double-entry bookkeeping for the benefit of the local economy.

Chapter 33

LOCAL SOLUTIONS: CITY-OWNED BANKS, COUNTY-OWNED BANKS, LAND BANKS AND EMINENT DOMAIN

"[P]rotesters in the Bay Area, especially Occupy San Francisco, have something their East Coast neighbors don't: a realistic plan aimed at the heart of banks. . . . It's called a municipal bank. Simply put, it would transfer the City of San Francisco's bank accounts—about $2 billion now spread between such banks as Bank of America Corp., UnionBanCal Corp. and Wells Fargo & Co.—into a public bank. That bank would use small local banks to lend to the community."

-- David Weidner, Wall Street Journal, December 2011[644]

Cities, counties, school districts, and universities all have pools of funds that could be used to capitalize their own depository banks. These banks could then extend credit for local purposes, slash the cost of local projects, serve as a source of revenue for the municipal government, and help with local mortgage crises. Public municipal banks are common in Europe and are now being explored by some U.S. cities and counties.

It is not just states that are handing their revenues over to Wall Street. By forming their own banks, municipal governments too could keep their revenues safe from the Wall Street casino, while putting them to work in their local communities.

San Francisco is one city exploring this possibility. David Weidner, writing in *The Wall Street Journal* in December 2011, called a proposal by San Francisco city supervisor John Avalos for a city-owned bank "the boldest institutional stroke yet against banks targeted by the Occupy movement." To the criticism that a city-owned bank would put public money at risk, Weidner wrote:

> Would you be surprised to know that most of the critics are bankers? That's why you don't hear them talking about the $100 billion they lost for the California pension funds in 2008. They don't talk about the foreclosures that have wrought havoc on communities and tax revenues. They don't talk about liar loans and what kind of impact that's had on the economy, employment and the real estate market—not to mention local and state budgets.[645]

Municipal revenues deposited in a city-owned bank would at all times remain available for withdrawal, just as they are in Bank of America. The difference would be that the loans backed by these funds would remain in the local community; the City of San Francisco, not Bank of America, would get the profits; and the city's revenues would not be at risk of confiscation when Bank of America, a major player in the derivatives casino, suffered a giant gambling loss.

Among other cities looking at establishing their own banks are Boston and Philadelphia. Mike Krauss, one of the founders of the Pennsylvania Public Bank Project, points out that the population of Philadelphia is more than twice that of North Dakota, and that the need there is great. Public funding has been slashed, schools have been closed, and infrastructure is in disrepair. A city-owned bank could reduce borrowing costs, generate revenues for the city, and create jobs.[646]

County Solutions:
Straightening Out the MERS Mess

Counties, too, are considering setting up their own banks. Many counties today have financial problems; and some smaller counties are governed by a mere handful of commissioners, who could get together and shake on a county-owned bank over lunch. Counties have been particularly hard hit by the housing crisis, not just from neighborhood blight and loss of property values but from the destruction of land title records.

Contributing to the problem is that over half the homes in America are now held in the name of an electronic database called MERS (Mortgage Electronic Registration Systems), the smokescreen behind which banks have been able to pull off a massive securitization scheme without worrying about such things as ownership and chain of title. According to property law attorney Neil Garfield, properties have been sold to multiple investors or conveyed to empty trusts; subprime securities have been endorsed as triple A; and banks have earned up to 40 times what they could earn on a paying loan, using credit default swaps in which they actually bet the loan would go into default.[647]

By its own admission, MERS is a mere place holder for the true owners, a faceless, changing pool of investors holding indeterminate portions of sliced and diced, securitized properties. The result has been not only to cheat counties out of millions of dollars a year in recording fees but to make a shambles of land title records.[648]

The identities of the true owners have been obscured so well, however, that their claims to title have been put in doubt. Jurisdictions differ, but some courts have held that MERS on the title records breaks the chain of title. According to one county auditor, "What this means is that . . . the institutions, including many pension funds, that purchased these mortgages *don't actually own them* . . . ."[649]

An interesting wrinkle in these holdings is that if MERS breaks the chain of title, then *no one* holds title to the properties. That could give the county an opportunity to reclaim them for the benefit either of the homeowners with "underwater" mortgages (loans with higher balances than the market value of their homes), or the local community in the case of properties that have been abandoned.

Lenders regularly use MERS to track loans, and the system serves as the representative of mortgage lenders across the country. Among other consequences of securitization is that underwater homeowners have no legitimate sellers with whom to negotiate. In August 2012, in a case called *Bain v. MERS, et al.*, the Washington State Supreme Court held that MERS can no longer file foreclosures in Washington because it is not the true owner of mortgage loans and is not a "beneficiary" under deeds of trust. The court observed that MERS has shielded investors, banks and servicers from accountability and liability:

> Critics of the MERS system point out that after bundling many loans together, it is difficult, if not impossible, to identify the current holder of any particular loan, or to negotiate with that holder. . . . Under the MERS system, questions of authority and accountability arise, and determining who has authority to negotiate loan modifications and who is accountable for misrepresentation and fraud becomes extraordinarily difficult.[650]

To help ease the plight of underwater homeowners, one solution under consideration is for counties to simply take ownership of the mortgages through eminent domain, clear title, and start over. Local governments can seize real or personal property if (a) they can show that doing so is in the public interest, and (b) the owner is compensated at fair market value.[651]

Land Banks and Eminent Domain

For blighted, abandoned and foreclosed properties, showing that taking the properties is in the public interest is easy enough. According to the U.S. Department of Housing and Urban Development (HUD) in a 20-page booklet titled "Revitalizing Foreclosed Properties with Land Banks":

> The volume of foreclosures has become a significant problem, not only to local economies, but also to the aesthetics of neighborhoods and property values therein. At the same time, middle- to low income families continue to be priced out of the housing market while suitable housing units remain vacant. . . .
>
> To ameliorate the negative effects of foreclosures, some communities are creating public entities — known as land

banks — to return these properties to productive reuse while simultaneously addressing the need for affordable housing.[652]

States adopting land bank legislation include Michigan, Ohio, Missouri, Georgia, Indiana, Texas, Kentucky, and Maryland. The HUD booklet notes that the federal government encourages and supports these efforts; but states can still face obstacles, including a lack of funds to acquire and restore the properties, and difficulties clearing title.

Both obstacles might be overcome by focusing on abandoned and foreclosed properties with a break in the chain of title, either due to MERS or through failure to transfer the promissory note according to the terms of the trust indenture. These homes might be acquired through eminent domain free and clear—free of cost and clear of adverse claims to title.

The county would initiate the process by giving notice in the local newspaper of intent to exercise its right of eminent domain. The burden of proof would then transfer to the bank or trust claiming title. If the claimant could not prove title, the county would take the property, clear title, and either work out a fair settlement with the parties (occupants, investors and servicers) or restore the home for rent or sale.

Even if the county acquired the properties without charge, however, it might lack the funds to restore them. Additional funds could be had by establishing a public bank serving more functions than just those of a land bank. In a series titled "A Solution to the Foreclosure Crisis," Michael Sauvante suggests that properties obtained by eminent domain can be used as part of the "tier 2" capital base for a chartered, publicly-owned bank, on the model of the Bank of North Dakota.[653] The county could deposit its revenues in this bank and use its capital and deposits to generate credit, as all chartered banks are empowered to do. This credit could then be used to finance property redevelopment and for other county needs, again on the model of the Bank of North Dakota.[654]

Sauvante adds that the use of eminent domain is often viewed negatively by homeowners. To overcome this prejudice, the county could exercise eminent domain on the mortgage contract rather than on title to the property. (The power of eminent domain applies to both real and personal property rights.) Title would then remain with the homeowner. The county would have only a secured interest in the property, putting it in the shoes of the bank. It could then renegotiate reasonable terms with the homeowner. This is something banks have often been unwilling or unable to do, since they have to get all the investor-owners to agree, a difficult task; and they have little incentive to negotiate when they can make more money on fees and credit default swaps on contracts that go into default.

Eminent Domain Proposals
for Underwater Homes

So far, homes that have been taken by eminent domain have been the sort of blighted, abandoned properties that are destroying neighborhood property values. Taking the mortgages of underwater homeowners in order to refinance them on easier terms is a more radical plan that is still being explored. The proposal is for the mortgages to be refinanced at their market value, with the investors recovering a portion but not all of their investments.

In 2012, the approach was studied by a Joint Powers Authority that was formed by the County of San Bernardino and the cities of Fontana and Ontario, California, to explore proposals to help struggling underwater homeowners with payments. In August 2012, a resolution was passed to consider plans in which the county would take underwater mortgages by eminent domain, then help the borrowers arrange mortgages with significantly lower monthly payments.[655]

Objections voiced at the August hearing included concerns over where the county would get the money for the purchases, and suspicions concerning the role of the private venture capital firm bringing the proposal. Would it make off with the profits and leave the county footing the bills?

After months of opposition from the finance industry, in January 2013 the plan proposed by the venture capital firm was finally rejected, although the five-member Joint Powers Authority board voted to continue soliciting proposals that could help underwater homeowners. What evidently killed the measure were threats from the mortgage industry that allowing local government to seize mortgage notes could have a chilling effect on lending, and concerns that the plan would undermine the security of loan agreements and impose losses on investors.

According to the venture capital firm, about thirty communities are still in talks to proceed with the plan, including Fontana, where fully half the homeowners in the city are underwater on their mortgages.[656]

Using Eminent Domain When Title Cannot Be Proven

A way around the objections to the plan rejected by the Joint Powers Authority might to be focus on properties with MERS in the chain of title, eliminate the private venture-capital middlemen, and proceed through a county land bank. The county might be able in this way to obtain a significant inventory of properties free and clear, while getting around the objection that using eminent domain to cure mortgage problems constitutes an unconstitutional taking of private property. In these cases there would be no owner from whom the property was taken, because no one would be able to prove clear title.

Without spending too much time on the legal issues, it is worth noting that the county would be in a different position from borrowers raising the "clouded title" defense to foreclosure—defendants on whom courts have not looked too favorably. The borrower is compromised by the fact that he signed a mortgage giving MERS the right to foreclose, and "a deal is a deal." But the county made no deal with MERS, and the county has a vested interest in maintaining clean title records. The burden in this case would be on MERS, the bank, or the investors to prove clear title rather than on the borrower to disprove it.

If MERS is not a beneficiary entitled to foreclose, as held in *Bain* and other cases, it is not entitled to assign that right or to assign title. Title remains with the original note holder; and in the typical case, the note holder can no longer be located or established, since the property has been used as collateral for multiple investors.

Putting the burden on MERS to prove title would overcome another snag in eminent domain proposals involving underwater homes. To make the proposals economically feasible, the mortgages would have to be purchased at less than fair market value, and that is a violation of eminent domain laws and due process. However, troubled mortgages with MERS in the title—which now seem to be the majority of them—could be obtained by counties or cities for no money at all.

Equitable Considerations: Sharing the Losses

Homeowners who paid much more for a home than it was worth as a result of the securitization bubble need a champion. They have little chance of challenging the legitimacy of their underwater mortgages on their own. Once the county or city has obtained title, it will be in a position to "do the fair thing," settling with stakeholders in proportion to their legitimate claims, and refinancing or reselling the properties as appropriate.

Opponents of eminent domain proposals say the result would be to rob Peter to pay Paul. But Peter today is getting 100 cents on the dollar, while Paul is bearing all the losses. The free-market argument is that the homeowners gambled and lost. However, they lost because it was *not* a free market. The banks and the investors got bailed out by the taxpayers. Where is the bailout for the homeowners? If federal bureaucrats won't make the banks and investors share the losses, county officials can and should.

What, then, is the remedy of the investors? Investors unable to trace the chain of title to the promissory note and deed of trust may have only an unsecured claim for monetary damages. Their remedy in that case is with the banks selling them the collateralized debt obligations (CDOs) protected with credit default swaps. The investors would need to collect either from the counterparties to those bets or from the banks that sold them a bill of goods.

Attorney Neil Garfield says the investors are unlikely to recover on abandoned and foreclosed properties in any case.[657] Banks and servicers can earn more when the homes are bulldozed (something that is actually happening in some counties) than from a sale or workout at a loss.[658] Not only is more earned on credit default swaps and fees, but bulldozed homes tell no tales. Garfield maintains that a third of the investors' money may have gone into middleman profits rather than into real estate purchases. "With a complete loss," he says, "no one asks for an accounting."

Attorneys for the banks naturally dispute these claims, and therein lies the problem with MERS: it all happens behind closed doors, making tracking and verifying what has gone on very difficult.

Meanwhile, not only homes and neighborhoods but 400 years of property law are being systematically destroyed. Bailing out reckless financiers and refusing to hold them accountable has led to a fundamental breakdown in the role of government and the court system. This can be righted only by holding everyone to the same set of laws, including bankers. Those laws include that a contract for the sale of real estate must be in writing signed by seller and buyer, that an assignment must bear the signatures required by local law, and that forging signatures (as in the "robo-signing" scandal) gives rise to an actionable claim for fraud.

State Legislative Eminent Domain Proposals

Variants of the county eminent domain approach have also been suggested at the state level. One version is in Hawaii, which has two bills for a state-owned bank pending as of March 2013—HB 1840 and HB 2103. Both bills passed the Hawaii House in March 2012. HB 1840 establishes a task force to review, investigate, and study the feasibility and cost of establishing a state-owned bank. HB 2103 directs the Hawaii housing and finance development corporation to establish and operate an interim purchase program for distressed residential properties encumbered by problematic mortgages until the bank of the state of Hawaii is operational.[659]

According to a report on HB 2103 from the Hawaii House Committees on Economic Revitalization and Business & Housing dated February 10, 2012:

> The purpose of this measure is to establish the bank of the State of Hawaii in order to develop a program to acquire residential property in situations where the mortgagor is an owner-occupant who has defaulted on a mortgage or been denied a mortgage loan modification and *the mortgagee is a securitized trust that cannot adequately demonstrate that it is a holder in due course.*[660]

In other words, the bill deals with distressed mortgages involving a break in the chain of title to the properties. The bill provides that in cases of foreclosure in which the mortgagee cannot prove its right to foreclose or to collect on the mortgage, foreclosure shall be stayed and the bank of the State of Hawaii may offer to buy the property from the owner-occupant for a sum not exceeding 75 percent of the principal balance due on the mortgage loan. The newly-formed bank of the State of Hawaii could then rent or sell the property back to the owner-occupant at a fair price on reasonable terms.

Arizona Senate Bill 1451 would do something similar for homeowners who are current on their payments but whose mortgages are underwater. Author and consumer activist Martin Andelman writes that the bill is a "revolutionary approach to revitalizing the state's increasingly water-logged housing market, which has left over 500,000 of Arizona's homeowners in a hopelessly immobile state." [661] The bill passed the Senate committee 6 to 0 in February 2012.

Senate Bill 1451 would establish an Arizona Housing Finance Reform Authority to refinance the mortgages of Arizona homeowners who owe more than their homes are currently worth. The existing mortgage would be replaced with a new mortgage from AHFRA in an amount up to 125 percent of the home's current fair market value. The existing lender would get paid 101 percent of the home's fair market value, and would get a non-interest-bearing note called a "loss recapture certificate" covering a portion of any underwater amounts, to be paid over time. The capital to refinance the mortgages would come from floating revenue bonds, and payment on the bonds would come solely from monies paid by the homeowner-borrowers. An Arizona Home Insurance Fund would create a cash reserve of up to 20 percent of the bond and would be used to insure against losses. That means the bill would cost the state nothing.

The idea is promising, but it could be taken a step further. The state could capitalize a publicly-owned bank, let it hold the homes as assets, and work with homebuilders, building trades, and others to maintain or improve the properties. The bank could then partner with local banks to get credit moving in the state's communities, again on the model of the Bank of North Dakota.

Chapter 34

FEDERAL SOLUTIONS: POSTAL BANKS, DEVELOPMENT BANKS, PUBLIC CENTRAL BANKS, AND NATIONALIZATION

While we have channeled capital into wars and debt, our competitors in Asia and Latin America have worked with infrastructure banks to lay a sound foundation for growth. As a result, we must compete not only with their lower labor costs but also with their advanced energy, transportation and information platforms, which are a magnet even for American businesses.

— Michael Likosky, "Banking on the Future,"
New York Times, July 2011

Public banking solutions are also available at the federal level. They include postal savings banks that provide people with a safe, convenient way to save; national public development banks, which have been instrumental in funding rapid economic development in many countries; and truly "national" central banks that use their power as lenders of last resort to underwrite the interests of the public and the economy rather than simply propping up the banking industry. Another federal solution gaining advocates today is outright nationalization of insolvent too-big-to-fail banks.

Capitalizing on the Possibilities of the Post Office

Banking services have been provided in post offices in many countries historically, including the United States. Federal postal banking offers not only convenience and security but an internationally proven way to maintain post office profitability.

Postal banking services were first offered in Great Britain in 1861. The postal banks were wildly popular, attracting over 600,000 accounts and £8.2 million in deposits in their first five years. By 1927, there were twelve million accounts—those of one in four Britons—with £283 million on deposit.

Postal banks then mushroomed in other countries. They were popular because they serviced a huge untapped market, the unbanked and underbanked. According to a Discussion Paper of the United Nations Department of Economic and Social Affairs:

> The essential characteristic distinguishing postal financial services from the private banking sector is the obligation and capacity of the postal system to serve the entire spectrum of the national population, unlike conventional private banks which allocate their institutional resources to service the sectors of the population they deem most profitable.[662]

Although serving low-income and rural populations does not sound particularly profitable, expanding to include postal financial services has actually been crucial in many countries to maintaining the profitability of their postal network. Letter delivery can be a losing proposition and often requires cross-subsidies from other activities to maintain its network. Public postal banks are profitable because their market is large and their costs are low. The infrastructure is already built and available, advertising costs are minimal, and government-owned banks do not reward their management with extravagant bonuses or commissions that drain profits away. Profits return to the government and the people.

Profits return in another way: money comes out from under mattresses and gets deposited in savings accounts, becoming "excess reserves" that the bank can use to purchase the bonds that fund government. The Japanese lead in this approach, with Japan Post Bank holding 20 percent of the national debt. (See Chapter 21.) The Japanese government has its own captive public lender that services the debt at low interest without risking the vagaries of the international bond market.

Japan Post Bank and New Zealand's Kiwibank were discussed at length earlier. Here are some other popular postal banks:

- **India's Post Office Savings Bank (POSB).** Now the largest banking institution in India, POSB was established in the latter half of the 19th century following the success of the postal savings system in England.[663] POSB is operated by the government of India and provides small savings banking and financial services. The Department of Posts is seeking to expand these services by creating a full-fledged bank that would offer full lending and investing services.[664]

- **China's Postal Savings Bureau.** After a 34-year lapse, this postal bank was re-established in 1986 with the assistance of the People's Bank of China. Savings deposits flooded in, growing at over 50 percent annually in the first half of the 1990s and over 24 percent annually in the second half. By 1998, postal savings accounted for 47 percent of China Post's operating revenues, and 80 percent of China's post offices provided postal savings services. As in Japan, the Postal Savings Bureau has served as a vital link in mobilizing income and profits from the private sector, providing credit for local development. In 2007, the Postal Savings Bank of China was set up from the Postal Savings Bureau as a state-owned limited company that provides postal banking services.[665]

- **Switzerland's Swiss Post** offers postal financial services that are by far its most profitable activity, balancing the heavy losses Swiss Post routinely suffers from its parcel delivery and the marginal profits it earns from letter delivery operations.[666]

- **Russia's PochtaBank.** In 2008, the head of the highly successful state-owned Sberbank stepped down to take on the task of revitalizing the Russian post office, including setting up PochtaBank in the Russian Post's 40,000 local post offices. The intent is for the postal banks to compete on an equal footing with private banks and with Sberbank itself.[667]

- **Brazil's ECT (Correios).** ECT, Brazil's national postal service, instituted a postal banking system in 2002 on a public/private model, forming a partnership with the nation's largest private bank (Bradesco) to provide financial services at post offices. The current partnership is with Bank of Brazil. ECT is one of the largest state-owned companies in Latin America, with an international service network reaching more than 220 countries worldwide.[668]

Time to Revive the U.S. Postal Savings System?

A movement is now afoot to restore banking services to the U.S. Postal Service. Self-funded throughout its history, the U.S. Post Office was pushed into technical insolvency in 2006, when Congress required it to prefund postal retiree health benefits for 75 years into the future. Critics of the legislation note that no other public or private company is required to carry that onerous burden.[669] They say the USPS has been targeted by elements in Congress bent on destroying the most powerful unions and privatizing all public services. That includes the school system and the post office, an institution that is as old as the country itself and is actually named in the Constitution.

On July 27, 2012, the National Association of Letter Carriers adopted a resolution at their National Convention in Minneapolis to investigate establishing a USPS banking system. The resolution pointed out that expanding postal services and developing new sources of revenue are important to the effort to save the post office and preserve living-wage jobs; that many countries have a successful history of postal banking, including Germany, France, Italy, Japan, and the United States; and that postal banks could serve the 9 million people who don't have bank accounts and the 21 million who use usurious check cashers, giving low-income people access to a safe banking system. "A USPS bank would offer a 'public option' for banking," concluded the resolution, "providing basic checking and savings—and no complex financial wheeling and dealing."

The now defunct U.S. Postal Savings System was quite successful in its day.[670] It was set up in 1911 to get money out of hiding, attract the savings of immigrants, provide safe depositories for people who had lost confidence in private banks, and furnish depositories with longer hours that were convenient for working people. The minimum deposit was $1 and the maximum was $2,500. The postal system paid two percent interest on deposits annually. It also issued U.S. Postal Savings Bonds that paid annual interest, as well as Postal Savings Certificates and domestic money orders.

Postal savings peaked in 1947 at almost $3.4 billion. The U.S. Postal Savings System was shut down in 1967, not because it was inefficient but because it became unnecessary after private banks saw the profit potential in the market the postal banks were serving. They raised their interest rates on deposits and offered governmental guarantees (FDIC insurance), just as the postal savings system had been offering earlier.[671]

Today, however, many banks are moving away from traditional banking services, and the market of the "underbanked" has grown again. In a 2009 survey, it included about one in four households.[672] Without access to conventional financial services, people turn to an expensive alternative banking market of bill-pay, prepaid debit cards, check cashing services, and payday loans. They pay excessive fees and are susceptible to high-cost predatory lenders. On average, a payday borrower pays back $800 for a $300 loan, with $500 going just toward interest. Low-income adults in the U.S spend over $5 billion annually paying off fees and debt associated with predatory loans.[673]

The rural population is another underserviced market. Rural banking services are more limited following the 2008 crisis; and with shrinking resources for obtaining credit, farmers are finding it increasingly difficult to stay in their homes.[674] Postal services themselves are being threatened in rural areas. A move to shutter 3,700 low-revenue post offices was halted in May 2012 only after months of dissent from rural states and their lawmakers.[675]

Another underserved segment of the population that could be serviced through postal banks is the U.S. military. Servicemen are often victims of loan sharks and payday loans. Alternatively, the U.S. military could follow the lead of the Mexican military, which provides full-service banking to its personnel through its own bank, Banjercito, the Mexican National Bank of the Army, Air Force and Navy.

Countries such as Russia and India are exploring not just depository but full-fledged lending services through their post offices;

but if lending to the underbanked seems too risky, a U.S. postal bank could be modeled on Japan Post, which uses the credit generated from its deposits to buy safe, liquid government bonds. That could still make the bank a win-win-win, providing income for the post office, inexpensive depository and checking services for the underbanked, and a reliable source of public funding for the government.

National Development Banks

Development banks have a mandate to provide finance to the private sector to promote development, insuring investment in areas in which the market would not otherwise invest sufficiently.[676] Successful national development banks discussed earlier include Brazil's BNDES and China's Development Bank, called "the most powerful financial institution in the world."[677] Others are the Japan Development Bank (once but no longer slated for privatization), India's Development Bank of India and Small Industries Development Bank of India, and Germany's KfW (Kreditanstalt für Wiederaufbau, meaning Reconstruction Credit Institute). German public development banks (called "special purpose banks") finance the greening of industry and lead banking groups in funding social institutions such as hospitals and other public works.

Development banks are underwritten by the government and can make long-term loans at low, fixed interest rates. They have been criticized as funding projects that are destructive to the environment in developing countries; for example, by funding hydroelectric dams that flood the Amazon and vast parts of China. But that is a policy issue. Combining the funding mechanisms of a development bank with U.S. environmental standards could turn this credit engine into a powerful tool for sustainable economic development.

The U.S. Reconstruction Finance Corporation operated on principles similar to a development bank. It recycled private investment money acquired through bond issues (debentures) into projects that increased employment and contributed to national development. The RFC was disbanded when the boost it gave to the economy was considered no longer necessary, but the U.S. economy is clearly lagging now. It may be time to look again at the idea of a U.S. federal bank aiming the firehose of national credit at the local economy, local businesses, and homeowners.

Some steps have been taken in that direction. The Coalition for Green Capital is working to set up green banks in ten states, and will work in 2013 to set up a national green bank to provide much of the funding for the state green banks.[678] A bipartisan bill was also introduced in the U.S. Senate in March 2011 to create an American Infrastructure Financing Authority, which would move private capital now sitting on the sidelines into much-needed infrastructure projects.[679] It would be funded like the RFC and its offshoots: it would get a one-time grant of federal money ($10 billion) and extend targeted loans and limited loan guarantees to projects that need a boost to get going but can pay for themselves over time—toll roads, energy plants that collect user fees, ports that impose fees on goods entering or leaving the country, and so forth. In a July 2011 article in *The New York Times* describing this bill, Michael B. Likosky wrote:

> . . . An infrastructure bank would not endanger taxpayer money, because under the Federal Credit Reform Act of 1990, passed after the savings and loan scandal, it would have to meet accounting and reporting requirements and limit government liability. The proposed authority would not and could not become a Fannie Mae or Freddie Mac. It would be owned by and operated for America, not shareholders.
>
> The World Bank, the Inter-American Development Bank, the Asian Development Bank and similar institutions helped debt-burdened developing countries to grow through infrastructure investments and laid the foundations for the global high-tech economy. For instance, they literally laid the infrastructure of the Web through a fiber-optic link around the globe. Infrastructure banks retrofitted ports to receive and process shipping containers, which made it profitable to manufacture goods overseas. Similar investments anchored energy-intensive microchip fabrication.[680]

Likosky thinks an infrastructure bank is critical to maintaining a healthy economy. He writes:

> For decades, we have neglected the foundation of our economy while other countries have invested in state-of-the-art water,

energy and transportation infrastructure. Our manufacturing base has migrated abroad; our innovation edge may soon follow. If we don't find a way to build a sound foundation for growth, the American dream will survive only in our heads and history books.

Public Central Banks

Also instrumental in the remarkable growth and development of some countries are central banks that are public not just in name but in function. They do more than just satisfy the liquidity needs of private banks that then lend at higher interest to individuals and governments, as "independent" central banks see their roles.

Central banks have only recently been declared independent of government. As Professor Tim Canova points out, in the 1940s even the U.S. Federal Reserve was enlisted in the service of government:

> The trend in central banking throughout the world for the last few decades has been to follow the U.S. lead in having an independent central bank, a central bank that is independent of elected government on their day to day operations. The problem is that independence has really come to mean a central bank that has been captured by Wall Street interests, very large banking interests. It might be independent of the politicians, but it doesn't mean it is a neutral arbiter. During the Great Depression and coming out of it the Fed took its cues from Congress. Throughout the entire 1940s, the Federal Reserve as a practical matter was not independent. It took its marching orders from the White House and the Treasury—and it was the most successful decade in American economic history.[681]

For governments to pull this off today, however, they may have to slip out of the regulatory straitjacket of the BIS and the Basel Committee. According to the BIS website, central banks in the Central Bank Governance Network are supposed to have as their single or primary objective "to preserve price stability."[682] "Price stability" is defined in monetarist terms, following the Milton Friedman dictum that "inflation is always and everywhere a monetary phenomenon."

Any increase in the money supply is considered to drive up prices. The monetarist prescription is to maintain a "stable" money supply even if that means burdening the people with ever-mounting debt. Central banks are discouraged from increasing the money supply by issuing money and using it for the benefit of the state, either directly or as loans; and to ensure that political considerations do not interfere with this mandate, central banks are required to be kept independent from government.

That is the alleged reason for insisting on central bank independence, but economist Henry C. K. Liu challenges it. In his 2002 *Asia Times* article "The BIS vs National Banks," he wrote:

> BIS regulations serve only the single purpose of strengthening the international private banking system, even at the peril of national economies. The BIS does to national banking systems what the IMF has done to national monetary regimes.
>
> . . . [Foreign direct investment] denominated in foreign currencies, mostly dollars, has condemned many national economies into unbalanced development toward export, merely to make dollar-denominated interest payments to [foreign investors], with little net benefit to the domestic economies.[683]

Liu maintains that by applying "the State Theory of Money" – the theory that national money supply should be created by governments rather than by private banks – "any government can fund with its own currency all its domestic developmental needs to maintain full employment without inflation." As Keynes pointed out, an increase in the money supply will have the beneficial effect of increasing demand, which will increase the production of goods and services, at least until full productive capacity is reached. At that point, price inflation can be prevented by pulling money back into the treasury with taxes and fees.

We have seen that countries that have tried this have usually been reined in by competing international financial interests, but some have escaped. China, which is too big to monitor or intimidate, still operates very successfully on the "public" or "national" central bank model, something it can get away with not only because of its size and economic clout but because it is discreet, at least pretending to play by the rules. Venezuela, Ecuador, Argentina and other Latin American countries are also using their central banks to more directly benefit the populace and the economy, quietly defying the neoliberal model.

Time to Nationalize Some Oversized Banks?

There is another way the government could fund the economy's credit needs through its own banks: by nationalizing insolvent too-big-to-fail banks. Nationalization is not a radical socialist proposition, as it has been characterized, Rather, it is what is *supposed* to happen when big banks go bankrupt. It is one of three options open to the FDIC when a bank fails. The other two are (1) closure and liquidation, and (2) merger with a healthy bank. Most failures are resolved using the merger option, but for very large banks, nationalization is sometimes considered the best choice for taxpayers. The leading U.S. example was Continental Illinois, the seventh-largest bank in the country when it failed in 1984. The FDIC wiped out existing shareholders, infused capital, took over bad assets, replaced senior management, and owned the bank for about a decade, running it as a commercial enterprise. In 1994, it was sold to a bank that is now part of Bank of America.[684]

What *is* a radical departure from accepted practice is Congress's acquiescence in an unprecedented wave of bank bailouts after the 2008 banking crisis. The taxpayers have taken the losses while the culpable CEOs have not only escaped civil and criminal penalties but have managed to make off with record bonuses. Banks backed by an army of lobbyists have succeeded in getting laws changed so that what was formerly criminal behavior is now legal.

In a July 2012 article in *The New York Times* titled "Wall Street Is Too Big to Regulate," Gar Alperovitz notes that the five biggest banks—JPMorgan Chase, Bank of America, Citigroup, Wells Fargo and Goldman Sachs—now have combined assets amounting to more than half the nation's economy:

> With high-paid lobbyists contesting every proposed regulation, it is increasingly clear that big banks can never be effectively controlled as private businesses. If an enterprise (or five of them) is so large and so concentrated that competition and regulation are impossible, the most market-friendly step is to nationalize its functions. . . .

Nationalization isn't as difficult as it sounds. We tend to forget that we did, in fact, nationalize General Motors in 2009; the government still owns a controlling share of its stock. We also essentially nationalized the American International Group, one of the largest insurance companies in the world, and the government still owns roughly 60 percent of its stock.[685]

In a February 2009 article in *Forbes* titled "Nationalize Insolvent Banks," economist Nouriel Roubini argued that "paradoxically, nationalization may be a more market-friendly solution to a banking crisis" than the alternatives. But by "nationalization" he meant:

> Outright government takeover (call it nationalization—or "receivership" if you don't like the N-word) of insolvent banks, to be cleaned after take over and then resold to the private sector.[686]

This type of nationalization, in which the government cleans up the asset and then sells it back to the private sector, Michael Hudson calls "Orwellian doublethink":

> Real nationalization occurs when governments act in the public interest to take over private property. . . . Nationalizing the banks along these lines would mean that the government would supply the nation's credit needs. The Treasury would become the source of new money, replacing commercial bank credit. Presumably this credit would be lent out for economically and socially productive purposes, not merely to inflate asset prices while loading down households and business with debt as has occurred under today's commercial bank lending policies.[687]

In a July 2012 article in the UK *Guardian* titled "Private Banks Have Failed—We Need a Public Solution," Seumas Milne maintained:

> Only if the largest banks are broken up, the part-nationalised outfits turned into genuine public investment banks, and new socially owned and regional banks encouraged can finance be made to work for society, rather than the other way round. Private sector banking has spectacularly failed—and we need a democratic public solution.[688]

Chapter 35

QUANTITATIVE EASING
FOR THE PEOPLE

"We make money the old fashioned way. We print it."

-- *Art Rolnick, former Chief Economist,*
Minneapolis Federal Reserve Bank

There is another solution to our economic woes that is available at the federal level. The Treasury could engage in a form of "quantitative easing" that actually gets money into the bank accounts of people, businesses and governments. If banks can borrow at 0.25 percent (the Fed funds rate) or 0.75 percent (the federal discount rate), why not people and local governments? That sort of solution could do more than just solve government budget problems. It could help address a cancer that is destroying the economy from within— the expectation that our money can and should "make money" without making any productive contribution to the economy.

Underlying the structural problems of our current monetary system is a financial parasitism in which money is expected to grow of its own accord, capitalizing on the "miracle of compound interest" and other money-making-money schemes. This mentality is not just the vice of Wall Street day traders. It infects us all. Government does not provide sufficiently for old age, sickness, or the increasing expense of higher education for our children. We feel we must save individually for these things; and no matter how much we save, we are never sure we have enough. Merely saving a bit from the paycheck each month won't do it. Our money needs to be invested so that it can "grow." But it can grow of its own accord only if money is taken from someone else or if the money supply is inflated; and investing the money means that it is vulnerable to being lost in "bad" investments. Even wealthy people can get wiped out in the stock market. We all live with a mindset of scarcity and want, always desiring more as a cushion, always nervous about the future.

And the future is getting more uncertain all the time. There hardly seem to be any good investments anymore. The interest rate on certificates of deposit and savings bonds is too low to add significantly to pensions, and the stock market is so vulnerable to manipulation that it is totally unpredictable. It used to be that you could "buy and hold"—buy good companies, invest in them, and hold the stocks for 20 years, watching them grow. But today, computers with high-frequency trading programs dominate 70 percent of the stock market and appear to be able to manipulate it more or less at will.

Interest rates are manipulated too, in part because the banking system is insolvent. Debt is leveraged on debt, with nothing backing the whole. Central banks push interest rates as low as they can go—but only for bankers, to give them the liquidity necessary to back their loans. Meanwhile, banks have generated derivatives with notional values in the hundreds of trillions of dollars. The money is simply not there to cover all the liabilities carried on bank balance sheets.

An insolvent banking system, in turn, means there can be no "free market." The market must be controlled. The central bank and the government's financial manipulators (sometimes called the "Plunge Protection Team") must support assets and interest rates that a truly free market would not support. The market rises and falls when these supporting institutions move them, not when the "market" would move of its own accord. There are artificial, manipulated booms and busts. The market is run up, investors are seduced into investing, and the market is plunged back down. Savings and investments get wiped out, progressively turning even the "haves" into "have nots." The people with money have less and less because there is no really safe place to save it; while the people who have nothing can get nothing, because there are no jobs, no low interest rates for them, and insufficient money flowing through the productive economy.

The long-held ideal of saving and investing the money for old age is no longer a reliable social safety net, and neither is the social security provided by the government. We need an Economic Bill of Rights that covers basic human needs, as Franklin Roosevelt urged in 1944. The government needs to provide these basic social goods if only to allow the nation's businesses to compete with other countries that do; but where is the money to be found? Western governments everywhere are broke – or they think they are. But there is an overlooked source of funds available to all sovereign governments: they can reclaim the power to create money from the banks and simply issue it themselves. Social crediters argue that governments *need* to issue additional money, just to fill the gap between what employers pay out collectively for wages, materials and interest and the collective cost of the products on the market.

Skeptics call this "funny money" and say that it cannot create productivity but will just create inflation. That argument, in fact, has kept the gatekeepers in control for centuries. We have seen, however, that national credit can be issued to fund public projects without inflating prices. Moreover, banks create money every day when they make loans. Money is not just created but is extinguished on the books of banks. When loans are repaid and new loans are not taken out to replace them, the money supply shrinks. According to a 2012 staff report on the website of the New York Federal Reserve, the money supply (M3) had at that time shrunk by $4 trillion from the beginning of the banking crisis in 2008.[689] That means that at least that much money could be added back in without creating price inflation. In fact it needs to be added back in, just to bring the money supply back to where it was earlier.

How is this "reflation" of the money supply to be done? Several alternatives have been proposed.

Central Bank Quantitative Easing

The solution of the Federal Reserve and other central banks has been massive quantitative easing to increase the "monetary base." The problem with this approach is that the money gets no further than bank reserve accounts. It is simply an asset swap between the central bank and commercial banks. The central bank gets the assets (federal securities or mortgage-backed securities) and the commercial banks get cash in their reserve accounts in place of those assets.

Reserves are used simply to clear checks between banks. They move from one reserve account to another, but the total money in bank reserve accounts remains unchanged. Banks can lend their reserves to each other, but they cannot lend them to us. As explained by Peter Stella, former head of the Central Banking and Monetary and Foreign Exchange Operations Divisions at the International Monetary Fund:

> [B]anks do not lend "reserves". . . . Whether commercial banks let the reserves they have acquired through QE sit "idle" or lend them out in the internet bank market 10,000 times in one day among themselves, the aggregate reserves at the central bank at the end of that day will be the same.[690]

This point is also stressed in Modern Monetary Theory. Professor Scott Fullwiler explains, "Banks can't 'do' anything with all the extra reserve balances. Loans create deposits—reserve balances don't finance lending or add any 'fuel' to the economy. Banks don't lend reserve balances except in the federal funds market, and in that case the Fed always provides sufficient quantities to keep the federal funds rate at its . . . interest rate target."[691]

That explains why the unprecedented quantitative easing programs now being conducted by central banks globally are not getting credit to the private sector and are not increasing the money supply. (See Figure 12.)

They aren't getting credit to the private sector, but they could. One possibility was put on the congressional table in May 2013, when Sen. Elizabeth Warren (D-Mass) introduced a groundbreaking bill called the "Bank on Students Loan Fairness Act." It would let students borrow directly from the government at the same rate that banks get from the Fed—0.75 percent. Sen. Warren said:

> Every single day, this country invests in big banks by lending them money at near-zero rates. We should make the same kind of investment lending money to students, who are trying to get an education.[693]

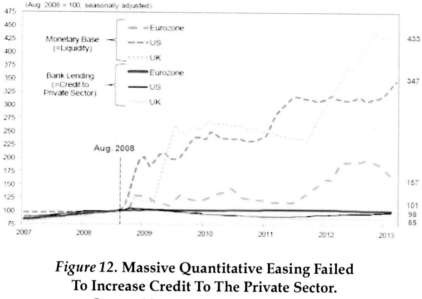

**Figure 12. Massive Quantitative Easing Failed
To Increase Credit To The Private Sector.**
Source: Nomura Research Institute,
based on FRB, ECB and Bank of England data.[692]

Critics quickly wrote off the bill as "a cheap political gimmick" that "confuses market interest rates on long-term loans (such as the 10-year Treasury rate) with the Federal Reserve's Discount Window (used to make short-term loans to banks), and does not reflect the administrative costs and default risk that increase the costs of the federal student loan program."[694]

That criticism would be valid if the lender were an ordinary private bank; but in this case, the proposed provider of funds is the U.S. Federal Reserve. It can expand its balance sheet by buying all the assets it likes, as we saw when it bought over $1 trillion in toxic mortgage-backed securities in QE1. The Fed is the "lender of last resort" and can write off its losses, just as the government of China can write off the bad debts of its government-owned banks.

The proposal is not radical or unprecedented. For more than twenty years, the Australian government has successfully funded students by giving out what are in effect interest-free loans. They are "contingent loans," which are repaid if and when the borrower's income reaches a certain level. New Zealand also offers 0 percent interest loans to New Zealand students, with repayment to be made from their incomes after they graduate.[695] If we had an Economic Bill of Rights, tuition for higher education would be provided by the government for free . In some countries it is nearly free today, and it was free or nearly free in this country in state universities in the 1960s.

The Trillion Dollar Coin

Another proposal for "reflating" the money supply that has been fertile ground in the media for jokes is for the Treasury to simply mint some trillion dollar coins. The idea is not, however, as ludicrous as it sounds. Today, the ability to mint coins is all that is left of the U.S. Treasury's money-creating power. If we the people want to reclaim that power so that we can pay our obligations when due, the Treasury will need to mint more than nickels and dimes. It will need to create some coins with very large numbers on them.

Somehow we have come to accept that it is less silly for the central bank to create money out of thin air and lend it at near zero interest to private commercial banks, to be re-lent to the public and the government at market interest rates, than for the government to simply create the money itself, debt- and interest-free. We have forgotten our historical roots. We have lost not only the power to create our own money but even the memory that we once had it.

The idea of minting large denomination coins to solve economic problems was evidently first suggested in the early 1980s by a chairman of the Coinage Subcommittee of the U.S. House of Representatives, who pointed out that the government could pay off its entire debt with some billion-dollar coins. The Constitution gives Congress the power to coin money and regulate its value, and no limit is put on the value of the coins it creates. In *Web of Debt* (2007), it was suggested that to solve the government's debt problems today, these would need to be trillion dollar coins.

In legislation initiated in 1982, however, Congress chose to impose limits on itself, by limiting the amounts and denominations of most coins. The one exception was the platinum coin, which a special provision allowed to be minted in any amount for commemorative purposes. In January 2013, in response to a pending federal budget ceiling crisis, attorney/blogger Carlos Mucha proposed issuing a platinum coin to capitalize on this loophole.[696]

Philip Diehl, former head of the U.S. Mint and co-author of the platinum coin law, confirmed that the coin would be legal tender:

> In minting the $1 trillion platinum coin, the Treasury Secretary would be exercising authority which Congress has granted routinely for more than 220 years . . . under power expressly granted to Congress in the Constitution (Article 1, Section 8).[697]

MMT co-founder Warren Mosler reviewed the idea and concluded it would work operationally. The funds would simply be new reserve balances at the Fed rather than new Treasury securities.[698]

Prof. Randall Wray explained that the coin would not circulate but would be deposited in the government's account at the Fed, so it could not inflate the circulating money supply. The budget would still need Congressional approval. To keep a lid on spending, Congress would just need to abide by some basic rules of economics. It could spend on goods and services up to full employment without creating price inflation (since supply and demand would rise together). After that, it would need to tax—not to fund the budget, but to shrink the circulating money supply and avoid driving up prices with excess demand.[699]

The Social Dividend

Another possibility for reflating the economy is the "social credit" option—issue a dividend that goes directly into the pockets of consumers, to be spent as they choose. This can be done electronically, just as the Fed conducts its quantitative easing electronically today. Consider this scenario:

Debit cards are created with a total value of three trillion dollars. They are drawn on the Treasury's account at the Federal Reserve, into which three newly-minted $1 trillion coins have been deposited. A card for $10,000 is given to each of the 300 million people in the United States, simply as a dividend for being alive in the twenty-first century, when mechanization has eliminated the need for a large portion of the human labor force. The cards are used over the course of the year, gradually increasing demand. The increased demand causes shopkeepers to put in more orders to suppliers, prompting the suppliers to produce more, hiring extra workers to get the work done; and all this productive output increases the goods and services available on the market.

Dangerously inflationary? No. Price inflation results when too much money is chasing too few goods and services; and in this case, goods and services will rise *along with* money ("demand"), keeping prices stable. When workers are unemployed and materials are available, adding money to the economy does not drive up prices but puts workers to work producing more goods and services.

A $3 trillion national dividend would not only not inflate prices; it might not even inflate the money supply. Money changes hands in the course of a year, multiplying taxable income; and the taxes return to the government. The possibilities were illustrated by this anecdote circulated on the Internet, suggesting how the Greek debt crisis might have been resolved:

It is a slow day in a little Greek village. The rain is beating down and the streets are deserted. Times are tough, everybody is in debt, and everybody lives on credit.

On this particular day a rich German tourist is driving through the village, stops at the local hotel and lays a €100 note on the desk, telling the hotel owner he wants to inspect the rooms upstairs in order to pick one to spend the night.

The owner gives him some keys and, as soon as the visitor has walked upstairs, the hotelier grabs the €100 note and runs next door to pay his debt to the butcher. The butcher takes the €100 note and runs down the street to repay his debt to the pig farmer. The pig farmer takes the €100 note and heads off to pay his bill at the supplier of feed and fuel. The guy at the Farmers' Co-op takes the €100 note and runs to pay his drinks bill at the tavern. The tavern keeper rushes to the hotel and pays off his room bill to the hotel owner. The hotel proprietor then places the €100 note back on the counter so the rich traveler will not suspect anything.

At that moment the traveler comes down the stairs, picks up the €100 note, states that the rooms are not satisfactory, pockets the money, and leaves town.

The money supply has not changed; but the whole village is now out of debt and looking to the future with a lot more optimism.

Substitute the government in this anecdote for the rich German tourist. The money changed hands five times, and each of the recipients owes taxes on it. In the United States, average effective federal tax rates for 2011 were close to 20 percent.[700] If the villagers in this anecdote were taxed at 20 percent, each producer or servicer would owe €20 to the government at the end of the year. The government would get the entire €100 back, and the money supply would not have changed. The system would be sustainable, just as the financial system was in colonial Pennsylvania.

True, taxes are only paid on net profits after deducting costs, so the percentage returning to the government would be lower than 20 percent of gross income. On the other hand, the average velocity of M1—coins, dollar bills and checkbook money—as of early 2013 was about 6.5, not 5, meaning it changed hands 6.5 times in the course of a year.[701] And the 20 percent taxation rate overlooks hidden taxes—the taxes at every stage of production of a product. When these are included in the total tax bill, fully 42 percent of U.S. income has been estimated to go to taxes.[702] When all this is factored in, the government's total outlay could well come back to it year after year, keeping the money supply stable and "sound."

We've seen the possibilities illustrated by the G.I. Bill, which provided education and low-interest loans for returning servicemen after World War II. For every 1944 dollar invested, the country received approximately $7 in return, through increased economic productivity, consumer spending, and tax revenues.[703]

Stimulating Economic Activity Without Exhausting Scarce Resources

What of the added use of natural resources that would be generated by all of this new economic activity? Would it not just further exhaust already limited supplies?

Perhaps, if the uses of the money were left entirely to the whims of commercially-driven shoppers. But if those uses were channeled in a directed way, there are many investment possibilities that either would not use natural resources or that could actually make resource use more efficient. Education, research and development can result in more efficient use of what we have. With proper funding, a whole range of natural energy alternatives could be developed, along with more efficient methods of recycling waste, restoring exhausted soils, growing foods in limited space, and so on.

A broad range of human services can also be expanded without using additional resources: eldercare, natural therapies, neighborhood cleanup, art, music, and sports, to name a few. Many a budding artist, writer or inventor could develop his or her potential, aided by a bit of subsistence level funding to cover the bills.

As with the G.I. Bill, investment in this sort of human potential could generate multiple returns, not just economically but in terms of enriching the quality of life of the people. When people can maintain their health and are well educated, their productive output will increase, allowing them to return more in the way of taxes and fees, and to take less in the way of medical, unemployment and disability support. They can also contribute more to society if they do not have to take care of their elders. "Human capital" is a capital investment like any other, with real economic returns.

Chapter 36

TOWARD A NEW THEORY
OF MONEY AND CREDIT

*"You never change things by fighting the existing reality.
To change something, create a new model that makes the old
model obsolete."*

--*Buckminster Fuller*

Banks serve critical functions in modern economies. They create our
circulating money supply in the form of credits and debits, and they
manage the flow of its circulation. This bank credit is the grease that
allows the wheels of industry to turn. The systemic flaw in the scheme
is that banks are privately owned and controlled, with a mandate to
serve the limited interests of their shareholders; and these interests
and the public interest often conflict. What is good for Wall Street is
not necessarily good for the economy.

"Independent" central banks overseen by secretive global
regulators abroad have been given a mandate to maintain the value
of the currency and the stability of the banking system. These could
be considered worthy goals—we need a stable currency and a stable
banking system—but they have been construed to mean preserving the
international banking system itself at all costs, without regard to the
needs of the people, the environment, governments, or social stability.
The private banking edifice is a massive piece of machinery with
the principal purpose of preserving itself. What is being preserved
is an extractive form of banking that is proving unsustainable and

has reached its mathematical limits. A parasite that devours its food source will perish along with the food source.

To be sustainable, a banking system needs a broader mandate, one that includes the needs of the people and of the earth itself. The simplest, most direct way to transition from an unsustainable to a sustainable banking system is to transform it into a public utility, responsive to the will and needs of the people.

Banks that operate as public utilities can direct credit to where it best serves the interests of the whole economy. They do not need to worry about maintaining their market share, and they have no incentive or authorization to gamble with depositors' money in the derivatives casino. They are highly unlikely to go bankrupt or lose their customers' money, because they have the full faith and credit of the government and the people behind them.

This is not just conjecture. Public banks globally have been found to be safer, sounder, and more productive to the overall economy than private banks.

The Need for a Copernican Revolution in Economics

Now that we have seen where our current system came from and how illusory and dysfunctional it actually is, we are in a position to consider a banking system that is simpler, more equitable, and more sustainable. In order to move from austerity to abundance, we need to reprogram and reboot the system to eliminate the systemic flaws arising from an antiquated conception of money and credit. The world long ago went off the gold standard, yet we still think of money as a "thing," something that must be borrowed from someone else who already has it. Banks do not have enough of this thing to cover their loans and investments, so they must engage in a continual shell game in which they advance credit and scramble to cover it with short-term loans, exposing them to the systemic risk of sudden and unpredictable withdrawals by the lenders.

All of the money to which we the people have access is now created by banks in the form of bank credit, except for the physical cash that composes only a very small portion of the circulating money supply.

Banks create this credit-money as needed in response to demand. Increases in bank credit increase the amount of money circulating in the money supply competing for goods and services; and every time the bank creates this imaginary bank credit on its books, it is allowed to collect tribute in the form of interest.

Banks can create credit in deposit accounts "out of thin air," but when the borrower writes a check on the account that is deposited in another bank, the issuing bank must find some existing pool of money from which to cover the outgoing check. Money that belongs to someone else but is sitting idle in an account somewhere can serve as loan money even if the depositor is not aware of it, because the bank, not the depositor, is considered to own the money once it has been deposited in the bank. The depositor just has a promissory note and the right to get the money back when he needs it. The bank knows it can find the money to cover its newly-created bank credits because most people keep their money in some account within the system, and the bank has access to the deposits of other banks through the reserve system.

The system is obviously artificial, a form of sleight-of-hand designed to make the bank appear to be lending existing money when it isn't. How artificial was highlighted in a May 2013 article in *Forbes* by Tim Worstall, who wrote:

> [B]anks settle their books at the end of the day. They might have lent out more than they took in deposits: or the other way around. But at 4 pm, 4.30 pm or so every bank's books must balance. So, those with excess funds lend to those with too little just overnight. The money's paid back in the morning and then the whole rigmarole is done again the next afternoon. OK, maybe this all sounds a bit silly but if they didn't do this then the system just wouldn't work as it does. Without it if you wanted to take your money out of the bank you would have to wait until someone had put some in: by being able to borrow from other banks this can be avoided.[704]

It is not only silly but deceptive. Why not just skip the step in which funds are shifted around to make the bank's books appear to balance when they don't, and set up a public system, in which any creditworthy borrower can get bank credit without the bank having to pretend to draw the money from somewhere else? Credit is merely a monetization of the borrower's promise to repay, a turning of his IOU into money. The true role of the bank is not to lend either its own money or its depositors' money but simply to verify the creditworthiness of the borrower and guarantee his credit to third parties.

A grocer might accept the IOU or promise to pay of his neighbor in return for groceries, because he knows he can trust the neighbor and knows where to find him. But the grocer does not trust the IOU of a stranger who might skip town. In a community currency system, participants create their own money and their own credit, "monetizing" their own promises to repay; but participants in those systems, too, can skip town. They lack the enforcement tools of chartered banks backed by governments.

What is needed is to combine the advantages of a national currency with the community currency model, in which participants create their money themselves simply by monetizing their own IOUs. This could be done by using the national currency in a mutual credit clearing system, one overseen by a network of public banks. The banks would be empowered to create money as "bank credit," backed not by gold or bits of mortgages but just by "the full faith and credit of the United States." The function of the bank would be simply to determine the creditworthiness of the borrower and turn his credit into the fungible tokens known as money, acceptable everywhere in trade. As a government agency, the public bank would have access to courts to enforce the loans and to sheriffs to collect on any collateral posted by the borrowers.

Credit is unlimited, as Denison Miller, first governor of the Commonwealth Bank of Australia, astutely observed a century ago. Money today is simply an agreement between parties, and we are not limited in the number of contracts or agreements into which we can enter. If more people want to agree on trading more goods and services, then more money should come into existence, and vice versa.

Money is backed today not by gold but by the full faith and credit of the people themselves. We the people are taking the risk that the credit will not be good, so we the people should be getting whatever fee is attached to generating this bank credit.

We need to return to the system of publicly-issued, publicly-monitored money and credit initiated by our forefathers. We need a banking system that is transparent, accountable, and overseen by public servants. Banking needs to become boring again, run by civil employees just doing their jobs, with no bonuses, fees, commissions or inside trades riding on how they manipulate the markets or their customers.

We as a community can create our own credit system, without having to engage in the sort of impossible pyramid scheme in which we're always borrowing from Peter to pay Paul and paying tribute in the form of compound interest for the privilege. We can avoid the pitfalls of privately-issued money with a credit system that is guaranteed not by "things" shuffled around furtively in a shell game vulnerable to exposure but by the community itself.

Money today is simply credit; and credit must come first, before services can be rendered or the products can be made that will generate the profits to pay back the loans. When credit is advanced by a bank, when the bank is owned by the community, and when the profits return to the community, the result can be a functional and efficient system of finance. By returning the profits generated by the credit of the nation to the nation and its taxpayers, banking can be made solvent, equitable and sustainable, an engine for feeding the economy rather than feeding off it.

GLOSSARY

Austerity: a policy of deficit-cutting by lowering spending done by reducing the benefits and public services provided, sometimes coupled with increases in taxes to show long-term fiscal solvency to creditors.

Bank money: Banks create deposits, known as "bank money," when they issue loans. They do this by simply crediting the borrower's account with a new deposit. The total amount of bank money increases when a bank issues a loan. When a loan is paid off, that amount of bank money vanishes. [705]

Bankrupt: unable to pay one's debts, insolvent, having liabilities in excess of a reasonable market value of assets held.

Bear raid: the practice of targeting the stock of a particular company for take-down by massive short selling, either for quick profits or for corporate takeover

Base money: Fiat money held by the private sector is known as the monetary base or "base money." The Fed issues base money when it buys securities from the public (mainly Treasury debt.) It pays by simply creating a deposit for the seller's bank at the Federal Reserve Bank [706]

Bills of credit: promissory notes or bills issued exclusively on the credit of the state.

Bill of exchange: an order made by one person to another to pay money to a third person. A common type today is the *check.* A check is a bill of exchange drawn on a banker and payable on demand.

BIS: The Bank for International Settlements -- a private banking organization headquartered in Basel, Switzerland. It regulates most of the world's central banks, which control national currencies; it functions as a bank for the world's central banks; sets rules, such as capital adequacy (Basel I,II, and III), for the world's banks; and trades in bullion, currencies, etc., on its own account and in coordination with the IMF and other international financial organizations.

BRIC(S): an association of leading emerging economies. As of 2013, the group's five members are Brazil, Russia, India, China, and South Africa.

Bubble: inflation in prices that is grossly out of proportion to underlying values.

Business cycle: a predictable long-term pattern of alternating periods of economic growth (recovery) and decline (recession).

Capitalization: market value of a company's stock.

Capital requirements: standardized requirements in place for banks and other depository institutions, which determine how much capital must be held for a certain level of assets (loans) through regulatory agencies such as the Bank for International Settlements, Federal Deposit Insurance Corporation or Federal Reserve Board.

Cartel: a combination of producers of any product joined together to control its production, sale and price, so as to obtain a monopoly and restrict competition in that industry or commodity.

Central bank: a non-commercial bank, which may or may not be independent of government, having some or all of the following functions: conduct monetary policy, oversee the stability of the financial system, issue currency notes, act as banker to the government, supervise financial institutions and regulate payments systems.

Check clearing: The movement of a check from the depository institution at which it was deposited back to the institution on which it was written. The Federal Reserve operates a nationwide check-clearing system. According to *About.com,* "When banks clear checks, the money is taken from a checking account and sent to the check recipient's account. The receiving bank requests funds from the check writer's bank, and if all goes well the money is transferred."

City of London: a London financial district, one of the leading centers of global finance.

Collateral: a borrower's pledge to a lender of specific property to secure repayment of a loan.

Colonial scrip: a paper fiat money issued by the colonies in the pre-revolutionary era up to 1775. It was a quite different money from the Continental currency issued during the American Revolution to fund the war effort, which depreciated rapidly. Since colonial scrip was not backed by gold or silver, the colonies could control its purchasing power. It was a revolutionary concept in economics. The conventional European mercantilist system of money required governments to borrow from banks and pay interest for those loans, gold and silver being the only recognized forms of money. In this debt-based money system, banknotes were "bills of debt." Colonial scrip consisted of "bills of credit" created by the government based on its own credit, so there was no interest to pay for the introduction of money into the economy. The system significantly defrayed the expenses of the colonial governments and helped maintain their prosperity. [707]

Commodity money: money that gets its value from the commodity from which it is made. Commodity money consists of objects that have value in themselves as well as in their use as money.

Community currency: Unconventional, non-government currencies that are used by groups with a common bond, such as members of a locality or association. They operate independently of banks, with credits and debits generated by the members themselves as they trade with each other.

Compound interest: interest calculated not only on the initial principal but on the accumulated interest of prior payment periods.

Countercyclical: An economic or financial policy is called "countercyclical" if it works against the cyclical tendencies in the economy. That is, countercyclical policies are ones that cool down the economy when it is in an upswing, and stimulate the economy when it is in a downturn.

Currency: Money in any form when in actual use as a medium of exchange, facilitating the transfer of goods and services.

Debt deflation: monetary deflation (shrinkage of the money supply) and price deflation (falling prices) following the bursting of an asset bubble. When debt remains although asset values have fallen, as in the 2008 mortgage and banking crisis, people must borrow less and pay down debts rather than spend. This causes the money supply to shrink and a downward spiral of recession.

Default: the failure to pay back a loan.

Deficit spending: government spending in excess of what the government takes in as tax revenue.

Deficit hawks: people who place great emphasis on minimizing government deficits, in particular reducing deficits by cutting government spending rather than by raising taxes.

Deflation: A contraction in the supply of money or credit that results in declining prices; the opposite of inflation.

Demand deposits: bank deposits that can be withdrawn on demand at any time without notice. Most checking and savings accounts are demand deposits.

Derivatives: Derivatives are financial contracts – bets – made on changes in some underlying commodity price, asset price, rate, index or event. The thing bet on does not have to be owned. Derivatives are used to increase financial leverage—the ability to benefit from price changes with minimum investment. They are sometimes sold to function as insurance, as with credit default swaps. Although purported to be a means of decreasing financial risk, critics say they actually increase risk.[708]

Discount: The difference between the face amount of a note or mortgage and the price at which the instrument is sold on the market.

Double-entry bookkeeping: a set of rules for recording financial information in a financial accounting system in which every transaction or event changes at least two different nominal ledger accounts.

Economic liberalism: the ideological belief in organizing the economy on individualist lines, such that the greatest possible number of economic decisions are made by private individuals and not by collective institutions. Economic liberalism opposes economic planning as an alternative to the market mechanism, and also generally opposes mixed economies.

European Central Bank (ECB): the central bank for the European Union (EU) and its currency, the euro. The ECB administers the monetary policy of the 17 EU member states, which constitute the Eurozone, one of the largest currency areas in the world. The ECB is thus one of the world's most important central banks.

Eminent domain: the power to take private property for public use by a state or municipality following the payment of just compensation to the owner of the property. The property is taken either for government use or by delegation to third parties who will devote it to public or civic use or, in some cases, economic development.

Equity: ownership interest in a corporation.

Equity market (stock market): a public entity for the trading of company stock (shares, equities) and derivatives at an agreed price.

European Stability Mechanism (ESM): an international organization which provides financial assistance to members of the Eurozone in financial difficulty. The ESM was established in September 2012 to function as a permanent firewall for the Eurozone, with a maximum lending capacity of €500 billion. All new bailout applications and deals for any Eurozone member state with a financial stability issue would in principle thereafter be covered by ESM.

Fannie Mae and Freddie Mac (Federal National Mortgage Association and Federal Home Loan Mortgage Corporation): these were privately owned, government-backed GSEs (government–sponsored enterprises). At the height of the real estate bubble, they held approximately $5 trillion worth of mortgages, implicitly guaranteed by the government. In danger of imminent bankruptcy in 2008, they were taken over by the federal government and their losses were "socialized."

FDIC (Federal Deposit Insurance Corporation): a U.S government-owned corporation operating as an independent agency created by the Glass-Steagall Act of 1933. It provides deposit insurance guaranteeing the safety of deposits in member banks, up to $250,000 per depositor per bank as of January 2012. The FDIC receives no Congressional appropriations. It is funded by premiums that banks and thrift institutions pay for deposit insurance coverage and from earnings on investments in U.S. Treasury securities. Under the leadership of Sheila Bair it played a leading role in financial sector clean-up after 2008.

Federal Funds rate: the overnight interest rate that banks charge each other.

Federal Reserve ("Fed"): the central bank of the United States, consisting of 12 regional banks, owned and controlled primarily by large private banks. The Fed functions as the bank for commercial and investment banks, holding their reserve deposits and clearing their checks. It is charged with regulating the U.S. money supply, mainly by buying and selling U.S. securities and setting the discount interest rate (the interest rate at which the Federal Reserve lends money to commercial banks). It has a dual mandate of controlling inflation and maximizing employment. Theoretically under the control of Congress, it is in fact not answerable to any branch of government, according to its former chairman Alan Greenspan.

Fiat money: money that derives its value from government regulation or law; state-issued money which is not convertible by law to any other thing (versus commodity money). The term derives from the Latin *fiat* --"let it be done."

Fiscal: having to do with government finance. *Fiscal policy* is the use of government taxation and spending to influence the economy.

Fractional reserve banking: a form of banking where a bank maintains a fraction of the total amount in its customers' deposit accounts as reserves of cash or deposits at the central bank to satisfy demand from depositors. Funds deposited at a bank are mostly lent out, and the bank keeps a fraction (called the reserve ratio) of those funds as bank reserves. Some of the funds lent out are subsequently deposited with another bank, increasing the reserves and deposit liabilities of that second bank, and allowing further lending. With a required reserve ratio of 10 percent, the original deposit can theoretically be the basis for ten times its amount in subsequent loans by various banks. That is the theory, but in fact banks make loans without regard to their reserves, simply by advancing "bank credit" on their books. (See Chapter 2.)

Fraud: a false representation of a matter of fact, whether by words or by conduct, by false or misleading allegations, or by concealment of that which should have been disclosed, which deceives and is intended to deceive another so that he shall act upon it to his legal injury.

Free trade: trade between nations unrestricted by any government controls. Critics say that in more developed nations, free trade results in jobs being "exported" abroad, where labor costs are lower; while in less developed nations, workers and the environment are exploited by foreign financiers, who take labor and raw materials in exchange for paper money the national government could have created itself.

Globalization: integration of the world economy. Critics of globalization say we should not submit to the *unconditional* "free trade" mode of globalization, but rather pursue *strategic* integration, promoting our competitive self-interest as do nations like China.

Gold standard: a monetary system in which currency is convertible into fixed amounts of gold.

Greenbacks: fiat currency issued by the U.S government during and after the Civil War. The *greenback movement* was a campaign, largely by persons with agrarian interests, to maintain or increase the amount of paper money in circulation after the war. Between 1862 and 1865, the U.S. government had issued more than $450,000,000 in paper money not backed by gold (greenbacks) to help finance the Union cause in the American Civil War. After the war, fiscal conservatives demanded that the government retire the greenbacks, but farmers and others who wished to maintain high prices opposed that move.

Hedge funds: investment companies that use high-risk techniques, such as borrowing money and selling short, in an effort to make extraordinary capital gains for their investors.

Hyperinflation: a period of rapid inflation that leaves a country's currency virtually worthless.

IMF (International Monetary Fund): A large international banking organization connected with the U.N. According to its site: "The IMF promotes international monetary cooperation and provides policy advice and technical assistance to help countries build and maintain strong economies. The Fund also makes loans and helps countries design policy programs to solve balance of payments problems when sufficient financing on affordable terms cannot be obtained to meet net international payments. IMF loans are short and medium term and funded mainly by the pool of quota contributions that its members provide." Critics say it is a tool of the Western banking system that keeps countries in debt and colonized by Western corporations.

Inflation: a persistent increase in the level of consumer prices or a persistent decline in the purchasing power of money, caused by an increase in available currency and credit beyond the proportion of available goods and services. Monetarists claim that inflation is caused by excess government spending; others say that its primary cause is private financial activities – excess lending, leverage, low (or high) interest rates, Fed money creation, and monopolistic control of prices.

Investment banks: banks that focus on investing -- selling securities and derivatives, etc. Unlike commercial banks, they do not take deposits or make commercial loans; but the lines have blurred with the 1999 repeal of the Glass Steagall Act, which prohibited the same bank from taking deposits and underwriting securities. Leading investment banks include Merrill Lynch, Salomon Smith Barney, Morgan Stanley Dean Witter and Goldman Sachs.

Keiretsu: The keiretsu system is the framework of relationships in postwar Japan's big banks and big firms. Related companies organized around a big bank (like Mitsui, Mitsubishi, and Sumitomo) which own equity in each other and the bank, and do business with each other. Similar economic groupings play a prominent role in the economies of Korea and China.

LBO (Leveraged Buyout): an acquisition, usually of a company, where the purchase price is financed through a combination of equity and debt and in which the cash flows or assets of the target are used to secure and repay the debt. As the debt usually has a lower cost of capital than the equity, the returns on the equity increase with increasing debt. The debt thus effectively serves as a *lever* to increase returns which explain the origin of the term LBO. Critics say LBOs are used to strip companies of assets, downsizing their workforces, eliminating their R and D, cutting wages, and confiscating their retirement funds, and thus have been a destructive, self-cannibalizing force in the U.S. economy.

Laissez-faire (French: "allow to do"): a policy of minimum governmental interference in the economic affairs of individuals and society. Laissez-faire was a political as well as an economic doctrine. The pervading theory of the 19th century was that the individual, pursuing his own desired ends, would thereby achieve the best results for the society of which he was a part.

Land bank: Land banks are governmental or non-governmental nonprofit entities that focus on the conversion of vacant, abandoned properties into productive use.[709]

Leverage: a general term for any technique to multiply financial gains and losses. Common ways to attain leverage are borrowing money and using derivatives. The more a company borrows, the less equity capital it needs, so any profits or losses are shared among a smaller base and are proportionately larger as a result. Hedge funds often leverage their assets by using derivatives. Derivatives transactions allow investors to take a large price position in the market while committing only a small amount of capital; thus the use of their capital is leveraged.

Liability: an obligation of an entity arising from past transactions or events, the settlement of which may result in the transfer or use of assets, provision of services or other yielding of economic benefits in the future. Customer deposits are liabilities to banks, but the loans banks make are considered assets.

LIBOR **(London Interbank Offered Rate):** the average interest rate estimated by leading banks in London that they would be charged if borrowing from other banks. LIBOR is widely used as a reference rate for many financial instruments in both financial markets and commercial fields around the world. In 2012, around 45 percent of prime adjustable rate mortgages and more than 80 percent of subprime mortgages were indexed to LIBOR. American municipalities also borrowed around 75 percent of their money through financial products that were linked to LIBOR. In June 2012, multiple criminal settlements by Barclays Bank revealed significant fraud and collusion by member banks connected to the rate submissions, leading to the LIBOR scandal.

Liquidity: the ability of an asset to be converted into cash quickly and without discount.

Money supply: the total amount of monetary assets available in an economy at a specific time.

Mercantilism: the economic policy that government control of foreign trade is of paramount importance. In particular, mercantilism demands a positive balance of trade. It dominated Western European economic policy and discourse from the sixteenth to late-eighteenth centuries. Its theory was developed in Renaissance Italy, was taken up by the British to build their empire, and was "a remarkably sophisticated attempt . . . to advance national economic development by means that would be familiar and congenial to the technocrats of twenty-first-century Tokyo, Beijing, or Seoul." (Ian Fletcher, *Free Trade Doesn't Work*, 2010.)

MERS (Mortgage Electronic Registration System): an American privately held company that operates an electronic registry designed to track servicing rights and ownership of mortgage loans in the United States. The financial industry, eager to trade in mortgage-backed securities, needed to find a way around the recordation requirements and fees of counties and states, thus MERS was born to replace public recording of mortgage titles with a private system. By 2007, MERS registered some two-thirds of all the home loans in the United States.

Monetarism: A theory holding that economic variations within a given system, such as changing rates of inflation, are most often caused by increases or decreases in the money supply.

Monetize: to convert government debt from securities into currency that can be used to purchase goods and services.

Money market: the trade in short-term, low-risk securities, such as certificates of deposit and U.S. Treasury Notes.

Money supply: the entire quantity of bills, coins, loans, credit, and other liquid instruments in a country's economy. "Liquid" instruments are those easily convertible to cash. The money supply has traditionally been reported by the Federal Reserve in three categories – M1, M2, and M3—although it quit reporting M3 after March 2006. M1 is what we usually think of as money – coins, dollar bills, and the money in our checking accounts. M2 is M1 plus savings accounts, money market funds, and other individual or "small" time deposits. M3 is M1 and M2 plus institutional and other larger time deposits (including institutional money market funds) and eurodollars (American dollars circulating abroad).

Montes pietatis: According to *The Catholic Encyclopedia,* "*Montes Pietatis* are charitable institutions of credit that lend money at low rates of interest, or without interest at all, upon the security of objects left in pawn, with a view to protecting persons in want from usurers. Being charitable establishments, they lend only to people who are in need of funds to pass through some financial crisis, as in cases of general scarcity of food, misfortunes, etc. On the other hand, these institutions do not seek financial profit, but use all profits that may accrue to them for the payment of employees and to extend the scope of their charitable work." They were first established in medieval Italy and England and were precursors of public savings banks.

Moral hazard: the risk that the existence of a contract will change the behavior of the parties to it; for example, a firm insured for fire may take fewer fire precautions. In the case of banks, it is the hazard that they will expect to be bailed out from their profligate ways because they have been bailed out in the past.

Multiplier effect: In monetary macroeconomics and banking, the money multiplier measures how much the money supply increases in response to a change in the monetary base. The theory is that the Fed can control the money supply in a leveraged way through increasing or decreasing bank reserves, which form the basis a multiple of loans because of fractional reserve lending. Critics say it doesn't work that way—that banks make loans regardless of reserves and the Fed is forced to supply them after the fact.

Non-performing loan: a loan that is in default or close to being in default. A loan is nonperforming when payments of interest and principal are past due by 90 days or more.

Notional value: on a financial instrument, the nominal or face amount that is used to calculate payments made on that instrument.

Oligarchy: government by the few, usually the rich, for their own advantage.

Open market operations: the buying and selling of government securities in the open market in order to expand or contract the amount of money in the banking system.

Overdraft: an overdraft occurs when money is withdrawn from a bank account and the available balance goes below zero.

Plutocracy: a form of government in which the supreme power is lodged in the hands of the wealthy classes; government by the rich.

Ponzi scheme: a form of pyramid scheme in which investors are paid with the money of later investors. Charles Ponzi was an engaging Boston ex-convict who defrauded investors out of $6 million in the 1920s, in a scheme in which he promised them a 400 percent return on redeemed postal reply coupons. For a while, he paid earlier investors with the money of later investors; but eventually he just collected without repaying. The scheme earned him ten years in jail.

Populism: a political philosophy supporting the rights and power of the people in their struggle against the privileged elite.

Proprietary trading: a term used in investment banking to describe when a bank trades stocks, bonds, options, commodities, or other items with its own money as opposed to its customers' money, so as to make a profit for itself. Although investment banks are usually defined as businesses which assist other business in raising money in the capital markets (by selling stocks or bonds), in fact most of the largest investment banks make the majority of their profit from trading activities.

Quantitative easing: an unconventional monetary policy used by central banks to stimulate the national economy when conventional monetary policy has become ineffective. A central bank implements quantitative easing by buying financial assets (loans or securities) from commercial banks and other private institutions in order to inject a pre-determined *quantity* of money into the economy. This is distinguished from the more usual policy of buying or selling government bonds to keep market interest rates at a specified target value. Quantitative easing increases the excess reserves of the banks, and raises the prices of the financial assets bought, which lowers their yield (interest rate).

Real bills: a notice of payment due, typically sent by the wholesale merchant to the retail merchant along with his shipment of goods. The value of the real bill, unlike that of most securities, increases day-after-day till maturity, which is at most 91 days away. By that time the goods itemized on the bill will have been sold to the ultimate consumer and disbursement of the proceeds will be in progress. The face value of the bill is the amount to be paid upon maturity. The bill does not represent a loan transaction: the wholesaler *is not* lending and the retailer *is not* borrowing. The credit is an inseparable part of the transaction, as confirmed by centuries and centuries of merchant custom.[710]

Repurchase agreement ("repo"): The sale or purchase of securities with an agreement to reverse the transaction at an agreed future date and price. Repos allow the Federal Reserve to inject liquidity on one day and withdraw it on another with a single transaction.

Reserve currency: a currency that must be held in significant quantities by many governments and institutions as part of their foreign exchange reserves. It also tends to be the international pricing currency for products traded on a global market, and commodities such as oil, gold, etc. The U.S. dollar has been the world reserve currency in the post-World War II era, but its role is being weakened, notably by the BRIC countries that have made agreements to trade among themselves and with other countries without using the dollar, and by Iran.

Reserve requirement: the percentage of funds the Federal Reserve Board requires that member banks maintain on deposit at all times.

Reserves: banks' holdings of deposits in accounts with their central bank, plus currency that is physically held in the banks' vaults (vault cash).

Savings bank: a financial institution whose primary purpose is accepting savings deposits.

Self-liquidating loan: a type of credit that is repaid with money generated by the assets it is used to purchase. The repayment schedule and maturity of a self-liquidating loan are designed to coincide with the timing of the assets' income generation. These loans are intended to finance purchases that will quickly and reliably generate cash.

Securitization: the bundling of pools of mortgages or other assets and turning them into "securities"-- tradable documents evidencing an ownership interest in a portion of a debt, which can be sold off to investors.

Shadow banking system: bank-like activities, mainly lending, conducted through *non-regulated* entities, including hedge funds, money market funds, and securitization vehicles. These institutions fund themselves through short-term sources such as unsecured debt, asset-backed debt, commercial paper, repos, etc., and use this funding to provide leverage for various activities ranging from securities trading to corporate finance. The shadow banking system also refers to unregulated activities by regulated institutions. It has been common practice for investment banks to conduct many of their transactions in ways that don't show up on their conventional balance sheet accounting and so are not visible to regulators. To the extent that investment banks do this, they can be considered part of the shadow banking system. The mortgage securitization process that led to the U.S. real estate bubble was dependent on the shadow banking system. Critics say that it is fundamentally flawed, and if left unregulated it will lead to another economic collapse.

Short sale: borrowing a security and selling it in the hope of being able to repurchase it more cheaply before repaying the lender. A *naked short sale* is a short sale in which the seller does not buy shares to replace those he borrowed.

Social credit: an economic philosophy developed by C.H. Douglas (1879–1952), a British engineer. Douglas observed that consumers collectively did not have enough income to buy back what they had made. He proposed to eliminate this gap between total prices and total incomes by augmenting consumers' purchasing power through a National Dividend. Each citizen would have a beneficial, not direct, inheritance in the communal capital. Douglas said that Social Crediters want to build a new civilization based upon absolute economic security for the individual.

SOE (state-owned enterprise): a business that is owned by the government and operated for profit.

Sparkasse: Savings banks in German-speaking countries are called *Sparkasse* (pl: *Sparkassen*). They work as commercial banks in a decentralized structure. Each savings bank is independent, locally managed, and concentrates its business activities on customers in the region in which it is situated. In general, savings banks are not profit-oriented. Shareholders of the savings banks are usually single cities or numerous cities in an administrative district.

Specie: coin; coined money; precious metal (usually gold or silver) used to back money.

State-guided capitalism: commercial (profit-seeking) economic activity undertaken by the state, with management of production in a capitalist manner, even if the state is nominally socialist. State capitalism is usually characterized by the dominance of state-owned business enterprises..

Structural adjustment: a term used by the International Monetary Fund for the changes it recommends for developing countries that want new loans, including privatization, deregulation, and the reduction of barriers to trade; a package of "free market" reforms ostensibly designed to create economic growth to generate income to pay off accumulated debt.

Tally stick: In medieval England, a hardwood "tally stick" was used as evidence of a financial transaction.. When a financial transaction took place, the stick would be notched. These obligations could be sold and traded, their validity being demonstrated with the matching halves of the sticks. The system was fraud-proof, since only two pieces of wood in England matched each other, and neither party could add a notch without the alteration being obvious. Tally sticks could function as money. The system continued in England until the early 1800s.

TBTF (too big to fail): a colloquial term used to describe certain financial institutions that are so large and so interconnected that their failure is widely held to be disastrous to the economy, requiring that they be supported by government when they face difficulty.

Time deposits: deposits that the depositor knows are being lent out and that he can't have back for a certain period of time.

Transaction deposit: a term used by the Federal Reserve for checkable deposits (deposits on which checks can be drawn) and other accounts that can be used directly as cash without withdrawal limits or restrictions. They are also called *demand deposits*, since they can be withdrawn on demand at any time without notice. Most checking and savings accounts are demand deposits.

Usury: the practice of lending money and charging the borrower interest, especially at an exorbitant or illegally high rate.

Vulture capitalist: an investor who uses the clauses of an investment deal in a company to seize ownership of the company or valuable parts of it outright. Unlike a venture capitalist who invests in a company likely to succeed in the marketplace and hence show a profit to the investor, a vulture capitalist looks to invest in a firm likely to fail to show a profit in the near term, triggering the takeover clauses that would result in forfeiture of some or all the assets of the company. The intent is to sell off the constituent parts and thus show a profit, while destroying or hobbling the company.

WTO (World Trade Organization): a world-wide supra-national trade-regulating organization that promotes *liberalization* (neo-liberal policies such as privatization). The stated aims of the WTO are to promote free trade and stimulate economic growth, but critics say it widens the social gap between rich and poor that it claims to be fixing; steadfastly ignores the issues of labor and environment; and is a tool of Western financial powers.

NOTES

INTRODUCTION

1. Woodrow Wilson, *Monopoly or Opportunity?* (1913), Vlib.us/Amdocs.
2. See Chapter 1.

CHAPTER 1

3. Thomas Hoenig, "A Turning Point: Defining the Financial Structure," FDIC, 17 April 2013, fdic.gov.
4. Dhani, "Deregulation--1987-1988: The rise of Alan Greenspan," The Barbers Chair, 13 Aug. 2012, dhani-thebarberschair.blogspot.com.
5. Evan Harris, "Clinton: I Was Wrong to Listen to Wrong Advice Against Regulating Derivatives," ABC News, 17 Apr. 2010.
6. Robert Teitelman, "The Case Against Favored Treatment Of Derivatives," The Deal Econom, 10 May 2011, thedeal.com.
7. "US Deposits In Perspective: $25 Billion in Insurance, $9,283 Billion in Deposits; $297,514 Billion in Derivatives," Zero Hedge, 19 Mar. 2013, zerohedge.com.
8. Margrit Kennedy, *Occupy Money: Creating an Economy Where Everybody Wins* (New Society Publishers, 2012).
9. "The 5 Percent Solution: How 5 Percent of the Workforce Generated 40 Percent of U.S. Business Profits and All of It Was a Ponzi Scheme," Finance My Money, 4 Jan. 2010, Financemymoney.com.
10. James Henry, "The Price of Offshore Revisited: Press Release," Tax Justice, 19 July 2012, Taxjustice.net; Nicholas Shaxson, *Treasure Islands: Uncovering the Damage of Offshore Banking and Tax Havens* (Palgrave Macmillan, 2012).
11. Kennedy, op. cit.
12. Table 7.11. "Interest Paid and Received by Sector and Legal Form of Organization," Bureau of Economic Analysis, 2 Aug. 2012, BEA.gov.
13. Mar Gudmundsson, "How Might the Current Financial Crisis Shape Financial Sector Regulation and Structure?" Bank For International Settlements, 23 Sept. 2008, bis.org.
14. Lane Kenworthy, "The Best Inequality Graph, Updated," Consider the Evidence, 20 July 2010, Lanekenworthy.net.
15. "About Interest Rates," Home Loan Learning Center, Mortgage Bankers Association, 21 Dec. 2012, homeloanlearningcenter.com.
16. Parija Kavilanz, "Small Businesses Not Crazy about Visa-MasterCard Deal," CNNMoney, 17 July 2012, money.cnn.com.
17. "Main Street Wins One In Congress," Meredith Advocacy Group, 13 June 2012, Meredithadvocacygroup.com.
18. "The Price of Offshore Revisited: Press Release," Tax Justice Network, 19 July 2012.
19. Alvin Rabushka, "Representation Without Taxation: The Colonial Roots of American Taxation, 1700-1754," Policy Review (Hoover Institution, Stanford University, Dec. 2003 and Jan. 2004); "The Colonial Roots of American Taxation, 1607-1700," ibid., Aug/Sept. 2002.
20. "BRICS: Working Together to Shape the Future," China Daily, 14 Apr. 2011, chinadaily.com.cn.

CHAPTER 2

21. Satyajit Das, *Extreme Money* (FT Press 2011), p. 238.
22. "Was Financial Terrorism Involved in the 2008 Crash?" Unified Patriots, 1 Mar. 2011, UnifiedPatriots.com.
23. Peter Dale Scott, "War, Martial Law, and the Economic Crisis," Global Research, 23 Feb. 2011, globalresearch.ca.

24. David M. Herszenhorn, Carl Hulse And Sheryl Gay Stolberg, "Day of Chaos Grips Washington; Fate of Bailout Plan Unresolved," The New York Times, 26 Sept. 2008, nytimes.com.

25. Tyler Durden, "How The World Almost Came To An End At 2PM On September 18," Zero Hedge, 8 Feb. 2009, zerohedge.blogspot.com.

26. Peter Rose, Sylvia Hudgins, *Bank Management & Financial Services* (New York: McGraw-Hill, 8th edition 2010), pages 419-29.

27. Ibid., page 357.

28. Ellen Brown, "Economic 9-11: Did Lehman Brothers Fall or Was It Pushed?", 7 Sept. 2009, webofdebt.com.

29. Elizabeth Shell, "How Bad Is the Current Stock Crash?" PBS News Hour, 11 Aug. 2011.

30. Michael Hudson, *The Bubble and Beyond* (Islet 2012), page 41.

31. Karen Aho, "If Your Landlord Is Facing Foreclosure, Stay Put," MSN Real Estate, Jan. 2012, Realestate.msn.com.

32. Reynolds Holding, "Breaking views: Guide for the Perplexed: Libor Litigation," Thomson Reuters News & Insight, 12 July 2012.

33. Matt Taibbi, "The Scam Wall Street Learned From the Mafia," Rolling Stone, 21 June 2012, Rollingstone.com.

34. Wayne Jett, "Big Banks Rig LIBOR," Classical Capital, 11 July 2012, Classicalcapital.com.

35. Jane Brunner, "Goldman Sachs Got Break, but Not Cities," SFGate, 16 July 2012, Sfgate.com.

36. "States, Localities Line Up Against LIBOR Criminality," LaRouche PAC, 17 July 2012, Larouchepac.com.

37. Tara Steele, "Louisiana Sues 17 Banks under RICO Laws for MERS Scheme," AGBeat, 19 Apr. 2012, Agbeat.com.

38. Ezra Klein, "Explaining FinReg: Shadow Bank Runs, or the Problem Behind the Problem," Washington Post, 26 Apr. 2010.

39. Gary Gorton, "Questions and Answers about the Financial Crisis," 20 Feb. 2010, Online.wsj.com.

40. Quoted in James Wesley, "Derivatives – The Mystery Man Who'll Break the Global Bank at Monte Carlo," SurvivalBlog.com, Sept. 2006.

41. "Shadow Banking System," Wikipedia.

42. "How Did the Banks Get Away With Pledging Mortgages to Multiple Buyers?" Washington's Blog, 26 Oct. 2010, washingtonsblog.com.

43. "Lawsuit Alleges That MERS Owes California a Potential $60-120 Billion in Unpaid Land-Recording Fees," Washingtons Blog, 24 Oct. 2010, Washintonsblog.com.

44. "Professors Black and Wray Confirm that Bear Pledged the Same Mortgage to Multiple Buyers," Washingtons Blog, 25 Oct. 2010, Washintonsblog.com.

45. Michael Rivero, "Bankers Gone Wild - How the U.S. Government Helped Wall Street Gang-rape America's Middle Class," What Really Happened, 28 Mar. 2012, whatreallyhappened.com.

46. Ellen Brown, "Time to Break Up the Too-Big-to-Fail Banks?" The Huffington Post, 15 Oct. 2010, TheHuffingtonPost.com.

47. Ann Pettifor, "The Broken Global Banking System," The Huffington Post, 3 Oct. 2010, TheHuffingtonPost.com.

48. Michael Hudson, "Banks Weren't Meant to Be Like This," Information Clearing House, 27 Jan. 2012, informationclearinghouse.info.

49. Yves Smith, "Why Do We Keep Indulging the Fiction That Banks Are Private Enterprises?" Naked Capitalism, 15 Sept. 2010, nakedcapitalism.com.

CHAPTER 3

50. S. Andrianova, et al., "There Should Be No Rush to Privatize Government-owned Banks," *VOX*, 20 Jan. 2010, VOXEU.org.

51. A. Micco, U. Panizza, "Public Banks in Latin America," Conference on Public Banks in Latin America: Myth and

Reality, Inter-American Development Bank, 25 Feb 2005.

52. "Financial Crisis Alters Russian Banks," *Forbes*, 16 Mar. 2010, Forbes.com; "Bank Regulation and Supervision," Research at the World Bank, The World Bank, June 2008, Econ.WorldBank.org.

53. "BRICS: Working Together to Shape the Future," China Daily, 14 Apr. 2011, chinadaily.com.cn.

54. Masaaki Kuboniwa, "Impact of Trading Gains on Economic Growth in BRICs for 1995-2010: Some Lessons from BRICs," Institute of Economic Research, May 2011, ier.hit-u.ac.jp.

55. Liam Halligan, "The BRIC Countries' Hainan Summit Could Make the G20 Redundant," The Telegraph, 16 Apr. 2011, telegraph.co.uk.

56. "Banking in BRIC Countries," Markets in Motion, 9 Aug. 2010, ftkmc.com.

57. Leahy, Joe, "Brazil's BNDES and Caixa Hit by Downgrades," Financial Times, 21 March 2013.

58. "World's 20 Safest Banks," Rediff, 4 May 2012, rediff.com.

59. *Jim O'Neill, "Building Better Global Economic BRICs,"* 30 Nov. 2001, Global Economics, Paper Number 66, Goldmansachs.com.

60. Ibid.

61. "Mutually assured existence: Public and Private Banks Have Reached a Modus Vivendi," The Economist, May 13, 2010.

62. Kurt Von Mettenheim, "Observations on Banking in BRIC Countries," Academia, 27 Nov. 2010, fgv.academia.edu.

63. Kurt Von Mettenheim and Oliver Butzbach, "Alternative Banking and Social Inclusion," IMTFI Blog: Institute for Money, Technology & Financial Inclusion, 5 Dec. 2011, blog.imtfi.uci.edu.

64. James A. Hanson, "The Role of State-Owned Financial Institutions: Policy and Practice," Worldbank, 26 Apr. 2004, info.worldbank.org.

65. Susanna Mitchell, "China Today--Restructuring the Iron Rice Bowl,"

JubileeResearch.org, 9 July 2003; He Qinglian, "China Continues to Borrow Despite Heavy Debt," Epoch Times, November 8, 2005.

66. Von Mettenheim, "Alternative Banking," op. cit.

67. Kurt Von Mettenheim and Maria Antonieta Del Tedesco Lins, *Government Banking: New Perspectives on Sustainable Development and Social Inclusion from Europe and South America* (Konrad Adenauer Foundation, 2008), page 196.

68. Panicos Demetriades, Svetlana Andrianova, Anja Shortland, "There Should Be No Rush to Privatise Government Owned Banks," 20 Jan. 2010, VOX, Voxeu.org.

69. Svetlana Andrianova, Panicos Demetriades, and Anja Shortland, "Is Government Ownership of Banks Really Harmful to Growth?" Brunel University, May 2009, brunel.ac.uk.

70. Scott Firsing, "BRICS Rise Much Faster than Predicted," Foreign Policy Association, 24 Nov. 2011, foreignpolicyblogs.com.

71. "India GDP Growth Rate," Trading Economics, 2011, TradingEconomics.com.

72. "Russia - Population - Historical Data Graphs per Year," Index Mundi, 1 Jan. 2011, indexmundi.com; "Low Inflation, GDP Growth Russia's Major 2011 Achievements – Medvedev," RIA Novosti, 27 Dec. 2011, en.rian.ru; Stefan Wagstyl, "Jim O'Neill: Russia Could Suprise Us All," Financial Times, 28 Nov. 2011, blogs.ft.com; "Jim O'Neill Gives An Ardent Defense Of The Most Controversial BRIC," Business Insider, 4 Apr. 2013.

73. Sean Williams, "Why Is Brazil an Emerging Market Economy?" The University of Iowa Center for International Finance and Development, Apr. 2011, ebook.law.uiowa.edu.

74. "New Cradles to Graves," The Economist, 8 Sept. 2012.

75. Anwar Nasution, "Indonesia's Banking System Still Needs Reform," Economic Policy, Indonesia, Regulation, eastasiaforum.org, 29 May 2013.

CHAPTER 4

76. "Lula Da Silva Proud to Lend Money to the IMF," Merco Press, 4 Apr. 2009, mercopress.com.

77. Vladimir Radyuhin, "For a New Order," Frontline: India's National Magazine, 7 Jan. 2008, hindu.com.

78. "BRICS," Wikipedia.

79. Halligan, op. cit.

80. Andrei Vernikov,"Russian banking: The state makes a comeback?" BOFIT Discussion Papers, Bank of Finland, Institute for Economies in Transition, 2009, ideas.repec.org.

81. Oxford Analytica, "Financial Crisis Alters Russian Banks," Forbes, 16 Mar. 2010, forbes.com.

82. Jason Corcoran, "Foreign Banks Are Fleeing Russia," Bloomberg Businessweek, 3 Mar. 2011, businessweek.com.

83. "In the Shadow of Giants," The Economist, 17 Feb. 2011, economist.com.

84. Philip Alexander and Guillaume Hingel, "Russian State Bank Dominance on the Cusp of Change," The Banker, 18 Jan. 2012, thebanker.com.

85. Corcoran, op. cit.

86. In the Shadow of Giants," op. cit.

87. Jason Bush, "Russia: The Bank That Roars," Bloomberg Businessweek, 28 Mar. 2005, businessweek.com.

88. "In the Shadow of Giants," op. cit.

89. "Russia's State Banks Seen Too Upbeat on 2012 Growth," Reuters, 19 Dec. 2011, reuters.com.

90. "BRIC-B," The Great Chessboard, 10 Dec. 2011, thegreatchessboard.wordpress.com.

91. "Brazil's President Lula: 'Father of the Poor' Has Triggered Economic Miracle," Spiegel Online, 23 Mar. 2013.

92. "Luiz Inácio Lula Da Silva," Wikipedia, 4 May 2012.

93. Von Mettenheim and Del Tedesco Lins, Government Banking, op. cit., page 161.

94. Gabriel Elizondo, "Brazil's Powerhouse Bank," Al Jazeera, 1 Dec. 2009, aljazeera.com.

95. Jayati Ghosh, "Development Banks Still Have a Role to Play, as Brazil's Success Shows," The Guardian, 28 Apr. 2013.

96. Ibid.

97. "Management Report – BNDES System," BNDES, 31 Dec. 2011, bndes.gov.br/SiteBNDES/export/sites/default/bndes_en/Galerias/Download/management_report1211.pdf.

CHAPTER 5

98. "Poverty in India," Wikipedia, 3 Jun. 2012.

99. "Bengal famine of 1943," Wikipedia, 5 Jun. 2012.

100. Jayati Ghosh, "Bank Nationalisation: The Record," People's Democracy, 05 June 201, pd.cpim.org.

101. Inder Malhotra, "Run over the Banks," The Indian Express, 10 July 2009, indianexpress.com.

102. Banjeree, ibid.

103. Ghosh, op. cit.

104. Pradip Biswas, "40 Years of Bank Nationalisation," India Current Affairs, 29 Oct. 2009, indiacurrentaffairs.org.

105. T.T. Ram Mohan, "Indira Gandhi the Reformer," The Economic Times, 21 Jan. 2010, articles.economictimes.indiatimes.com.

106. "Nationalised Banks in India," I Love India, 05 June 2012, iloveindia.com.

107. Gerard Caprio, Jonathan Fiechter, Michael Pomerleano, and Robert E. Litan, "The Future of State-Owned Financial Institutions," Brookings, Sept. 2004, brookings.edu.

108. Banjeree, op. cit.

109. Mohan, op. cit.

110. Biswas, op. cit.

111. Ghosh, op. cit.

112. Nirmal Chandra, "Is Inclusive Growth Feasible in Neoliberal India?" Networkideas, Sept. 2008, networkideas. org.

113. Ibid.

114. Swaminathan S. Anklesaria, "India Weathers 12 Months of Financial Crisis," Swaminomics, 13 Sept. 2009, swaminomics.org.

115. C. P. Chandrasekhar, "The Importance of Public Banking," Frontline, 25.25, 19 June 2008, hindu.com.

116. Ibid.

117. "India Survived Slowdown Because of Nationalization," Pak Tea House, 28 June 2009, pakteahouse.net.

118. Mohan, op. cit.

119. Jayati Ghosh, "One-Way Street," Frontline 14.26, 27 Dec. 1997, frontline. in; "The Foreign Threat in Banking," Frontline 19.05, 02 Mar. 2002, frontline.in.

120. G. Srinivasan, "Negative Signal," Frontline 29:02, 28 Jan. 2012, frontline.in.

121. Ibid.

122. Arvind Subramanian, "Why Is Inflation in India so Stubbornly High," Rediff Business, 28 July 2010, business.rediff. com.

123. Abhijit Neogy and Tony Munroe, "India Inflation Mounts, May Cause Another Rate Increase," The China Post, 15 Sept. 2011, chinapost.com.tw.

CHAPTER 6

124. Brian Wang, "China and the World's Emerging Middle Class," Next Big Future, 15 Aug. 2008, nextbigfuture.com.

125. Eamonn Fingleton, In the Jaws of the Dragon (St. Martins 2008), page 98.

126. Ibid, page 145.

127. Ibid, page 151.

128. "Institutional Arrangement," The People's Bank of China, 21 June 2012, pbc.gov.cn.

129. "How the China Development Bank is Rewriting the Rules of Finance: Debt, Oil and Influence," Brookings, John L. Thornton China Center, 18 April 2013, Brookings.edu.

130. Andrew Szamosszegi and Cole Kyle, "An Analysis of State-owned Enterprises and State Capitalism in China," U.S.-China Economic and Security Review Commission, 26 Oct. 2011, uscc.gov.

131. Sophie Beach, "Just How Powerful Are China's State-Owned Firms?" China Digital Times, 26 Oct. 2011, chinadigitaltimes.net.

132. James Galbraith, The Predator State (Free Press 2008), pages 112, 154.

133. Rachel Armstrong et al., "Factbox - Ownership Restrictions on Banks in Asia," Reuters, 2 Aug. 2011, in.reuters. com; John Manley, "China Defends Foreign Bank Ownership Limit at WTO," Reuters, 02 Nov. 2009 blogs.reuters.com.

134. Szamosszegi, op. cit.

135. Ibid.

136. Stanley Lubman, "China's State Capitalism: The Real World Implications," Berkeley Law - Op-Eds, 1 Mar. 2013, law.berkeley.edu.

137. Harry Broadman, "The Chinese State as Corporate Shareholder," International Monetary Fund, Sept. 1999, Imf.org.

138. "State Capitalism in China: Of Emperors and Kings," The Economist, 12 Nov. 2011, Economist.com.

139. Szamosszegi op. cit.

140. "China's Postal Savings Bank to Play Key Role in Spreading Rural Wealth," China Briefing, 26 Feb. 2009, china-briefing. com.

141. Loretta Chao and Jason Leow, "Buying Into China's Land Rush," The Wall Street Journal, 18 Jan. 2008, Online.wsj.com.

142. Adam Hersh, "Chinese State-Owned and State-Controlled Enterprises," Center for American Progress Action Fund, 15 Feb. 2012, americanprogressaction.org.

143. "5 Reasons China Will Crash in 2011," The Street, 24 Dec. 2010, thestreet.com.

144. Samah El-Shahat, "China Puts People before Banks," Al Jazeera, 14 Aug. 2009, aljazeera.com.

145. "How Bad Is China's Debt Crisis?", China Worker, 12 April 2013, chinaworker.info.

146. Ibid.

147. Ibid.

148. "China Moves to Temper Growth," WSJ, 4 Mar. 2013, online.wsj.com.

149. "China to Raise Budget Deficit by 50 Percent to Boost Demand," Business Week, Bloomberg News, 4 Mar. 2013, businessweek.com.

CHAPTER 7

150. Michael Hudson, "Debts and Indebtedness in the Neo-Babylonian Period: Evidence from the Institutional Archives," *Debt and Economic Renewal In The Ancient Near East*, vol. 3 (Columbia University 1998), academia.edu.

151. Ibid.

152. "Writing System," Wikipedia.

153. "History of Sumer," Wikipedia.

154. "Sumerian Background and History," Crystalinks.com, citing Wikipedia, "History of Sumer," and C. Freeman, *Egypt, Greece, and Rome* (Oxford, England: Oxford University Press, 1996).

155. "History of Sumer," op. cit.

156. "Gilgamesh Flood Myth"; "Noah's Ark," Wikipedia.

157. Bernard Lietaer, *The Mystery of Money* (2000, 2003), pages 33-44, novigroshi.org.

158. Ibid., citing Gerda Lerner in *The Origins of Patriachy* (1986).

159. Michael Hudson, "The Creditary/Monetarist Debate in Historical Perspective," published as "The Cartalist/Monetarist Debate in Historical Perspective" in *The State, The Market and The Euro* (London: Edward Elgar, 2003); Michael Hudson, "Reconstructing the Origins of Interest-bearing Debt," in *Debt and Economic Renewal in the Ancient Near East* (CDL Press, 2002).

160. Hudson, "Debts and Indebtedness in the Neo-Babylonian Period," op. cit.

161. Michael Hudson, "How Interest Rates Were Set, 2500 BC – 1000 AD," michael-hudson.com, 24 Mar. 2000.

162. Hudson, "Debts and Indebtedness in the Neo-Babylonian Period," op. cit.

163. "Cuneiform," Ancient Scripts, 30 Mar. 2012, AncientScripts.com.

164. "Ancient Mesopotamian Units of Measurement," Wikipedia.

165. Lietaer, op. cit.

166. Ibid.

167. "The Origins of Coinage," British Museum, 20 Apr. 2012, britishmuseum.org.

168. "Define Shekel," shekel.askdefine.com.

169. "History of Banking," Wikipedia.

170. "Hammurabi's Code," Script Bay, Mar. 2009, Ramanraj.blogspot.com.

171. *The Britannica Guide to Numbers and Measurement* (The Rosen Publishing Group, 2010), page 205, books.google.com; Elizabeth Stone, et al., *Adoption in Old Babylonian Nippur and the Archive of Mannum-mešu-lissur, vol. 3, Mesopotamian Civilizations* (Eisenbrauns, 1991), page 8, books.google.com.

172. K.V. Nagarajan, "The Code of Hammurabi: An Economic Interpretation," International Journal of Business and Social Science (May 2011), ijbssnet.com.

173. Hudson, "Debts and Indebtedness in the Neo-Babylonian Period", op. cit.

174. Ibid.

175. Hudson, "How Interest Rates Were Set," op. cit.

176. Richard Hoskins, *War Cycles, Peace Cycles* (Lynchburg, Virginia: Virginia Publishing Company, 1985), page 2.

177. Michael Hudson, "The Lost Tradition of Biblical Debt Cancellations," michael-hudson.com.

178. J. Dunn, "Prices, Wages and Payments in Ancient Egypt," TourEgypt.net.

179. "The Ancient Egyptian Economy," The Saylor Foundation, saylor.org.

180. Bernard Lietaer, "Community Currencies: A New Tool for the 21st Century," transaction.net.

181. "History of Banking," Wikipedia.

182. Richard Werner, *Princes of the Yen* (New YorkCity: East Gate Book, 2003), pages 40-42.

CHAPTER 8

183. Peter Spufford, *The Power and Profit* (New York City: Thames & Hudson, 2002), page 39.

184. Ibid., page 40.

185. Ibid., page 34.

186. Charles Dunbar, ,"The Bank of Venice," Quarterly Journal of Economics, vol. VI (Harvard University Publishers, 1892), page 314.

187. Spufford, op. cit., pages 44-45.

188. Dunbar, op. cit., page 330; Spufford, op. cit.

189. Emmanuel Beeri, "Monti Di Pieta," Jewish Virtual Library, 2008, jewishvirtuallibrary.org.

190. See Deuteronomy (New World Translation), 15:6 -- "[Y]ou will certainly lend on pledge to many nations, whereas you yourself will not borrow; and you must dominate over many nations, whereas over you they will not dominate." 23:19 -- "You must not make your brother pay interest . . . ." 23:20 -- "You may make a foreigner pay interest, but your brother you must not make pay interest."

191. Umberto Benigni, "Montes Pietatis," *The Catholic Encyclopedia. Vol. 10* (New York: Robert Appleton Company, 1911), 3 Aug. 2012, newadvent.org.

192. Spufford, op. cit., page 42.

193. Charles Dunbar,"The Bank of Venice," Quarterly Journal of Economics, vol. VI (Harvard University Publishers, 1892).

194. Ibid., pages 310-335.

CHAPTER 9

195. Nicholas Apostolou and D. Larry Crumbley, "The Tally Stick: The First Internal Control?" ACFEI News, Spring 2008, bus.lsu.edu.

196. Chris Cook, "The Myth of Debt," Herald Scotland, 10 Mar. 2013.

197. Apostolou and Crumbley, op. cit.

198. M. T. Clanchy, *From Memory to Written Record, England 1066-1307* (Cambridge, Mass., 1979), page 96; see also Page 95, n. 28, pl. VIII.

199. Dave Birch, "Tallies & Technologies," Journal of Internet Banking and Commerce, arraydev.com; "Tally Sticks," yamaguchy.netfirms.com.; Carmack & Still, op. cit.; "Tally Sticks," National Archives, 7 November 2005, nationalarchives.gov.uk.

200. Richard Hoskins, *War Cycles, Peace Cycles* (Lynchburg, Virginia: Virginia Publishing Company, 1985), page 39.

201. Peter Spufford, *Money and Its Use in Medieval Europe* (Cambridge University Press, 1988, 1993), pages 83-93.

202. Hoskins, op. cit., pages 37-45, 59-61.

203. James Walsh, *The Thirteenth: Greatest of Centuries* (New York: Catholic Summer School Press, 1907), Chapter 1.

204. "Poverty and Pauperism," Catholic Encyclopedia, online edition, 2003, newadvent.org.

205. Hoskins, op. cit., pages 37-45, 59-61.

206. Patrick Carmack, "The Money Changers, Part III," Dollar Daze, 18 Oct. 2007, http://dollardaze.org/blog.

207. Stephen Zarlenga, *The Lost Science of Money* (Valatie, New York: American Monetary Institute, 2002), pages 266-69.

208. Patrick Carmack, Bill Still, "The Money Masters: How International Bankers Gained Control of America" (video, 1998), text at mailstar.net/money-masters.html.

209. Ibid.

210. J. Lawrence Broz, Richard Grossman, "Paying for Privilege: The Political Economy of Bank of England Charters, 1694-1844," econ.barnard. columbia.edu (Weatherhead Center for International Affairs, Harvard University), January 2002, page 11.

211. Zarlenga, op. cit., page 228.

212. "Sveriges Riksbank," Wikipedia.

213. Carroll Quigley, *Tragedy and Hope* (Macmillan, 1966), page 49.

214. "The Bank of England," British History Online, british-history.ac.uk.

215. Broz, et al., op. cit.

216. "Tally Sticks," op. cit.; R. Hoskins, op. cit.

CHAPTER 10

217. Sir Adrian Cadbury, "A Talk in the Faith Seeking Understanding Series," May 2003, Leveson.org.uk.

218. Cadbury, ibid.

219. "Pennsylvania" in H. W. Elson, *History of the United States of America* (New York: MacMillan, 1904).

220. Elson, ibid.

221. lson, ibid.

222. Jason Goodwin, *Greenback* (Westminster: Penguin Books, 2003), page 43.

223. Ibid.

224. H.A. Scott Trask, "Did the Framers Favor Hard Money?" 2002, lcwatch.com/special69.shtml.

225. Benjamin Franklin, "A Modest Enquiry into the Nature and Necessity of a Paper Currency," *Encyclopædia Britannica*, britannica.com.

226. Benjamin Franklin, "The Writings of Benjamin Franklin: Philadelphia, 1726-1757," The History Carper, historycarper.com.

227. Edward Burke to the House of Commons, April 14, 1774, quoted in Retford Currency Society, *Currency, Agriculture and Free Trade* (London: Simpkin, Marshall and Co., 1849).

228. Goodwin, op. cit.

229. Alvin Rabushka, "Representation Without Taxation: The Colonial Roots of American Taxation, 1700-1754," Policy Review (Hoover Institution, Stanford University, December 2003 and January 2004); "The Colonial Roots of American Taxation, 1607-1700," ibid, Aug/Sept 2002.

230. Ibid.

231. "Colonial Scrip," Friends of the American Revolution, 20 Jan. 2013, 21stcenturycicero.wordpress.com.

232. "The Currency Act," Timelines, 30 Mar. 2012, Timelines.com.

233. "The Currency Act," UShistory.org, 30 Mar. 2012; "The Stamp Act Controversy," ibid.

234. Alexander Del Mar, *History of Monetary Systems* (1895), quoted in Stephen Zarlenga, *The Lost Science of Money* (Valatie, New York: American Monetary Institute, 2002), page 378.

235. William Smyth, Jared Sparks, *Lectures on Modern History: From The Irruption Of The Northern Nations To The Close Of The American Revolution* (B.B. Mussey and Co., 1849), page 639, books.google.com.

236. J.W. Schuckers, *Finances and Paper Money of the Revolutionary War* (Philadelphia: J.Campbell & Son, 1874), quoted in S. Zarlenga, op. cit., pages 380-81.

237. S. Zarlenga, op. cit., pages 377-87; Patrick Carmack, Bill Still, op. cit..

CHAPTER 11

238. Alexander Hamilton, *Works*, Part II, page 271, quoted in G. Edward Griffin, *The Creature from Jekyll Island* (Westlake Village, California: American Media, 1998), page 316.

239. Zarlenga, op. cit., pages 385-86.

240. Goodwin, op. cit., pages 95-115.

241. Alexander Hamilton, "Article 1, Section 8, Clause 2: Report on Public Credit," Electronic Resources from the University of Chicago Press Books Division, 1790, press-pubs.uchicago.edu.

242. Alexander Hamilton, "Report on a National Bank," 13 Dec. 1790, Britannica.com.

243. Hamilton, ibid.

244. Hamilton, ibid.

245. Zarlenga, op. cit., page 380.

246. Michael Kirsch, "Nicholas Biddle and the 2nd Bank of the United States," 4 July 2012, larouchepac.com.

247. Michel Chevalier, quoted in Kirsch, ibid.

248. David Cowen, "The First Bank of the United States," EH.net, 01 Feb. 2010.

CHAPTER 12

249. Louis Even, In This Age of Plenty, Chapter 49, "The History of Banking Control in the United States," Michaeljournal.org.

250. "The First Bank of the United States 1791-1811," San Jose State University, sjsu.edu.

251. "The Second Bank of the United States," PhiladelphiaFed.org, December 2010.

252. Richard Cook, We Hold These Truths: The Hope of Monetary Reform (Denver, Colorado: Tendril Press 2008), Pages 94-5.

253. "The Second Bank of the United States," op. cit.

254. Ibid.; Kirsch, op. cit.

255. "National Bank Act," Wikipedia.

256. Nelson Hultberg, "The Future of Gold as Money," Gold-eagle.com, 1 Feb. 2005, citing Antal Fekete, Monetary Economics 101; "Real Bills Doctrine," Wikipedia.

257. "Real Bills Doctrine," ibid.

258. "National Bank Act," op. cit.

259. Federal Reserve Bank of St. Louis, "A Lesson from the Free Banking Era," Regional Economist, 1996.

260. Douglas Clement, "Interview with Gary Gorton," The Federal Reserve Bank of Minneapolis, Dec. 2010, MinneapolisFed.org.

261. Kirsch, op. cit.

262. "Abraham Lincoln's 'Bank War,'" Anton Chaitkin, Executive Intelligence Review, 30 May 1986.

263. Richard Pettigrew, Triumphant Plutocracy: the Story of American Public Life from 1870 to 1920 (Kessinger Publishing 2007). For a detailed history of the publication of this document and the Hazard Circular, see http://www.yamaguchy.com/library/clark/shylock_12.html.

264. "National Bank Act," Wikipedia.

265. John Kenneth Galbraith, Money: Whence It Came, Where It Went (1975).

266. "National Bank Act." Wikipedia.

267. "Interview with Gary Gorton," op. cit.

CHAPTER 13

268. Edward Griffin, The Creature from Jekyll Island, p. 476, citing Charles Lindbergh Sr., The Economic Pinch (1923).

269. United States of America. Committee on Banking and Currency, "Hearing on H.R. 2233 An Act to Amend the Federal Reserve Act" (Washington DC: United States Government Printing Office, 1947), Fraser Economic Library and Archives, fraser.stlouisfed.org.

270. "Interest Expense on the Debt Outstanding," Treasury Direct, 6 Mar. 2013, treasurydirect.gov.

271. J.W. Smith, "Private Banks Creating Money Is Really Only a Circulation of Money," The Institute for Economic Democracy, ied.info.

272. Ann Pettifor, "The Broken Global Banking System," The Huffington Post, 03 Oct. 2010, huffingtonpost.com.

273. "Money supply," Wikipedia.

274. J.W. Smith, op. cit.

275. Ibid.

276. Congressman McFadden on the Federal Reserve Corporation, Remarks in Congress ,1934, home.hiwaay.net.

277. J.W. Smith, op. cit.

278. Margaret Rouse, "Federal Deposit Insurance Corporation (FDIC),"

Search Financial Security, May 2011, searchfinancialsecurity.techtarget.com.

279. Don Taylor, "U.S. Government Stands behind Deposits," Bankrate, 23 Apr. 2008, bankrate.com.

280. Beardsley Ruml, "Taxes for Revenue Are Obsolete," American Affairs (8.1 (1946): 35-39), home.hiwaay.net.

CHAPTER 14

281. Walker F. Todd, "History of and Rationales for the Reconstruction Finance Corporation," The Federal Reserve Bank of Cleveland, 1992, clevelandFed.org.

282. "Reconstruction Finance Corporation," Gale Encyclopedia of U.S. History, answers.com

283. Richard Freeman, "How Roosevelt's RFC Revived Economic Growth, 1933-45," EIREconomics, 17 Mar. 2006, larouchepub.com.

284. Laurence B. Robbins, Assistant Secretary of the Treasury, "Final Report on the Reconstruction Finance Corporation," Fraser Economic Library and Archive, 6 May 1959, pages 21, 33, 45, 161, fraser. stlouisfed.org.

285. Jesse Jones, Fifty Billion Dollars: My Thirteen Years with the RFC, 1932-1945 (Macmillan, 1951).

286. Jeffrey Orr, "Self Liquidating Loans pay for themselves," 5 Jun. 2011, moneychanges.org; Jeffrey Orr, "How the RFC Worked - The Real Cause of Economic Recovery," 7 May 2011, moneychanges.org.

287. Patricia Decker, and Robert Porterfield, "Bay Bridge Unparalleled Bridge, Unprecedented Cost," San Francisco Public Press, 8 Dec. 2009, sfpublicpress. org.

288. "Tolls and Traffic," Bay Area Toll Authority, 19 Mar. 2013, bata.mtc.ca.gov.

289. Decker and Porterfield, op. cit.

290. Marshall Auerback, "The Real Reason Banks Aren't Lending," The Huffington Post, 10 Apr. 2010, TheHuffingtonPost. com.

291. "New Deal," The History Channel website, Mar 19 2013, history.com.

292. Frederick Soddy, Wealth, Virtual Wealth, and Debt: the Solution of the Economic Paradox (Unwin Brothers, Ltd. 1926) page 196, abob.libs.uga.edu.

293. John M. Keynes, The General Theory of Employment, Interest and Money, Marxists Internet Archive (1936), marxists.org.

294. Hyman Minsky, quoted in Walker F. Todd, "History of and Rationales for the Reconstruction Finance Corporation," op. cit.

295. Franklin D. Roosevelt, "State of the Union Address," 11 Jan. 1944.

296. M. Paulsell, "GI Bill created generation of business leaders," Columbia Tribune, 3 Jul. 2009, columbiatribune.com.

CHAPTER 15

297. Jack Lang, The Great Bust: The Depression of the Thirties (McNamara's Books, Katoomba, 1962).

298. David Kidd, "How Money Is Created in Australia," 14 Jul. 2001, p2pfoundation. net/Commonwealth_of_Australia_Bank.

299. R. Hawtrey, Trade Depression and the Way Out (London, 1931).

300. R. Hawtrey, The Art of Central Banking (Frank Cass & Co. Ltd, 1932).

301. Dr. H. C. Coombs, In an Address at Queensland University, 1954.

302. Reginald McKenna, "Extraordinary Quotes for the Times We Live In," Market Watch, The Wall Street Journal, 27 July 2008, marketwatch.com.

CHAPTER 16

303. Edward Epstein, "Ruling the World of Money," Harper's Magazine, Nov. 1983, harpers.org.

304. "Otto Niemeyer," Wikipedia.

305. A. J. Millmow, The Power of Economic Ideas : The Origins of Macroeconomic Management in Australia, 1929-39, (ANU E Press, ebook, 2010), page 66.

306. "The Bank for International Settlements," Wikipedia.

307. Carroll Quigley, *Tragedy and Hope,* (Macmillan, 1966), page 324.

308. Alfred Mendez, "The Network," The World Central Bank: The Bank for International Settlements, http://copy_bilderberg.tripod.com/bis.htm.

309. Quigley, op. cit., page 324.

310. "BIS – Bank of International Settlement: The Mother of All Central Banks," 2009, hubpages.com.

311. Epstein, op. cit.

312. Ibid.

313. Joan Veon, "The Bank for International Settlements Calls for Global Currency," News with Views, 26 August 2003.

314. Steve Waddell, "Global Finance and the Role of Responsible Investors," in *Responsible Investing in Times of Turmoil* (Springer Netherland 2011).

315. Ibid., reproduced with permission.

316. Ibid.

CHAPTER 17

317. "Bank of Canada," Wikipedia.

318. Mackenzie King, quoted in "Of Primary Concern to Every Canadian," Independent Party Canada, 21 June 2012, independentpartycanada.com.

319. Kerry Bolton, "Breaking the Bondage of Interest: A Right Answer to Usury, Part 3," Counter-Current, 14 Aug. 2011.

320. William Krehm, *A Power Unto Itself: The Bank of Canada* (Stoddart Publishing Company 1993), page 3.

321. William Krehm, "A Monetary Education for MPs," Economic Reform, May 2008.

322. Krehm, *A Power Unto Itself,* op. cit., page 57.

323. Krehm, ibid., pages 56-57.

324. Will Abram, "Money: The Canadian Experience with the Bank of Canada Act of 1934," 9 Aug 2009.

325. J. Gilbert Turner, "The Hospital Insurance and Diagnostic Services Act: Its Impact on Hospital Administration," Canadian Medical Association Journal 78.10 (CMAJ, 1958), ncbi.nlm.nih.gov; Donna Wilson, "Principles of the 1984 Canada Health Act" (University of Wollongong, 2000), uow.edu.au.

326. Bolton, op. cit.

327. "History of the Basel Committee and Its Membership," Bank For International Settlements, 21 June 2012, bis.org.

328. Ibid.

329. Paul Hellyer, "Economics for Boomers." Roads Less Travelled, 3 Mar. 2007, pipalya.com.

330. William Engdahl, *The Gods of Money* (edition.engdahl 2009) Pages 265-273.

331. "Nixon and Domestic Issues," AP U.S. History Topic Outlines.

332. James Cumes, *The Demon Money,* (kindle edition: Amazon.com: Books. 1 Jan. 2013).

333. "Gross Canadian Federal Debt, 1867-2008," 24 Apr. 2010, pomiec.blogspot.com.

334. Ron Thompson and Jeff Greenberg, "1993 Report of the Auditor General of Canada," Office of the Auditor General of Canada, 1993, oag-bvg.gc.ca.

335. Adam Taylor, "Til' Debt Do Us Part? - With a Plan Ottawa's Debt Can Be Eliminated," Enter Stage Right, 23 Oct. 2006, enterstageright.com, confirmed by Hon. Paul Hellyer from official sources, April 2012.

336. Ibid.

337. Kerry Bolton, "Breaking the Bondage of Interest: A Right Answer to Usury, Part 4," Counter-Current, 10 Aug. 2011.

CHAPTER 18

338. "What is Social Credit All About?" Douglas Social Credit Secretariat, 2013, douglassocialcredit.com/about.php.

339. From private correspondence with Derryl Hermanutz, cited with permission.

340. "Social Credit Party of Canada," 04 Feb. 2013, Wikipedia.

341. Frances Hutchinson, *Understanding the Financial System: Social Credit Rediscovered* (Charlbury, U.K.: Jon Carpenter Publishing, 2010), pages 129-30.

342. Ibid., page 166.

343. Ibid., pages 187-88.

344. Ibid., page 149.

345. Reproduced with permission from private correspondence in February and March 2013.

346. D. Finch and Alberta Treasury Branches, *Albertans Investing in Alberta, 1938-1998* (Alberta Treasury Branches, 1999).

347. Alberta Publicity Bureau *These Are the Facts: An Authentic Record of Alberta's Progress, 1935-1948* (A. Shnitka, King's Printer, 1948).

348. "Social Credit: Fall from Power," HCF Alberta Online Encyclopedia, University of Alberta, 8 Dec. 2010, wayback.archive-it.org.

349. Finch, op. cit.

350. "ATB Faces New Reality," The Edmonton Journal (CanWest MediaWorks Publications Inc., 12 Oct. 2007), canada.com.

351. "ATB Financial," 17 Jun. 2012, Wikipedia.

CHAPTER 19

352. K.R. Bolton, "Funny Money," Alternative Right, The National Policy Institute, 13 Sept. 2011, alternativeright.com.

353. Kerry Bolton, "Breaking the Bondage of Interest: A Right Answer to Usury, Part 4," Counter-Currents, 10 Aug. 2011.

354. Ibid.

355. C. Firth, *State Housing in New Zealand,* (Ministry of Works 1949) page 7, quoted by Stan. Fitchett, "How to Be a Billionaire," *Guardian Political Review* (Winter 2004), page 25.

356. Margrit Kennedy, *Interest and Inflation-free Money* (1995), discussed in Deidre Kent, "Margrit Kennedy Inspires New Zealand Groups to Establish Regional

Money Systems," McKeever Institute of Economic Policy Analysis (2002), Mkeever.com

357. Rodney Shakespeare, *The Modern Universal Paradigm* (2007), pages 95-96.

358. S. Fitchett, The New Zealand Guardian Political Review (2004).

359. Stuart Jeanne Bramhall, "The IMF—A Global Protection Racket," E-Zine Articles, 3 Apr. 2010, ezinearticles.com.

360. "More about Us," Kiwibank, 15 Mar. 2012, kiwibank.co.nz.

361. Peter Wilson, "Key Promised Nine times to Never Sell Kiwibank – King," Guide to Money (Digital Advance, 3 June 2010), guide2.co.nz.

CHAPTER 20

362. Kerry Bolton, "Breaking the Bondage of Interest: A Right Answer to Usury, Part 4," Counter-Currents, 10 Aug. 2011.

363. C. H. Douglas, "Sydney Speech 1934," The Social Creditor 87.3 (2011): 51, douglassocialcredit.com.

364. Stephen Goodson, "The Real Reason the Japanese Attacked Pearl Harbor Prime," The Barnes Review, Nov. 2008.

365. Bolton, op. cit.

366. A. Hitler, Reichstag speech, January 30, 1939, R de Roussy de Sales (ed.) op. cit., pp. 457-458.

367. Bolton, op. cit.

368. A. J. P. Taylor, *The Origins of the Second World War* (New York: Fawcett Premier, 1961), p. 105.

369. H. W. S. Russell, The Duke of Bedford, *Propaganda for Proper Geese* (England, ca. 1939), pp. 3-4.

370. Goodson, op. cit.

371. Hays, Jeffrey. "Changes In The Japanese Military: Revising The Peace Constitution And Addressing Threats From China And North Korea," Facts and Details, 2009.

372. Goodson, op. cit.

CHAPTER 21

373. Peter Alford, "Japan's Post Bank Takes up Bonds Slack," The Australian: Business, 8 Apr. 2010, theaustralian.com. au.

374. Uwe Vollmer, Diemo Dietrich, and Ralf Bebenroth, *Behold the 'Behemoth': The Privatization of Japan Post Bank* (Kobe University, Feb. 2009), rieb.kobe-u.ac.jp.

375. "Japan's Debt Sustains a Deflationary Depression," Bloomberg, 25 Mar. 2013.

376. Peter Myers, "The 1988 Basle Accord - Destroyer of Japan's Finance System," Mailstar, 6 Sept. 2001, mailstar.net/basle. html.

377. Ibid.

378. Ibid.

379. *"Princes of the Yen* - Book Synopsis: Japan's Central Bankers and Their Battle to Transform the Nation," profitresearch. com.

380. "Behold the Behemoth," op. cit.

381. "Japan Post," Wikipedia.

382. Tabuchi, Hiroko, "News Analysis; In Japan, A Tenuous Vow to Cut," The New York Times, 2 Sept. 2011, nytimes.com.

383. Tejvan Pettinger, "List of National Debt by Country," Economics Help, 7 Sept. 2011, economicshelp.org; A. Gary Shilling, "Japan's Debt Sustains a Deflationary Depression," Bloomberg, 4 June 2012, bloomberg.com.

384. Ben Schott, "Country & State Credit Ratings," The Big Picture, 4 Feb. 2010, ritholtz.com.

385. Joe Weisenthal, "It Begins: Japanese Post Bank Urged To Diversify Away From Government Bonds," Business Insider, 2 Feb. 2010, businessinsider.com.

386. David Faber and Kyle Bass, "If a Japanese Sovereign Debt Default Was Predicted Before, What Will Happen Now?", The Political Commentator, 14 Mar. 2011, politicsandfinance.blogspot. com.

387. Christian Caryl, "Japan's Rebound," Foreign Affairs, 19 Mar. 2011, foreignaffairs.com.

388. "Japan Post Bank," Banks Daily, 30 September 2012, Banksdaily.com.

389. Conspiracy buffs may recognize the name. See "Former Japanese Finance Minister Heizo Takenaka - 'Japan Was Threatened With An Earthquake Machine,'" 15 March 2011, the-tap. blogspot.com; "Scalar Weapon Used To Cause Haiti Quake," January 21, 2010, europebusines.blogspot.com.

390. Anthony Rowley, "Selling Japan Post," Highbeam Business, 1 Mar. 2006, business.highbeam.com.

391. "Postal Shake-up," The Economist, 4 Oct. 2007, economist.com.

392. Hans Greimel, "Japan Post Office Will Top Citigroup as World's Largest Financial Institution," USA Today, 29 Mar. 2007, usatoday.com.

393. Peter Alford, "Japan's Post Bank Takes Up Bonds Slack," The Australian: Business, 8 Apr. 2010, theaustralian.com. au.

394. Ibid.

395. Michiyo Nakamoto, "Japan Set 'to Freeze' Sale of Post Bank," CNN.com 20 Sept. 2009, studentnews.cnn.com.

396. American Chamber of Commerce in Japan. et al. "Joint Statement on Japan Post Reform," Insurance Europe, 10 May 2010, insuranceeurope.eu.

397. Michiyo Nakamoto, "Private Sector Nervousness Rings Japan's Postal Bank," Financial Times, 20 May 2010, ft.com.

398. Greimel, op cit.

399. "Japan Post Bank May Branch out to London," Daily Yomiuri Online, 17 Dec. 2010, yomiuri.co.jp.

400. Chris Cook, "The Aftershock Doctrine," Asia Times Online, 18 Mar. 2011, atimes. com.

401. Christian Caryl, "Japan's Rebound," Foreign Affairs, 19 Mar. 2011, foreignaffairs.com.

CHAPTER 22

402. Chalmers Johnson, "Japanese 'Capitalism' Revisited," JPRI Occasional Paper No. 22 (August 2001), jpri.org.

403. Robert Locke, "Japan, Refutation of Neoliberalism," Post-Autistic Economics Review, Issue 23, 21 Mar. 2005, paecon.net.

404. Ibid.

405. Hazel Henderson. "Japan at the Crossroads, August 2001," Hazel Henderson.com, 30 Aug. 2001.

406. Richard Werner, "MP & Banking Expert Call For Change to BoE Policy," Policy News, University of Southhampton Management School, 8 Feb. 2012.

407. "*Princes of the Yen* - Book Synopsis: Japan's Central Bankers and Their Battle to Transform the Nation," profitresearch.com.

408. Brian Bremner, "Japan's Central Bank Is Pressed to Boost Money Supply," Bloomberg News, 2 Jan. 2013, businessweek.com.

409. Eamonn Fingleton, *In the Jaws of the Dragon: America's Fate in the Coming Era of Chinese Dominance* (New York: Thomas Dunne /St. Martin's, 2009), page 94.

410. Locke, op. cit.

411. Ibid.

412. Fingleton, op. cit., page 9.

413. "Economy of South Korea," Wikipedia.

414. Fingleton, op. cit, page 105.

415. Ha-Joon Chang, *Bad Samaritans*, page 14.

416. Fingleton, op. cit., page 109.

417. Alice Amsden, "Taiwan's Economic History," *Modern China* 5.3 (1979): Jstor. org, 15 Jan. 2010.

418. Fingleton, op. cit., page 101.

419. Russell Flannery, "Taiwan's Banking Failure," Forbes, 23 Aug. 2009.

CHAPTER 23

420. Kurt Von Mettenheim, Maria Antonieta Del Tedesco Lins, *Government Banking: New Perspectives on Sustainable Development and Social Inclusion From Europe and South America* (Konrad Adenauer Foundation, 2008), Academia.edu.

421. David R. Henderson, "German Economic Miracle," *The Concise Encyclopedia of Economics*, 2008, econlib.org.

422. Geoff Riley, "EU Economics: Germany Leads Euro Zone Revival," Tutor2u, 25 Feb. 2011, tutor2u.net.

423. D. Henderson, op. cit.

424. Peter Dorman, "What Is Public Capital?" EconoSpeak, 16 July 2011), econospeak.blogspot.com.

425. David Fairlamb, "Banking: It's Brussels vs. Berlin," Bloomberg Businessweek, 15 Nov. 1999, businessweek.com.

426. Kurt Von Mettenheim and Olivier Butzbach, "Alternative Banking and Social Inclusion," IMTFI: Institute for Money, Technology & Financial Inclusion, 5 Dec. 2011, blog.imtfi.uci.edu.

427. Ibid.

428. "German Public Bank," Wikimedia Foundation.

429. "Alternative Banking," op. cit.

430. Richard Werner, "The Case for Local Banking," YouTube, 06 Jan. 2013.

431. Von Mettenheim, et al., op. cit., page 116.

432. Von Mettenheim, et al., op. cit.

433. Ralph T. Niemeyer, "Commission's Dirty Task: Westlb Devoured By Private Banks," Crom Alternative Exchange Association, 3 July 2011, cromalternativemoney.org.

434. Michael Lewis, *The Big Short: Inside the Doomsday Machine*, (W.W. Norton, 2010), page 67.

435. James Kanter, "To Curb Abuses, Europe Pushes for Centralized Supervision of Banks," The New York Times, 1 Sept. 2012.

436. "Europe Takes an Important Step Forward on Banking," Bruegel, 13 Apr. 2013.

437. "Agreement Reached on Single Supervisory Mechanism," RTE.ie, 19 Mar. 2013.

438. Pierre, Gilles, "Single Supervisory Mechanism: Get Ready for the New Supervisory Landscape!" ABBL.lu, Luxembourg Bankers' Association, 26 Mar. 2013.

CHAPTER 24

439. Jim Willie, "The Coming Isolation of USDollar," 27 Dec. 2012, GoldenJackass. com.

440. Cullen O. Roche, "Understanding the Modern Monetary System," Pragmatic Capitalism, 5 Aug. 2011, pragcap.com.

441. Paul Craig Roberts, "Just Another Goldman Sachs Take Over," Counterpunch, 28 Nov. 2011.

442. "Erin Gone Broken Bank: The 2nd EMU Nation That Didn't Need a Bailout Get's Bailed Out Within Months, Next Up," ZeroHedge, 22 Nov. 2010.

443. Brian Gorman, "Europe Shares Fall after Moody's Ireland Downgrade," Reuters, 17 Dec. 2010, reuters.com.

444. Landon Thomas Jr., "As the Bailouts Continue in Europe, So Does the Flouting of Rules," *New York Times*, 29 Nov. 2012.

445. Bernard Lietaer and Christian Asperger et al., *Money and Sustainability:The Missing Link* (Triarchy Press, 2012).

446. Ibid., page 126.

447. Ibid.

448. Richard Douthwaite, "Deficit Easing – an Alternative to Severe Austerity Programmes in the Eurozone," Smart Taxes, Nov. 2011, smarttaxes.org.

449. Mark Weisbrot, "There Is Another Way for Bullied Ireland," The Guardian, 19 Nov. 2010, guardian.co.uk.

450. "How the Fed Could Fix the Economy— and Why It Hasn't," webofdebt.com, 13 Apr. 2013.

451. Marcus Walker, David Gauthier-Villars, and Brian Blackstone, "Europe's Leaders Pursue New Pact," Wall Street Journal, 28 Nov. 2011, online.wsj.com.

452. Ellen Brown, "Forget Compromise: The Debt Ceiling is Unconstitutional," 31 July 2011, webofdebt.com.

453. Marcus Walker, et al., op. cit.

454. "Treaty Establishing the European Stability Mechanism," European Council, 25 Mar. 2011, european-council. europa.eu, See "European Stability Mechanism = Debt Slavery," Red Ice Creations, 21 Dec. 2011, redicecreations. com.

455. "There Is Life After the Euro!", Helga Zepp-LaRouche, 8 June 2012, EIR.

456. "EU Finance Ministers Push Through ESM Treaty in Fishy Fly-by-Night Move," ZeroHedge, 24 Jan. 2012, zerohedge.com.

457. Ellen Brown, "Government by the Banks, for the Banks: The ESM Coup D'Etat in Europe," 1 July 2012, webofdebt.com.

458. Simon Thorpe, "The Insanity of ECB Lending - How Goldman Sachs Has Already Taken over," Simon Thorpe's Ideas, 31 Dec. 2012, simonthorpesideas. blogspot.com.

459. "How to Use the Rule of 72," WikiHow, 12 June 2012, wikihow.com.

460. Genevieve Signoret, "Article 123 of the Lisbon Treaty Is Quite Clear," La Carpeta Monetaria, 15 Nov. 2011, lacarpetamonetaria.com.

461. "Iceland Wins Case On Deposit Guarantees," Wall Street Journal, 21 Jan. 2013, online.wsj.com.

CHAPTER 25

462. Alejandro Micco and Ugo Panizza, "Public Banks in Latin America," Argentina Ministry of Economy and Public Finances, 25 Feb. 2005, cdi.mecon. gov.ar.

463. Michael Hudson, "Financial Predators v. Labor, Industry and Democracy," 2 Aug 2012, michael-hudson.com.

464. "Hyperinflation in the Weimar Republic," Wikipedia.

465. Kurt Von Mettenheim and Maria Antonieta Del Tedesco Lins, *Government Banking: New Perspectives on Sustainable Development and Social Inclusion from Europe and South America* (Konrad Adenauer Foundation, 2008).

466. "Venezuelan banking crisis of 2009–2010," Wikipedia, 26 Apr. 2011.

467. Kiraz Janicke, "Venezuelan Government Takes Over Three Banks, Sanctions Ten More," Venezuelanalysis, 19 Jan. 2010, venezuelanalysis.com.

468. Frank J. Daniel, "Rising Hindu Nationalist Seeks Moderate Image with Fast," Reuters, 17 Sept. 2011, blogs.reuters.com.

469. "Venezuela: Banks," Economist Intelligence Unit, 4 July 2011, eiu.com.

470. Rachael Boothroyd, "Venezuela Increases Banks' Obligatory Social Contributions, U.S. and Europe Do Not," Venezuelanalysis, 23 Apr. 2012, venezuelanalysis.com.

471. Banco Nacional Del Ejército Fuerza Aérea Y Armada, S.N.C., 13 Apr. 2013; Nacional Financiera : Otros , 13 Apr. 2013, banjercito.com.

472. Von Mettenheim and Del Tedesco Lins, Government Banking, op. cit., Page 37.

473. Von Mettenheim and Del Tedesco Lins, Government Banking, op. cit., Page 137.

474. "ECLAC Praises BancoEstado for Increasing Loans during the Crisis," Bancoestado, 5 Jan. 2010, en.corporativo.bancoestado.cl.

475. "China Loans and Oil Prices Boost Ecuador Economy Two Years after Default," MercoPress, 26 June 2011, en.mercopress.com.

476. Rebecca Ray and Sara Kozameh, "Ecuador's Economy Since 2007," Center for Economic and Policy Research, May 2012, cepr.net; Rebecca Ray, "Is Ecuador's Economic Policy a Non Neo-Liberal Alternative?", Interview by Paul Jay, The Real News, 7 June 2012, therealnews.com.

477. Frederick Soddy, *Wealth, Virtual Wealth, and Debt: the Solution of the Economic Paradox*, (Unwin Brothers, Ltd. 1926), page 196, abob.libs.uga.edu.

478. "The man with the mighty microphone," Economist, 9 Feb. 2013, economist.com.

479. "Uruguay Economy Expands 6.8 percent in the First Quarter and Domestic Demand, 8.3 percent," MercoPress, 21 July 2011, en.mercopress.com.

480. "Snapshot of the Uruguayan Financial System," PwC, 2008, pcw.com.uy.

481. Filipe Carvallo M., "Uruguay," Moody's Global Banking, July 2008, moodys.com.ar.

CHAPTER 26

482. "Printing Money Does Not Lead to Inflation, Argues Argentine Central Bank President," MercoPress, 26 Mar. 2012, en.mercopress.com.

483. James Petras, "Argentina: Why President Fernandez Wins and Obama Loses," James Petras Website, 30 Oct. 2011, Petras.lahaine.org.

484. James Petras, "Egypt and Argentina: The Right-Left Alliance," Global Research, 10 Dec. 2012, globalresearch.ca.

485. Viviana Alonso, "Ten Years Of Privatization Made Argentina's Crisis Worse," Monitor, 14 Jan. 2004, albionmonitor.com.

486. Dennis Small, "Argentina Proves," Executive Intelligence Review, 8 Feb. 2002.

487. Laura D'Amato, et al., "Contagion, Banks Fundamentals or Macroeconomic Shock?" Banco Central de la Republica Argentina, July 1997, Bcra.gov.ar.

488. Stephen DeMeulenaere, "A Pictorial History of Community Currency Systems," 2000, socioeco.org.

489. Petras, "Argentina," op. cit.

490. Larry Rohter, "Argentina's Economic Rally Defies Forecasts," New York Times, 23 Dec. 2004.

491. Jorge Altamira, "The Payment to the IMF Is Embezzlement Committed Against

Argentina," Prensa Obrera no. 929, 2005; Cynthia Rush, "Argentina, Brazil Pay Off Debt to IMF," Executive Intelligence Review, 30 Dec. 2005; Dennis Small, "'Vulture Funds' Descend on Dying Third World Economies," Executive Intelligence Review, 10 Oct. 2003.

492. "Argentine Peso," Answers.com; "Banco Central de la Republica Argentina," Wikipedia.

493. "Tucking into the Good Times," Economist.com, 19 Dec. 2006.

494. Ibid.

495. Brian Byrnes, "Inflation Downplayed as Argentina Recovers," CNN, 21 Oct. 2011, articles.cnn.com.

496. Mark Weisbrot, "Cristina Kirchner and Argentina's Good Fortune," The Guardian, 22 Oct. 2011, guardian.co.uk.

497. Petras, "Argentina," op. cit.

498. "Banking in Argentina," Wikipedia.

499. Rick Rowden, "The Shots Heard Round the World," Democracy Lab, 3 July 2012, foreignpolicy.com (paraphrased).

500. "Argentine economic crisis (1999–2002)," Wikipedia; "Argentina Inflation Rate," Trading Economics, Aug. 2012, tradingeconomics.com.

501. Mark Weisbrot, et al., "The Economic Success Story and Its Implications," Cepr.net, Dec. 2010.

502. Juan Forero, "Fight over Argentina's Inflation Rate Pits Government against Private Economists," The Washington Post, 02 Nov. 2011, washingtonpost.com.

503. Petras, "Egypt and Argentina," op. cit.

504. Dave Truman, "Argentina: A Case Study in How an Elite Political Dynasty Is Used to Further the New World Agenda," Endthelie.com, 27 Dec. 2012.

505. James Petras, "Egypt and Argentina: The Right-Left Alliance," Global Research, 10 Dec. 2012, globalresearch.ca.

CHAPTER 27

506. John Perkins, "Libya: It's Not About Oil, It's About Currency and Loans," Johnperkins.org, 29 Apr. 2011.

507. Cyril Svetitsky, "Bombing of Libya - Punishment for Ghaddafi for His Attempt to Refuse U.S. Dollar," Лучший.ЖЖ.РФ, 28 Mar. 2011, kir-t34. livejournal.com.

508. Judson Berger, "U.N. Council Poised to Adopt Report Praising Libya's Human Rights Record," Fox News, ,28 Feb. 2011, foxnews.com.

509. "CIS Countries," Windows to Russia, 18 Nov. 2008, windowstorussia.com.

510. "AFP: Libya Warns of Disaster If 'Great Man-Made River' Hit," Google News, 3 Apr. 2011, google.com/hostednews.

511. Robert Wenzel, "Libyan Rebels Form Central Bank," Economic Policy Journal, 28 Mar. 2011, economicpolicyjournal. com.

512. Alex Newman, "Libyan Rebels" Create Central Bank, Oil Company," The New American, 30 Mar. 2011, thenewamerican.com.

513. Edmund L. Andrews and Clifford Marks, "Libya: Why a Two-Percent Oil Producer Is Rattling Global Markets," NationalJournal, 24 Feb. 2011, nationaljournal.com.

514. "Proof: Libyan Invasion Planned 10 Years Ago!", Ascertain the Truth, 1 Apr. 2011, ascertainthetruth.com.

515. "Organization and Governance," Bank For International Settlements, 19 Dec. 2011, bis.org.

516. "Rogue State," Wikipedia.

517. Kenneth Schortgen Jr., "America's True Reason for Attacking Libya Becomes Clear with New Central Bank," Examiner, 30 Mar. 2011, examiner.com.

518. Patrick Henningsen, "Globalists Target 100 percent State Owned Central Bank of Libya," The Market Oracle, 28 Mar. 2011, marketoracle.co.uk.

519. Anh Van, "Gaddafi Control Holds Nearly 144 Tons of Gold - Libya Has

the 25th Largest Gold Reserves in The World," Newsessentials Blog, 25 Mar. 2011.

520. Willie, Jim, "Historic Collapse of Corrupt Monetary System Gritty Questions," Market Oracle, 27 Feb. 2013.

521. "Central Bank of Libya," Wikipedia.

522. See, e.g., "Converting Our Transportation Fuel Needs to Use Alcohol," Alcoholcanbeagas.com.

523. Corbett B. Daly, "Clinton on Qaddafi: "We Came, We Saw, He Died,""" CBSNews, 20 Oct. 2011, cbsnews.com.

524. "The Morals of Money-Lending," *The World Guide*, Henciclopedia.org.uy.

525. Carol J. Williams, "No Imminent Threat of a Nuclear-armed Iran, Experts Say," Los Angeles Times, 3 Aug. 2012.

526. "Treaty on the Non-Proliferation of Nuclear Weapons," Wikipedia.

527. William Engdahl, "Why Iran's Oil Bourse Can't Break the Buck," *Asia Times Online*, 10 March 2006.

528. Ibid. See also Julian Phillips, "Gold Positive: Iran Wants Yen from Japan Not the U.S. $ for Oil," www.goldseek.com, July 27, 2007.

529. Rodney Shakespeare, *The Modern Universal Paradigm* (2007), pages 63-64.

530. Achin Vanaik, "Cancel Third World Debt," *The Hindu*, August 18, 2001.

531. Carroll Quigley, *Tragedy and Hope: A History of the World in Our Time* (New York: Macmillan Company, 1966), page 324.

532. Haitham Al-Haddad and Tarek El-Diwany, "The Islamic Mortgage: Paradigm Shift or Trojan Horse?" Islamic Finance, Nov. 2006, islamic-finance.com.

533. "Riba," Wikipedia.

534. "Impact of the Grameen Bank on Local Society," rdc.com.au/grameen/Impact.html.

535. "Why War with Iran Would Spell Disaster," Al Jazeera English, 12 Sept. 2012.

536. John Perkins, "Libya: It's Not About Oil, It's About Currency and Loans," 29 Apr. 2011, Johnperkins.org.

CHAPTER 28

537. Peter Myers, "The 1988 Basle Accord – Destroyer of Japan's Finance System," http://www.mailstar.net/basle.html (updated 9 Sept 2008).

538. "OCC Approves Basel II Capital Rule," Comptroller of the Currency Release, 1 Nov. 2007.

539. Vinny Catalano, "FAS 157: Timing Is Everything," vinnycatalano.blogspot.com, 18 March 2008.

540. Bruce Wiseman, "The Financial Crisis: A look Behind the Wizard's Curtain," Canada Free Press, 19 March 2009.

541. See Ellen Brown, "Credit Where Credit Is Due," 11 Jan. 2009, webofdebt.com.

542. John Berlau, "The International Mark-to-market Contagion," 10. Oct. 2008, OpenMarket.org.

543. "What People Are Saying About Fair Value Accounting," American Bankers Association, aba.com (2012).

544. Jon Danielsson, et al., "An Academic Response to Basel II," LSE Financial Markets Group Special Paper Series, May 2001.

545. Marilyn Barnewall, "What Happened to American Sovereignty at G-20?", 18 Apr. 2009, NewsWithViews.com.

546. Ellen Brown, "Basel III: Tightening the Noose on Credit," Web of Debt, 16 Sept. 2010, webofdebt.com.

547. David Dayen, "Biggest Banks Already Qualify Under Basel III Reforms," FDL, 13 Sept. 2010, Firedoglake.com.

548. Greg Keller and Frank Jordans, "Basel III Rules: Banks Given Until 2019 to Fully Comply with Global Regulations," Huffington Post, 13 Sept. 2010.

CHAPTER 29

549. "How Did Iceland Recover? Report From Davos," Beyond Money, 13 Apr. 2013.

550. Raul Meijer, "Cyprus Bank Run, Who's Next?", The Market Oracle, 13 Mar. 2013.

551. Michele Kambas, and Karolina Tagaris, "Cyprus Lawmakers Reject Bank Tax; Bailout in Disarray," Reuters, 19 Mar. 2013.

552. Tim Worstall, "There's Something Very Strange About The Cyprus Bank Haircut. Very Strange Indeed," Forbes, 31 Mar. 2013.

553. Russel Norman, "National Planning Cyprus-Style Solution – Greens," Voxy, 13 March 2013, Voxy.co.nz.

554. See, e.g., Singh, Dalvinder, "Banking Regulation of U.K. and U.S. Financial Markets" (Epub 2007), Google Books, page 83; "Fractional Reserve Banking," Wikipedia; Edward Harrison, "On Claims of Depositors, Subordinated Creditors and Central Banks in Bank Resolutions," 19 Mar. 2013; "Are Uninsured Bank Depositors in Danger?", Felix Salmon, 13 February 2009, Felixsalmon.com.

555. "Key Attributes of Effective Resolution Regimes for Financial Institutions," Financial Stability Board, Oct. 2011.

556. "Recovery and Resolution Planning: Making the Key Attributes Requirements Operational Consultative Document," Financial Stability Board, Nov. 2012.

557. Kevin Hoskin and Ian Woolford, "A Primer on Open Bank Resolution," Reserve Bank of New Zealand: Bulletin, Vol. 74, No. 3, Sept. 2011.

558. "National planning Cyprus-style Solution – Greens," Green Party, Fuseworks, 19 Mar. 2013, nz.news.yahoo.com.

559. "Submission to the Reserve Bank of New Zealand on the Open Bank Resolution – IT Pre-positioning consultation document," New Zealand Bankers Association, 4 October 2011.

560. Federal Deposit Insurance Corporation and the Bank of England, "Resolving Globally Active, Systemically Important, Financial Institutions," Bank of England, 10 December 2012.

561. John Butler, "Someone Has to Pay - Will it Be You?", Financialsense.com, 4 Apr 2013.

562. See "Bank Of America Dumps $75 Trillion In Derivatives On U.S. Taxpayers With Federal Approval," Seeking Alpha, 28 Oct. 2011.

563. "The Derivatives Market's Payment Priorities as Financial Crisis Accelerator," Stanford Law Review, Volume 63, Issue 3, March 2011.

564. Robert Teitelman, "The Case against Favored Treatment of Derivatives," The Deal Economy, 10 May 2011, thedeal.com.

565. "Naked Capitalism," Naked Capitalism RSS.

566. "World Derivatives Market Estimated as Big as $1.2 Quadrillion Notional, as Banks Fight Efforts to Reign it in," Naked Capitalism RSS, 26 March 2013.

567. Ron Galloway, "70 Trillion Reasons JP Morgan Is Too Big," The Huffington Post, 18 May 2012.

568. "The Dodd-Frank Act," International Association of Risk and Compliance Professionals, risk-compliance-association.com.

569. Statement by FDIC Chairman Sheila Bair at the Quarterly Banking Profile Press Conference. Federal Deposit Insurance Corporation, 27 Aug. 2009.

570. Laura Bruce, "How the FDIC Pays for Bank Failures," Bank Rate, 16 October 2008, Bankrate.com.

571. "The Coming Major Bank Insolvency," Toritto's Blog, 19 October 2011, open.salon.com/blog/toritto.

572. Steven D., "Why the FDIC Is Upset With Bank of America's Derivatives Transfer Despite Dodd-Frank," Daily Kos, 2 November 2011, dailykos.com.

573. Elaine Magliaro, "Bank of America & The Great Derivatives Transfer," Jonathan Turley, jonathanturley.org.

574. William Black, "Not With a Bang, but with a Whimper: Bank of America's Derivatives Death Rattle," The Daily Bail, 19 October 2011, thedailybail.com.

575. Edward Harrison, "Buiter: Most European Banks are Zombies," Credit Writedowns, 30 March 2013, Creditwritedowns.com.

576. Luke Baker, "After Cyprus, Eurozone Faces Tough Bank Regime - Eurogroup Head," Reuters, 25 March 2013, uk. reuters.com.

577. "Bernanke Fails to Answer Concerns about a Cyprus-Style Seizure of American Bank Deposits," WashingtonsBlog.com (21 Mar. 2013).

578. "Slaughtering Sacred Cows: It's the Turn of the Unsecured Creditors Now," William Buiter's Mavercon, 18 March 2009, blogs.ft.com/maverecon.

579. "The Commodity Customer Coalition Objects to JP Morgan's Super-Priority Protection Over MF Global Customers," Zero Hedge, 15 November 2011.

580. "America the Battlefield: Confirmed — DHS to Banks: Seizures of Private U.S. Bank Accounts and Safe Deposit Boxes Forthcoming," America the Battlefield: Confirmed, 3 April 2013, americathebattlefield.blogspot.com.

581. "H.R.129 - Return to Prudent Banking Act of 2013," Congress, 3 January 2013, beta.congress.gov/.

582. Sen. Bernie Sanders, "Too Big to Jail?" The Huffington Post, 28 Mar. 2013, thehuffingtonpost.com.

583. Paul Craig Roberts, "Collapse At Hand," 5 June 2012, paulcraigroberts.org.

584. Tim Worstall, "The Financial Transactions Tax Will Just Kill The Banking Economy," Forbes, 8 May 2013, forbes.com.

585. George Zornick, "Financial Transactions Tax Introduced Again-Can It Pass This Time?" The Nation, thenation.com.

CHAPTER 30

586. G. Edward Griffin, The Creature from Jekyll Island (Westlake Village, California: American Media, 1998), p. 140-153.

587. "Detractors of Adam Smith's Real Bills Doctrine," 13 July 2005, Safehaven.com.

588. "Jim Rickards: A New Gold Standard Will Mean $16,000-$44,000 Gold," 7 Aug 2011, Silver Doctors.

589. "The National Emergency Employment Defense (NEED) Act of 2011, HR 2990," American Monetary Institute, 21 Sept. 2011, monetary.org; Ben Dyson, "Full-Reserve Banking (In Plain English)," Feb. 2012, positivemoney.org; "The Chicago Plan Revisited," Jaromir Benes and Michael Kumhof, Aug. 2012, imf. org; "IMF Authors Get Full Reserve Wrong," Ralphonomics, 13 Aug. 2012, ralphonomics.blogspot.co.uk.

590. Dyson, "Full-Reserve Banking," op. cit.

591. Ben Dyson, "Dirk Bezemer on Positive Money: A Response," 17 April 2013, positivemoney.org.

592. Benes and Kumhof, op. cit.

593. Zoltan Pozsar, et al., "Shadow Banking," Federal Reserve Bank of New York Staff Reports, Staff Report No. 458, February 2012, newyorkfed.org.

594. Marshall Auerback, "'The Chicago Plan' Does Not Deserve to be Revisited," macrobits.pinetreecapital.com, 23 Oct. 2012; Bill Mitchell, "100-percent Reserve Banking and State Banks," Bill Mitchell - Billy Blog, Bilbo.economicoutlook.net, 12 Jan. 2010.

595. "Chartalism," Wikipedia.

596. Matthews, Dylan, "Modern Monetary Theory, an Unconventional Take on Economic Strategy," Washington Post, 19 Feb. 2012.

597. Warren Mosler, "Proposals," Mosler Economics, moslereconomics.com.

598. Warren Mosler, "Proposal posted on October 2nd, 2008," moslerecononomics. com.

599. Ellen Brown, "How the Fed Could Fix the Economy—and Why It Hasn't," 24 Feb. 2013, webofdebt.com.

CHAPTER 31

600. Josh Harkinson, "How the Nation's Only State-Owned Bank Became the Envy of Wall Street," Mother Jones, 27 Mar. 2009.

601. Catarina Saraiva, et al., "California Markets Second-Biggest Taxable Bond Sale of 2010," Bloomberg, 25 Mar. 2010.

602. Timothy A. Canova, "The Public Option: The Case for Parallel Public Banking Institutions," New America Foundation, June 2011, growth.newamerica.net.

603. "State Revenue Changes from 2008 to 2009," Tax Foundation, 13 May 2010.

604. "North Dakota Land for Sale," Land Central, 20 Mar. 2012, landcentral.com; Carla Fried, "Why North Dakota May Be the Best State in the Country to Live In," Yahoo! Finance, CBS MoneyWatch, 31 Mar. 2011, finance.yahoo.com; "Failed Bank List," FDIC, 20 Mar. 2012, fdic.gov.

605. Eric Fox, "Bubbling Crude: America's Top 6 Oil-producing States," MSNBC, 8 June 2011, msnbc.msn.com.

606. "North Dakota Unemployment," Department of Numbers, 2 May 2013, deptofnumbers.com.

607. "Bakken Formation," Wikipedia.

608. "Big Tax Break for ND Residents?", WDAZ, 13 Aug. 2012.

609. Canova, op cit.

610. Ibid.

611. Jason Judd and Heather McGee, "Banking on America: How Main Street Partnership Banks Can Improve Local Economies," Demos.

612. Eric Hardmeyer, "Bank of North Dakota Annual Report: President's Message," Bank of North Dakota, 21 Mar. 2012, banknd.nd.gov.

613. "Bank of North Dakota Sets Profit Record for 7th Year," Inforum, 20 Apr. 2011, inforum.com.

614. "Washington State Bank Analysis Center for State Innovation," Center for State Innovation, Dec. 2010, stateinnovation. org.

615. Josh Harkinson, "How the Nation's Only State-Owned Bank Became the Envy of Wall Street," Mother Jones, 27 Mar. 2009, motherjones.com.

616. "Navigating for Today, Anchor for Tomorrow: Annual Report 2011," Bank of North Dakota, 2011.

617. Harkinson, op. cit.

618. "Calpensions," calpensions.com.

619. "CalPERS Earnings Fall Way Short," LoanSafe, CalPERS Earnings Fall Way Short, Comments.

620. "Wall Street Firms Earned $1.1 Billion Managing Investments for Calpers," Bloomberg, 9 Apr. 2013.

621. "Navigating for Today, Anchor for Tomorrow: Annual Report 2011," Bank of North Dakota, 2011.

622. Josh Harkinson, "How the Nation's Only State-Owned Bank Became the Envy of Wall Street," Mother Jones, 27 Mar. 2009, motherjones.com.

623. Stephen Gandel, "Thousands of Banks May Disappear," CNNMoney, Cable News Network, 09 Nov. 2012.

624. Jim Morrow & Ira Dember, "Hurricane Sandy & The Great Red River Flood: How the Public Bank of North Dakota Saved Grand Forks," Sky Valley Chronicle, Washington State News, 15 Apr. 2013.

CHAPTER 32

625. "State Activity, Resource and Contact Info," Public Banking Institute, 21 Mar. 2012, publicbankinginstitute.org.

626. Publicbankinginstitute.org/; publicbankinginstitute.org/faqs.htm; papublicbankproject.org/faqs; demos. org/publication/banking-america-how-main-street-partnership-banks-can-improve-local-economies.

627. "Financials," Bank of North Dakota, 31 Dec. 2010, banknd.nd.gov.

628. State of California, State Treasurer, 55th Annual Report Fiscal Year 2010-2011, By Bill Lockyer, treasurer.ca.gov.

629. banknd.nd.gov.

630. Standard & Poor's, "Bank of North Dakota Rating," Bank of North Dakota, 27 July 2010, banknd.nd.gov.

631. Treasurer.ca.gov/bonds/debt/201011/summary.pdf

632. Tom Hagan, "Letters to the Editor, Maine Pays Double for I-95 Upgrades," The Portland Press Herald, 3 Dec. 2011, pressherald.com.

633. Kyle Hence, "Where Are R.I. Revenues Being Invested? Not Locally," ecoRInews, 26 Jan. 2012, ecori.org.

634. "Capital Adequacy Ratio," Wikipedia.

635. Michael Sauvante, "State Owned Banks: DBA vs. Separate Corporation, Regulatory Oversight and Risks," Commonwealth Group.

636. Burhouse, Feid, French, and Ligon, "Basel and the Evolution of Capital Regulation: Moving Forward, Looking Back," Federal Deposit Insurance Corporation, 13 January 2003.

637. "CA CAFR Shows $600 Billion Tax Surplus, 1 percent Criminals Cover-up, Demand 'Austerity,'" Washingtons Blog, 12 Apr. 2013.

638. Anthony Pesce, "California Budget Balancer," Los Angeles Times, 15 Nov. 2010, latimes.com; treasurer.ca.gov/pmia-laif/performance/sum_invest_data.pdf.

639. "Governor Proposes Yet Another Scheme To Raid State Transit Funding," California Transit Association, 8 Jan. 2010, caltransit.org.

640. Scott Baker, "We Have to Rescue Our Own Darn Economy, Because Obama and the Party of No Won't," OpEdNews, 04 Nov. 2010, opednews.com.

641. Center for State Innovation, 21 Mar. 2012, stateinnovation.org; "Washington State Bank Analysis Center for State Innovation," op cit.; "Oregon State Bank Analysis - Revised Center for State Innovation," Center for State Innovation, Dec. 2010, stateinnovation.org.

642. Heather C. McGhee and Jason Judd, "Banking On America," Demos, 21 Apr. 2011, demos.org.

643. Ibid.

CHAPTER 33

644. David Weidner, "Occupy Shocker: A Realistic, Actionable Idea," The Wall Street Journal, 1 Dec. 2011, online.wsj.com.

645. David Weidner, "Dump Your Bank," Market Watch, 6 Dec. 2011, marketwatch.com.

646. Jason Sibert, "Can Public Banks Help Fix Local Finance?," 8 May 2013, newgeography.com.

647. Neil Garfield, "Should Bankers Go to Jail?", Livinglies, 20 Aug. 2012.

648. Shannon Finnell, "County Could Recover Mers Fees," 2 May 2013, eugeneweekly.com.

649. David Dayen, "Register of Deeds John O'Brien Releases Forensic Study, Finds Mass Fraud in Foreclosure Docs," FDL, 30 June 2011, news.firedoglake.com.

650. "Bain (Kristin), Et Al. v. Mortg. Elec. Registration Sys., Et Al., No. 86206-1,"Courts.wa.gov, 16 Aug. 2012.

651. "Eminent Domain," Wikipedia.

652. U.S. Department of Housing and Urban Development, "Revitalizing Foreclosed Properties with Land Banks," U.S. Office of Policy Development and Research, Aug. 2009, huduser.org.

653. Ellen Brown, "North Dakota's Economic 'Miracle' – It's Not Oil," Web of Debt, 31 Aug. 2011, webofdebt.com.

654. "A Solution to the Foreclosure Crisis," Main Street Matters, 2011, mainstreetmatters.us.

655. "San Bernardino Moves Forward with Eminent Domain Plans," National Mortgage News RSS, 23 Mar. 2013.

656. "San Bernardino County: Eminent Domain Mortgage Solution Rejected," Breaking News, 23 Mar. 2013.

657. Neil Garfield, "How Long Do We Just Sit and Boil?", Livinglies's Weblog, 21 Dec. 2011, livinglies.wordpress.com.

658. "There Goes the Neighborhood," CBSNews - 60 Minutes, CBS Interactive, 18 Dec. 2011, cbsnews.com.

659. "State Owned Financial Institutions 2012 Legislation," National Conference of State Legislatures, 23 Mar. 2013.

660. Committees on Economic Revitalization & Business and Housing. Letter Regarding A Bill for an Act Relating to the Bank of the State of Hawaii, State of Hawaii, Twenty-Sixth State Legislature, 10 Feb. 2012, capitol.hawaii.gov.

661. Martin Andelman, "It's Unanimous! AZ's SB 1451 Passes Senate Banking Committee," Mandelman Matters, Feb. 2012, mandelman.ml-implode.com.

CHAPTER 34

662. Mark J. Scher, "Postal Savings and the Provision of Financial Services," Rural Finance, Dec. 2001, ruralfinance.org.

663. "Indian Postal Service," Wikipedia.

664. "Govt. Scouting Consultant to Set up Post Bank of India," The Indian Express, 1 May 2012, indianexpress.com.

665. "Postal Savings Bank of China," Wikipedia, 17 Jan. 2012.

666. Scher, op. cit.

667. Constantine Rusanov, "Shakeup at Sberbank," Russia Profile, 1 Jan. 2008, russiaprofile.org.

668. "Correios," Wikipedia.

669. "Default Committed by Congress, Not by USPS," NALC Bulletin, 26 July 2012, nalc.org.

670. "United States Postal Savings System," Wikipedia.

671. Robert Guttmann, How Credit-Money Shapes the Economy (M.E. Sharpe, 1995)

672. "FDIC National Survey of Unbanked and Underbanked Households," FDIC, 3 May 2010, fdic.gov.

673. "Bank the Unbanked," Applications For Good, 9 Sept. 2012, applicationsforgood.org.

674. "How Is Credit Affecting Family Farmers Right Now?", FarmAid, May 2010, farmaid.org.

675. Hope Yen, "Closing of Rural Post Offices Put off to Study Other Ideas," The Washington Times, 9 May 2012, washingtontimes.com.

676. "Development Finance Institution," Wikipedia.

677. "How the China Development Bank is Rewriting the Rules of Finance: Debt, Oil and Influence," Brookings, 18 April 2013, Brookings.edu.

678. William Pentland, "The Case For A Green Bank," Forbes, 11 Jan. 2012, Forbes.com.

679. U.S. Congress, "S.652 as Introduced in Senate Building and Upgrading Infrastructure for Long-Term Development," Open Congress, 17 Mar. 2011, Opencongress.org.

680. Michael B. Likosky, "Banking on the Future," The New York Times, 13 July 2011, Nytimes.com.

681. "CBR: Federal Reserve Reform, Tim Canova (220)," YouTube, 31 Jan. 2012.

682. Paul Moser-Boehm, "The Relationship Between the Central Bank and the Government," Bank For International Settlements, 15 Mar. 2006, bis.org.

683. Henry CK Liu, "The BIS vs National Banks," Asia Times Online, 14 May 2002, atimes.com.

684. Thomas S. Mondschean, "Nationalize Broken U.S. Banks," Bloomberg Businessweek, Feb. 2009, Businessweek.com.

685. Gar Alperovitz, "Wall Street Is Too Big To Regulate," The New York Times, 23 July 2012, Nytimes.com.

686. Nouriel Roubini, "Nationalize Insolvent Banks," Forbes, 12 Feb. 2009, Forbes.com.

687. Michael Hudson, "Orwellian Doublethink: 'Nationalize the Banks.' 'Free Markets.'", Global Research, 23 Feb. 2009, Globalreasearch.ca.

688. Seumas Milne, "Private Banks Have Failed: We Need a Public Solution," The Guardian, 03 July 2012, Guardian.co.uk.

CHAPTER 35

689. Zoltan Pozsar, et al., "Shadow Banking," Federal Reserve Bank of New York Staff Report No. 458, February 2012, ny.frb. org.

690. Isabella Kaminska, "The Base Money Confusion," FT Alphaville, 3 Jul. 2012.

691. "Naked Capitalism," Naked Capitalism RSS, 25 Mar. 2013.

692. "Richard Koo on the Ineffectiveness of Monetary Expansion," 2 May 2013, Zerohedge.com.

693. "Elizabeth Warren: Student Loans Should Have Same Rate Big Banks Get," Huffington Post, 8 May 2013.

694. William Jacobson, "Brookings: Elizabeth Warren student loan proposal 'embarrassingly bad' and 'a cheap political gimmick,'" Legalinsurrection. com, May 20, 2013.

695. See Ellen Brown, "Student Loans: The Government Is Now Officially in the Banking Business," 31 March 2010, webofdebt.com.

696. Ryan Tate, "Meet the Genius Behind the Trillion-Dollar Coin and the Plot to Breach the Debt Ceiling," 1 Jan. 2013, wired.com.

697. Cullen Roche, "Philip Diehl, Former Head of the U.S. Mint Addresses Confusion Over the Platinum Coin Idea," Pragmatic Capitalism, 8 Jan. 2013, pragcap.com.

698. Warren Mosler, "Joe Firestone Post on Sidestepping the Debt Ceiling Issue with Coin Seigniorage," 20 Jan. 2011, moslereconomics.com.

699. "L. Randall Wray — Update on Trillion Dollar Coin: Not Inflationary," 8 Jan. 2013, mikenormaneconomics.blogspot. com.

700. "Baseline Tables: Effective Federal Tax Rates by Cash Income Level," Tax Policy Center Urban Institute and Brookings Institution, 8 Feb. 2012, taxpolicycenter. org.

701. Velocity of M1 Money Stock (M1V), FRED, Q1 2013, stlouisfed.org.

702. "Taxes," Arizona Libertarian Party, 20 Apr. 2012, azlp.org.

703. M. Paulsell, "GI Bill created generation of business leaders," 3 Jul. 2009, columbiatribune.com.

CHAPTER 36

704. Tim Worstall, "The Financial Transactions Tax Will Just Kill The Banking Economy," Forbes, 8 May 2013, forbes.com.

GLOSSARY

705. WF Hummel, "Money: What It Is, How It Works," Money Basics, wfhummel. cnhost.com/moneybasics.html.

706. Ibid.

707. "Colonial Scrip," Friends of the American Revolution, 21stcenturycicero. wordpress.com.

708. "Primer Derivatives," Financial Policy Forum, 2002, financialpolicy.org/ dscprimer.htm

709. "Land Banks," hud.gov.

710. Antal Fekete, "Real Bills Visited," Financial Sense, 26 July 2010, financialsense.com.

INDEX

CPSIA information can be obtained at www.ICGtesting.com
Printed in the USA
BVOW04s1221130614

356215BV00024B/212/P

9 780983 330868